# A BRIEF HISTORY OF ISRAEL'S ECONOMY

## 120 Years Of Economic Development—And Perspectives For The Future

# A BRIEF HISTORY OF ISRAEL'S ECONOMY

## 120 Years of Economic Development—And Perspectives for the Future

DAVID BRODET

VALLENTINE MITCHELL
LONDON • CHICAGO

*First published in 2025 by Vallentine Mitchell*

Catalyst House,
720 Centennial Court,
Centennial Park, Elstree WD6 3SY, UK

814 N. Franklin Street,
Chicago, Illinois,
IL 60610 USA

**www.vmbooks.com**



British Library Cataloguing in Publication Data:
An entry can be found on request

ISBN 978 1 80371 080 8 (HB)
ISBN 978 1 80371 081 5 (EB)

Library of Congress Cataloging in Publication Data:
An entry can be found on request

To my dear parents Hinda and Ezechiel

My wife Nora

My children Eyal and Dana

My grandchildren Micheal and Maya

# Contents

**Part Four: A New Economic Regime: 1986–2019**



**Part Five: Towards a Civilian Economy**



**Part Six: The Foundations of the "Kingdom"**



**Part Seven: The Coronavirus Pandemic and Challenges for the Future**

# Author's Foreword

This book explores somewhat more than a century of the development of the economy of the Land of Israel and the State of Israel as an integral part of the epic story of the Jewish struggle to establish and maintain an independent homeland. During this century of economic activity and development, the foundations were laid for Israel to become what it is today—a developed economy and one of the most advanced countries in the world.

My three decades of work in the Israeli government, the many lectures I have given on the Israeli economy at different academic institutions in Israel over the past 50 years, the articles I have written for various newspapers and journals, and my involvement in the Palestinian economy through my role in managing the economic negotiations between Israel and the Palestinian Liberation Organization (PLO) that resulted in the Protocol on Economic Relations for implementing the Oslo Accords (1993–1994), are but some of the many hands-on experiences that have fueled the writing of this book. In addition, my various roles on government-appointed committees and in the private and the third sectors have also enriched this book, providing me with a unique, multifaceted perspective on Israel's economic history and development. Undoubtedly, my professional life has given me a front-row seat with many opportunities for direct involvement in a number of formative and defining moments in the development of Israel's economy. I lived through Israel's rampant inflation and economic crisis between 1978 and 1985, a dark period that became known as the country's "lost decade." During this difficult period, I was privileged to play a role in implementing the government's far-reaching 1985 Economic Stabilization Plan, serving as project manager for the most "unorthodox" element of these reforms—the implementation of price controls. This period taught me a great deal about how to handle economic crises.

I took a break from government service for about four years (1987–1991) to serve as the Chief Financial Officer of Israel Aerospace Industries. In the wake of the decision by the Israeli government on August 30, 1987, to cancel the Lavi fighter plane program, I returned to the Ministry of Finance, where I served as the State Budget Director between 1991–1994. I served as the Ministry's Director General between 1995 and 1997, fascinating years that saw the mass Aliyah (immigration) to Israel of Jews from the former Soviet Union, and a series of far-reaching, essential reforms and changes to the Israeli economy that transformed it from a centralized public regime to an open and competitive market economy. This period also saw key political developments with the Palestinians and Israel's neighbors, including the Oslo Accords of 1993 and 1995, and the Israel-Jordan peace treaty in 1994. During 1993–1994, I was responsible for managing Israel's negotiations with the Palestinians, which resulted in the signing of the Protocol on Economic Relations on April 29, 1994. This was a vital, formative period for Israel's economy.

My experiences outside the government have provided me with a rich and diverse perspective on various aspects of Israel's economy and society. In addition to having served as chair of the board at Ben-Gurion University, Hadassah Academic College, and Hadassah Hospital. I also served as chair on several government-appointed public committees, including the committee to assess Israel's defense budget (in the wake of its second war with Lebanon in 2006), and the committee on capital market reform. During my decade as chairman of Bank Leumi during 2010–2019, the global and Israeli banking industry underwent dramatic changes in technology and regulation. The numerous lectures I gave in academia during this period were an engaging and professional way to keep abreast of these processes and informed about the Israeli economy.

In all my senior roles, I experienced the dramatic changes and transformations that unfolded across broad swathes of Israel's economy and its society, and was involved, often directly, in many fascinating processes that helped shape and develop the Israeli market.

Economics is not about numbers and data. Neither do economists undertake controlled research in laboratories to test their theories and ideas. Rather, economics is about decision-making in complex, highly constrained situations. It is about providing people and businesses with incentives to help them achieve their goals in various areas of life. All this requires considerable deliberation and responsibility. Economic policy is about values, not just cost-benefit calculations.

This book discusses the key events in Israel's economic history, in particular the major decisions taken at crucial stages in the development of the country's economic and social policies. I have studied, and seen firsthand, the institutional systems whose foundations were rooted in the pre-state Jewish Yishuv. These institutions served as an important bedrock for Israel's economic development and were the secret of the success of the Jewish economy in the pre-state Land of Israel.

In writing about past events, we are influenced by our awareness of the present. Writing history allows one to better see what is taking place in the here-and-now—and to look ahead and consider the future. The past more than one hundred years of Israel's history have been filled with economic activity and have witnessed rapid, dramatic shifts from one reality to another. Writing about over a century of this history has enabled me to take a long perspective and gain a deeper understanding of the lengthy processes that have taken place within, and shaped, Israel's economy.

The history of Israel's economy is a compelling story about the building of a national economy and the development of a country. Founded with the aspiration to become a leading country like any other, and to shake off the "not-so-normal" aspects of its existence, Israel and its economy have frequently developed in unconventional ways, sometimes making it difficult for Israel to rid itself of unwanted aspects the past. From the early days of the Jewish Yishuv, Israel has been rooted in entrepreneurship, invention, and creativity, qualities that have helped it make impressive achievements. However, these achievements should not blind us to the "shadows" of Israel's continuing challenges, some of which are typical of any developed nation, which will accompany Israel for the foreseeable future.

The Israeli economy faces a complex reality over the coming years—including, among other issues, external security, the Palestinian threat, as most dramatically seen in the 2023 Gaza War, and demographic challenges from the country's rapidly growing populations which have yet to fully share in efforts to acquire the basic education needed to move forward in a technological and global world. Without this training for all its citizens, the trajectory of Israel's economy could change course, from an impressive success toward a slowdown—or in an extreme case, even a crisis.

Also in 2023, Israel faced a constitutional crisis as its government expressed the intention to take steps to weaken its independent judiciary. These moves also posed a serious threat to Israel's entrepreneurship and creativity. Over the last hundred years, Israel has demonstrated a great ability to cope with many sorts of threats and challenges. The question now arises—will this ability be enough to allow Israel to tackle these, and other, threats and challenges in the future?

This book is intended for anyone —not just professional economists or economics students—interested in learning more about the development of Israel's economy and experiencing the successes and setbacks of this unique nation's fascinating economic journey, with a view to understanding the challenges it faces in the future.

David Brodet, Jerusalem, June 2024

# PART ONE

# THE ECONOMY OF THE PRE-STATE YISHUV, 1918-1948

## 1

## The National Economic Dimension

### From a "Distribution" Economy to a Productive Economy

Throughout the nineteenth century and in the first years of the twentieth, the Land of Israel was poor and underdeveloped, ruled by an ineffectual Ottoman government. It was a remote province, considered part of southern Syria, a land without natural resources. Beginning in the 1830s, the Ottoman Empire underwent a process of decentralization that strongly affected the region's economic development in the second half of the century, allowing the local populations to advance. The Ottoman-ruled Land of Israel was not densely populated, but neither was it empty. Most of its inhabitants were Arabs who made a living by working the land. In 1882, under Ottoman rule, the Old Yishuv numbered around 24,000 Jews and was concentrated in the so-called Four Lands—the cities of Jerusalem, Hebron, Tiberias, and Safed—and in the agricultural settlements (moshavot[1]) that were established during this period. The Jewish community mainly survived on donations from Diaspora Jews (the "distribution—charity-based—economy") and had almost no productive economic activity. During this period, it was the Arabs who were the producers of goods and providers of services. The Arab population numbered around 200,000[2] and grew from the mid-nineteenth century as a result of waves of migration from Egypt to the coastal plain (Jaffa and Gaza), during the reigns of the Egyptian rulers Muhammad Ali Pasha and his son Ibrahim Pasha (from 1805–1848), as well as immigration from Syria in the north, both fueled by the crumbling of the Ottoman Empire and the resulting search for economic opportunities.

In the nineteenth century, individual Jews began immigrating to the Land of Israel. They brought some capital with them and began to engage in economic development. Among them were Rabbi Avraham Shlomo Zalman Zoref (known as the Rashaz) and his grandson Yoel Moshe Salomon, and others who sought a life of labor. These pioneers sparked the exodus of Jews beyond the walls of Jerusalem's Old City, and in 1878 established the first moshava, Petah Tikva (known as Em HaMoshavot—the mother of the moshavot). This was a continuation of the transformation that had taken place in the lives of the Jews of Jerusalem with the establishment of the Mishkenot Sha'ananim (the Peaceful Dwellings—the first Jewish settlement outside of the walls of the Old City) in 1860, with the funding and support of a figure impressive in his work and generosity, the philanthropist and entrepreneur Moshe Montefiore, with help from the American businessman and philanthropist Judah Touro. In the second half of the nineteenth century, Montefiore worked to strengthen and expand Jerusalem's Jewish community outside the Old City walls, through a new model of philanthropy that emphasized productive aid – "helping people to help themselves" – in contrast to the "charity handouts" that had traditionally supported the Old Yishuv's religious, conservative, and zealous community. At the same time, the Alliance Israélite Universelle (Universal Israel Alliance), founded in France in 1860 to promote Jewish self-sufficiency and self-defense, helped Charles Netter establish an agricultural college, Mikveh Israel, in 1870, which became a productive base for agriculture. These economic ventures played an important role in the national revival project. This was the beginning of the struggle of the new pioneers against the Old Yishuv[3] and against the charity handouts on which its Ashkenazi communities were based.

The Jewish national renaissance began in Europe in the middle of the nineteenth century, influenced by the wave of national ideas and the creation of nation states sweeping Europe. The Jews, most of whom lived in Europe, suffered from poor living conditions and constant persecution especially Eastern Europe. They were disappointed that Europe's emancipations and enlightenment had failed to remedy the rising antisemitism on the continent. In the 1880s, the influence of national currents in Europe sparked the establishment of the Hovevei Tsiyon (Lovers of Zion) movement in Eastern Europe in the early 1880s, which began to take steps to realize Jewish nationalism. It would later become the Zionist movement, the goal of which was to establish a political framework for the Jewish people.

While organized Jewish immigration to the Land of Israel had secular foundations it did not arise out of a negation of Judaism. Rather, it posed a sharp—but constructive—criticism, seeking to change the lives of the Jewish people through productive labor and encourage a nation marked by practical activity alongside spiritual creativity. The first institutionalized—as opposed to individual—immigration began in 1881 and 1882 and is considered the beginning of Jewish settlement in the Land of Israel in the modern period. It centered on the First Aliyah—immigration from Russia and Yemen, each with its own motivation. In Eastern Europe, the Bilu organization (whose name is an acronym based on a verse from Isaiah (2:5), *Beit Ya'akov Lekhu Veneikha* ("House of Jacob, let us go [up]") was the first organized movement that called for Jews to immigrate to the Land of Israel. The Bilu pioneers were few in number but were fired by strong ideological motivations and were imbued with a yearning for nationhood, including immigrating to the Land of Israel. In the 1880s, Bilu brought some 15,000 Jews to the Land of Israel as part of the First Aliyah. Their intention was to live in the land, not to die and be buried there, as had been the case for many years. As the pattern of aliyah shifted in favor of youth who wanted to live and work in the Land of Israel, a new period dawned for the Jews in that land, and economic considerations began to gain significant weight in the daily life of the Yishuv. The Jews of this aliyah worked the land as a way of life and as a source of livelihood; developing an economy through cultivation of the land, and pursuing a productive life based on agriculture.

In this same period, from 1882 until the outbreak of the First World War in 1914, there was also a mass immigration of about a third of the Jews living in Eastern Europe—some two million people—to the United States. Immigration to the Land of Israel and building a Jewish homeland was seen as a marginal concern, and certainly not relevant for those who had chosen to build their futures in America. Indeed, the minority of Jews who chose to migrate to the Land of Israel had a distinct nationalist and/or socialist ideological leaning.

Baron Edmond James de Rothschild is another noteworthy figure in the development of the Yishuv's economy. His exceptional generosity—he was known as HaNadiv ("the Generous One")—was indispensable to the establishment and development of the agricultural moshavot in the Land of Israel during this period. Baron de Rothschild organized philanthropic schemes to aid a multitude of business ventures, and supported the first moshavot of Zikhron Yaakov, Rishon LeZion, Yesud HaMa'ala, Rosh Pina,

Mazkeret Batya, Nes Ziona, and Mishmar HaYarden. Indeed, it is doubtful whether these moshavot would have survived without his financial assistance.

Working in agriculture represented a dramatic change in the lives of the Jews; this shift can undoubtedly be seen as an expression of the pioneers' desire to take control of their own fates. Baron de Rothschild purchased land from the Turkish government and private individuals, and together with the Jewish Charitable Association (JCA) founded by Baron Hirsch, and the Palestine Jewish Colonization Association (PJCA), he doubled the amount of land owned by Jews. Baron de Rothschild, who was also known as Avi HaYishuv (Father of the Yishuv), sponsored the moshavot through a philanthropic guardianship working with a network of officials who often created friction with the settlers. However, the Baron's support made possible the development of the moshavot during their first twenty years of existence, helping establish an agricultural and industrial base for wines, oil, and perfumes, until they became self-supporting economic enterprises. The winery that Baron de Rothschild built in Rishon LeZion in 1892 was the largest and most sophisticated of its day in the Middle East and still operates today as the Carmel Winery.

The Zionist movement was officially established at the First Zionist Congress in Basel in 1897. This was a watershed moment on the road to creating a Jewish national home and to transforming the Jews into citizens responsible for their own destinies and not subject to the whims of other nations or people. Within this novel, institutionalized Zionist activity, the beginnings of a Jewish national framework were created. Although there was, as yet, no territorial goal, a common vision and distinct goals and objectives for the Jewish people were defined. The first Zionist Congress set in motion the political tradition of elections and representation that would become the cornerstone of the Yishuv's political culture at the start of the twentieth century, in terms of the creation and election of key institutions. It was this culture that gave rise to the political pluralism and the multiple parties that characterized Jewish life in the Land of Israel, and became the foundation of Israeli society after 1948, continuing to this very day. The Zionist idea sparked the imagination of Diaspora Jews. Zionist activity was focused on political, social, and economic action—not on empty statements. Theodor Herzl, (1860–1904) is unquestionably considered the father of Zionism—the movement not merely for an independent Jewish life, but for a Jewish homeland in the Land of Israel. Herzl and his ever-growing supporters sought socioeconomic change, aided by new scientific and technological developments as well as by fundraising.

All this, they were convinced, would lead to the establishment of a modern state in which progress and nationalism would form the bedrock of a Jewish national home. Herzl was inspired by these technological innovations and sought to harness them to benefit the Zionist revolution. He called for enterprise and private capital, while advocating a public mechanism to curb the shortcomings of capitalism. While Herzl was not a socialist, he recognized the need for solidarity, defining his vision for it in his book *Altneuland* as a socioeconomic regime that he dubbed "mutualism"—incorporating shared ownership of the land and natural resources, a mixed economy, an agricultural and industrial cooperative, national service, medical insurance, and old age insurance funds. Herzl advocated an economic regime that combined the concepts of capitalism and socialism, capitalist freedom and competition, and socialist equality and justice. He believed in free enterprise, cooperatives, and state ownership, just as he believed in the principles of a welfare state before it became a widely accepted concept. Herzl was not a "visionary" or a dreamer, but a leader who drew a blueprint for a new society that was idealist, but not utopian.[4]

At the Second Zionist Congress in Basel in 1898, it was decided that there was a need for a financial arm[5] to raise economic resources for the development of the Land of Israel. As a result, the Jewish Colonial Trust was founded in London in 1902 (with an initial capitalization of £58,000) and became the parent company of the bank of the Zionist movement, the Anglo-Palestine Bank, the aim of which was to promote settlement financing in the Land of Israel. In this, it was a combination of a commercial and an investment bank. The intention was to create a mechanism that would operate independently from the body politic and be run as a business for all intents and purposes. The bank that opened its first branch in Jaffa in 1903 is known today as Bank Leumi LeIsrael, the name given to it upon the establishment of Israel and today Israel's largest bank. Its role was central to the development of the Yishuv.

At the Fifth Congress in Basel in 1901, the Jewish National Fund was established as an arm to purchase land—without land purchases and the establishment of the kibbutzim and moshavot, the success of the Zionist enterprise was uncertain. The Seventh Congress in Basel in 1905 decided to support the agricultural settlements and industrial activities in the Land of Israel. At the Eighth Zionist Congress in The Hague in 1907, the Palestine Office was established, its purpose to direct and manage all settlement activities of the Zionist movement. The Palestine Office was headed by Arthur Ruppin (1876–1943), an economist and sociologist who would become a central figure in the economic development of the Land of Israel, establishing the physical, planning, and economic infrastructures of the Yishuv in these formative years. It was Ruppin who designed the Zionist settlements, rural and urban, and who worked systematically to purchase land and regional settlements, influencing the location of land purchases and the layout of the settlements.

Against the backdrop of the spread of socialist ideas among the intelligentsia in Russia in particular, and in Europe more generally, young people with a socialist and national ideology immigrated to the Land of Israel during the Second Aliyah, which began in 1904. These young people helped save the Zionist project that was in decline after Herzl's death, viewing the realization of its ideas in the Land of Israel as a personal, social, and national expression. Their form of Zionism, Socialist Zionism, combined the idea of national liberation with emancipation from the exploitative capitalist order. These young people were content to live on little, and, resisting support from Baron de Rothschild, they established kibbutzim and developed cooperative ideas of mutual aid in health, workers' canteens, culture, and education. It was their aspiration to change the status of the Jew in exile to that of a proud Jew who toils for a living by working the land, tilling and plowing, living a creative life—the very antithesis of the exile, alienated from the land

Degania, as the first of the kibbutzim (established in 1909), was an important landmark in this process. Its foundation was a milestone in Zionist efforts to develop cooperative economic life, efforts that gained pace over the next decades in the kibbutzim, moshavim,[6] and cooperative associations that were so crucial to the twentieth century Jewish economy. Also in 1909, the city of Tel Aviv was founded. Tel Aviv represented a different settlement model. The goal was similar to that of the communal settlements—realizing a creative and independent Jewish life—but the approach was quite different. In Tel Aviv, a bourgeois vision prevailed, whereby residents would make their livings independently, from industry, construction, and services. This concept was actually well-suited to the backgrounds of most of the Jews who immigrated to the Land of Israel, who were certainly not all socialists.

These two settlement models, as well as other variations, created a fascinating mosaic for the geographic and social distribution of the Yishuv. By 1914, on the eve of the First World War, there were 47 Jewish rural settlements that represented a significant shift in the composition of the Jews, their occupations, and their places of residence. At this time, the Yishuv numbered about 85,000, but its population decreased during the war due to deportation and emigration. By the end of the war, when

General Allenby led British forces into the Land of Israel, the Yishuv had shrunk to around only 57,000 people.

The Zionist movement went about establishing the nation-building enterprise from the ground up. A prime example is Eliezer Ben-Yehuda (1858–1922), born in Eastern Europe and part of the First Aliyah to the Land of Israel in 1881, who revived the Hebrew language. Ben-Yehuda, who learned Hebrew from the age of three in his Jewish elementary school, was responsible for developing a Hebrew education system and teaching institutions. As a result of his incomparable drive and the immense success of his undertaking, already, the first Hebrew school was founded in Rishon LeZion in 1887, and the first Hebrew kindergarten opened in the same city in 1897. Six years later, a second Hebrew kindergarten opened in Jerusalem. These kindergartens, which taught in Hebrew, instilled the language in the children's homes. It would be these kindergarten children who served in the vanguard of the Zionist revolution, essentially fighting the "War of the Languages" with "Ezra," the Relief Organization of German Jews advocating for German as the language of instruction the Land of Israel. Indeed, Hebrew proved itself a successful vehicle for creating an Israeli identity. In 1912, two seminaries were established for training teachers and kindergarten teachers—the Lewinsky Seminary in Neve Tzedek in Tel Aviv, which was the first institution to teach Zionist ideology in Hebrew, and the Beit Midrash for Hebrew Teachers founded by David Yellin in Jerusalem. These institutions emerged victorious in the War of the Languages. At that time, there were 20 kindergartens and 36 schools in the Land of Israel. The revival of Hebrew is one of Zionism's great achievements and formed the foundation of the Hebrew school system. In 1922, the educator Yosef Azaryahu created an organized, comprehensive Hebrew curriculum for all elementary education in the Land of Israel. This is a tangible example of the power of ideas and language to build institutions and tools that can serve as a success factor in nation- and state-building.

During this period, the Arab-Palestinian population lived mostly in villages, making a living by working the land. However, Arab agriculture was traditional, with low productivity rates. Lacking modern tools, it used very simple work methods and had almost no livestock. The Jews' foray into agriculture had a positive, albeit gradual effect on the economy of the Land of Israel. Arab institutions were underdeveloped, and far removed from the modern processes and new ideas that were taking hold in Europe. The Jewish "storm" that had arrived Ottoman Palestine troubled the local Arabs, and by the end of the Ottoman period, they viewed the small number of immigrants as a threat. Fear of the nascent Jewish economic and national progress centered on "Hebrew labor"[7] and land purchases, which aroused the ire of the local Arabs, who feared Jews replacing them in agricultural work and buying land that they were working. Already in 1908, the first nationalist-motivated harassments of the Jews of Jaffa erupted; these would become the start of a reaction of violence and terror to the Yishuv's advances, rather than a reaction based on economics.

## Notes

1. The moshavot were founded in the last quarter of 19th century as rural settlements in the Land of Israel and later evolved into urban settlements.
2. According to data taken from the great Ottoman census, as published by the late Prof. Kemel H. Karpat, Emeritus Distinguished Professor of History, University of Wisconsin, there were about 200,000 Arabs living in Ottoman Palestine in 1893.
3. The Old Yishuv refers to the body of veteran Jewish inhabitants living in the Land of Israel before the first wave of immigration in the late 19th century.
4. Binyamin Ze'ev Herzl. (1973) The Jewish State. Jerusalem, Zionist Library Publishing House.
5. See: N. Halevi (Ed.) (1977). Bankai Leuma Bhitchadashuta: Toledat Bank Leumi LeIsrael ("A Banker for a Nation in Renewal: The History of Bank Leumi LeIsrael." Jerusalem, Masada.
6. The moshavim were rural settlements where the land was privately owned but worked cooperatively, in contrast to the kibbutzim, where the division of the land and revenues were cooperative.
7. This refers to the Zionist vision of having Jews work in all professions and branches of the economy, expressed in their preference for hiring Jews rather than non-Jews in the Land of Israel.

# 2

# The British Mandate

After the fall of Turkey at the end of the First World War, and the ensuing partition of the lands of the defeated Ottoman Empire among the Allied Powers,[1] the efforts of the Jews and the Zionist movement to create a political and economic basis for the Yishuv gained momentum. Against the background of this new map of the Middle East came the greatest achievement of Jewish-Zionist diplomacy—the 1917 Balfour Declaration, the official British declaration confirming the Jewish people's right to a homeland in the land of Palestine. Chaim Weizmann (1874–1952), the man who worked to achieve it, transformed Herzl's vision into reality, and succeeded in allying Zionist goals with British interests to achieve vital recognition for the Zionist project. Weizmann, later to become Israel's first president, is often referred to as the "King of the Jews" because of his wisdom and diplomatic skills in presenting the Zionist narrative and mobilizing support for it.

The Balfour Declaration was a watershed moment for the Zionist movement in its efforts to obtain political recognition for a Jewish national home and settlement in the Land of Israel. It was the "kosher certificate" that gave an official seal of approval to the Jews' claims to a national home. With the end of the First World War, which had been fought by all sides fueled by slogans exalting the right to national self-determination, an opportunity arose for Zionism, as the national movement of a persecuted, stateless people, to act on the international stage. Britain, having emerged victorious in the war, and with its religious-Biblical sensitivity to the Jews' connection to their homeland, declared the right of the Jewish people to establish a national home in the Land of Israel. The Declaration emerged out of British recognition of the plight of the Jews and their connection to their historical homeland, as well as their wanting the Jews to be on Britain's side at the end of the war for political, economic, and strategic reasons. British recognition lent international legitimacy to the struggle for Jewish rights, sparking an almost messianic wave of enthusiasm in the Jewish world, and motivating Jews to settle in the Land of Israel.

The Declaration was included in a letter written on November 2, 1917 by British Foreign Secretary Lord Balfour to Lord Rothschild, the chairman of the Zionist Federation of Great Britain and Northern Ireland, and stated that:

> *His Majesty's government views with favor the establishment in Palestine of a national home for the Jewish people, and will use their best endeavors to facilitate the achievement of this object, it being clearly understood that nothing shall be done which may prejudice the civil and religious rights of existing non-Jewish communities in Palestine, or the rights and status enjoyed by Jews in any other country.*[2]

It can safely be stated that the Balfour Declaration and the British Mandate for Palestine were responsible for the creation of Palestinian nationalism. When the region was divided between Britain and France, the Land of Israel was separated from Syria. Previously, the Arabs living in the Land of Israel had considered themselves as southern Syrians and their country as southern Syria. The British government sympathized with the revival of the Jewish people in their land, and established their capital in Jerusalem, in accordance with the Christian tradition, which is similar to the Jewish tradition in this respect.

The development of the Jewish economy had already begun accelerating in the wake of the early 20$^{th}$ century establishment of the Anglo-Palestine Bank and the Jewish National Fund (JNF) as an executive arm for purchasing land in the Land of Israel. After the First World War, the Zionist movement was faced with the need to reconsolidate its organizational structures and devise plans of action to fulfill Zionist economic policy, with an emphasis on raising public capital.[3,4]

At the 1923 Zionist Congress in Carlsbad, Menachem Ussishkin (1863–1941) was elected as head of the JNF and became the driving force behind economic activity in the Yishuv. And even as land was being purchased and settlements established, intellectual and cultural endeavors were not overlooked. The 1920s saw the establishment of two institutions of higher education, which served as a basis for strengthening the Yishuv. In 1923, the Technion opened in Haifa,[5] intended as a technical school modeled on the German technological college run by the Ezra organization. The Hebrew University of Jerusalem opened in 1925, more a decade after the Eleventh Zionist Congress in Vienna in 1913 passed a resolution to establish a university in Jerusalem as a center for higher education and advanced knowledge in the Jewish community. Attesting to the momentous occasion, the Hebrew University of Jerusalem's inauguration was attended by Lord Balfour, Chaim Weizmann, and Albert Einstein. It is notable that all this took place in a community of some 100,000 people[6] over 100 years ago, within the course of a decade. These higher education institutions were a continuation of the development of the primary and secondary education system spearheaded by Ben-Yehuda. The National Committee, the Jewish representative body during the Mandate period, provided an elementary education to the entire Jewish community in the Yishuv as early as the 1920s. Education and learning were the foundations of Jewish society, and, together with its educated immigrants, formed the basis for its high-quality human capital. The education system, including higher education were important elements in the socioeconomic power of the Yishuv. At the same time, the Chief Rabbinate for the Jews of the Land of Israel, headed by the important and influential figure Rav Kook (1865–1935), was founded in 1921. While it was not a Zionist body, the Chief Rabbinate was part of the institutional fabric of the Yishuv that was developing in the Land of Israel.

Meanwhile, a fierce debate was being waged within the Zionist movement between two schools of thought, which would become the two main historical strands of the Zionist movement. The socialist pioneer movement saw settlement and economic development "from the ground up" as the correct way to realize the ideas of Zionism. The Revisionist movement, in contrast, saw the political (and later the military) struggle as key to realizing Zionism. These differences formed the core of a critical dispute in the Yishuv and the Diaspora about the political and socioeconomic nature of a future Jewish state in the three decades between the start of the British Mandate and the founding of the State of Israel.

The socialist movement emphasized the social and economic aspects of cooperative settlement and agriculture, and advocated the development of Jewish pioneers who would work and produce. In 1917, its leader, David Ben-Gurion (1886–1973), who at that time had no official role, realized that, despite the importance of the Balfour Declaration, the success of the Zionist project depended on Zionist settlement in the Land of Israel, where they would experience the challenges of work and creativity. Meanwhile, the Revisionist movement, led by Ze'ev Jabotinsky (1880–1940), saw a firm and determined stand against the Arabs through the so-called Iron Wall[7] as the main way forward to bring the Arabs to recognize the establishment of a Jewish state in the Land of Israel, including the East Bank of the Jordan. They believed that the Iron Wall would protect the Zionist project, and that, over time, the Arabs would become convinced they had no power to crush it, at which point there would be room for mutual concessions. Jabotinsky believed that urban settlement was as important to the Zionist project as were cooperative-agricultural efforts. He advocated a liberal economy and elements of bourgeois social welfare that he expressed in five basic principles: food, clothing, education, medicine, and housing—a safety net that would empower each person to flourish according to his ability.

Clearly, the Zionist-Socialist movement captured the hearts of many young Eastern European Jews, gaining momentum from two major events that took place in close succession. The Balfour Declaration of November 2, 1917 spurred national Zionist vision in the Land of Israel, while the Great October Socialist Revolution in Russia on November 7, 1917 was an extraordinary historical event, an ideological revolution with a social and economic component that succeeded in overthrowing the Tsarist regime. These two very different events formed the foundations of the Zionist-Socialist movement, which would become a dynamic and influential current in the Yishuv during the years of the British Mandate.

In 1920, at the start of the Third Aliyah (1919–1923), the Histadrut (General Organization of Workers in Israel) was established. This was a unique organization designed not only as a professional trade union to protect the rights of workers against employers, but also as a body that provided social and economic services. The Hevrat HaOvdim (Workers' Company), the economic wing of the Histadrut, was founded as a worker-owned cooperative, and served as a holding corporation of companies involved in building national infrastructure, combining building the country's infrastructure and developing a socialist approach to strengthen the working class. The Histadrut established institutions and companies, the most prominent of which were its financial arm Bank Hapoalim (1921), today Israel's second-largest bank, Solel Boneh as an economic arm for investments in construction and industry (formed into a separate industrial arm, Koor, in 1944), and a health insurance fund[8] as a health service.

The large-scale activities and plans of the small Yishuv (which comprised fewer than 100,000 Jews) may have seemed grandiose, but in retrospect, they point to a powerful vision that led to impressive economic developments, including the creation of economic institutions and business activities that would form the basis for the establishment of the State. Under its slogan "one more dunam, one more goat," the Zionist movement called for the development of a productive economy. This involved creating a national home as a territorial refuge for Jews, but also molding the Jew into a productive individual—the very antithesis of the Diaspora Jew, eking out a meager livelihood.

A census conducted by the British in October 1922 showed that the population of Land of Israel numbered 753,000, including 84,000 Jews (the Jewish population had returned to what it had been on the eve of the First

World War) and 599,000 Muslims. Christians and other residents numbered 79,000 inhabitants, a population density of 27 per square kilometer. During the Third Aliyah, some 35,000 Jews from Eastern Europe arrived in the Land of Israel (some chose to migrate because of the bad economic situation in Poland), most of them imbued with a pioneering spirit and a strong Zionist and socialist ideology.

The establishment of the Jewish Agency in the Land of Israel in 1929 as a local branch of the World Zionist Organization was a key step in the formation of Jewish leadership in the Land of Israel. The Jewish Agency became the central institution of the Yishuv, the highest level of the Yishuv "corporation" with its multiple component bodies. Politically, economically, and socially, the Jewish Agency became the organized, institutional basis of the Yishuv. In uniting the Yishuv's disparate activities, it catalyzed a significant shift that transformed the Yishuv into an active national collective.

The Arabs of the Land of Israel began to unite and gain a national identity through their struggle against the Jewish national movement,[9] and the Balfour Declaration that posed a challenge to the local Arab population. Nationalist sentiment among the Arabs of the Land of Israel was a novelty. Without the British Mandate, Palestinian nationalism may never have been created, since Palestinian society did not consider the idea of a sovereign state as its central goal. They saw themselves as part of the Arab people. As a young political community, it did not have organizational skills or governmental culture, and did not devote efforts to forming a socioeconomic concept alongside state-political formation. The local Arab national movement was based on the traditional socioeconomic structure (with feudal elements) of a number of well-to-do families who held political and economic status and influence. The old Arab families (al-Husseini, al-Nashashibi, al-Dajani, al-Khalidi, al-Jabari, al-Shawwa, al-Alimi) were afraid to engage excessively in formulating an economic plan, fearing that the socialist ideology that had gripped Europe might undermine their economic and political status among the Arab public. This approach was typical of most of the Arab world, with the exception of Egypt, where other processes took place.[10] The Palestinians did little to build economic institutions for economic development in the Arab settlement, despite seeing how a small Jewish community manifested considerable economic and social activity and entrepreneurship. The Yishuv succeeded in bringing immigrants, buying land, building settlements, developing agriculture and other branches of the economy, building community economic institutions, and developing an economically and socially supportive environment for advanced health and education services.The economic behavior of the Arab community prior to the establishment of Israel was passive, and its national efforts were based on engaging in political activity (through the Arab Higher Committee) relating to the Arab world and implementing a strategy of violence toward the Yishuv.

Clashes between the two communities in the economic arena began with the Jewish labor issue. The socialist-Zionist movement, rather than adhering to the socialist ideal of universalism, preferred employing Jews over Arabs. The economy of the Yishuv was affected by the extent of Jewish immigration, and as the number of immigrants grew, often replacing Arab workers, tensions with the Arab community increased. Meanwhile, in Palestinian politics, there was a split not on an ideological basis (as there was among the Jews), but on the basis of family loyalty—the main factor in political activity.

Among the two leading Arab families, the Al-Nashashibi family supported the British (and were prepared to compromise), while the al-Husseini family were extremists and supported Nazi Germany. The Arab leadership tried to prevent the plan to establish a Jewish national home through violent riots. In 1920–1921, a series of anti-Jewish riots took place in Jerusalem and Tel Hai. In the aftermath of the riots, the Haganah arose as a Jewish military force and defender of the Yishuv, and over time, would become the basis of the military force in the War of Independence and the Israel Defense Forces (IDF). In 1921, also in the wake of these events and in an attempt to calm the situation, Herbert Samuel, the first High Commissioner of Palestine, ordered a temporary suspension of Jewish immigration to British Mandate Palestine. A commission of inquiry—the Haycraft Commission—was established in 1921 to investigate the riots. It was upon the commission's recommendation that Winston Churchill, then the British Secretary of State for the Colonies, drafted the Churchill White Paper[11] of June 3, 1922.

In the 1920s, two waves of Jewish immigration arrived on the shores of British Mandate Palestine. The first of these, the Third Aliyah, lasted from after the First World War until 1925. This was a pioneering, formative aliyah with a socialist approach, which propelled the development of the moshavim and agriculture. During the Fourth Aliyah (1925–1930), some 80,000 immigrants arrived. Most, bourgeois immigrants from Poland, some of whom came due to economic crises in Poland, strengthened the urban settlements. At the same time, thousands of immigrants from Iraq and Yemen arrived. Tel Aviv developed into a large city, and the Yishuv in Jerusalem and Haifa also expanded. The number of kibbutzim and moshavot increased, and the areas of land purchased from the Arabs also grew. These two waves of immigration increased the numbers of the small Yishuv and drove home to the Arabs of the Land of Israel the meaning of the return of the Jews to their homeland.

The national conflict erupted into severe violence in 1929, when Jewish settlements were attacked by Arabs (the bloodiest riot occurred in Hebron in 1929). The riots consolidated the identity of the national struggle between the two populations and shaped the contours of the national conflict.[12] In the wake of the riots, the British issued the Passfield White Paper on October 20, 1930, following the Hope Simpson Enquiry[13] which argued that Jewish immigration and settlement should be restricted due to water shortages. The Yishuv rejected the findings of the Enquiry and its conclusions, on the grounds that the amount of water in the Land of Israel was actually much greater. Water was an important production factor for the agricultural sector and vital to both Jews and Arabs. The tension between the two communities did not subside, Jewish immigration continued, and the Yishuv's economic development—both public and private—intensified. In less than a decade, the Yishuv doubled in size, and in 1931, numbered around 175,000 Jews. The British were under constant pressure from the Arabs protesting the Balfour Declaration and the preferences in ongoing governance given to the Jewish community. The Arab position did not recognize any Jewish right to Land of Israel, and with the British government not unanimous in its support of the Balfour Declaration, the Arabs felt they could pressure those British who did not support the creation Jewish state.

The leadership of David Ben-Gurion, who headed the Histadrut from 1921 to 1933, and then the Jewish Agency from 1933 until the establishment of Israel in 1948, was the driving force in the creation of the independent state and the development of a Jewish economy as an institutional and productive infrastructure for the new national economy. In addition to the Jewish Agency, the Histadrut continued gaining economic power, which was the basis for Mapai's (Mifleget Poalei Land of Israel—Workers' Party of the Land of Israel) political power. Mapai had been the leading political party since 1933, and controlled the Jewish Agency and the Histadrut, which in turn comprised the organizational-institutional infrastructure of the Yishuv.

The development of the Yishuv's economy was rapid in terms of land purchases, settlements, and agriculture, which comprised the "ground floor" of the new national home. The "upper floors" comprised the development of industry, business, social services, higher education institutions, and public institutions, which were significant milestones in building the soon-to-be State of Israel. The Jewish Agency maintained its political department,[14] as a political component for the establishment of a Jewish national home and led the Yishuv. In retrospect, we can see that a Yishuv of around 100,000 Jews established civil society institutions in the 1920s, and about a decade later, when the Yishuv had swelled to some 300,000 people, it put in place the functioning institutions of the soon-to-be State.

The Jewish-Arab conflict is a national, cultural, and religious conflict. However, the economic aspect was a critical factor at many points in the long and complex journey of the Yishuv to independent statehood. Economic competition and economic conflict between the Jewish and Arab communities in British Mandate Palestine became integrated into their struggles with the British government in an attempt to influence it and recruit it to each side. The British, with their colonial experience, saw their role as maintaining a stable government. British contributions were felt throughout the region, from their desire to establish their rule in the Land of Israel in order to bolster their status in the wider Middle East. The British built roads, a seaport in Haifa, an airport near Lod, and an oil refinery in Haifa (which, when completed in 1940, was the third largest in the world), and oil pipelines, all as part of a comprehensive strategy to control oil in the Middle East. The British also helped establish an electricity company, and built army camps and police stations, infrastructure that served both the Jewish and the Arab communities.

The relative lack of assertive intervention of the British in the ongoing communal lives of the population in the Land of Israel worked in favor of the Jews, who, through their initiative and creative power, integrated better with the concept of British institution building. The Jewish economy, which was built on European models and closely related to the British concept, used its power better than did the Arab economy. The British administration, despite all its problems, allowed the Yishuv to grow and become stronger. The Yishuv, regardless of the British colonial establishments, built independent institutions to run efficiently, while the Palestinian national movement developed almost none, which harmed its ability to build a leadership and institutions befitting the Arab population. This lack of leadership and institutions led the Palestinians to be highly dependent on Arab states, which dictated their path. At the decisive point, in 1947–1948, the Palestinians' lack of leadership or functioning institutions in contrast to the Jews' leadership and strong institutions were key factors in the Jewish victory in the War of Independence.

## Notes

1. Great Britain, France, Russia, Italy and the United States.
2. The importance and centrality of this statement led historian Avi Shlaim to write in his book, Lion of Jordan: The Life of King Hussein in War and Peace (2007) that "My own view is that the Balfour Declaration was one of the worst mistakes in British foreign policy in the first half of the twentieth century." Only such an important statement could create such an overwhelming and extreme reaction. It is from the historian that we learn about the importance of the historical movement. In Shlaim's opinion, the Declaration was a great injustice to the Arabs of the Land of Israel and the cause of the prolonged conflict between Jews and Arabs ever since. There is no doubt that the Balfour Declaration is an important crossroads and milestone for all the developments that took place in later years.
3. Jacob Metzer (1979). A National Fund for a National Home. Yad Ben Tzvi, pp. 1019–1021.
4. In 1920, the National Committee was elected by the Assembly of Electors as the representative of the Jewish settlement, in which capacity it operated until the establishment of the Jewish Agency in 1929.
5. In 1901, the Fifth Zionist Congress called for the establishment of a technical school in the Land of Israel. In 1907, Paul Natan from the Ezra association visited the Land of Israel and decided to initiate the establishment of the school. The cornerstone for the first building was laid in Haifa in 1912.
6. Similar to the size of Eastbourne in England.
7. Ze'ev Jabotinsky coined this term in his two-part essay The Iron Wall, published in the Russian-language Jewish journal Rassvet in Berlin in November 1923. It is considered the conceptual basis of Jabotinsky's Zionist vision of the Jewish people standing as an "Iron Wall" to secure their presence in the Land of Israel and was highly influential in the development of the Iron Wall approach of the Revisionist arm of the Zionist movement.
8. In 1921, health insurance funds that had operated since 1911 merged into the General Health Insurance Fund of Hebrew Workers in the Land of Israel.
9. Yehoshua Porath (1976). Growth of the Palestinian National Movement, 1918-1929. Tel Aviv, Am Oved.
10. Egypt was semi-independent from 1928.
11. The White Paper, published in June 1922, was the first of three official papers laying out Britain's policy regarding the future of the Land of Israel under British Mandate rule.
12. Hillel Cohen. (2013). 1929: Year Zero of the Jewish-Arab Conflict. Jerusalem, Keter Books.

13. The White Paper, published in June 1922, was the first of three official papers laying out Britain's policy regarding the future of the Land of Israel under British Mandate rule.
14. See: Moshe Yegar. (2011). History of the Political Department of the Jewish Agency. Jerusalem, Bialik Institute.

# 3

# Economic Building Blocks

The Zionist Congress in Carlsbad in 1923 declared that, in establishing a National Home, the Jews should maintain good relations with the Arab population. In 1933–1934, the idea was raised by some Zionist leaders to develop a project in Hula in collaboration with local Arab dignitaries. At the local level, sheikhs and *mukhtars* (village leaders) supported the Jewish immigration in anticipation of economic development.[1] However, talks with the British about joint economic development met with national Arab resistance and did not develop into meaningful relations.

From the earliest days of the Mandate, the Jewish leadership continued to reinforce and develop the economic and social capabilities of the Yishuv. The struggle for Hebrew labor and the push for Jewish sovereignty over the Land of Israel increased tensions with the Arab population and intensified the national conflict. Although there was no formal cooperation with the Arab population, Jewish economic development created jobs and resulted in the immigration of Arabs from Syria, Egypt, and Transjordan to Mandatory Palestine.

In 1936, the Arab population of Mandatory Palestine, under the leadership of Hajj Amin al-Husseini, the head of the Arab Higher Committee, initiated a series of general strikes and violent uprisings (the "Great Revolt", *al-Thawra al-Kubra*) against the British and the Yishuv. The Great Revolt (1936–1939) was a national-Palestinian struggle with a religious impulse, the goal of which was to reverse Britain's support of a Jewish National Home and the right of the Jews to immigrate to the Land of Israel. This was the first, broad organization of the Arab population against the Mandatory government and the Jews. The Arab effort was aimed at damaging economic life and harassing the Jewish settlements, creating an economic boycott of the Yishuv, blocking the port of Jaffa from serving the British and the Yishuv, damaging Jewish agricultural crops and Jewish transportation (hence the development of the *Notrim*—Jewish auxiliaries, mainly police—with British support), and also causing damage to the Mandatory government. The Great Revolt claimed hundreds of Jewish victims, mostly civilians going about their daily lives. It came amid rising Jewish immigration, increasing land purchases from the Arabs, and

Arab fears regarding the strengthening of the Jewish National Home and its economic power, which was developing apace. In 1936, on the eve of the Great Revolt, the Yishuv numbered about 350,000, having doubled its population in six years (1931–1936) thanks to the Fifth Aliyah that began in 1930, most of whom were Jews who fled Germany and Central Europe amid the Nazis' rise to power. It was this increase in population that laid the foundations for the development of a modern economy. The aim of the Great Revolt was to prevent the expansion of the Yishuv and to discourage Jews from immigrating to the Land of Israel.

The outbreak of the Great Revolt was a cause of concern for the British government. Consequently, it established a Royal Commission of Inquiry in 1936.[2] William Ormsby-Gore, Colonial Secretary in the Neville Chamberlain government, appointed Lord William Robert Peel to chair the Commission, which was tasked with investigating why the Great Revolt had broken out and how to resolve the conflict, and with examining the functioning of the Mandatory government along with its commitment to Arabs and Jews.

The Jewish leadership across the spectrum—Chaim Weizmann, Ze'ev Jabotinsky, and David Ben-Gurion—spoke to the Commission of the historical rights of the Jews to the Land of Israel, based on the Balfour Declaration. They emphasized the loyalty of the Jews to the British and demanded the immediate establishment of a Jewish state in all of the Land of Israel. The Arabs initially refused to cooperate with the Peel Commission, in protest against British refusal to agree to their demand to stop Jewish immigration. Responding to pressure from Arab states, a delegation led by Hajj Amin al-Husseini agreed to appear before the Commission. There, al-Husseini claimed that the Jews were taking land from the Arabs and sought to erase all traces of the religious and historical rights of the Muslims to Mandatory Palestine. The Arabs presented the Great Revolt as a protest against the British policy of supporting the establishment of a Jewish National Home. The Arabs' demands included that the British cease support for the Jewish National Home, end Jewish immigration, ban the transfer of Arab land to Jews, end the Mandate, and recognize Palestine as an Arab base for an independent national government.

With the aim of finding a fundamental solution, The Peel Commission focused on the roots of the conflict and not just on the events of the Great Revolt. Its report, published in July 1937, shows that the Commission had accepted that there were conflicting national ambitions in Mandatory Palestine and that there was no chance for Jews and Palestinians to enjoy a shared life through the establishment of one state for the two peoples:

> *There is no common ground between them... They differ in religion and in language. Their cultural and social life, their ways of thought and conduct, are as incompatible as their national aspirations.*[3]

Its conclusion was that there should be a treaty system based on the Iraqi-Syrian precedent, with partition into two states—one Jewish and one Arab—both under British supervision, but not fully independent, like Egypt—with a new Mandate for an enclave that would incorporate Jerusalem and Bethlehem[4] and include a corridor to the sea at Jaffa. The Peel Commission also recommended that the development of a Jewish national home be frozen, (in all Eretz Israel) and that Jews should be allowed to purchase land only in the area designated for a Jewish state, which would include about a fifth of the territory of the western area of Mandatory Palestine. In Chapter 10 of the Peel Report, when discussing recommendations for Jewish immigration under the status quo of the Mandate (i.e., not under a partition), the Commission recommended that, "If immigration under the existing Mandate is thus to continue, its volume should no longer, in our view, be determined solely by 'economic absorptive capacity'"[5] and advised that:

> *There should now be a definite limit to the annual volume of Jewish immigration. We recommend that Your Majesty's Government should lay down a "political high level" of Jewish immigration to cover all categories. This high level should be fixed for the next five years at 12,000 per annum, and in no circumstances during that period should more than that number be allowed into the country in any one year. The political maximum having been fixed the High Commissioner should receive instructions to the effect that he may use his discretion to admit immigrants up to the maximum figure, but subject always to the economic absorptive capacity of the country.*[6]

However, under its recommendations for what should be done in terms of Jewish immigration if its Partition Plan were agreed, the Peel Commission recommended that, *ahead of partition:*

> *Instead of the political "high level" recommended in Chapter X, paragraph 97, there should be a territorial restriction on Jewish immigration. No Jewish immigration into the Arab Area should be permitted. Since it would therefore not affect the Arab Area and since the Jewish State would soon become responsible for its results, the*

> *volume of Jewish immigration should be determined by the economic absorptive capacity of Palestine less the Arab Area.*[7]

The Commission recommended a population transfer and land exchange. In its recommendations for partition the Commission determined that the territory of the Arab state should encompass the area currently mostly inhabited by Arabs and that the Jewish state should be allotted the area inhabited mostly by Jews, which would allow for the settlement of new immigrants (with limitations). Two new principles emerged in the Commission's recommendations: partition and limitations on Jewish immigration. Following the Commission's report, Jewish settlement was accelerated in empty areas (the "Tower and Stockade" settlement method[8]), with the intention of annexing them to the Jewish state. This is the basis of the ethos of "the settlements shall determine the borders."[9]

The Arabs rejected the Peel Plan and renewed their struggle against the Jews and against British rule even more vigorously, engaging in acts of severe violence against military installations and Jewish settlements. The Jewish community was disappointed with the British for their backtracking and rejection of the Balfour Declaration, which they had seen as a promise to establish an independent Jewish state. The British explained that they saw the Balfour Declaration as general and not as a concrete promise. The British turnaround resulted from a *realpolitik* approach, which could not ignore the Arab majority population or the British aim of getting closer to the Arabs in preparation for a confrontation with Germany in order to dissuade the Arabs from supporting Nazi Germany.

Opinion in the Yishuv was divided regarding the Peel Plan for partition. Some saw it as a once-in-a-lifetime opportunity to establish a state, while others thought it was a disaster and the death knell of the Zionist enterprise, fearing that there would not be enough room for the millions of Jews who would want to immigrate.

In view of the rejection of the Peel Plan by the Palestinians and the Arab states, and the mixed reactions of the Zionist movement toward it, the British government distanced itself from it, and sent a second Commission—the Woodhead Commission, technically known as the Palestine Partition Commission—to conduct investigations in Mandatory Palestine from April to August 1938. The Woodhead Commission concluded that the Peel Plan's partition recommendations were impractical and proposed to considerably expand the territory that would remain under British mandatory rule at the expense of areas that had been designated for the Jewish and Arab states.

Opposition from both Jews and Arabs led the British to abandon the recommendations of both Commissions. The British saw that there was no agreement between the two sides. In February 1939, the British government convened the St. James's Conference in London, a round table with Jewish (Jewish Agency and Zionist Organization) and Arab leaders, to formulate an alternative solution. However, the conference ended without producing any results. On May 17, 1939, the British government published a third White Paper (McDonald), contradicting the British promises of the Balfour Declaration to establish a Jewish national home, and claiming that:

> *His Majesty's Government believe that the framers of the Mandate in which the Balfour Declaration was embodied could not have intended that Palestine should be converted into a Jewish State against the will of the Arab population of the country.*

The 1939 White Paper added that:

> *The objective of His Majesty's Government is the establishment within 10 years of an independent Palestine State in such treaty relations with the United Kingdom as will provide satisfactorily for the commercial and strategic requirements of both countries in the future.*

And that: "Within ten years, the Land of Israel will become an Arab state with a Jewish minority."

Britain accepted the Arab position and abandoned the Yishuv to its fate during a difficult period for the Jewish people in Europe. It established two main limitations, on Jewish immigration and the purchase of land:

> *Jewish immigration during the next five years will be at a rate which, if economic absorptive capacity permits, will bring the Jewish population up to approximately one third of the total population of the country.*

Regarding land transfers, the 1939 White Paper stated that:

> *The Reports of several expert Commissions have indicated that, owing to the natural growth of the Arab population and the steady sale in recent years of Arab land to Jews, there is now in certain areas no room for further transfers of Arab land, whilst in some other areas such transfers of land must be restricted if Arab cultivators are to maintain*

> *their existing standard of life and a considerable landless Arab population is not soon to be created. In these circumstances, the High Commissioner will be given general powers to prohibit and regulate transfers of land.*

The violence of the Great Revolt and the recommendations of the Peel Plan and Woodhead Commission engendered a shift in the Jewish leadership, which went from seeking to realize the establishment of a Jewish National Home in the Land of Israel to agreeing to the principle of partition. The 20th Zionist Congress in Zurich in 1937 empowered the leadership (Weizmann and Ben-Gurion) to continue negotiations with the British government on the principle of partition, even if it rejected the outline proposed by the Peel Plan. This decision came amid a rising tide of antisemitism and an acute threat to European Jews with the Nazi rise to power in Germany, coupled with the need to find a territorial base for a Jewish revival.

In their drive for an independent state, the Yishuv leadership faced the challenge of the Peel Plan's recommendations that Jewish immigration be limited. In particular, the Yishuv had to contend with the claims that there was no room for additional Jewish immigrants in the Land of Israel because the Yishuv's economy was limited in terms of its absorption capabilities. The conclusions of the Peel Committee about the need to limit the number of Jewish immigrants as well as the absorption capacity of Jews presented a challenge to the Jewish leadership. For the first time, an economic question had arisen in Jewish-Arab public discourse and in official debates in the United Kingdom. The question of the possible capacity of the Land of Israel to contain Jews and Arabs focused the economic debate in Britain and in the Yishuv regarding the economic development capacity of the Yishuv and its relationship to Jewish immigration. In retrospect, the debate was irrational and far-fetched, and failed to take into account real economic processes and the use of this economic argument by the British was both naïve and cynical. Their determination to impose limits on Jewish immigration, which became a principle of British policy, disturbed and worried the Yishuv.

The 1939 White Paper was a waiver of the obligations of the Mandate, apparently on an economic basis, referring to the absorption capacity of an additional population in the Land of Israel.

The debate over the economic absorptive capacity of Mandatory Palestine was already controversial at the time the 1939 White Paper was published and, in retrospect, completely unfounded. The economic component was simply a "rational" way to justify the recommendations for the shift in British policy toward the Yishuv and would become a central motif of British policy.

## Building the Jewish Economy

In response to the restrictions on Jewish immigration and settlement, a "flash" method was developed for the establishment of "Tower and Stockade" settlements, and the purchase of land from Arabs continued apace to ensure a physical basis for the absorption of Jewish immigrants. Arab violence and the Peel Plan's recommendations regarding partition were the impetus that led the Yishuv to make determined moves to build a Jewish economy that was decoupled from, and independent of, the Arab economy. Until this point, the Yishuv's strategy had followed the principles set out by Arthur Ruppin in 1908 of buying land and settlements in unpopulated, peripheral areas. This was a strategy of settlement, not of constructing an independent Jewish economy. Nonetheless, it became an essential step in transitioning to the next stage, which began with the outbreak of the Great Revolt and involved the development of an independent Jewish economy that would form the basis for a future Jewish state. The Yishuv leadership demonstrated their ability to develop a strategy that could adapt to the new circumstances. Reliance on the Arab economy could have been a stumbling block in the Yishuv's development, and therefore it was a good idea to reduce this dependence.

Zionism, which advocated that the Jewish people had the right to possess all of the Land of Israel, had reached a crossroads, having to choose whether to become a liberation movement for the Land of Israel, or for the people of Israel (in other words, the Jews). Ben-Gurion decided that the fate of the people of Israel came before that of the Land of Israel. This was the moment to realize a policy for the decoupling of the Jewish economy from the Arab economy, and to build an independent economic base for the Jewish National Home, even if this involved partitioning the Land of Israel.

The Fifth Aliyah, from 1930–1939, which comprised Jews from Germany (the so-called Yekkes), Austria, and Czechoslovakia, brought about 250,000 immigrants to the Land of Israel. The Yishuv was transformed into a combination of a rural population in the kibbutzim and moshavim, and a growing urban population in Tel Aviv, Jerusalem, and Haifa. The contribution of the Fifth Aliyah, rich as it was in human and financial capital, was a significant factor in helping the Yishuv build an independent economy. With these new immigrants, there were approximately 450,000 Jews in the Land of Israel on the eve of the Second World War.

While most countries of the world were facing a serious economic crisis, which had begun with the stock market crash in New York at the end of 1929, the Land of Israel was enjoying a boom period. German Jews had immigrated with money, human capital, technology, management skills, fashion, architecture, and culture. They brought to a pioneering society, mostly Eastern European in origin, an urban bourgeois tradition and the advanced European economy of the time. Their contribution to the burgeoning economy of the Yishuv was unparalleled thanks to their high levels of education, their modern knowledge that enriched the economy, and the academic world that developed with the arrival of scholars from the best universities in Germany. Many opened businesses in trade, industry, and banking. In Haifa, a cluster of industrial plants sprang up. These plants, which were very large for their time, were the fruits of the Jewish Agency's policy of encouraging industry and of the JNF's land purchases in Haifa Bay. Haifa was chosen as a center of industry because of its deepwater port for shipping, its British-built airport, and because it was the focus of a great deal of activity by the Mandatory government. In Haifa, German and Central European Jews founded factories such as the Shemen Oil Factory (today Shemen Industries, Israel's largest manufacturer of edible oils), the Nesher Haifa cement plant (now Israel's leading cement manufacturer), and the Lime and Stone Production Company Ltd. (Israel's leading aggregate producer, running quarries and factories), as well as flour mills.

Beginning in 1937, a decision was made (by the Jewish Agency) to build an independent infrastructure for the Yishuv. A new port in north Tel Aviv served as a replacement for the Arab-controlled Jaffa port and was a key milestone in the development of the independent Jewish economy, since the port facilitated the import and export of goods (oranges) and the exit and entry of Jews. At the same time, close to the new port, the Sde Dov airport was constructed in north Tel Aviv in 1938, which enabled free movement by air and greater security. Sde Dov airport was named after Haganah chief and aviation pioneer Dov Hoz. In 1937, Levi Eshkol, with the help of Pinchas Sapir, founded the Mekorot water company to provide an independent water infrastructure for Jewish settlements in arid areas. The supply of water was a clear political statement for national existence. In the same year, the British granted permission for the construction of the Reading power station in north Tel Aviv, which provided electricity to

Jewish residents of the area. The British government indirectly—and sometimes directly—helped the Yishuv to carry out these and other measures for economic autonomy, since it was otherwise occupied dealing with the Arab violence. The British in effect facilitated the Jews' development of key infrastructures like the Tel Aviv Port, the Sde Dov airport, the Reading power station, and separate water lines for Jewish settlements, since none of these activities could have been undertaken if the British had opposed them, and so in effect the Mandatory government assisted the Yishuv to establish economic autonomy.

The Yishuv's leadership saw the development of independent infrastructures and the establishment of economic and social institutions as key milestones on the journey to statehood. In the wake of the Great Revolt, the Palestinian economy was damaged while the Jewish economy grew stronger. In this period, the leaders of the Yishuv called for a boycott of Arab products and a preference for Jewish products. The Palestinians lost the Jewish market and were not prepared to make the necessary adjustments to compensate for this.

Despite the strong settler ideology of the Hapoalim and Histadrut parties, not all Jewish immigrants engaged in settlement and agricultural activity. Immigrants from the big cities of Poland, Germany, and Czechoslovakia imported their European bourgeois values and developed the urban infrastructure of the Yishuv, which grew in parallel to the rural, agricultural settlements. During this short period, Tel Aviv advanced considerably (due to the Jewish private sector). A minority of the money came from the Zionist movement's fundraising efforts abroad, but most came from Jewish immigrants who brought private capital with them from Germany, Austria, Czechoslovakia, and Poland. Industry, services, and banking businesses were opened in Haifa, which at this time was economically stronger than Tel Aviv. Jerusalem also became stronger economically, thanks to its status as the capital of the Mandatory government, which invested in modern town planning, and developed the Hebrew University, as well as the Jerusalem Academy of Music and Dance and the Bezalel Academy of Art and Design. Despite the Zionist revolutionary ethos of the time, the Jews in these urban settlements lived bourgeois, modest, lives. At the end of the British Mandate period, about 70% of the Yishuv was concentrated in the three largest cities, with 43% in the Tel Aviv metropolitan area alone—there were almost no medium or small towns.

The development of the private sector and private entrepreneurship alongside the Histadrut and its enterprises became a catalyst for diversifying and strengthening the economy on its path towards independence. The 1930s saw the emergence of several companies that would later become large and significant players in the Israeli economy, including Elite, Strauss, Osem, Teva, and Israel Discount Bank—all fruits of the private entrepreneurship that developed in in parallel with the institutionalized, public initiatives of Histadrut. The large privately owned textile factory, ATA, the first company in Israel to manufacture textiles locally, was not only a clothing company but also served as a powerful a symbol of national formation, mobilizing the Jewish public to wear civilian khaki "uniforms." The diamond businesses that emerged in Netanya in the 1940s are another example of an industry that was born through private entrepreneurship and grew into a powerful economic sector.

## Institutions

The strength of the Yishuv came not only from its wide-ranging economic activities, but also from its development of organized institutions. Since the First Zionist Congress, an institutionalized political discourse had developed that manifested itself in a multiparty system and open political debates. The Yishuv's democratic ecosystem included elected parties and assemblies, as well as voluntary professional institutions that together formed an active part of the struggle for statehood. This institutional infrastructure also adopted European traditions of democratic processes and civil society institutions, which, as partners in the national struggles to achieve statehood, helped lay the foundations for the future Jewish state. The Yishuv's first elected assembly in the Land of Israel was formed in 1920, and its second in 1926; even at this early stage, the assembly involved around 20 political parties.

Civil and professional bodies were also founded. The Association of Craft and Industry was founded in 1908, and the Physicians Association in January 1912, which was the first Jewish union of free professionals, and also the first scientific society in the Hebrew Yishuv (it would later become the Hebrew Medical Association in the Land of Israel). Teachers had organized themselves from the end of the nineteenth century, before founding the Teachers Union in 1928. In that same year, a football association was founded, which was admitted to FIFA in 1929 (a similar process occurred for the Palestinians in 1932). The Lawyers Association was founded in 1930, followed by the Association of Certified Public Accountants and Auditors in 1931. The Securities Exchange Bureau, the forerunner of the Tel Aviv Stock Exchange, was established in 1935 (the Tel

Aviv Stock Exchange in its current form was established in 1953). The Association of Engineers was founded in 1937. Women's associations were also extremely active and were dual purpose: promoting the status of women and becoming partners in the national struggle. Among the most prominent women's organizations were Meshek Hapoelot ("Women Workers", an early stage of Irgun Hapoalot ("Organization of Women Workers") in the best tradition of the socialist Histradrut) and Histradrut Nashey Mizrachi ("Union of Mizrahi Women," founded 1919), the Hapoelot ("The Woman Worker") movement (founded 1921), Mizrachi Poelot (1935), and affiliates of Jewish women's organizations in the United States and the United Kingdom, as well as the Women's International Zionist Organization (WIZO) and Hadassah, the Women's Zionist Organization of America, which operated in the fields of society, welfare and the status of women. These groups were not only professional associations, but also formed the basis of an economic and social fabric that strengthened social involvement and exerted a powerful influence on the nature of the economy and society of the Yishuv.

These new, thriving political bodies and civil professional institutions reflected the vitality and strength of the Yishuv in its national struggle. Jewish society in the Yishuv was mobilized and showed solidarity with its leadership. For its part, the Yishuv leadership did not hesitate in turning to the people to help it raise funds for national purposes, through the "settlement tax" that was introduced in 1938 to finance the defense of the Yishuv. Levied and collected by the Jewish Agency, the "settlement tax" was a voluntary taxation for security purposes and was born from a sense of shared destiny and solidarity.

## Growth

The period of the Second World War was one of growth and prosperity for both the Arab and Jewish economies thanks to the British, who used Mandatory Palestine as a supply center and large-scale military rear infrastructure for its war effort in the Middle East. Relatively speaking, the Jewish economy benefitted more from the boom, because it fully mobilized to help the British in the war effort, including by recruiting volunteers for the British Army in its fight against the Germans, and through Jewish companies like Solel Boneh ("Paving and Building," a construction company founded in 1921), which participated in the war effort. Jewish companies built infrastructure for the British in their wartime activities, including outside Mandatory Palestine, which in turn strengthened the capabilities of the Yishuv. The Jewish economy grew significantly during the war, while the Yishuv turned a blind eye to the British anti-Jewish policy of limiting the quota of Jews allowed to immigrate to Mandatory Palestine. The decision to develop an independent Jewish economy, population growth, and the great demand created as a result of the war powered a great leap forward in the Jewish economy and helped put in place a sound infrastructure for its later independence.

The Yishuv was marked by greater economic and social equality than the Palestinian population, as a result of its ownership structure and the high proportion of public capital invested in its economy, the development of which was based on entrepreneurship and public investments by the Histadrut, the Jewish Agency, the settler movements, and the Mizrachi and Hapoel HaMizrachi movements. There was also a parallel thriving private sector of trade, services, finance, and small and midsize industry. The Arab economy, on the other hand, was based on a handful of wealthy families (some of whom lived in Syria and Lebanon), whose wealth came from land ownership and control over new economic activities such as citrus growing, industry, services, and construction, while the general population did not enjoy the fruits of the economic growth in Mandatory Palestine. The Palestinian economy experienced a slow transition from a traditional to a capitalist economy, and wealth was concentrated in the hands of the few traditional families who controlled the means of production—the bourgeoisie and the effendis versus the fellahin and the tenant farmers. The concentration of capital in private hands and a very small number of public economic institutions meant that the transformation of the Arab economy was slow. There was a population shift from the villages to the cities, especially Jaffa and Haifa, in places close to Jewish population centers, where there was a demand for workers. Meanwhile, the Arab leadership was engaged in political protest activities, and turned its energies against the very actors that had brought about the economic transformations in Mandatory Palestine—the British Mandatory government and the Yishuv.

The decoupling of the Jewish economy from that of the Arabs harmed traditional Arab agriculture. The Arabs had previously competed with the Yishuv in sales of agricultural produce, some of which the Arabs had previously sold to the Yishuv for Jewish consumption. Jewish agriculture was based on vegetables, fruits, dairy, and poultry. The major agricultural innovation in the 1930s was citrus growing, which both Jews and Arabs engaged in following pioneering work by the Templars. Citrus growing, in particular, represented modern agriculture that opened up exports to Europe. From the 1930s, citrus exports were the pride of the Yishuv and one of its symbols (Jaffa). Jewish fruit attracted higher prices than Arab fruit (more than a shilling a box) because of its higher quality, (mostly a result of the improved methods for orchard cultivation used by the Jewish growers, and their strict criteria for only selecting the best-quality fruit for export). In 1938, citrus exports comprised 84% of total exports and before the war, in 1939, about 15 million crates were sent to Europe.

The rapid growth of the Jewish population and the economic development indirectly affected the Arab economy, and these positive effects would have been even greater without the events of 1936–1939 Great Revolt. Arab industry lagged behind the industrial transformation in the Yishuv. Investments in the Arab economy were lower than those in the Jewish economy, and this affected employment and wages. The Arabs concentrated on basic consumer goods, food, clothing, construction materials, and quarrying

The Jewish economy grew stronger in the 1940s and competed not only with the Palestinian economy, but also with neighboring Arab countries in terms of exports. In January 1946, the Secretary General of the Arab League (which had been established in March 1945 with encouragement from the British), Said Abdul Rahman Azzam Bey, announced a boycott on Jewish goods produced in the Land of Israel, banning their export to Arab states. This boycott was not a Palestinian initiative but was intended to protect industries in neighboring countries. Although the boycott made it possible to respond to the plight of the Palestinians, it also served the Arab economic interests in the region. The boycott barely harmed Jewish production, and purchases by Palestinians and Arab states did not stop. However, it did encourage the Saudis to create an alternative route for the Trans-Arabian Pipeline (TAPLINE) through Syria to Sidon in Lebanon, abandoning the original plan for it to terminate at refineries in Haifa, in order to harm the British and the Yishuv.

The unequal economic development of the Arab and Jewish sectors was the result of several sociopolitical and economic processes.[10] The Palestinian movement focused on a violent struggle against the Jewish national movement, alongside the political activity in the greater Arab world. The size of the Arab population engendered a sense of power and the belief that victory would be achieved through demographic advantage, and thus there was no need to rely on economic power. They saw agriculture as their main economic strength and preserved traditional agricultural technologies, which perpetuated poverty among the fellahin. The large landowners (of whom there were very few) planted orchards and the fellahin became auxiliary laborers (tenant farmers). The concentration of capital among just a few individuals produced a large disparity between the elite and the masses, which prevented them from identifying with their leadership.

The disparities between the two national movements were clear. Accelerated industrial development and a high level of entrepreneurship in the Yishuv, which took better advantage of British government policy, fundamentally changed the power equation between the Yishuv and the Palestinians. The Yishuv had a strong and determined leadership, while the Palestinian leadership was divided. The Grand Mufti of Jerusalem, Mohammed Amin al-Husseini, who collaborated with Hitler and Mussolini and whom the British and Americans considered illegitimate, left the country for Berlin and was not allowed to return after the war. No alternative leadership emerged. The Jewish community also gained strength by participating in the British war effort, gaining military experience in the Jewish Brigade and other units with the Allies.

In the 1940s, the Yishuv was well-developed in terms of socioeconomic parameters such as low infant mortality (its rates resembled those in Europe), as well as literacy and education, including the quality of its higher education institutions. With the establishment of the state, about 10% of Jews had a higher education and about 30% had graduated high school. Between 1920–1948, the Jewish economy grew at an average rate of over 5% per capita. The growth was financed by donations raised by the Zionist movement and from capital donated by the immigrants themselves. According to research by Prof. Yaakov Metzer, the Yishuv's economy was ranked 15$^{th}$ in the world while the Palestinians were ranked 30$^{th}$.

During the two decades from 1927–1947, the Jewish population in the Land of Israel grew from about 150,000 to about 650,000, while the Jewish economy grew at an average annual rate of 12%, with a per capita growth rate of 5% per annum.

The Zionist leadership looked to the future and worked tirelessly to prepare for the moment of truth when the Second World War would end and the time would be ripe for the establishment of a Jewish state. The Holocaust, the true extent of whose horrors was only fully revealed in 1944–1945, was a catalyst for accelerating the political claim to a Jewish state. But the terrible losses of the Holocaust did not change the desire or stop the preparations of the Yishuv's leadership to establish a Jewish state, and even strengthened its willingness to partition the land to that end. The Arabs understood the strategic significance of the loss of Jewish potential in Europe and hardened their stance against the establishment of a Jewish state.

In the summer of 1945, the Labour Party came to power in the United Kingdom and tightened British immigration policy regarding Mandatory

Palestine. The Jewish call to open the gates of the Land of Israel to Holocaust survivors was at the heart of the policy of its national institutions and boosted the immigration enterprise that culminated in the well-publicized voyage of the ship *Exodus* in 1947. Amid the political debates and the immigration row, U.S. President Harry Truman called for restrictions on Jewish immigration to Mandatory Palestine to be lifted. Additional attempts were made within the framework of the Anglo-American Committee (1946) and the Morrison-Grady Plan (1946) to address the conflict between the Jews and the Palestinians and the question of partitioning Mandatory Palestine. In 1946, after the establishment of the United Nations, the United States and other countries recommended that the matter be transferred to the United Nations. Britain, which had adapted to the new geopolitical reality of its declining power, now had to contend with the political struggle of the Jewish Agency and the intensification of the armed struggle led by the Etzel and Lehi revisionist movements, which put London in a predicament. Eventually, in 1947, Britain agreed to transfer the question of Mandatory Palestine to the United Nations and the international community.

Despite the 1939 White Paper limiting Jewish immigration and land transfers and despite the Arab violence, the Jewish leadership stuck to its strategy of buying land and establishing new settlements. British Foreign Minister Ernest Bevin's prohibition on immigration did not stop the Yishuv's leaders from attempting to create settlements, and between 1945–1947, even as the restrictions on Jewish settlement tightened, 50 new settlements were established. These proved crucial in determining the partition map in 1947 and ultimately shaping the borders of the State of Israel. Along with these settlement activities, there were also ongoing efforts to develop security. A logistical system was created to prepare the Yishuv for the inevitability of military conflict, and Ben-Gurion trained the Haganah as the military force of the Yishuv in preparation for the expected war.

## The Kibbutzim

In the pre-State Yishuv, a special type of Jewish agricultural settlement—the kibbutz—was developed. The first kibbutz, Degania Alef, was founded in 1909. As noted in Chapter 1, the kibbutz (plural: kibbutzim) is a form of agricultural settlement unique to Zionism, the Yishuv, and Israel, and reflects Jewish aspirations for settlement in the Land of Israel, based on socialist values, equality, and economic and ideological cooperation. The kibbutz is a society founded on the values of work, solidarity, democracy, and equality—in essence, a free association of people for the purposes of settlement and communal life. Each kibbutz has a mutual guarantee between its members, and advocates a society based on shared work, economy, consumption, welfare, culture, and education. The kibbutz model of shared ownership and mutual efforts challenged economic thinking regarding the concept of the market economy and the incentives that motivate the individual in contrast to an economic model based on public money, which is the money of others.

The kibbutzim were a vital tool for the realization of Zionism, and the kibbutz movement was on the front lines of Zionist efforts to establish a Jewish state in the Land of Israel. The kibbutzim established settlements in the soon-to-be-state, including in frontier areas, and maintained large areas under difficult living conditions. Their pioneering work was integrated into their cooperative lifestyle and earned them enormous prestige, which raised the kibbutz to the pinnacle of the Yishuv's ethos. Their residents, known as kibbutzniks, were considered the social elite of the Yishuv. This elite status securing them key positions in the Yishuv and in the leadership of the nascent State of Israel. With the contributions of the kibbutzim to settlement, security, immigration, and immigrant absorption far exceeding their demographic weight, they became the economic and social backbone of Israel in its first years of independence.

In the 1920s, Jewish settlers began to establish communal moshavim as an alternative to the kibbutzim. In the moshav, members work their own land, but cooperate with one another by sharing the purchase and use of farm equipment, including large, expensive items (e.g., tractors, combines, trucks). The moshav members also cooperate in marketing produce, and through various forms of mutual guarantees.

The kibbutzim also played a decisive role in the establishment of the Palmach,[11] the Haganah's elite fighting force, and in defining the borders of the future Jewish state. Toward the end of the 1930s, when it became clear that there was an intention to partition Mandatory Palestine between the Jewish and Arab populations, the Yishuv leadership established dozens of kibbutzim on the frontiers of the territory to increase the likelihood that these areas would be incorporated into a future Jewish state. Many of these kibbutzim were established overnight, using the Tower and Stockade method. In 1946, at the end of Yom Kippur, 11 kibbutzim were established overnight in the northern Negev, as part of a strategic move by the Yishuv leadership.

By the time that the State of Israel declared its independence in 1948, the proportion of kibbutzniks in the Jewish population had reached a peak of about 7%. However, after the State was established it, others gradually came to take over many of the duties that the kibbutzim had previously fulfilled, such as army commanders and government members and ministers; as the prestige of the pioneers faded, so did their motivation to continue carrying the burden of national tasks. The kibbutzim had to come to terms with their new status as islands of communal life in a capitalist society and a market economy. They gradually declined in importance until the economic crises they faced in the 1980s.

The first challenge the kibbutz movement faced following Israel's declaration of independence was how to absorb the hundreds of thousands of new Jewish immigrants from Arab countries and North Africa. Many kibbutzim hired these Mizrahi immigrants to work in the fields and expand the kibbutz infrastructure. These new Mizrahi workers were often housed in the development towns that sprang up near the older kibbutzim. Although the kibbutzim identified ideologically with the proletariat, a long-standing estrangement grew between the residents of the new development towns and those of the neighboring kibbutzim.

## Notes

1. Isaiah Friedman (2012). British Pan-Arab Policy: 1915–1922: A Critical Appraisal. Jerusalem, Magnes Press.
2. The Peel Commission was established in August 1936. Its full report can be accessed here: ECF - Economic Cooperation Foundation: Peel Commission Full Report (1937) - English.
3. Peel, W. et al. (1937), "Report of the Palestine Royal Commission," UNISPAL, available at http://unispal.un.org/pdfs/Cmd5479.pdf.
4. Ibid., p. 381.
5. Ibid., p.306, paragraph 96.
6. Ibid, p. 306, paragraph 97.
7. Ibid., p. 393.
8. "Tower and Stockade" was the name given to a series of operations to construct agricultural and fortified Jewish settlements during the events of 1936–939.
9. A modern rewording of the Torah verse: "very place whereon the sole of your foot shall tread shall be yours." Deuteronomy, 12:24.
10. See Avraham Cohen, The Economy of the West Bank and Gaza, 1922–1930. Givat Haviva, 1986.
11. This was a special military force (similar to a commando force) within the Haganah that was founded in 1941—the Plugot Mahatz ("Striking Forces"), from which came the acronym "Palmach."

# 4

# From Yishuv to State

## The UN Partition Plan—November 29, 1947

After failing to formulate a plan for the future of Mandatory Palestine, the British returned the Mandate to the United Nations, the successor to the League of Nations. On May 15, 1947,[1] The United Nations created UNSCOP (the United Nations Special Committee on Palestine), which included representatives from 11 countries who traveled to Palestine on June 16, 1947 to conduct investigations and make recommendations for possible solutions to the problem of Mandatory Palestine.

As world powers began to realize the sheer scale of the Holocaust and contend the question of the huge number of desperate Jewish refugees in Europe, the need to find a quick solution to the Jewish National Home became increasingly evident. In August 1947, UNSCOP decided by majority vote to recommend the partition of Mandatory Palestine into two states, one Jewish and one Arab, and an international territory, rather than creating one state for two peoples (the minority had voted in favor of establishing a federation). The international community saw the Jewish people's right to an independent state as natural, moral, and historical. UNSCOP's plan was accepted by a majority of votes in the UN General Assembly on November 29, 1947 (Resolution 181).

According to the USCOP plan, Mandatory Palestine would be divided into a Jewish state, an Arab state, and an international territory that would be administered by the United Nations and that would include Jerusalem and Bethlehem.[2] This situation was intended to last for ten years with an option to extend. The plan gave the Jewish state about 56% of the territory and the Palestinians about 43%. The territories under international administration, Jerusalem and Bethlehem, comprised about 1%. The partition did not coincide precisely with the distribution of residents, and it was intended that there would be a small population of Palestinians in the Jewish state and a handful of Jews in the Palestinian state. The lack of continuity in the distribution of Jewish settlements created a problematic partition of Mandatory Palestine into three areas that connected at two points.

The difficulties inherent in partitioning the infrastructure of Mandatory Palestine provided the basis for UNSCOP's recommendations for Jewish-Arab cooperation. UNSCOP advocated the creation of an "economic union" in which the two states would maintain a common economic infrastructure, despite their political separation, including in the internationally administered territories of Jerusalem and Bethlehem. The economic union would maintain a customs union and a common currency, and would share land, water transport, seaports and airports, and communications infrastructure. The Jewish state would have an outlet to the sea in Haifa, and the Arab state in Jaffa. The economic organizing principle was that it was impossible to maintain complete economic separation between the two states in view of their proximity and convoluted borders that were not formed by natural or artificial barriers, as well as the lack of territorial continuity. The proposed international zone of Jerusalem and Bethlehem increased the complexity of the partition and highlighted the impossibility of creating an effective economic separation.

In just a short period of about 50 years since the birth of the Zionist Organization in 1897, the State of Israel was born, thanks to a pragmatic Zionist establishment and the willingness of a few to settle in the Land of Israel, amid maneuvering within the politics throughout that period. The Zionist movement and the Jewish community accepted the partition proposal, albeit with regret, for the sake of peace between the two peoples and so that an independent Jewish State could finally be established and provide asylum to Jews. The Arab leadership, however, rejected the plan completely.

In reality, the war for control of the Land of Israel began on November 30, 1947 and ended on May 14, 1948, with the British serving as the formal rulers of the territory during this time. The population in the Land of Israel at the beginning of 1948 numbered about 1.9 million—1.1 million Muslims, 150,000 Christians, and about 650,000 Jews.

## The Founding of the State

Despite its importance, the UN resolution, and the legitimacy it conferred to the establishment of an independent Jewish state, did not in itself establish the State of Israel. In reality, the State of Israel was established as a result of the Yishuv's ability to defend itself, and to build a functioning society and economy.

Arab violence prevented the original UN partition plan from being implemented as agreed.

In reality, the War of Independence was a battle between two populations that had been in a state of hostilities for some time. The Yishuv had developed and prepared itself for a decisive struggle and was ready for battle. Its leadership proved itself capable of marshalling the Yishuv to fight for independence, through mobilizing its community resources and developing its institutions. This was all done in partnership with the civilian home front in the rural and urban settlements for the benefit of the national effort and management of logistics. With its success in harnessing its human capital and more sophisticated means of warfare, the Yishuv was able to counter the Palestinians' numerical advantage. The big test for the Yishuv and its leadership was the sudden shift from armed conflict against Palestinian militias to a full-scale war against invading Arab armies. The Yishuv as a community had already demonstrated impressive organizational and economic ability, which, together with the courage of its leadership, empowered its fighting men and women to go to battle and win a difficult war. The rear assisted the front at close quarters. The War of Independence was not just about establishing an independent Jewish state, it was a battle for life and home. The Palestinians were not prepared for war and relied on their superior numbers and support from neighboring Arab states. The Palestinian leadership, which had already failed to develop legitimacy and effectiveness, collapsed. It could not create an orderly military command and was unprepared for a military and logistical struggle against the more advanced capabilities of the Jewish forces. The war led to the collapse of Palestinian society, with its elites abandoning the fight, while the masses fled in fear or after expulsion.

There were two parts to the 1948 war—the battle against the Palestinian militias (which were far less organized than the Palmach, Etzel, Lehi and Haganah) in a civil war (November 1947–May 1948), and the war against the surrounding Arab armies (May 1948–January 1949). At the beginning of 1949, the strength of the Israeli military versus that of the Palestinians and Jordanians was clear. The military and logistical power of the newly independent Israel was at its peak and numbered around 100,000 combatants (out of a total Jewish population of about 750,000). The success of the Yishuv and the newly independent Jewish state was not only in its quantitative strength, but in its development and mobilization of an organized and functioning civil and military force. The ability, know-how, and power that the Yishuv developed through its institutions and leadership enabled its victory in the War of Independence. In the historical debate between the two major currents of the Zionist movement, the faction that had supported and accomplished settlement and nation-building "from the ground up" had emerged the victor, although the competing national movement, in its fight against the British, contributed to the armed struggle that preceded the War of Independence.

The end of the War of Independence in March 1949 by signing of a series of armistice agreements with Jordan, Egypt, Syria, and Lebanon, was a watershed moment and defining milestone in the history of Zionism and Jewish nationalism. An independent Jewish political entity with internationally recognized borders was created. However, these borders were not the same as those proposed in the UN patriation plan. The territory of the newly independent Israel was about 78% of British Mandate Palestine, compared with the 56% allocated to it by the UN. There was no international zone in Jerusalem or Bethlehem. The borders in themselves had no military, topographical, economic, historical, or religious advantage. However, because they were agreed in the armistice agreements, they became international fact as the borders of the State of Israel.

The administration of the new Jewish state was based on the national institutions that were put in place three decades before it was formally established. Between October 1947 and April 1948, the Situation Committee[3] made a special effort to fill the gaps in government institutions that had arisen with the departure of the British. The Situation Committee is another example of the practical thinking that guided the Yishuv's leadership, who understood the need to build institutions and government to manage an independent Jewish state effectively and address the major challenges that faced it in terms of security, absorbing large numbers of immigrants, and developing an economic infrastructure and a national economy. Political and other professionals undertook extensive planning and executive efforts to create government departments by merging the Yishuv's institutions with the system of governance put in place by the Mandatory government. While the Yishuv's institutions had executive management experience in some areas of governance, other areas were new to them. The Situation Committee's recommendations were implemented during the War of Independence, when a response to immediate issues was needed, even if this meant temporarily setting aside longer-term questions. The development of Israel's government administration took a long time after its declaration of independence, and the initial foundations laid by Ben-Gurion had an effect for many years. The announcement of Israel's new currency (the Israeli pound) on August 17, 1948, now detached from the British pound, was the second most important political and economic act of sovereignty.

The Arab decision to go to war in protest at the UN partition plan created the Nakba[4] and the Palestinian refugee problem. The Palestinian urban culture that had developed before 1948 was damaged, and the image of the Arab population in Israel as a rural, fearful, underdeveloped, politically unrepresented, and culturally peripheral population dependent on the economy of the Jewish city was established.[5] Those who remained did not process the defeat, and for years denied their new reality. They were required to build a new community, cut off from the Arab world under Israeli rule, and in the shadow of an ongoing national conflict.

This short chapter recounts the political achievements surrounding the creation of the State of Israel. These were all made possible by the astounding economic growth and development of the pre-State Yishuv. More will be discussed on this nexus between the political and the economic in coming chapters.

## Notes

1. UNSCOP—United Nations Special Committee on Palestine.
2. When Israel annexed Jerusalem in 1967, the mayor of Bethlehem, Elias Bandak announced that, under these conditions, he had no viability, and therefore he had no choice but to join Jerusalem as well because of the traditional socioeconomic link between Jerusalem and Bethlehem. Bethlehem's connections to Jerusalem were very strong, and since Israel had annexed Jerusalem, Bandak also wanted the city to have the same status as Jerusalem, that is, to be annexed to Israel. At that time, Bethlehem was a majority Christian city, and its major industry was tourism. Bandak feared that the split between Bethlehem and Jerusalem would harm Christian tourism.
3. Prior to the establishment of the State, the Situation Committee was established by the Jewish Agency to prepare public administration.
4. The Nakba ("Catastrophe") was the departure, fleeing, or deportation of 700,000 Palestinians during the Israeli War of Independence (1948).
5. Haim Yacobi and Tovi Fenster (2006), An Israeli City or a City in Israel? Bnei Brak, Hakibbutz Hameuchad.

# PART TWO

# A MOBILIZED SOCIETY AND ECONOMY: 1948–1973

## 5

## The Challenges of the New State

### A New State

The Palestinians joined their Arab neighbors in a war against the nascent Israeli state, only to find themselves scattered as refugees (some fled the horrors of the war, some heeded the calls of Arab leaders and left, and others were expelled as a result of the circumstances of the war) in dispersed, separate communities in various Arab states, without their own country, without status, and lamenting their disaster (the Nakba)

The story of Israel's economy is part of the tale of Israel's establishment. This is an epic tale, and like every epic, features various challenges, heroic struggles, and also traumas. Israel's impressive development and economic achievements were the result of the hard work and tremendous dedication of its leadership and citizens over a long period. Its mobilized society and economy were driven by the first generation of Israelis to savor their independence and sovereignty during the first quarter century of the state. This was a special, pioneering, and unique period, and it would shape the legislation and structure of many different areas of the Israeli economy and society for over seven decades. During these years, for example, compulsory education law and labor laws were enacted, major projects were conducted in diverse areas (among them water infrastructure, ports, defense industries), while governance procedures and economic and social norms were established. This initial period of progress and optimism came to an end with the bloody conflict of the 1973 Yom Kippur War, followed by an ensuing economic crisis that led to soaring inflation. These events, in turn, set in motion drastic political and economic changes.

Returning to its early years of statehood, Israel had been faced by an existential threat that the Arab states would mobilize in a joint effort to destroy it. Israel's strategic goals then were to rapidly shape the territorial sovereignty that emerged from the outcome of the War of Independence, prevent the return of Palestinian refugees, and rapidly settle new immigrants in the lands between the original borders of the partition plan and the 1949 armistice line.

Two main factors shaped Israel's character and development in these early days: the hostile environment surrounding it, and the fact that most of its citizens were new immigrants. Opposition to the existence of a Jewish state in the region forced Israel to devote a large part of its resources to security and condemned it to economic isolation from its neighbors (the Arab boycott). As a country of immigrants, Israel was preoccupied, economically and socially, with building a national identity. The task was to coalesce into a single nation the tens of thousands of immigrants who poured into its borders from various countries, with different cultures and languages. The sociopolitical beliefs of the founding generation, accompanied by their desire to consolidate their manifestos, as well as the heavy security burden, all helped determine the direction of Israel's economic policy, including the large-scale government involvement in the economy and its preference for cooperative action (including through the trade unions and agricultural sectors). In its first decades of independence, Israel was a mobilized society with a high level of social cohesion. Its nationalist and Zionist ethos placed public interest at the forefront of society, over and above personal interests and individual self-expression.

Two main factors shaped the character and growth of the people of Israel in their own state – the rapid population expansion fueled by waves of immigration, and the rapid growth of the economy. Between 1948 and 1973, the country's population tripled in size, total GDP increased tenfold, and per capita GDP grew fourfold. Per capita GDP grew at an average annual rate of 5.7 percent, and total GDP by over 10 percent. These rapid rises were achieved thanks to an impressive increase in productivity (an average of 4.4 percent per annum). This was an extraordinary achievement, even on an international scale. The rapid population growth created new jobs on a large scale, and the economy operated at full employment for most of this period. Israel became known around the world as an economic miracle. One of the factors behind this rapid growth was long-term political and economic stability – the former under Prime Minister David Ben-Gurion, the latter under the tenures of two Ministers of Finance, Levi Eshkol (in office 1952–1963) and Pinchas Sapir (in office 1963–1968; 1969–1974), who between them led the economy for more than 20 years. Both radiated stability, commitment, political understanding, judgment, and responsibility.

The state was deeply involved in all areas of the economy, including investments, production, foreign trade, capital markets, importing capital, and foreign currency reserves. The government played a central role in building Israel's society and economy, but there was also an economic price to pay. Over the years, the economy suffered from a constant external imbalance (a deficit in the balance of payments), far-reaching dependence on external aid, rigid economic systems, and dependence on the government bureaucracy. It is common to view this stage in Israel's growth as its "nation-building phase." This was expressed in Israel's desire to prove that, as a newly independent state, it was able to produce everything it needed like some other new countries. This was the backbone of the new state's pride, and instilled self-confidence and respect in its new citizens, since, despite the scarcity of foreign currency reserves, it was able to meet the challenges of production and development. This pride resulted in Israel producing almost everything it needed – even cars – during these first pioneering years, albeit not always efficiently, or in an economically viable manner. Nevertheless, having a productive society and economy was an important achievement and goal. These factors also sowed the seeds of tension between autarky (a closed, self-sufficient state) in the short term and openness in the long term. What was important was production for the short term, the supply of necessary products, and the pride of creation and fulfillment.

The State of Israel was not accepted by the Arab world and this reality meant Israel was cut off from any economic ties with neighboring Arab countries, having with them only relations of hostility and enmity instead. The Arab League declared an economic embargo on Israel and set up a mechanism in Damascus to monitor countries and companies and warn them against investment in or economic relations with Israel.

From the day it was founded, Israel faced serious economic challenges due to its position as a geopolitical island surrounded by hostile Arab states. While its outlet to the Mediterranean, and later to the Red Sea, opened Israel's economic and trade relations with the rest of the world, the initial (direct) and the secondary and tertiary (indirect) Arab boycotts presented difficulties to Israel in its early years. Many international actors avoided ties with the new state in order not to lose access to the populous and influential Arab oil and banking markets. Israel's need to address the Arab boycott helped shape and forge its economy at the very start of its development, forcing it to be competitive, creative, and talented in dealing with its unique problems.

The largest undertaking of the newly independent Israel was the absorption of Jewish immigrants from all over the world (between 1948 and 2022, around 3.4 million Jews would immigrate). In its early years, Israel experienced enormous economic difficulties in absorbing these immigrants, who doubled the population of the new state in less than four years. By the end of 1951, the Jewish population in Israel numbered approximately 1.4 million, twice that of 1948. When Israel declared its independence in May 1948, the Jewish population numbered 650,000—double that of 1936 and more than ten times what it had been at the start of British Mandatory Palestine in 1917. With the establishment of the State of Israel, around 180,000 Arabs remained in the State of Israel. Around 710,000 left either voluntarily or by force.

The establishment of the state in 1948 did not alter the pattern of behavior of the "mobilized economy and society" that had characterized the Yishuv, and the Israeli leadership continued in this manner for at least the first three decades of Israel's existence. In 1955, amid the worsening of the security problem of the Palestinian fedayeen (nationalist guerillas or militants), the government did not hesitate to ask the public for donations through the *Keren HaMagen* ("Defense Fund"), which raised funds for weapons for the IDF. This received a strong positive response. The fundraising efforts raised public morale and created a sense of cohesion amid the dangers that the country was facing. The public felt it was a partner in these security efforts.

The State of Israel's establishment resulted from a combination of a number of historical, political, cultural, social, and military processes. The development of economic power was an important factor in the building of the state. The Zionist strategy had been successful in two major projects. The first was increasing the Jewish population in the Land of Israel to such a critical mass that no solution other than partitioning the land into two states for two peoples was possible. The second success was building a modern, growing, dynamic economy open to the global economy, a domestic economy that was proactive, with developed institutions and capable leadership. The Yishuv's great achievement throughout the years was its success in taking advantage of time and opportunities to create powerful security, economic, and societal structures, and move toward the realization of its national goals.

Amidst the economic struggle that took place in the Land of Israel between the Jewish community and the Palestinians since the end of the nineteenth century lay the achievement of the Jewish Yishuv in building economic power. The Jewish population in Israel in 2022 was over a hundred times greater than it had been in 1922. Thanks to the large waves of immigration, the population had increased steadily, without harming growth. Israel is an example, perhaps the only one of its kind, of a country that has maintained both rapid population growth and rapid economic growth, and over a long period, partly because of the large amounts of foreign aid from global Jewry, as well as from Germany and the United States, but largely due to its determined economic policy that focused on growth and employment. From a historical perspective—a bird's eye view, as it were—Israel's economy can be said to have demonstrated great flexibility in the way it transitioned between economic strategies. While these strategies did not pass without crisis, they usually succeeded in making the quantum leap to the next level.

# 6

# Building the Economy

## The Tempestuous Years

In 1973, as Israel celebrated its 25th Independence Day, its per capita GDP stood at about $13,000 per capita (at 2021 prices): similar to that of some smaller European countries (e.g., Austria or Belgium), and even higher than that of Japan. This achievement was the result of Israel's economic policy in the country's first 25 years of statehood, during which the foundations of the Israeli economy were laid.

These early years were very difficult, chiefly as a result of two events that had a considerable impact on the economy: the harsh and bloody War of Independence against invading Arab armies, and the influx of hundreds of thousands of immigrants from what was referred to as "70 countries," although the actual number was 120. When Israel declared its independence, the Yishuv had a population of some 650,000 Jews (plus another 180,000 Palestinians). In less than four years, some 700,000 new immigrants poured into the new state, doubling the population between May 1948 and the end of 1951.

Security and immigration costs were to prove a challenge and a heavy burden for the nascent state. Israel's acute scarcity of foreign currency reserves following British limitations on the pound when they left Mandate Palestine made it harder for the government to address these challenges, and this affected imports of food, raw materials, fuel, weapons, and the equipment for investment that was so necessary to creating employment. Victory in the War of Independence, which had claimed so many lives, was finally secured in April 1949 upon the signing of the Armistice Agreements between Israel, Egypt, Lebanon, Jordan, and Syria, formally declaring an end to the hostilities. Until then, Israel's conscription efforts had been at their peak. By early 1949, there were about 100,000 people – some 15 percent of the Jewish population of Israel – actively serving in the Israeli military. As soon as Israel declared its independence, with the war still raging, Holocaust survivors from the displaced populations of Europe began pouring into the country. So, too, did immigrants from the Middle East and North Africa in a mass Jewish exodus from the Muslim world, including Jews from Iraq (including many brought to Israel in Operation Ezra and Nehemiah, 1951–1952) and Yemen (including many brought in Operation Magic Carpet, 1949–1950), who were torn from their communities in the wake of Israel's declaration of independence. Their requirements were modest, but the state still needed to provide food, clothing, housing, employment, healthcare, and education – and it had no resources to absorb these immigrants properly. In the absence of adequate housing for the hundreds of thousands of new immigrants, 132 transit camps of tents, huts, and shacks were erected as temporary solutions for a quarter of a million people and provided shelter for them during the harsh winters of 1950 and1951.

When the British Mandatory government left the Land of Israel, it also left behind empty coffers. As a result, the new Israeli state set out on its economic journey on the verge of bankruptcy, as, because of British moves, it had no foreign currency to buy food, oil, raw materials, and more. On February 22, 1948, three months before Israel declared independence, the British had excluded the Palestine pound (the currency of British Mandatory Palestine) from the sterling area and blocked its accumulated sterling balances. Israel continued to peg its currency to the sterling but without British backing. The per capita GDP of the Yishuv, on the eve of Israel's declaration of independence, was about $4,500 (at 2021 prices), which was still relatively high compared to the Palestinian community and even small European countries. In 1949–1951, GDP fell as a result of mass immigration, but by 1954, this trend had reversed, and Israel's GDP per capita began to rise.

In the period of 1948–1954, management of Israel's economy was entirely in the hands of the Ministry of Finance, which was responsible for all branches of economic policy, fiscal and monetary. However, this economic management had to be undertaken under the dark cloud of Israel's foreign currency reserve shortage, which created the need for administrative management, rationing, price controls, and strict foreign currency controls. In addition, there were other pressing concerns—including a serious lack of educational resources for schoolchildren, with schools operating in two shifts due to a classroom shortage. This was accompanied by a teacher shortage, and young women soldiers just out of high school themselves were often brought into schools to teach. Meanwhile, the health system was also struggling to cope under the heavy load that had been placed on its existing infrastructures.

The main thrust of Israel's administrative policy was austerity. During 1949–1954, this policy affected the supply of food, clothing, furniture, and other basic goods. These were allocated through a system of vouchers and points at subsidized prices, replacing free market mechanisms. The government copied this model from a weakened post-war Britain, which had introduced rationing in the aftermath of the Second World War. Israel saw black markets and profiteering emerging alongside these administrative mechanisms, enabling those with means to purchase what they could not buy in the state-regulated system. This led to suppressed inflation, whereby the prices of the controlled goods were cheaper than free market prices. Nonetheless, for the government, the most important thing was to create a mechanism that could supply everyone with basic necessities at an equal price, so that no one would go hungry. The unpopular policies of austerity and rationing were a necessary evil for the poor as well as the rich, creating a sense of solidarity in the country. The price was bureaucracy, protectionism, and corruption. The easing of austerity began in 1954, when new sources of foreign currency reserves were created through money that came from Germany, Israeli bonds, and philanthropy, and in 1959, the policy was formally abolished.

Eliezer Kaplan was the Minister of Finance responsible for leading Israel's economic policy in these early years. Kaplan was in office during the turbulent period of war, mass immigration, and acute foreign currency reserve shortages, and dealt with the economic difficulties of 1948–1951 "with his bare hands." During his tenure as Minister of Finance, dozens of agricultural settlements were built, as well as a network of roads that connected the settlements to the center of the country. Above all, Kaplan provided for the needs of the population with the meager resources he had at his disposal. The slowing of the great wave of immigration at the end of 1951 enabled the government to begin planning an economic policy and present a wide-ranging plan at the start of 1952. This task was undertaken by Israel's second Minister of Finance, Levi Eshkol, following Kaplan's death at the end of June 1952.

Presented in 1952, Eshkol's plan addressed the issue of suppressed inflation, the budget deficit that accompanied the austerity policy, and price controls. The acute foreign currency reserve shortage mandated a sharp devaluation of the Israeli lira against the dollar, a reflection of the government's late understanding of the need to adjust the price of foreign currency to its scarcity. Beyond devaluing foreign currency, Israel adopted a policy of protectionism over imports, which involved serious distortions in taxes and incentives. This move helped subsidize exports as well as the establishment of scores of factories that were able to employ a large number of workers, most without prior experience in industry or agriculture, thereby both reducing unemployment and providing an answer to the shortage of goods. The government's policies achieved their main goals of controlling the current account deficit in the balance of payments, engineering rapid growth, supplying basic goods, lowering unemployment, and building an industrial base that employed about a quarter of all workers. The process also introduced a distorted effective exchange rate system into the production system.

***

A particularly difficult issue with which Israel had to contend immediately upon declaring independence was the supply of fuel.[1] This was a complex problem for the newly independent state, even greater than that of the scarcity of foreign currency reserves. The supply of oil to British Mandatory Palestine had come via pipeline from Iraq to the refineries in Haifa. However, with the outbreak of the Arab-Israeli War in 1948, this source was cut off, and Israel found itself without fuel not only for its war efforts, but for its civilian needs as well. In short, without oil, it was impossible to maintain the state or to win the war.

In its early years of statehood, Israel made considerable efforts to procure oil. The country's leadership found itself having to maneuver between the interests of Britain and oil producers in the Middle East to ensure a fuel supply. Complex operations and convoluted stratagems were employed to obtain the oil without which Israel could not have continued to exist. Petroleum supply would remain a complex issue for years to come. In the 1950s, efforts were made to forge ties with the Shah's regime in Iran to transfer oil through the Straits of Tiran to the port of Ashkelon on the Mediterranean coast – a move that also benefitted Tehran by helping it export oil to the West. This arrangement lasted until the Iranian Revolution in 1979. Israel's dependence on oil remained a central economic and political factor in forming government policy. The 1979 peace agreement with Egypt contained an important clause for the supply of crude oil in exchange for Israel's relinquishment of the Alma oilfield in the Gulf of Suez.[2] Only with the discovery of natural gas in the 2000s would a new era begin for Israel's energy policy, creating opportunities that turned a central strategic problem into just one of many economic issues.

## Organization and the Great Leap Forward

During the turbulent years of 1948–1954 and the rapid growth period of 1955–1965, foreign currency reserve shortages continued to be a fundamental problem, pushing the government to resort to a significant devaluation in February 1962, when the official exchange rate of the Israeli lira against the dollar rose from 1.8 – 3. However, this nominal devaluation did not result in the desired economic outcome in terms of improving the balance of payments. Instead, it caused inflationary pressures that neutralized the effectiveness of the real devaluation, and there was no resulting improvement in the balance of payments. The lesson Israeli leaders learned from these events was that, in order to improve the balance of payments, increase the price of imports, and stimulate exports, there needed to be a real change in the exchange rate. The economy has since undergone several nominal devaluation events that, due to price increases in production inputs, did not result in a real devaluation.

The 1950s and 1960s were years of building numerous large-scale national construction and development projects, among them the Port of Ashdod, the Dead Sea factories, the National Water Carrier of Israel (used to transfer water from the Sea of Galilee to the center and south of the country), and the creation of a merchant fleet and Israel's defense industries. Some of these projects were funded by reparations from Germany and World Bank loans. The end of the reparations payment arrangement in 1964 and the cessation of the World Bank loans for big projects, on the grounds that Israel had already become a developed country resulted in a decrease in capital imports to Israel. The Israeli leadership feared that the country would be hit by another foreign currency reserve shortage that would harm growth. Despite the development of import-substituting industries and exports, excess imports continued to rise, posing a major problem for economic policymakers. In 1965, fears of foreign currency reserve shortages pushed the government to introduce a moderated, proactive economic policy, intended to reduce demand for foreign currency and free up production, thus boosting exports and increasing the country's foreign currency reserves. The state budget for 1965 thus aimed to slow down economic activity and divert production from domestic goods to exports. In reality, by reducing government investments, the government caused a sharper recession than it had originally intended. As a result, unemployment soared to a record high of 11 percent in 1966, while GDP increased by only 1.6 percent in the same year. The resulting recession prevented any continuation of the rapid growth that the economy had enjoyed for over a decade.

Despite the recession, the Six-Day War of 1967 was proof that the immense efforts invested in developing the Israeli economy over the previous two decades had resulted in strategic economic resilience. It had also created a significant economic disparity between Israel and its neighbors. The IDF's impressive military successes in the Six-Day War were achieved with a military force that had been developed over the years based on a strong economy that also contributed to the 1968 military victory. Here was the practical proof, demonstrated through a real-world test, that Ben-Gurion's decision to balance defense spending with investments in the economy and society was justified. The economy was strong, in spite of the recession, and the army was well-equipped and ready for action.

After the Six-Day War, the economy emerged from recession quickly, due to an increase in defense spending and the replenishment of stocks. Recovery was also bolstered by a rise in public optimism in the wake of the great victory that had followed the anxiety during the many days of waiting for the anticipated breakout of hostilities. In addition, world Jewry mobilized to help Israel, before and after the war, with grants and loans in foreign currency that enabled the country to survive the war and recover from it quickly.

The economic situation had now shifted from one extreme to another. A small devaluation in the currency rate in November 1967, following the depreciation of British sterling against the dollar (even though the lira was not pegged to the sterling) had a positive effect on exports and contributed to the recovery of the economy. This is an example of a "modest" devaluation (16 percent), which caused a positive real devaluation, due to unemployment and the recession, which in turn curbed the increase in imports without eroding the profitability of exports.

Already by 1969, the economy had bounced back to full employment and rapid growth. During 1971–1973, growth stood at over 12 percent per annum, and the standard of living However, defense costs also increased as a result of the extensive deployment of the IDF and the War of Attrition that involved fighting between Israel and Egypt, Jordan, and the Palestine Liberation Organization (PLO) between 1967 and 1970. These events increased the budget deficit and balance of payments, resulting in inflationary pressures and rising social disparities. Unemployment stood at less than three percent, prompting the government to finally agree to allow Palestinian workers to enter the Israeli labor market in September of 1970. Thus opened a new chapter of unemployment and dependence on foreign labor.

## Notes

1. Gili Dinstein, The Clerk, Kinneret-Zmora-Bitan, 2020.
2. See "Israel Gives Up an Oilfield to Egypt in Biggest Sacrifice for Treaty Yet," The New York Times, Nov. 26, 1979. https://www.nytimes.com/1979/11/26/archives/israel-gives-up-an-oilfield-to-egypt-in-biggest-sacrifice-for.html.

# 7

# Economic Strategy

## Survival

It cannot be said that, upon its establishment, Israel had a clear, well-thought-out strategy for economic development or for providing goods and services to its existing population and the large waves of new immigrants arriving on its shores. What the Yishuv's leadership did have was a "super strategy"—to realize the nation's destiny by establishing a sovereign Jewish settlement in the Land of Israel, one that could receive immigrants and maintain its people's security. The new Jewish state was born into a reality in which it had no natural resources nor allies, whether historical, geopolitical, strategic, or in terms of shared values. Israel faced enormous uncertainty in the first few years of its existence, due to both the imposing numbers of immigrants who flooded into its borders and to the military challenges that it had to face as soon as it declared its independence.

However, the Israeli leadership, led by Prime Minister David Ben-Gurion, did have clarity of thinking and a strategic, logical plan of action guided by key principles that the new state needed to achieve in these difficult and risky first years. These entailed devoting most of the resources that could be mobilized to building economic and social strength alongside building security capabilities. These principles served as the foundations of the resolute decisions taken by the young state's leadership in building the state and its economy. It was against this background, for example, that Ben-Gurion signed the Reparations Agreement with Germany—his motive was to facilitate the development of the economy. To reinforce this strategy, the leadership had a firm belief in the righteousness of their chosen path, as well as in their ability and determination to act decisively in the face of the enormous challenges that lay ahead. They were sure that they could sway public opinion and lead the Israeli masses along this path, without needing to resort to populism.

The main mission of the newly independent State of Israel was to create a normal, stable country for the Jews who were immigrating to it. This was no easy task, not least in light of the sheer diversity of the tens of thousands of immigrants arriving on its shores, who came from different countries, spoke different languages, and had very different cultural backgrounds. Most came because they were fleeing hardship in their countries of origin, and not because they were motivated by Zionist ideology or by a desire to be pioneers. The one ambition uniting most of these immigrants was their fervent wish to live in a sovereign state, where they could take charge of their own destinies.

It is impossible to overlook the economic hardships that Israel faced in its first years, and especially the feelings of fragility that characterized this period. Nonetheless, Israel's leaders, driven by their great vision and determination, did not refrain from taking risks and imposing tough, collective measures to manage the economy. In the first three years of Israel's independence, the government had to contend with a war, a precarious security situation, and a huge population increase due to immigration. During this short period, some 700,000 new immigrants arrived in Israel, slightly more than the number of Jews living in British Mandatory Palestine on the eve of Israel's declaration of independence. There is no precedent for such immigration rates anywhere in the world. No country in history has ever doubled its population in less than four years, certainly not while fighting for its very existence. As noted previously, the government had to supply the basic needs of this growing population with the few natural resources it had available, and amid an acute scarcity of foreign currency reserves.

## Import substitution strategy

Throughout 1952 and 1953, Israel's leaders made a series of major economic decisions that would affect the country's economic development for decades to come. They developed a far-reaching economic strategy, which is reflected in the economic plan presented in July 1952 by the new Minister of Finance, Levi Eshkol. Eshkol's plan centered on devaluing the currency to make imports more expensive and to stimulate exports, with the aim of overcoming the main problem faced by the economy—the acute shortage of foreign currency reserves. Indeed, this shortage was the basis of the rationale behind the government's strategy of developing import-substituting industrial plants, and its strict rules on importing finished goods and encouraging local production. Under this policy, the government also imposed strict administrative import bans and high import taxes, with the aim of stimulating the domestic production of all possible products using the minimum amount of imported raw materials. The development of an independent industrial and agricultural production capacity was intended to supply basic necessities to a growing population that desperately needed them. By building industries that were protected from imports, the government also answered another pressing need—providing employment for the new immigrants. At the same time, the government took a number of actions to increase capital imports by opening channels for grants and loans from world Jewry and from West Germany.

Additionally, the government directed many new immigrants to live in the moshavim, among other places, so that they could work to provide agricultural produce for themselves and for the rest of the population of Israel. Hundreds of moshavim and kibbutzim were established for this purpose within the agricultural sector. In 1958, the number of people employed in agriculture reached a peak of about 18 percent of the total workforce (compared to just one percent in 2023). This was accompanied by the development of industry in both the country's well-established and its new cities, all officially protected by high customs rates, and based on labor-intensive production and simple technologies. These new factories produced basic goods that replaced imports at low standards but with minimum use of imported inputs (foreign currency). This not only provided a response to consumer demand, but helped drive large-scale employment in industry, agriculture, and construction. At this stage, attention was not necessarily paid to considerations of efficiency or viability. Rather, the goal was to develop a system of industrial production at almost any cost. This would provide speedy employment solutions and help train new immigrants for a productive working life, chiefly as agricultural workers and manual laborers in industry and construction.

The severe foreign currency reserve shortages helped engender a national economic ethos that the new Jewish state had the technical know-how to produce literally everything itself, even when it was not necessarily beneficial to do so. The principle of "comparative advantage"[1] had no meaning. The tens of thousands of new immigrants who were quickly absorbed into industry and agriculture were a source of pride and satisfaction to the new state. The phrase "for the first time after two thousand years of exile" was echoed in all areas of life, including with regard to the economy: there were, "for the first time after two thousand years of exile," industrial laborers and factories, farmers, and construction workers. In the late 1950s, about one-quarter of the total workforce was employed in industry. In essence, this was Israel's industrial revolution—replete with factories, mass production, and the clamor of machinery. The government chose to invest in water infrastructure, electricity, land reclamation and drainage, road construction, and establishing new settlements instead of increasing the standard of living and even instead of building suitable and permanent housing. In short, the state suppressed private consumption in favor of investing in agriculture, industry, and infrastructure.

Both veteran Israelis and new immigrants shared in the initial experiences of building the state, economy, and nation. They understood the significance of living at a time where the defining experience was creating a brand-new state that was fulfilling the historical vision of "Shivat Zion" ("return to Zion)," a term often used to refer to the event when Jews returned to Israel from the Babylonian exile, following the decree by Cyrus the Great of Persian. In these early days, the drive to build the economy was an inseparable part of the public's enthusiasm for building a state and fulfilling its dream of sovereignty and independence. Growth in the first two decades post-independence was over 10 percent in real terms per year, and about 5.5 percent per capita. These were unprecedented rates even in a world that was experiencing rapid growth following the Second World War: Israel was seen as an "economic prodigy" even compared to Germany and Japan, which themselves were experiencing impressive growth.

The government was involved in financing, setting prices, subsidies, and entrepreneurship. Preference was given to the wider public sector—the government, the Histadrut, and the Jewish Agency, dividing much of the work between them. Nevertheless, the government also encouraged the private sector, and was keen on encouraging foreign investment, mainly from world Jewry, to diversify sources of financing and entrepreneurship. Foreign investors were few and far between, however, and affluent Diaspora Jews preferred to donate to fundraising campaigns and buy State of Israel Bonds rather than invest directly in Israel. Israel's enjoyed rapid growth in its first years following independence not because of foreign investment, but because of its extensive construction of infrastructure, including roads, power plants, a merchant fleet, the Ashdod port, the National Water Carrier, and water and drainage projects for the extensive agricultural sector, financed in part by bonds purchases and other foreign funds, such as German reparations.

The construction industry was vital, not least because of the need to provide permanent housing solutions for the hundreds of thousands of immigrant families living in temporary accommodation, but also to build public institutions, industrial plants, and infrastructure. The number of people employed in construction in those early years amounted to about ten percent of the total workforce, a high rate that reflected the importance of industry, and served as an indicator of economic activity.

Israel was not only concerned with the development of industry and physical infrastructure for housing. Many resources were invested in developing the education system to meet the overwhelming needs for education services for the growing population, the importance of which was also reflected in the enactment of the Compulsory Education Law (1949). One of the first laws legislated by the first Knesset, it was passed despite the country's difficult economic situation. Israel's healthcare system also expanded considerably as the country's population swelled and relied on the state hospitals that had operated under the British Mandatory government, as well as on the already existing Hadassah Hospital and the Histadrut Health Fund, which served as the basis of the healthcare system growing population.

The government's economic policies were met with lively and often heated public and professional debate. Some saw these policies as socialist because of the extensive involvement of the state in the management of the economy, and thus opposed them on ideological grounds. Others saw them as practical—the only way to supply basic needs to the population. Mapai, the party that governed in the first decades of the state, continuing its leadership since the 1930s, did employ socialist rhetoric and terminology, but in practice, its economic policies were not socialist. Rather, they were realistic and pragmatic. Led by Ben-Gurion (and Minister of Finance Eshkol), the government's economic strategy was designed to address the challenges of employment, the supply of goods, and economic growth, and fulfill the government's state-building project. This involved finding ways to absorb the huge waves of immigrants and turn them into productive citizens within the so-called "melting pot" of the new state. These new immigrants were urged to shed their old Diaspora identities and adopt the values of the hegemonic population that had guided the Yishuv and now the government of the independent State of Israel. In essence, this was a great social experiment. The tremendous efforts to absorb these immigrants were certainly not free from errors, injustices, discrimination, misunderstandings, prejudices, and a hegemonic cultural and value perception that would also affect the second and third generations of Israelis. Yet, under the conditions faced by the poor, besieged new State, which had endured a bloody war, the government was simply not able to give the immigrants what it did not have in the first place. Under the circumstances, the state's achievements should be seen as an unparalleled accomplishment.

Economic policy in the 1950s and 1960s was rooted in the political stability that was a hallmark of the governments in those decades. Levi Eshkol and Pinchas Sapir each served about 11 years as Minister of Finance. The definitive policy decisions of the 1950s would determine the development of the economy's foundations and infrastructure for the first four decades of Israel's existence, and in some cases even longer. Their economic strategy produced real growth, from 1952–1973, of over 10 percent on average per annum, and 5.5 percent on average per annum in per capita GDP. From a historical perspective, the first ten years of Israel's independence was a formative decade that shaped the generations to come. The great challenges faced by the nascent state required an economic policy that was appropriate for its time, under the unique circumstances of that era. The first years of independence were a unique period of state-and-nation-building both accomplished using governmental and Histadrut mechanisms that had a high capacity to deliver, and led by a determined, capable leadership that enjoyed popular support and solidarity. Key to the success of the economic policy of these turbulent, formative years was gaining the people's trust in the country's leadership, not least since the government had to prioritize national needs at the expense of citizens' private standard of living.

Israel's most impressive achievements was the absorption of immigrants from all over the world - what is called in Hebrew "Kibbutz Galyot," the ingathering of all the exiles. The 350,000 Holocaust survivors who had flooded into Israel by the early 1950s, along with hundreds of thousands of new immigrants from Middle Eastern countries, and joined the existing population of the old Yishuv, created a vibrant, multicultural society. There was certainly no lack of problems—indeed, some are still ongoing today—but the merging of immigrants from Eastern Europe and the Middle East created the melting pot and rich mosaic of human diversity that characterizes Israel. This was a complex social process that was neither easy, nor perfect. Its echoes still resonate to this day. Yet the economic results were impressive, which have found expression in recent years in the emergence of the concept of the "Start-Up Nation." These qualities revealed themselves in Israel's very first years of existence through its ambition to become a first-world economy. Israel was able—despite the hardships experienced by its population in the early years of statehood—to reject the gratifications of consumption and "extravagance," and instead focused its resources on building economic and social infrastructure as a basis for growth and creating an advanced economy. This was the secret of its success—a unique phenomenon that would probably be difficult to reproduce.

## Geographic strategy

The aim of Israel's geographical strategy was to disperse the population within the new state and develop the economy in order both to absorb the waves of immigrants and settle the new territories gained in the War of Independence. There was a tacit acknowledgement that if Israel did not immediately succeed in settling the territories it had taken control of during the War of Independence, they would not remain in Israeli hands.

These new territories, together with the huge increase in population, led the government to prepare a master plan for the dispersion of the population in 1951. Known as the "Sharon Plan" after Arieh Sharon, the architect who developed it, this was Israel's first national master plan, and it would define the country's character (and create not a few of its problems). The Sharon Plan was intended to fulfill certain national imperatives—political, security, and territorial.

Sharon's master plan called for the creation of new cities and hundreds of settlements across the entire new Israeli space, from the north to the south. It dictated a Israel's geographical organization in terms of land use, infrastructures, and the dispersed development of the country beyond the central Tel Aviv-Jerusalem area. The logic behind the plan was to convert uninhabited territories into settlements that could guard against security threats, create defenses along the borders of the young state, and to develop agricultural lands to provide basic fresh foodstuffs—vegetables, fruit, and livestock—to feed the growing population.

When the state was established, there were very few medium-sized or small urban settlements outside of the three big cities of Jerusalem, Tel Aviv, and Haifa. The government sought to create a balanced urban hierarchy that changed the polarized urban arrangements of these three large urban centers, by creating small, medium, and large towns alongside the agricultural settlements, and medium-sized towns that would exist in a continuous chain between village and city. Under the population dispersion policy, as outlined in what was known as the Sharon Plan or the "New Towns Program," dozens of urban settlements of varying sizes were built, as well as a network of roads connecting them, thereby changing the status quo of the three large metropolitan cities. The creation of these development towns[2] resonated with contemporary thinking that opposed large, densely populated cities. This, then, was the basis for Israel's urbanization.[3]

To secure the sovereignty of the young state, the leadership believed that the Negev and Galilee should be settled so that the new territories annexed to the state during the war would not remain empty, and that many people were needed to accomplish this. This policy was viewed as positive and necessary, and resulting in an impressive achievement of settling the new immigrants and populating new areas of the country, including the sensitive, empty, and neglected frontier lands. In retrospect, however, it is apparent that, despite the dispersion of the immigrants to the development towns in Israel's periphery, the majority of the population continued to reside along the coastal plain.

Israel was founded at a time when the world was dominated by the modernist trend in city planning and architecture—the Brutalist movement that suited the mythology and values that characterized Israeli society at the time: fast construction, simplicity, directness, and an emphasis on the authentic expression of materials, born out of a commitment to fair housing that would be as equal as possible and serve the masses. Since the land was owned by the state, it was easy for it to carry out its plans quickly. This is how the neighborhoods of uniform row housing projects came to be built: similar to workers' housing in the suburbs of European cities, they were designed as a solution to the housing shortages in the coastal plains, the Jerusalem hills, the Negev desert, and in the center of the country. The neighborhoods themselves were often populated according to the ethnic background of the immigrants dispersed to them.

In the first 30 years, the government adopted a policy of urban dispersion and rural settlement—a policy that was not supported by an adequate road and rail transport infrastructure. The argument was that it would have been more effective to invest in strengthening existing settlements; instead, there was a proliferation of small development towns, many of which were unable to support themselves financially for quite some time. The policy of population dispersion led to a flood of immigrants being transferred into these problematic development towns. Most of these immigrants originated in Mizrahi cultures, and suffering from low socioeconomic status in Israel, they lacked the cultural power to resist their relocation. Since that period, this policy has been subject to considerable criticism. In addition to objections to the settlement of Mizrahi immigrants in development towns, arguments have been raised that too many development towns were created, or that government should have settled the immigrants in the old, established cities. Other groups also criticized the treatment, Instead of Mizrahi, not familiar to the reader, immigrants who came from Arab states. who were excluded from the Zionist narrative of nation-building in the heroic days of the 1950s and 1960s. It is difficult to judge the decisions of the young country's leaders by today's standards.

These are profound issues, and some of the reaction responses to them are insights borne from hindsight. The important point is that these problems should be addressed and corrected, that historical consciousness needs to change, and that there must be a recognition of the injustices caused to the immigrants. Acknowledging these injustices does not delegitimize the special national and Zionist actions of those years, or the impressive achievements of Israel's economy.

## Government involvement

The government's involvement in economic development in the early years of statehood was an unavoidable necessity in view of the great challenges that faced the young country. The situation in the years immediately post-independence was one of acute "market failure." The markets struggled to provide solutions to the reality of an ongoing war, the absorption of hundreds of thousands of immigrants, the huge shortage of foreign currency as well as goods and services, and a not yet developed private sector. The economy simply could not operate according to normal market forces. To prevent chaos, the government had no choice but to be involved in almost every area of life. A legitimate question was—for how long should this situation prevail? The answer is a complex one.

Ben-Gurion, upon assuming the post of prime minister, emphasized the consolidation of statehood in the newly independent Israel, and decided that it was the government that should lead the economic, geographic, and urban development of the state. He feared that otherwise nothing would be done, and the future of the fragile, new state would be jeopardized. Statism dictated much of Israel's economic steps, just as it did in other areas of life. These policies did not stem from a strict socialist ideology of state control of the means of production, as opposed to the capitalist concept of private financiers. The government adopted a statist policy of involvement in the economy on the grounds that this was the only way a national economy could be built. At this point, there was no practical alternative that involved private capitalists who could help lighten the heavy load of developing the country, as no private financiers were forthcoming with offers of help.

In the summer of 1950, Israel decided to pivot to the West, when it supported the United States rather than the Soviet Union in the Korean crisis. This decision had both political and economic motives, as Ben-Gurion faced strong internal opposition against the government's economic policy from the Mapam[4] party, which had communist and socialist leanings. Ben-Gurion, believing the economy should rely on both private and public involvement, bolstered his more moderate position by deciding not to take the side of the Soviet Union, the communist superpower. In practice, there were also struggles between the government and the Histadrut. The Histadrut was more "loyal" to the socialist approach than was the government. In view of the Histadrut's size and centrality in the pre-state economy, the government saw it as a partner in the economy and in social enterprises, such as through the Histadrut-owned *Kupot Cholim* (health funds) in healthcare and the *Hevrat HaOvdim* (the Society of Workers, the economic arm of the Histadrut), in economic development. However, the government also saw the Histadrut as an adversary that was hindering the consolidation of the state economy. The Histadrut was involved in health services through the "kupot holim" and in education through its educational track. The Jewish Agency and the Zionist Organization were also useful public entities involved with bringing in immigrants, assisting with their initial absorption, and helping to establish agriculture and waterworks. In fact, these two organizations provided most of the services to the Jewish community until the state was able to do so. For a government that was perceived as socialist, at no stage did it make any attempt to adopt a communist ideology.

The government did not hesitate to support the encouragement of private investors from Israel and abroad, as another arm in building the economy and creating sources of employment. The government courted foreign private investors so that they would bring entrepreneurship and capital to the development of the economy. Some argued that there was over-encouragement of private investors, who brought almost no private capital but received generous assistance from the government. The government encouraged the private sector in areas where it thought this was appropriate, such as dentistry and some other trades, but there were areas that the government considered should not have private sector involvement, such as infrastructure, pensions, education, health, and security.

In a reality where the government was the driving force behind entrepreneurship and financing, the almost inevitable outcome was the nationalization of the capital markets. For forty years, the government mobilized public savings to allocate capital to meet its goals. The Histadrut benefited from being the preferred recipient of state capital. As the owner of most of Israel's pension funds, the Histadrut secured a large portion of the country's retirement savings to use for the development and investment goals of its economic arm, Hevrat HaOvdim. This situation undoubtedly served political ends. In addition, most of the capital that flowed into the country from overseas (via fundraising campaigns, bonds, reparations, World Bank loans, etc.) went to the government and public institutions to build public infrastructure.

Political opposition to the country's economic policies came mainly from the General Zionists and Herut (Freedom) political parties, and to a lesser extent from academics from the Hebrew University's Economics Department (which in the 1950 and 1960s was the main source of scholars in economics), who supported a free market economy. They were united in challenging the government's policy but did not offer any realistic practical alternative to the problems the country was facing. The General Zionists were the leading capitalist party of post-independence Israel. They were staunch supporters of a liberal economy and free markets, and firmly opposed the government's involvement in the economy, criticizing the distortions caused by state intervention, such as the concentration of power in the Histadrut and the priority given it in resource allocation, as a policy disgrace. They openly declared their support for a free market liberated from state intervention and based on private entrepreneurship. Together with Herut, the General Zionists opposed the Histadrut on economic and political grounds. They advocated a free-market housing rental market, and opposed state intervention in the form of subsidized housing or rent controls. The ideas of the General Zionists and their close circles were supported by the urban and bourgeois public.

Israel was facing challenges that few, if any, other countries had ever experienced. Its development strategy was determined by constraints and limitations, and much less by ideology. There was simply no other practical strategy to build large-scale production capacity and create jobs quickly, especially amid such an acute shortage of foreign currency reserves. The strategy to build a labor-intensive (i.e., in order to create employment for immigrants) import-substituting industry with simple technologies, and to implement foreign exchange controls, import bans and tariffs, stemmed from pragmatism and not so much from ideology. There is no doubt that state intervention in the economy created distortions that had a political dimension. But the historical question remains open—would it have been possible to manage Israel's economy in these years via free market policies and low government intervention, and also absorb a million immigrants and build the economy? Israel's economic performance was very good, in terms of growth, employment, building infrastructure, and centralized social systems. Could even better results have been achieved? It is difficult to say. In later years, free market ideas became the economic reality of the country. There is a time for every idea, and a time for every stage of economic development. The question of how long the state should have been involved in the economy is debatable—some have argued 20 years, and some 30 years. But there is a consensus that it should not have lasted for any longer than that.

Long-term, significant state intervention in Israel's early years created a situation in which the government had to take on numerous roles, making it difficult for it to function properly. The government, of course, was in charge of determining economic and social policy—now a necessary and accepted role for every government in the world, even in free market economies. It was also extensively involved in the economy as the owner of state companies, some of which were monopolies in their fields (e.g., electricity, water, communications, energy), and thus found itself embroiled in conflicts of interest that required oversight and monitoring. The government appointed the regulators whose role it was to supervise competition, maintain standards, and more, but in practice, regulation was weak, unprofessional, and disorganized. As a result, state dominance was total. As the owner of assets, the state operated without any oversight of its decisions and actions. As a significant purchaser of goods and services in health, security, and energy, there was a high potential for conflicts of interest. It was obvious that such a reality could not continue for many years. As the economy grew, and these economic complexities increased, it became clear that other arrangements were needed, and state involvement should be reduced. This would take place during the serious economic crises and reforms of the 1980s.

## Economic and social institutions

International experience has shown that successful countries have professional and efficient institutions that, together with the political leadership, create the balance and integration necessary to build a functioning economy and society. In its first years following independence, Israel relied on the institutions of the "soon-to-be-state" and those of the British Mandatory government. This already represented quite a lot. For some 30 years before the establishment of the state, the Yishuv leadership built a functioning "soon-to-be-state" for the Jewish community within British Mandatory Palestine. This "state within a state" had a democratic life, a settlement movement, a disciplined and relatively large militia, education, health, and banking systems, industrial and water infrastructure, a seaport, and airport, and construction plants. These institutions were built by the Yishuv according to the values that were important to them. Unique systems were created—the health funds, the kibbutzim, the moshavim, and the pension funds. The Histadrut was a trade union and also a large economic concern with extensive economic and social activity. The Jewish Agency, headed by Ben-Gurion, an outstanding leader in terms of his organizational ability and political savvy, added a dimension of self-government through its political department and national treasury.

The government took over the institutions of the British Mandatory government, its transport and energy infrastructure, courts, postal services, and police. The institutions of the British Mandatory government had served the entire population of British Mandatory Palestine, both Arabs and Jews. Yet it would be the institutions of the Yishuv that set the tone in the newly independent Israel, not those of the British colonialist system. The institutions of the British Mandatory government mainly served the governmental needs of the British, even if they were important in providing services to the population, and they needed to be adapted to the new reality.

Ben-Gurion did what was necessary to make the transition from a "soon-to-be-state" to a functioning state, including transforming the leadership of a national liberation movement to that of an independent country that was conscious of its statehood. He fought to realize this statehood—through the army (by dissolving the Palmach and Lehi organizations), and in education (by dissolving the Histadrut's workers' education scheme). This resulted in a fusion of political cultures: that of the Jewish leadership, most of whom came from Eastern Europe, British colonial tradition, and the culture that had developed in the Yishuv. The result was a fusion in two areas: one, a culture of struggle had to adjust to the need to maintain normal life; and second, the culture of institutions and the collective had to make room for individual needs.

One of Ben-Gurion's first actions as prime minister in July 1948 was to implement a 1947 proposal to establish a Central Bureau of Statistics. This move was an expression of Ben-Gurion's understanding that gathering professional and reliable data is central to decision-making, and was part of a series of formative events that showed forward thinking regarding the needs of the nascent state. The government's first major civilian operation was its policy of austerity and the rationing of basic goods via the Ministry of Rationing and Supply headed by Dov Yosef (Bernard Joseph). The shortages of foreign currency and the waves of immigrants entering the newly independent state posed an enormous challenge to the government, particularly in terms of ensuring food provision to the growing population.

The first Minister of Finance, Eliezer Kaplan, had served as the treasurer of the Jewish Agency since 1933. However, Jewish Agency treasurers had never needed to contend with the macroeconomic management of an independent country. Clearly, the Ministry of Finance of a sovereign state must address far more complex problems than those faced by the Jewish Agency. In the chaotic early years of statehood, the Ministry of Finance had to wrestle with the daunting challenges of absorbing masses of new immigrants amid an acute foreign currency reserve shortage, while simultaneously adopting measures to address immediate hardships. The second Minister of Finance, Levi Eshkol, built up the Ministry of Finance, and in 1952 established the Budgets Department as a separate office from the Treasury (the Accountant General). The Budgets Department was (and is) responsible for setting the state's economic policy by producing its budget. In the same year, an organized annual state budget was presented for the first time. Eshkol also organized the taxation system.

The year 1954 saw the establishment of two new and important institutions, both essential to an organized state. The first was the Bank of Israel as a central bank responsible for the country's monetary management and the supervision of its banking system. In the absence of a central bank, the role had been assigned to the Anglo-Palestine Bank, the bank of the Zionist movement. On August 17, 1948, the Anglo-Palestine Bank issued Israeli lira banknotes and coins. This was the second phase of sovereignty after the declaration of independence. The Anglo-Palestine Bank, which was renamed Bank Leumi L'Israel in 1951, continued to serve as a central bank for currency purposes until the Bank of Israel was established in 1954. The second institution to arise in 1954 was the National Insurance Institute as a social security institution, the concept of which had been developed prior to Israel's independence.

The development of Israel's general and economic administration took time. In 1959, the Israel Land Administration was founded. Social legislation was created, including the Hours of Work and Rest Law (1951), the State Education Law (1953), the Employment of Women Law (1954), and the Collective Agreements Law and Settlement of Labor Disputes Law (both 1957). The first governments were small, and government ministries (and ministers) numbered less than 15. Ministries were established in response to the needs of the hour—e.g., the Ministry of Rationing and Supply, the Ministry of Minority Affairs, and the Ministry of Religions and War Victims (which in 1951 became the Ministry of Welfare). The major ministries were: Foreign Affairs, Defense, Finance, Education, Justice, Health, Interior, Police, Trade and Industry, Labor (which included Housing), and Transport.

The success of Israel's economy has been partly attributed to the high quality of its government institutions, which were staffed by people dedicated to the concept of nation-building. The fabric of Israel's institutions was developed gradually, along with an evolving national ethos. This was the case with the law enforcement bodies of the police, the state prosecutor's office, and the courts, which were able to curb the government's tendency to take care of its own narrow concerns at the expense of the interests of the public. A dynamic democracy was built, one that was able to publicly criticize and penalize those who failed in their tasks (including through the Office of the State Comptroller, tasked with auditing government bodies), and over the years, institutions "with teeth" developed that were well able to curb conflicts of interest. This process of institution building was not without its challenges, in particular regarding addressing organizational and political obstacles. It was achieved through hard work, perseverance, and experience. In this way, Israel built its civil service and functioning government agencies. The public administration was initially staffed by an "old boys' club" from the controlling Mapai party, but over the years, it developed into a professional civil service, with a tradition of public servants. Despite the socialist tradition, these institutions gradually adopted codes of conduct that protected private property, establishing rules for contracts, competition, and profit, as exist in market economies.

## Israeli Arabs

After the establishment of the state, it became clear that the new government was also responsible for the Arabs who remained within the borders of the State of Israel after the War of Independence. The Arab society was shocked by the change that had occurred in its position, from a majority in British Mandatory Palestine to a minority in the new Jewish state. Most of its leadership fled during the war, and those who remained were mostly in villages engaged in agriculture. Most of the Arabs who had lived in urban areas left the new state, and the elite fled. The defeat of the Arabs in the war left a small, weakened minority. In 1949, after the armistice agreements were signed with neighboring Arab states, there were about 180,000 Arabs in Israel, about 22 percent of the population, but their proportion decreased with the arrival of hundreds of thousands of immigrants in the 1950s. This was a poor population, preoccupied with survival, and was not involved in the main tasks of the state. This was a traditional society centered on the village, subsisting on agricultural and small-scale trading. Arab women's participation in the economy was very low—less than ten percent until the 1980s—a characteristic of traditional societies where women's educational level is low and their place is considered to be in the home. The educational level of Arab-Israeli men at that time was also low, and the overall standard of living was less than the average standard of living in Israel.

From 1948–1966, the Palestinians living in Israel were subjected to martial law that limited their freedom of movement, their ability to exercise independent economic activity, and many civil rights. The sense of vulnerability and lack of self-confidence of the young state regarding threats of a "second round" and the lack of recognition of its legitimacy by the Arab world led the new Israeli government to, among other things, isolate the "internal threat"—the Arabs of Israel. The Arab population within Israel saw itself as subordinate and discriminated-against tenants, and hardly contributed to Israel's economy. As a result, they barely benefitted from the growth boom that Israel experienced in its first few decades.

In November 1966, Prime Minister Levi Eshkol lifted the military rule over the Arab population in Israel, and from that moment there began a slow and gradual process of integrating the Arab minority into the economy—a process that has yet to be completed. The younger generation, who did not directly experience the events of 1947–1949 but heard of them only from their parents and grandparents, began to demand more rights from the state. The proportion of Palestinian residents of Israel in the Israeli population has increased over the years, reaching about 16 percent in 2022 (and about four percent of residents of East Jerusalem). The Arabs have become a large sector that the Israeli economy cannot ignore. On the contrary, recognition that the state needs to fully integrate this population into the economy has grown, a process that began, albeit with ups and downs, in the 1990s and continues to this day.

## Notes

1. This principle recognizes that every economy in the world seeks to specialize in certain goods and/or services in order to gain a "comparative advantage" in free trade with other countries.
2. Today, many of these development towns, built with the intention of modernizing the country and encouraging economic growth, have not thrived and are considered part of the economic periphery that lags behind the rest of the country.
3. This thinking has been attributed to the architect Eliezer Brutzkus, the urban planner who headed the government's Research and Survey Department after the establishment of the State Planning Department in 1948.

4. Mifleget HaPoalim HaMeuhedet (United Workers Party).

# 8

# Security

The pair of words "security and economy" has accompanied the economy of the State of Israel from the beginning of its existence and even earlier, and it continues to be relevant for the foreseeable future. The unique geopolitical situation of the State of Israel has created ongoing security challenges that have burdened Israeli society and its economy with exceptionally high security expenditures. Israel's economy and its national security *have* always been mutually interdependent—and will continue to be so for the foreseeable future. When the country was born amid the storm of fire and blood of its War of Independence (the First Arab-Israeli War, 1948–1949), Israel's defense expenditures stood at an astonishing 40 percent of total GDP. Its first years of statehood unfolded under the shadow of great uncertainty about Israel's survival due to constant security threats. These also threatened to overshadow its urgent major state and nation-building projects—absorbing the massive waves of new immigrants that began arriving on its shores, building a functioning economy and society, settling the land, dispersing the population, and developing key civilian infrastructures. The existential threat to Israel in its early years of statehood was very real. It is little surprise, then, that Israeli defense spending has always been exceptionally high compared with that of developed Western countries. Israel's high defense expenditure created (and still creates) a financial burden for the population and is the subject of an ongoing debate over the country's national priorities. The refrains (immortalized in a popular song) "cannons instead of socks" and "tanks instead of tractors,"[1] have been Israeli cultural leitmotifs from the early days of statehood. The young State of Israel needed to contend with the immediate needs of building a nation and an economy.

In its early years of statehood, Israel's first prime minister and minister of defense David Ben-Gurion established a clear defense doctrine that integrated and balanced the country's economic and security needs. Ben-Gurion adopted a policy of taking calculated risks, with the aim of developing Israel's economy and society as foundations for creating national resilience. In doing so, he understood that national security is not just about military might, and that the strength and resilience of a state hinges on finding a proper balance between investing in military power and building a stable economy and society. Israel's first premier was well aware that the resilience of the country's citizens, its public health, the education of its youth, and the development of infrastructures to permit free movement on land, sea, and air were also crucial elements in ensuring national security.

In December 1952, despite the precarious security situation and threats from Israel's neighbors to start a "second round" of the Arab-Israeli War, Ben-Gurion did not hesitate to refuse a request by IDF Chief of Staff Yigael Yadin for increases to the defense budget. The prime minister was willing to accept Yadin's resignation over this budget dispute, despite appreciating his Chief of Staff as a man who, to a large extent, had shaped the organizational structure of the IDF's regular and reserve forces. Ben-Gurion took risks. Despite the very real security threats facing Israel, he chose to direct its limited resources to absorbing immigrants, developing infrastructure, and establishing basic civil systems, out of a belief that maintaining a functioning society and a robust economy were essential components of the state's national security efforts.

Israel adopted the "people's army" model of compulsory military service for both men and women, with high public conscription rates and high levels of reserve service for decades after completion of compulsory military service. Ben-Gurion believed the "people's army" was a good model for a "melting pot" that could unite a heterogeneous population into a single nation. The relative economic equality in the population of those years made it easier for the government to instill a sense of solidarity among its citizens about bearing the economic and security burden of the new state.

Defense spending, from the end of the War of Independence to the Six-Day War (1949–1967) stood at about 9 percent of GDP (including defense imports of military equipment), with the exception of 1956–1957, during the Suez Crisis (the Second Arab-Israeli war). Israel's other budgetary priority was developing the economy and society. The high growth rate of the economy of about 10 percent per year on average made it possible to increase defense spending at a similar rate.

In practice, Israel's security expenditure, in the sense of the total cost to the economy, was much higher than the official defense budget recorded in the national accounting. Compulsory military service, which delayed young people from acquiring a profession and entering the labor market, had an alternative economic cost estimated at around three to four percent of GDP. However, military service also made a positive contribution to the economy by providing draftees with skills that improved their human capital.

Israel's great military victory in the Six-Day War of 1967, for example, was not only the result of its military might and capabilities, but also of its economic strength. Even with Israel's victory in the Six-Day War, defense spending soared in its aftermath to over 10–12 percent of GDP. This was due to the fact that Israel could not translate its military victory into diplomatic results; security threats continued to plague the country. The increase in defense spending created budgetary pressures, sparking debates in government and among the public over Israel's national priorities, the security burden, and its socioeconomic implications. One series of events that illustrated this conflict were the dramatic 1971 protests by the Israeli Black Panther movement, a group of young, second-generation Jewish immigrants from North African and Middle Eastern countries, protesting discrimination against Mizrahi Jews.

## Security as a "Public Good"

Security is a product that fulfills all the characteristics of a "public good," characterized by the fact that market forces cannot provide it effectively ("market failure"). Only the state can create and provide security—private parties cannot do so. Therefore, if not for the state, there would be no security. Security is a good that is freely consumed by the entire public, regardless of whether they actively choose to do so or not. Furthermore, if one citizen consumes it, others are not prevented from also consuming it; security is a good provided to all citizens, regardless of the "amount" of security that each individual requires. Even citizens who do not pay taxes benefit from the security provided by the state. It is impossible to prevent its consumption. The cost of security is financed from taxes levied on citizens, and the state is responsible for allocating an appropriate budget to sustain it.

While it is easy to measure the direct cost of a defense budget, it is much harder to quantify its actual benefits. The asymmetry between defense spending and the benefits of that spending is largely related to the fact that, while direct defense costs are directly quantifiable, its benefits are intangible. Defense spending benefits are measured in terms of deterring and preventing future wars, shortening the duration of potential hostilities, reducing damage, and also in terms of the military and political outcomes at the end of the fighting. Because these events are hypothetical, the probability of their occurrence is uncertain, and it is difficult to say exactly what level of budget is required to prevent or contend with them. Deterrence is important for creating economic certainty and reducing

Israel's "risk premium" to make it more attractive to potential investors and high-quality immigrants. The asymmetry between the economic benefit of security and its cost has been an integral issue in the economic-security debate throughout Israel's history.

However, one thing is clear—there is a mutual interdependence between the economy and security. Adequate security is a precondition for a functioning society and economy, and a functioning society and economy are essential to financing the defense budget. Defense spending ensures the normal operation of the economy by reducing security risks and increasing certainty, stability, and a sense of security for all market actors—including consumers, investors, and exporters. Thus, the benefits of defense spending can be expressed on three levels: deterrence (preventing wars, reducing the duration of hostilities, and reducing the damage caused by war); providing ongoing security including by thwarting attacks on the home front and thus preventing disruptions to everyday life; and, finally, through the contribution of defense research and development to defense exports and civilian applications of defense technologies.

High defense spending has helped turn Israel's defense industry into a very influential player in the market. Notwithstanding the importance of defense spending and its economic contribution to the country, the security reality in Israel also has negative economic consequences. Israel's "risk premium" has been very high for many years, and this has affected the willingness of foreign entrepreneurs and investors to conduct business in Israel. Defense spending has also negatively affected taxation rates, public debt, and the allocation of resources for civilian needs. Israel's ongoing need for high defense expenditure make the need for good security and economic risk management all the more important. This is particularly the case in the current age of globalization, where a deviation in defense spending from globally accepted norms impairs Israel's ability to compete. Stable and sustainable economic growth enable Israel to set aside resources for security (as a sort of "insurance premium"). The government also has to finely balance the allocation of national resources between defense and civilian needs, so that the country is able to contend with military threats but also has room for sustainable economic growth. In retrospect, Israel has managed to achieve a proper balance between its security challenges and socioeconomic needs. The exception is the period following the Yom Kippur War, when the great increases in the country's defense budget burdened the economy, stifling the growth of the economy and public services.

## The "Theory of Rounds"

Even before the establishment of the State, David Ben-Gurion had laid out an organized plan for the Yishuv's security-economic strategy in British Mandatory Palestine. He believed that the Yishuv needed to take advantage of every lull between the inevitable rounds of violent conflict to develop its economy and society. This, in essence, is Ben-Gurion's "Theory of Rounds," and Israel's first premier would continue to rely on it as part of his defense doctrine in the first years of statehood by taking calculated security risks in order to establish the new country's economy and society. In setting the historical goals, first of building a Jewish home and then of creating the State of Israel, Ben-Gurion and his fellow Zionists never intended that all the resources of their poor, nascent state would be allocated to security and defense. Rather, the strategic goal of the Jewish State was to absorb mass waves of immigration, consolidate a high-quality society, and build a prosperous economy—even in the face of the security threats that periodically erupted into rounds of violence.

Ben-Gurion's defense doctrine and his "Theory of Rounds" was based on a concept of security based on "three pillars"—early warning, deterrence, and military decision.[2] Early warning relies on good intelligence to prepare for any situation. Deterrence is intended to maintain the lulls between the rounds in order to build the state's society, economy, and culture. Ben-Gurion knew that Israel would be forced to carry out periodic rounds of violence as a result of the conflict with the Palestinians and its neighbors. The lulls between these rounds would be used to grow, develop, establish the country's strength, and reinforce its economic, social, cultural, and technological foundations. These periodic rounds of violence were designed to meet the challenge of war, and to attain and create deterrence for as long as possible. All this with the knowledge that when the effects of the deterrence wear off, the next round will begin. As the lulls between the rounds increased, there would be time to allocate resources to strengthen the country's infrastructure. This is how the State of Israel was built amid the security threats that faced it: military intensification on the one hand, and risk management, the use of political tools, and redirection of resources into socioeconomic growth and development on the other.

Ben-Gurion's "Theory of Rounds" depends on several principles. First, victory in each round of violence, which provides a further increase in Israel's deterrence by undermining the adversary's confidence in his ability to achieve a significant military victory. Second, after each round, Israel must repair any damage and build its strength for the next round. Third,

Israel must use the lulls between rounds to build its economic and social strength and develop the country to make it an attractive option for new immigrants and for its existing population, thus deterring them from leaving. At each stage, it is extremely important for Israel to try to use strategic political means to avoid military action.

On average, there have been rounds of violence every decade between the Jews and the Arab states and Palestinians in the West Bank and Gaza during the twentieth century, from the period of the Yishuv prior to Israeli independence, and continuing after the establishment of the State. Israel's nation-building efforts have been dogged by ongoing struggles, including several violent and harsh armed confrontations that were intended to threaten Israel's existence. For the better part of a century, there has been a strategic lifecycle of rounds of violent conflict interspersed with relatively quiet lulls, during which Israel carried out the bulk of its state-and-nation-building, and attained its great economic and social achievements, absorbing the great waves of immigration, establishing physical and social infrastructures, developing culture and creativity, and establishing its position in the world. The decade from 1957 through 1967, during which there was no military conflict, was a significant one. During this period, the masses of new immigrants shaped themselves into a nation and a functioning society amid rapid economic growth and development. By the end of this ten-year period, Israel had achieved international economic parity with other nations, and its economy was on the verge of becoming that of a developed country.

In the balance sheet of national resilience, the long-term successful integration of civilian and defense spending is notable for its success. Damage to market stability is, ultimately, also damage to Israel's military capacity and its ability to withstand future violent conflict. There has been just one period when Israel did not maximize the principle of building the economy, and that was after the Yom Kippur War. The surprise and shock experienced by the nation at the start of that conflict precipitated a severe counterreaction by Israel's political and military establishments, that then allocated large amounts of resources to security, thereby upsetting the delicate balance. The economic price was severe, and the period from 1974–1985 would become known as the "lost decade."

The pattern of rounds of violent confrontations would continue even after the Yom Kippur War. In 1982, there was a conflict with the PLO in Lebanon. In 1991, Israel was attacked by Iraq during the first Gulf War. From the end of the 1980s, there were rounds of clashes with the Palestinians in the two intifadas. In 2006, Israel fought the Second Lebanon

War against Hezbollah, and there were operations against the Palestinians in Gaza following the 2005 disengagement: Cast Lead (2008), Pillar of Defense (2012), Protective Edge (2014) and Guardian of the Walls (2021) and Gaza war (2023-2024). In the 2000s, there was a complex confrontation with Iran, which remains a major military (nuclear) threat to Israel that has preoccupied every area of Israel's security establishment.

Israel's geopolitical situation in the Muslim and Arab Middle East has made it impossible to secure a decisive strategic victory over its enemies, even if it has been able to deliver successful blows on the battlefield. Israel's victories, including its impressive achievements in the Six-Day War, did not break the will of the Arabs to continue their fight. However, there has been a gradual shift in the attitude of the Arab world towards Israel that began in the late 1970s in the wake of the Yom Kippur War. Realizing the power of Israel's military and the high cost of continuing hostilities, Egypt signed a peace agreement with Israel on March 26, 1979, following the 1978 Camp David Accords. Years later, on October 26, 1994, Jordan signed the Wadi Araba Treaty, establishing mutual diplomatic relations with Israel. In 2020, the Abraham Accords were signed normalizing relations between Israel and the United Arab Emirates, Bahrain, Sudan, and Morocco, which do not have borders with Israel. These political agreements notwithstanding, Israel is still required to maintain a strong military capability and cannot relinquish its security capabilities as long as the Middle East remains a politically unstable region.

## Israel's Defense Industries

From its very first years of statehood, Israel's defense industries have played a key role in the country's defense system and economic infrastructure and are an essential component of its national security. Israel Military Industries (also known as Ta'as)[3] was created in 1933, some 15 years prior to Israel's declaration of independence. The Rafael Armament Development Authority[4] was founded as the country's research and development defense laboratory upon the establishment of the State, while Israel Aerospace Industries (IAI) was created as the Bedek Aviation Company in 1953 and functioned as an aircraft testing institute. These industries were established out of a recognition that, in view of its geopolitical situation, Israel had no choice but to maintain an independent defense base for both routine and emergency situations. Israel's defense industries ensured a regular and independent supply of arms, and provided the country with the ability to develop innovative military products that could give it an advantage over any aggressors by providing an element of surprise on the battlefield. Since their creation, Israel's defense industries have undergone many changes and crises, and continue to be a key industrial-technological-security component of Israel's defense capabilities and economy. An important turning point in Israel's defense industrial complex occurred in the wake of the Six-Day War, when France imposed a temporary arms embargo on Israel. In response to this move, Israel felt it necessary to make large-scale investments to expand and develop new domestic arms manufacturers. These included several small factories and subcontractors that would later develop into important companies in both the defense and civilian arenas (such as Elbit Systems). These investments reflected the advanced industrial and technological developments taking place in Israel. During the two decades from 1967 to 1987, Israel's defense industries grew to attain a high market value, and their upkeep and support became part of the high security burden on the economy.

Such high security costs contributed to an imbalance between the country's defense spending and its economy. This was reflected in the government's decision to cancel its IAI Lavi project to construct a fighter aircraft in 1987. The cancellation of the Lavi enabled Israel to partially divert resources from defense to civilian needs, as reflected in reduced defense budgets and increased civilian budgets. The government-owned defense industries were streamlined by the broad economic changes that occurred in the wake of the economic crisis and the 1985 Economic Stabilization Plan. Since then, Israel's defense industries have become very active in the international markets, and defense exports have become a key aspect of Israeli diplomacy and a means of achieving its security interests.

Although Israel's defense spending has had negative economic externalities, over the years, Israel's defense industries have provided positive externalities in terms of technology transfer and the development of human capital, which has contributed to the development of advanced civilian mid-tech and hi-tech industries. In 2022, Israel's defense industries are an important aspect of Israeli manufacturing and exports. The key to managing the relationship between Israel's defense and civilian industries is to achieve a proper balance between the two. Israel's defense budget is, in essence, an "insurance premium" that makes it possible to facilitate the economic growth that, in turn, ensures that the country can generate and allocate the resources necessary to maintain security. It is this delicate balance that allows Israel to deal with military threats, while sustaining socioeconomic growth and development.

## Notes

1. "Shirut", Lyrics to the song "Cannons Instead of Sock," Noah Ensemble, (mako.co.il).
2. Charles D. Freilich, "Israel's Classic Defense Doctrine," in Israeli National Security: A New Strategy for an Era of Change (New York, 2018; online ed., Oxford Academic, 22 Mar. 2018), https://doi.org/10.1093/oso/9780190602932.003.0002.
3. Later renamed IMI Systems, the company was acquired by Elbit Systems in 2018.
4. Currently Rafael Advanced Defense Systems Ltd.

# 9

# The Great Constraint—Israel's Foreign Currency Reserves Crisis

When the British departed in May 1948, the Mandatory government failed to leave sufficient foreign currency reserves for Israel to address its immediate major challenges. Chief among them were the supply of food and basic goods to the country's growing population and defense procurement for its army in their fight against Arab armies. Indeed, most of the economic crises that Israel faced in its first five decades of statehood were related to this issue.

The government formulated economic plans in an attempt to overcome the constraints created by the foreign currency shortages. In Israel's first years of statehood, its foreign currency reserves were very tightly managed, and considerable "acrobatics" were required to address immediate challenges and supply the population's basic needs. The foreign currency reserves crisis hampered economic development and growth in the first years of statehood, forcing Israel to adopt difficult decisions and make unconventional moves. Foreign currency scarcity was the main reason for Israel's policies of rationing and austerity, which the Israeli public, accepted with great understanding—a reflection of their commitment to the national state-building project.

The health of Israel's foreign currency reserves was to dictate the pulse of its economy and of government decisions for many years. One of Israel's most difficult and painful decisions was to accept a Reparations Agreement with the Federal Republic of Germany, seven years after the Holocaust. As Israel wrestled with the decision of whether to accept reparations from Germany, the country endured stormy public and political debates, sometimes accompanied by violent and angry demonstrations. Israel had to contend with moral questions about accepting money from a country that had a grim past with the Jews, while also considering its need to build a safe haven for the Jewish people. For the West Germans, the Reparations Agreement was important to its future rehabilitation and enabling it to return to the fold of the international community. Eventually, the

Reparations Agreement was signed on September 10, 1952 by Israeli Foreign Minister Moshe Sharett and West German Chancellor Konrad Adenauer (the Communist German Democratic Republic (East Germany) refused to bear any responsibility for the crimes of the Nazis). Under the terms of the Agreement, the West German government undertook to transfer 3.45 billion Deutsche Mark (around $800 million) in reparations to Israel for the unimaginable suffering of the Jews in the Holocaust. The reparations were paid mainly in goods[1] (the real value of which is estimated at about $20 billion at 2022 prices), spread over a dozen years. West Germany paid the reparations to the government of Israel as the legitimate representative of the Jewish people for the costs of "resettling so great a number of uprooted and destitute Jewish refugees" after the war, as well as for compensating individual Jews who were displaced and lost their property due to the actions of the Nazis."[2]

Israel's perception regarding the use of German reparations was that the monies were intended for the good of the collective. The ethos was of "the State above all, and national goals before survivors." The import of foreign capital in the form of reparations partially solved the foreign currency reserve shortages that were suffocating Israel, thus allowing it to grow and develop and extricate itself from the difficult economic situation that had plagued it from the outset. The goods that Germany transferred to Israel were mostly investment products for developing Israeli agriculture, industry, transport infrastructure, and for the establishment of the National Water Carrier and power plants.

In parallel to the Reparations Agreement, in 1951, West Germany also signed a personal compensation agreement with Jewish organizations on behalf of the Jewish people, for Jews as individuals.

Israel's foreign currency needs were immense, and many efforts were directed to reaching out to American Jews, the world's largest and wealthiest Jewish community, to encourage transfers of dollars to Israel from the United Jewish Appeal (UJA), a Jewish philanthropic umbrella organization. Founded in 1939 by the Zionist movement, the UJA originally helped fund settlements in the Land of Israel. Later, together with the American Jewish Joint Distribution Committee, it helped Jewish refugees in Europe after the Holocaust. Following Israel's declaration of independence, the UJA collected funds for the needs of the new State.

Also in 1951, Israel made a special, creative effort to raise its foreign currency reserves with the launch of State of Israel Bonds (officially known as the Development Corporation for Israel). The idea was for Israel to sell bonds to the Diaspora (mainly in the United States) to raise capital for investment in developing the country. The bonds carried a high interest rate that reflected the risk associated with investing in Israel. Jews with means, who cared about Israel's economic growth, bought the bonds and identified with big projects such as the national carrier, the seaports (Ashdod, Haifa and Eilat), power plants, and in later years, immigration from Ethiopia and the Soviet Union. Between 1951–2022, approximately 37 billion dollars were raised in total from Israel Bonds.

Raising foreign currency through fundraising appeals, bonds, reparations, and personal compensation made it possible for Israel to finance infrastructure investments and the immediate needs of its population. This had a positive effect on the economy. In 1953, an investment boom began that would change Israel's economy, sparking a period of extraordinary growth that would last through 1965. However, the ongoing scarcity of foreign currency reserves would continue to be a dark cloud casting a shadow over Israel's economic policy until the start of the twenty-first century.

## The Exchange Rate

Faced with the reality of a built-in deficit in the balance of payments, Israel pursued a policy of a fixed exchange rate with adjustments every few years via nominal devaluations and close supervision of the foreign exchange market. Foreign currency was a product in short supply, and under free market conditions, its price had to rise, meaning more Israeli lira (later the New Israeli Shekel) were required to purchase one dollar (or any foreign currency). Israel did not allow this process to occur naturally, and free market conditions were outlawed in its foreign exchange market. This was due to fears that a large devaluation of the Israeli lira against foreign currencies would lead to sharp rises in the cost of imported goods, especially foodstuffs. Therefore, Israel resorted to a carefully managed formal devaluation policy, rather than the major adjustments in the exchange rate that the reality of the foreign exchange situation called for.

In 1948, Israel's exchange rate was pegged to the pound sterling. At the time, the exchange rate of the Israeli currency to the dollar was 1:4, the same as the exchange rate between the pound sterling and the dollar. When the British adjusted the sterling exchange rate to the dollar in September 1949 to a ratio of 1:3, Israel did the same with the lira. It was clear that this exchange rate did not reflect Israel's true economic situation. The government was afraid to carry out a large devaluation of the lira lest basic products became more expensive, and the population have difficulty buying them, even with the rationing and points system that was in place. It was only in February 1952 that Israel recognized the need to carry out a large nominal devaluation of the exchange rate against the sterling, which was necessitated by the real value of the lira. Pegging the Israeli currency to the sterling was formally abolished at this time and Israel set three official exchange rates (a unique event) for the Israeli currency against the dollar. These were: 0.7:1 (for foreign currency transfers), 1:1 (for imports) and 1.8:1 (for exports). This was an unconventional step, which, according to the rules of the international exchange rate system at the time, had to be approved by the International Monetary Fund. The measures were intended to be temporary, and gradually, the government consolidated the official exchange rate, so that by the end of 1954, the nominal exchange rate stood at 1.8 lira to the dollar. This was a devaluation of hundreds of percentage points which had to be carried out due to the scarcity of Israel's foreign currency reserves.

Alongside nominal devaluation, Israel imposed import bans and multi-rate import taxes (duties, sales taxes, and other levies), and introduced export incentives, so that in practice, the effective real exchange rate was higher than the official rate. Israel had different import tax rates for different goods, services, and industries.

The multiple effective exchange rates and import bans were intended to protect import-substitute industries and provide jobs. The growing population created increased demands for basic consumer goods including food, clothing, furniture, construction products, and housewares, which were supplied by import-substituting factories. This policy protected Israeli manufacturers from overseas competition, and created a convenient business infrastructure for in which entrepreneurs could establish industrial plants. Effective exchange rates differed for the various industries, development areas, and sometimes even for specific goods. The administrative exchange rate regime was strict, rigid, and distorted.

The nominal devaluation took place a decade later, in February 1962, when the lira decreased in value against the dollar from 1.8 lira to 3 lira to the dollar. This new exchange rate was also not an equilibrium exchange rate in a free foreign exchange market. Only through foreign exchange controls and restrictions on the demand for foreign currency (such as restrictions on purchasing foreign currency when traveling abroad) was this situation made possible.

These formal and effective exchange rates existed in varying degrees until the end of the 1980s. Until this time, these "maneuvers" continued, with administrative government interventions maintaining the gap between the formal and the effective exchange rates in imports and exports, causing economic distortions. As the economy opened up to activity following international agreements, Israel had to abandon these methods of operation, which were prohibited in international trade. Israel's ambition to integrate into the global economy required it to adopt the rules of the international economy and transition to a single official exchange rate for exports and imports and other financial operations. It would take half a century from Israel's declaration of independence for a free foreign exchange rate policy to be established.

## A Closed Market

Israel was a small economy and an isolated "island." Since Israel did not pose an economic threat to any other country, it could take drastic protectionary measures against imports, even though these went against the grain of post-World War II international principles supporting market openness and increased global trade. Because of the small scale of its trade, Israel failed to take into account the effects of being closed and the resulting lack of reciprocity in relation to imports versus exports. The wider world operated under the Bretton Woods money management system of the International Monetary Fund, led by the United States as a superpower, and based on the dollar as the international reserve currency. Israel defined itself as politically part of the West during the Cold War, joined international organizations, and was assisted by the World Bank in the construction of its Ashdod port and other infrastructure projects.

However, as a small economy without natural resources, Israel could not pursue a total autarkic policy, even in the short term. It needed to import basic foodstuffs (such as sugar, grains, and rice) and basic raw materials (in particular, fuel and metals). Its economic policy was managed in accordance with the amount of foreign currency reserves that the market possessed at the time. There was an almost total ban on importing finished products. Even the expansion of capital imports in the form of donations from world Jewry and reparations from West Germany did not meet Israel's foreign currency needs. Exports were limited and even before Israel's declaration of independence, the authorities had worked hard to expand the Yishuv's traditional export industries of citrus fruits and diamonds. However, this was not enough to meet the demands of the market, which needed foreign currency for investment, raw materials, and consumption.

The scarcity of Israel's foreign currency reserves produced two successive economic strategies. The first, from the early 1950s, was the development of import-substituting industries, and the second, from the 1980s, was the development of export industries. Replacing imports proved relatively easy, while the development of exports required complex moves—international agreements, a technological industrial base, and high-quality personnel that took time to develop. The structural and fundamental solution to this challenge was based on developing exports that would provide revenues for financing imports. The initial development of import-substituting industries provided an infrastructure for developing the country's export industries. Israel had not pre-planned this economic-industrial strategy. Rather, it was an emerging activity, driven by an understanding that the economy needed to be export-oriented to ensure stable and sustainable growth and employment and high living standards. This strategy gradually matured from the 1970s, in the wake of trade agreements with the European Common Market for agriculture, the export of processed food, clothing, and traditional goods.

Israeli agriculture had always been protected through subsidies and non-tariff protections (estimated at about around 6 billion NIS in 2021). Israel imported almost no fresh agricultural produce, since Israeli agriculture enjoyed a special status, both politically and economically, in the ethos of the State. In the early years, agriculture was an important source of employment (in 1958, about 18% of the total workforce was employed in agriculture), and a basis for exports (mainly citrus fruits). In later years, fresh agricultural exports expanded to include vegetables and other fruits, and Israel's agricultural industries grew. This growth and innovation have continued through today, with Israel having developed a relative advantage in various fresh agricultural products (including strawberries and flowers), and in related industries, such as the irrigation industry (drop irrigation systems). Only at the start of the twenty-first century did these long-term processes mature, resulting in the improvements in Israel's foreign reserves and the removal of the foreign currency restrictions which had choked the Israeli economy since its birth. Instead of carrying a dollar debt, Israel accumulated large foreign currency reserves, and its economy became a loan economy. A new era had dawned for Israel's foreign currency reserves.

## From a Closed to an Open Economy

Despite its closed economy policy, the understanding that Israel needed to open up to the world, especially in terms of foreign trade, began percolating among academics and policy makers. It was becoming clear that as a country lacking in natural resources and raw materials, and requiring large imports of food, raw materials, investments, and fuel, Israel needed a strategy of developing its export industries in order to attain long-term economic independence.

International openness accelerated with the establishment of the European Common Market in 1957, a development that threatened Israeli exports, in particular of citrus fruits and their industrial by-products. Israel realized that the Common Market would make it harder to export to Europe, and that Israel's rigid closed market policy was incompatible with its desire to receive concessions from Europe, as international trade requires reciprocity. Countries that limit imports must expect that exports will be limited in return. Despite Israel's tendency to hoard foreign currency reserves and favor import-substituting industries, it had no choice but to develop exports and maintain a favorable system with the European Common Market.

In the early 1960s, Israel began discussions with the Common Market, its main export market due to its geographical proximity and traditional ties. Israel's goal was to achieve special concessions that would allow it to develop its exports. With this in mind, the Ministries of Finance, Trade and Industry, Agriculture, and Foreign Affairs began conducting negotiations with Europe for special arrangements, and in 1965, Israel signed an initial "preferential trade agreement" with the Common Market. This allowed special concessions for the gradual entry of Israeli exports into Europe, without the need for symmetry and reciprocity of imports. These export concessions were granted to Israel based on it being considered a developing country.

The continuing relationship between Israel and Europe led to the signing of a free trade agreement with the Common Market in 1975. This was a dramatic development and a strategic, political, and economic turning point, from which Israel began the slow, and gradual, and ultimately structural process of leaving behind its closed market policy in favor of openness. The free trade agreement initiated a policy of exposure to exports and the rationalization of Israel's industry. Israel shifted its approach of absolute protectionism of industrial production in favor of a policy of production according to comparative advantage. The reduction of Israeli import tariffs on Common Market goods was gradual and would come to an end 14 years later in 1989, when the Israeli market was opened to full competition for duty-free European industrial products from what had now become the European Union.

This was a strategic move that shifted the Israeli market toward export-oriented growth. Its free trade agreement with Europe, were a reflection of its new open market policy, industrial specialization, and global outlook. Indeed, while the "Israeli mind" knew how to produce everything in the 1950s and 1960s, Israel had not yet grasped the concept that what can be produced is not necessarily what is worth producing. Import-export policies require specialization, division of labor, and relative advantage vis-à-vis trading partners. This understanding, which finally matured in the 1960s, was gradually implemented in the 1970s and 1980s. This was an important step toward Israel's adoption of a professional economic approach, albeit one that interfered with short-term domestic political considerations due to the closure of inefficient factories and the resulting worker layoffs. Although Israel had a public, centralized orientation in its first decades of statehood, it was also open to long-term thinking and recognized the need to develop an export strategy and openness to imports.

The agreement with the European Common Market was a prelude to a free trade agreement with the United States in 1985 and to additional agreements in later years. In 1991, the recognition of the openness of foreign countries regarding trade led Israel to implement a significant unilateral reduction of tariffs and to begin its increasing openness to trade with the whole world. From the 1990s, Israel adopted a policy of an open market and integration into globalization, a position that is well-suited to a small economy with few natural resources. This move was an important step in Israel's journey to globalization and membership in the "club" of developed countries.

## Notes

1. Hans-Peter Schwartz (1995). Konrad Adenauer: A German Politician and Statesman in a Period of War, Revolution and Reconstruction: From the German Empire to the Federal Republic, 1876–1952 (Vol. 1). Berghahn Books.
2. Agreement between the State of Israel and the Federal Republic of Germany, September 10, 1952, Preamble (https://treaties.un.org/doc/Publication/UNTS/Volume%20162/volume-162-I-2137-English.pdf).

# 10

# Growth Factors

## Major Trends in the Workforce

Thanks to the demographics of the Jewish immigrants to British Mandatory Palestine, on the eve of Israel's declaration of independence, the Yishuv had a relatively high level of education, comparable to populations in developed European nations. However, the mass waves of immigration in Israel's first years of statehood brought many thousands of new citizens with low levels of education and skillsets that were unsuited to their new country's productive economy of agriculture, industry, and construction.

By the end of 1951, immigration had slowed. As Israel began to implement its new economic plan in 1952, its focus was on creating employment order to provide households with an income and meet demands for basic goods and services. In the 1950s and 1960s, Israel's economic policy directed immigrants into what were the three productive sectors: manufacturing, agriculture, and construction. As a result, almost half of the total workforce was employed in these sectors. Israel's agricultural sector absorbed many of the costs of supplying the growing population with food, and played a role in creating the Zionist ideal of the "new Jew" engaged in productive, useful labor. Israel's manufacturing and construction industries also created sources of income for the growing population. The decline in unemployment after 1955 was an indicator of Israel's success in creating jobs—indeed, providing hundreds of thousands of new immigrants with productive employment in these sectors should be viewed as a significant achievement. After all, it was no easy task to integrate the masses of newcomers from different countries and working cultures into unfamiliar jobs.

As discussed, in developing its manufacturing base, Israel created an import-substituting industry that produced basic goods using unskilled, intensive labor, simple technologies, and minimal equipment and machinery. Within a decade of independence, Israel's manufacturing industry had become a leading market sector, and many unskilled new immigrants had acquired the skills to work in it through "on-the-job" training schemes. This was a rapid and intense industrial and labor revolution.

Throughout the 1950s and 1960s, Israel promoted the idea of labor above all, and the concept that being unemployed should not mean being idle. Rather than making transfer payments, the state provided the unemployed with productive "workfare" jobs in areas such as forestry, archeological digs, and road construction. This preference for transfer payments and relief over welfare was an ideological position that stemmed from Israel's long-held Zionist belief in the importance of labor. Unemployment insurance became part of Israel's national insurance plan only in 1972, in the wake of the great recession of 1966–1967.

By the 1960s, Israel had already begun to see shifts in employment patterns and workforce skills. More educated immigrants began arriving from Eastern Europe. In addition, its education system, including post-secondary and higher education, began producing skilled young people. The technological level of Israel's manufacturing industry also increased, thanks to investments in machinery and equipment, which led to greater demand for skilled labor to operate the new modern industrial production lines. Workers who had been absorbed into low-level manufacturing jobs in the 1950s had by this time gained experience and more skills and had advanced to management positions. Israel created organized professional training schemes to prepare skilled workers for manufacturing, which also helped contribute to economic growth and high productivity.

The demand for skilled labor was also growing in Israel's service industries, particularly in healthcare, education, and business. The increase in the importance of educated (higher as well as post-secondary) laborers was a reflection of the increasing importance of the service sector, especially with the more comprehensive development of the country's public services. These changes altered the balance of manufacturing industries (agriculture, industry, and construction) in the economy from their peak in the 1970s in favor of the service economy. The growth of the service sector also had an impact on female participation in the labor market. In Israel's early years of statehood, the majority of the workforce was male. As the economy developed and Israel's service industries grew, along with the standard of living and education, the participation of women in the labor market also rose, and they quickly integrated into new employment opportunities. Jobs suitable for women, particularly in the public services, such as nursing, and favorable conditions for part-time work were created, which made it easier for women to integrate into the labor market.

This dynamism in training and improving the skills of the workforce to meet modern needs was an important factor in Israel's economic growth and high levels of productivity, particularly in view of the fact that the majority of its workforce had no prior manufacturing experience. By the 1970s, Israeli industry had begun to be competitive internationally and viable. Israel had trained and improved the skills of its immigrants, enabling it to grow economically and join the developed world. If at the dawn of the twentieth century, the Yishuv had triggered a "second industrial revolution" by developing and operating production lines, by the time of Israel's independence in the mid-twentieth century, a "third industrial revolution" was underway. Also, in the 1970s, Israel's defense industry had begun to adopt sophisticated equipment and modern technologies, and more developed civilian industry based on the new technologies soon followed in its wake.

In 1970, workers from the Occupied Palestinian Territories were allowed to participate in the economy for the first time. This dramatic change was the result of low unemployment rates of around three percent. Labor shortages in the agriculture, industrial, and construction sectors opened the doors for the employment of laborers from the Occupied Palestinian Territories, and in a relatively short time, their numbers grew to about six percent of the total workforce in Israel. This was part of the great change in the Israeli labor market following the Six-Day War.

It was only in the 1980s, following the 1985 Economic Stabilization Plan in response to a serious economic crisis, that the Israeli market made significant progress towards overcoming its fundamental problems and achieving economic independence. The economic crisis of the 1980s was the result of structural defects and not just of failed policies. The structural changes and basic reforms that were carried out in the wake of the 1985 Economic Stabilization Plan created conditions for a revival of the economy and changes in the composition of the workforce from unskilled to skilled labor.

A number of factors led to a shift in the composition of the workforce from unskilled manual labor to skilled service labor. These included the end of the policy of excessive protectionism of import-substituting industries and the completion of the exposure of export industries to international competition in the late 1980s. At the same time, Israel experienced a rising standard of living and an increased demand for services. There was increased recognition that as Israel's workforce was its only natural resource, a high value should be extracted from it, and that the market should specialized according to relative advantages and for exports.

The 1990s saw Israel implement a development and growth policy that exploited its increasingly highly educated workforce, which received a boost with the influx of skilled immigrants from the Soviet Union. The improvement in the skill level of Israel's workforce coupled with the population's increasing expectations for satisfying and rewarding employment boosted international trade, as Israel's export industries enjoyed increased innovation and improved technology. Rising exports helped improve the balance of payments, which in turn had a positive effect on employees' compensation.

The "Zionist model" that for many years had advocated redesigning the Jewish workforce and adapting it to a "normal" structure (Ber Borokhov's "inverted pyramid," for turning Jews into productive laborers, as discussed in Chapter 1), had changed. The policy—which began in the pre-state Yishuv but gained momentum in the first years of statehood—of encouraging employment in "productive" albeit unsophisticated industries typical of developed countries at the time (manufacturing, agriculture, and construction), underwent an upheaval, leaving behind the traditional Zionist attitudes toward creating Jewish work and workers. Indeed, the achievements of Israeli economy before the 1980s had proved that there was no truth in the claim that the Jewish people were not ready for a "normal" workforce structure. The proportion of workers in "productive" industries in Israel was now similar to that in developed countries. However, while Israel was still encouraging employment in these market sectors, Western Europe and North America had undergone a process of de-industrialization, and a transition to knowledge and technology-based sectors at the interface between manufacturing and services, as the high-tech industry began combining hardware and software.

This international trend also precipitated a sea change in Israel. The shift away from manufacturing toward a knowledge-based economy were well-suited to a country with few natural resources, since such an economy depended on the one resource Israel did have—an educated workforce. Since the 1990s, Israel's economic development has been driven by an increasingly skilled workforce, as well as innovation, and creativity, and included both "veteran" Israelis and new immigrants. The new "normal" employment structure reflected historical employment trends of Diaspora Jews—that is, a preference for employment in service and creative industries, coupled with a global outlook. These shifts were a major boost to Israel's economic strength, helping to address its long-standing weak point—the balance of payments.

## Investments and Capital

In its first years of statehood, Israel favored long-term economic development over short-term needs, reflected in its preference for investments over consumer goods, and in its efforts to focus on building "productive" industries even if this meant neglecting to improve the public's standard of living. For example, this policy resulted in Israel not constructing permanent housing for some groups of immigrants, leaving them in difficult conditions in temporary transit camps. The preference for prioritizing investment in economic and market development rather than in private consumption was a direct result of the scarcity of Israel's foreign currency reserves, which the government had to use for establishing infrastructures to accelerate growth and provide mass employment. In the 1950s and 1960s, government investment in developing infrastructure to develop the economy stood at about five percent of Israel's GDP. This high rate of investment, demanded by a new country that had experienced a sudden leap in population, made it possible to build the widescale infrastructure that had simply not existed when Israel declared its independence in 1948.

Since it lacked capital imports, Israel financed these investments through domestic national savings, in particular via high private household savings (that is, by encouraging low private consumption). Insufficient domestic savings would have meant that Israel would not have been able to invest in infrastructure development, which would have meant slower economic growth, and insufficient jobs for the growing population due to lack of capital imports. Although living standards were not high, households still managed to save even when living in austere conditions. Many Israelis were used to hardship, and there was a high public awareness, supported by some government incentives, of the need to put money away "for a rainy day." Private savings helped fuel government investment in the economy, in infrastructure, and in business, and thus helped stimulate rapid growth. The high rate of domestic savings and investments in the 1950s and 1960s would not be repeated in the 1970s and 1980s, when the increased import of foreign capital would finance high public consumption (mainly for security), and from the 1990s, private consumption. In the decade from 2010–2019, national savings stood at 12–13 percent of GDP, a reasonable rate in international terms.

## Encouraging Capital Investments

To accelerate the development of the private sector, in the 1950s and 1960s, Israel designed new policies for encouraging private investments. Despite the dominance of the public sector, the government was quite eager to encourage private capital to stimulate development and entrepreneurship. Entrepreneurship and knowledge were essential for a young country without industrial or export experience. The government in particular wanted private investment to improve what had become known as the "periphery"—the less developed and less prosperous regions outside the wealthier coastal plain.

In the 1950s, Israel had no transparent, clear, or uniform criteria for encouraging private investment. Instead, ministers and government officials made ad hoc decisions, largely out of a desire to obtain the maximum level of investment in the minimum possible time. The government provided incentives to individual investors in the form of tax breaks, cheap loans, grants, and protectionism via import taxes or import bans, including by making individual guarantees. These measures were also needed as compensation to foreign investors for losses incurred as a result of the Arab boycott of Israel. The government's ultimate aim was simply to increase private investment and stimulate growth, employment, and encourage population dispersion outside of the central coastal plain.

In 1959, Israel enacted the Encouragement of Capital Investments Law,[1] whose stated aim was to "attract capital to Israel and to encourage economic initiative and investments of foreign and local capital" with a view to, among other things, developing the productive capacity of the economy, improving the balance of payments, and aiding immigrant absorption, including population dispersal and job creation. The law included criteria for encouraging investments as well as for development areas. Later, export criteria were added. Since then, the law has undergone many changes, but initially, its main criteria were encouraging investments in machinery, equipment, and buildings.

In the 1980s, Israel began to realize the benefits of encouraging investment in research and development (R&D), because of its positive externalities on the economy. In 1984, Israel passed the Encouragement of Research and Development Law, which was intended to encourage investments in R&D with a view to stimulating growth and employment in Israel's knowledge and technology-based industries. Unlike earlier incentives for investment in machinery and buildings, grants were now given for R&D projects to develop new technologies that could become engines of growth, with an emphasis on exports. Since the 1990s, Israel has shifted from focusing solely on encouraging physical capital investment to also encouraging R&D and marketing. The return on investment of R&D to the economy as a whole is much higher than the return seen by private investors because of the high risk associated with this type of activity. Over the years, Israel has increasingly recognized the value of encouraging innovation in traditional industries, not only in technological ventures.

For quite some time, Israel favored encouraging investment in manufacturing rather than in the service sectors and incentivized the export of goods rather than services. Industry was seen as productive and tangible, with strategic resilience. The huge shift—indeed, a revolution—in industry in the second half of the twentieth century, amid the growing importance of technology and especially information technology, also changed the attitudes regarding government incentives. Software development has become as important as that of any physical product, while the definition of industry has become blurred in terms of the distinction between goods and services. A good example of this can be seen in the incentives granted to Intel when it began operations in Israel in the late 1980s, which to a large extent determined and redefined Israel's high-tech industry. Intel's contributions, both direct and indirect, to the Israeli high-tech industry affected the definition of industrial products. They also led to the creation of policies, which, unlike those of the past that had encouraged traditional goods, now incentivized a broad definition of goods and services, physical capital, R&D, and innovation.

## Growth, Development, and Productivity

The Israeli economy, despite having to contend with foreign currency reserve shortages, an unstable security situation, large waves of immigrants, and poor infrastructure, experienced incredible growth from 1948–1973, with a real annual average of over ten percent, a per capita growth of about 5.5 percent, and productivity per employee growth of around 5 percent per annum. In the post-Second World War era, Israel was considered a global economic prodigy. Such a high rate of economic growth, in a country whose population had tripled almost overnight, was indeed a remarkable, even unique achievement. Although Israel had started from a very low point, there was still no other economy in the world that managed to develop at such a high rate and in such a short period of about 25 years.

By the mid-1950s, Israel's market reached full employment, even though its new immigrants did not come from agricultural or industrial backgrounds. Israel itself was surprised at the speed of its transition from a developing to a developed country. Japan and West Germany, both on the losing side of the Second World War, also enjoyed high growth rates, partially thanks to generous American aid under the Marshall Plan. Unlike Israel, however, these two nations were already developed industrial countries with advanced human capital and technological and managerial knowledge, and their economies were able to rely on organizational and technological know-how they had gained before the war.

In the 1930s, the Yishuv in British Mandatory Palestine had developed industries based on those of Europe, thanks to the influx of new immigrants who had come from developed countries like Germany, Austria, and Czechoslovakia during the "Fifth Aliya." These highly educated immigrants brought with them entrepreneurial experience and management skills. The new businesses they helped create relied on the Yishuv's three major banks, which symbolized the three pillars on which its economy (and later that of Israel) rested—national capital (Bank Leumi), union capital (Bank Hapoalim), and private capital (Bank Discount). The industry that developed in the 1950s, after Israel's independence, with the heavy involvement of the government and the Histadrut, was mostly based on public capital, and the government was responsible for encouraging private entrepreneurs for rapid industrial development. The desire to produce everything domestically also led to ambitious ventures that verged on megalomania, such as Israel's short-lived automobile industry of 1955–1975.

The government also encouraged industry based on natural resources. In October 1951, the Israeli government nationalized Palestine Potash, now part of the Fertilizers Division of Israel Chemicals Ltd, became a factory for the production of potash, magnesium, and bromine, as well as other minerals in the Negev (mostly phosphates). Along with developing its natural resources, the government saw strategic importance in advancing the country's defense industries to boost its ability to supply defense products.

From the 1970s, Israel saw changes in its industry, as capital investments and modern production methods increased and the proportion of export industries increased. This trend was strengthened with Israel's signing of free trade agreements with the European Common Market and European Free Trade Area countries that promised concessions for Israeli exports. Israel's industry was spread across its established urban centers as well as the new development towns. Industrialization even penetrated the kibbutz movement, which diversified its activities from agriculture to industry. In the 1980s, knowledge and technology-intensive industries based on innovation and R&D began to thrive. This period saw the heyday of companies like Elbit System, Elscint, a medical imaging company, and Scitex which produced products and systems for the graphic design and printing markets.

The trade agreements of the 1990s and the policy of exposure to exports changed the image of Israeli industry from one that was fairly basic to one characterized by modern, skilled technology and innovation, which became competitive with import products in the export markets. This was indeed the start of the "start-up nation." The accelerated development of Israel's high-tech industry completely changed the country's mix of industrial establishments and labor composition, shifting the balance from traditional to advanced industry and from unskilled to highly skilled, educated labor. The development of Israeli industry has been a long journey that began with protected, inefficient factories reliant on mass, unskilled labor, and that after a long learning curve of a quarter of a century, created a vital, competitive basis for the Israeli economy.

## Note

1. kns3_investments_eng.pdf (knesset.gov.il).

# 11

# Quality of Life in a Mobilized Economy

Israel is a society of immigrants—but it is quite distinct from most immigrant societies. Unlike in other countries, immigration to Israel is not restricted by an individual's capital, education, skills, or age. Rather, every Jew has the right to immigrate and settle in Israel.

From a historical perspective, Israel's great achievement was to become a functioning and open democratic society in spite of its wars and complex security situation, and the fact that most of its immigrants came from non-democratic states in Eastern Europe or the Middle East. The concept of democracy was an important element of the young state's ethos and was instrumental in mobilizing its population for its security and economic efforts. The solidarity among most of Israel's residents in supporting its state-building efforts stemmed from their shared sense of belonging, of being partners in achieving these lofty national goals. Israel's main aim in its first years was to forge from its disparate population of new immigrants a strong "imagined community" with a sense of shared destiny, instilling in these new citizens the novel (for them) concepts of statehood and the symbols of national pride and sovereignty.

Despite the ostensibly socialist character of Israel's economic policies, with its high levels of public concentration and involvement during its first years of statehood, it never developed into a full-fledged, ideologically socialist economy. Israel's centralized statist economy (with distortions) developed as a result of historical circumstances and far from being a free market fueled by private capital, neither did it resemble the closed markets of the Eastern Bloc or the developing economies of Asia. Israeli economic policy was certainly one of state interventionism. Given that many in the new state were poor and struggling immigrants with no capital, the public considered state interventionism a basic need. In the absence of private capital and entrepreneurs, most accepted that Israel's economic development rested on public capital and public initiatives, and that reality dictated that its market, at least in its first years, be closed and state directed. However, the dynamics of adjusting to economic realities led relatively quickly to the development of an open, globally oriented market.

During Israel's first years of statehood, private consumption was low, a direct result of its preference for investing its scarce foreign currency reserves in national infrastructure. Even so, the level of public services—in particular health, education, and social security—were high relative to the country's state of economic development. This was a legacy of the pre-State Yishuv, which had benefitted from a sound social safety net thanks to its strong sense of social solidarity.

The Yishuv's education system had been built in several stages and created a solid foundation of education and shared values for Israel. Israel's healthcare system was based on the Clalit Kupat Holim community health fund, as well as on other smaller health funds. In the British Mandatory period, the Hadassah organization had established a number of hospitals that, together with those run by the British Mandatory government, had created the basis for a high-quality medical infrastructure. The American Jewish Joint Distribution Committee and its Malben program, established in 1949 to care for aged and disabled immigrants, formed the bedrock of Israel's nursing and old age care institutions. Mishan, founded in 1931, had been the primary institution for old age care provision in the Yishuv. The elderly represented a relatively small population, but still one that needed care. After May 1948, Israel suddenly found itself having to provide services for a huge influx of immigrants, a situation that demanded a sudden threefold increase in the capacity of its education and health systems. In addition, special attention had to be given to the new immigrants, whose needs differed from the residents of the old Yishuv.

The young country quickly enjoyed genuine social achievements. The new state soon enacted labor laws that limited working hours and stipulated rest days. Israel had a social security system based on the National Insurance program founded in 1954, which itself had emerged from ideas developed in the pre-State Yishuv. All of Israel's pension funds were part of the Histadrut trade union system, which had a progressive approach toward workers' rights. Overall, social rights in the early years of Israeli statehood were consistent with its economic capacity, and formed the foundations for the higher standards that would later develop into a welfare state.

The first seeds of Israel's higher education system were planted in the 1920s during the British Mandatory period. It operated according to European standards—unsurprising, given that most of its academic staff had immigrated from Europe. It provided a high-quality academic research infrastructure through its major institutions (the Technion, the Hebrew University and the Weizmann Institute), as well as through teachers' colleges, all of which met the needs of the small Yishuv. Alongside these institutions, there was extensive cultural activity, including in theater, literature, music, journalism, and sport that helped provide extra meaning and vitality to the difficult life in a new country.

Economically, culturally, and socially, in particular because of its vibrant and mobilized civil society with its extensive creative, cultural life and strong heritage, Israel belonged to the developed world. This despite the fact that its per capita GDP was more akin to that of a developing country. Even during the difficult years of the 1950s, Israel wanted to be counted among the world's advanced and developed nations. It might not be an easy journey, but its direction was clear.

The government sought to create a social "melting pot," that would turn all new immigrants, whatever their origins, into the Zionist concept of the "new Jew." Freed from the habits and complexes of the Diaspora, these new Israeli citizens would become productive workers—farmers, industrial laborers, construction workers, or soldiers—as part of the drive to create a new society. The government sought to create a proletariat through which it could transform Israel into a normal, functioning society. This was a "mobilized society," engaged in realizing the Zionist challenge of creating a model state. From this determination arose the emphasis on the collective, while at times losing sight of the needs of the individual within the great enterprise that was the State of Israel. The miracle of the resurrection of the Jewish nation justified any short-term suffering, and the hardships of the present were seen as worth bearing for the cause of fulfilling the Zionist vision of a good future. A life of equality in poverty was worth living if it meant achieving the miracle of statehood. Everyone was equal—everyone was poor, or at least content with very little. The "rich" were ashamed to appear as such. The important word was "meaning."

This Utopian vision encountered real human, cultural, and social limitations. The policies of austerity and rationing were dictated by Israel's scarcity of foreign currency reserves, but also stemmed from a national ethos of modesty and frugality. Socialist culture was anti-consumerist. Even when the foreign currency reserves crisis eased, the public mood and government perception still supported the idea of a modest lifestyle without ostentation, where people were content to have little and happy to save.

In the 1950s, Israel was a relatively egalitarian society. The first disparities began to appear in the 1960s, when Israeli Holocaust survivors began to receive personal compensation payments from Germany, raising their standard of living without any need to obtain income from work, As the economy became more sophisticated and differential compensation began for jobs requiring education, professional knowledge and management skills, disparities in income and consumption grew between the educated and uneducated populations. The willingness of the public to be content with little dissipated. Private consumption increased, and with it came the consumption patterns of developed economies. Israel became "normal,", in both its positive and negative meanings. The initial enthusiasm for the vision of creating a "model" state gradually faded. These idealistic and Utopian ideas seemed too pure and lofty, perhaps to be found only in academic theories and in dreams.

Income disparities widened, along with inequalities due to ethnicity, largely associated with location—residency in the old established cities (largely home to a wealthier, Ashkenazi population) versus the newer development towns (largely home to a poorer, Mizrahi (North African and Middle Eastern) population). These disparities became even greater during the 1970s, when Israel enjoyed an economic boom of over 11 percent growth per annum following the Six-Day War (1968–1973) coupled with low unemployment rates of about three percent. However, the growth did not affect all the country's residents equally, and the poorer populations, particularly those from Mizrahi backgrounds, felt excluded from the rise in living standards enjoyed by the largely Ashkenazi population of the central coastal plain. In the peripheral regions in the south and north, residents were still suffering from inadequate health systems and infrastructure. The euphoria and unequal growth caused rising disaffection and anger among the Mizrahi population, marking the start of their class and cultural consciousness.

## The Black Panthers

The Black Panthers movement was born in 1972, after a series of angry demonstrations in Jerusalem in the previous year. The protesters demanded better housing and an end to discrimination over the benefits that they believed immigrants from the Soviet Union and United States were receiving preferentially.

The Black Panthers, a group of young people from the Musrara neighborhood of Jerusalem, declared that they would be "like the Black Panthers of the United States, because we are Black and oppressed." The movement was born amid a global wave of social protests—such as France's student revolt and the protests in the United States against the Vietnam War and for civil rights. The sense of deprivation and anger over the lack of a future and exclusion from the Zionist narrative led young Mizrahi Jews to protest against Israel's social policies. This was a time of euphoria and feeling a sense of "empire," perhaps even invincibility, after the great gains of the Six-Day War. The Black Panthers raised the flag of social revolution and ignited a debate: is it possible to raise two flags—of security and society—at the same time? The concept still prevailed that citizens should "sacrifice" living standards in the here-and-now for the sake of the Utopian vision of building the country. The sense of deprivation felt by the Mizrahi Jews was partly due to objective factors of low education and skills, and partly due to the attitudes of older residents toward newcomers.

The government realized—albeit a little late and constrained by the protests—that it needed to regulate the state's social expenditure and make up for the shortcomings in how immigrants had been treated in the early days of independence. The government adopted a social agenda in light of the recommendations of the Prime Minister's Commission on Children and Youth At-Risk (also known as the Katz Commission after its chairman, Israel Katz, the director general of the National Insurance Institute). The Commission formulated plans for housing, education, and transfer payments to promote an agenda in line with the principles of the welfare state that were gaining momentum in Western Europe.

Earlier social protests in 1959 in Haifa's Wadi Salib neighborhood, sparked by the shooting of a Moroccan immigrant by police, were much more limited in their impact on social policy. In the 1950s, Israel was still struggling with basic subsistence, and income disparities were limited. Following the Wadi Salib riots, a program of income tax reductions began based on the number of children in a family, reflecting the government's understanding of the problems of the citizens who came from Arab countries, as well as its desire to better integrate them into the larger society. The Black Panthers' protests were more effective than the Wadi Salib riots, and led to major changes in social policy, not least because by the time of these protests, Israel was already a more established economy, and the younger generation of immigrants from North Africa and the Middle East were more self-confident than the previous generation. The Black Panther protests were more damaging than the Wadi Salib riots, and there was more social openness by the time they occurred. Both sets of protests, however, occurred against a background of discrimination and frustration and a feeling of exclusion from mainstream Israeli society.

In 1972–1973, in the wake of the recommendations of the Katz Commission, civilian public spending increased considerably. Israel believed in its ability to carefully and gradually adopt a policy that would bring the country to resemble a European welfare state. The rapid economic growth of the early 1970s gave rise to hopes that this positive direction of travel would help facilitate the expansion of social services as part of Israel's state and economy-building efforts. However, the increased public spending, coupled with the high security budget, put great pressure on the state's coffers, creating huge demands that manifested themselves in overemployment, with the demand for workers exceeding the supply, inflationary pressures, and an increase in the current account deficit.

Following the Yom Kippur War in October 1973, Israel found itself having to stretch all its resources to provide security and respond to social needs. The war was difficult and expensive, sparking an unprecedented rise in defense spending to 25–30 percent of GDP. Despite this, over the next decade, Israel did not adjust government spending to cope with this new reality of soaring defense costs. Social spending, which had been on the rise before the war, continued to be relatively high after it was over. Together, Israel's defense and civilian public spending in the late 1970s and early 1980s reached 65–75 percent of GDP, which was very high compared to other countries. The budget deficit soared to 10–15 percent of GDP. There was also a considerable increase in public debt in Israel and abroad. This is the essence of the economic crisis that led to the "lost decade" of 1974–1985, the most prominent manifestation of which was the inflationary spiral of the early 1980s.

## Construction and Housing

Construction was a major part of the Israeli economy in its first decades of statehood, and its weight in terms of GDP and employment was relatively high, at about 10 percent. Construction projects included housing, public buildings, infrastructure, and factories. In the first two decades of independence, Israel's built-up areas (mainly for housing) more than doubled as a result of the mass waves of immigration. The construction industry was hit by the recession of 1966–1967, during which time it completed large projects but experienced no investments in new projects of a similar size.

Even during the British Mandatory period there had been an acute housing crisis, largely as a result of legal and illegal immigration to the Land of Israel. The waves of immigration of the 1920s and 1930s increased the size of the Yishuv fivefold, and as a result, there was a constant need for new housing stock. Construction activity was simply insufficient to create the required number of homes, leading to soaring housing prices and rents and creating an economic problem. In response, the British Mandatory government created a "fair rent" model, which imposed a regulatory regime on the rental market. The Yishuv adapted the British approach and developed a "key money" (security deposit) system, in which landlords demanded compensation for the erosion of their incomes as a result of rent controls. The amount of "key money" was determined by the market. Even in the pre-State period, "key money" rates were discussed in the same way that rent and mortgage prices are today. The "key money" system continued to be widespread in the 1950s and 1960s, but changes in the industry, particularly the large supply of "shikunim"—neighborhoods of low-cost housing – by the government led to its gradual disappearance, and there are almost no rent controlled apartments in Israel today.

In Israel's first decade of statehood, some 900,000 people immigrated to its shores and urgently needed housing. Israel temporarily solved the housing crisis by building transit camps, mainly on the edges of old settlements, or in towns and villages abandoned by Palestinians. In 1951, there were 132 transit camps housing around a quarter of a million Israelis. The transit camps all but disappeared from the landscape in the 1960s after a period of intense housing construction.

Israel's construction market was affected by government schemes to provide low-cost housing for the growing population, through the construction of housing projects in new cities and neighborhoods. Government aid helped those who immigrated to Israel with nothing, and the state helped about 70 percent of the population to own apartments, thanks in part to the government selling apartments it built or owned to the public. The reparations from West Germany from the 1950s provided an impetus for high level construction and created disparities and inequality in consumption and housing.

In the 1960s and 1970s, there was an improvement in residential construction, and Israel experienced a process of suburbanization and urban sprawl that allowed car travel between city centers to housing projects and settlements in the suburbs. There were no land shortages, due to the feeling that Israel was an empty land. There was no issue with overcrowding, as land was plentiful, and neighborhoods of detached homes were built for the middle classes.

After the recession of 1966 and the Six-Day War, Israel's construction industry experienced renewed momentum in building residences and infrastructure. Roads were paved, and military bases, hotels, industrial plants, and public buildings were built. This was one of the reasons for the high growth of the early 1970s. The shortage of construction workers led Israel to issue work permits for laborers from the Occupied Palestinian Territories, whose entry into the labor market caused changes in the makeup of employment in the industry. Many Israelis left construction, and Palestinians (and, in later years, foreign workers) comprised the majority of construction workers in Israel. This phenomenon had implications for low productivity in construction, and for the dependence between the Occupied Palestinian Territories and Israel.

# PART THREE

# THE "LOST DECADE" AND THE 1985 ECONOMIC STABILIZATION PLAN: 1974–1985

## 12

## Upsetting the Balance

### The Significance of the Yom Kippur War

The period between the Six-Day and Yom Kippur Wars (1967–1973) were challenging years in Israel's short economic history. In the wake of its great military victory in the Six-Day War, Israel's sense of strength, even invincibility, soared to new heights. Overnight, it had become a regional power, now infused with a near messianic-religious fervor. A country that had suffered severe anxiety over its security and even existence in the days preceding the Six-Day War had miraculously become, within just six short days, a victorious nation, strong and powerful. The years that followed, until the shock of the Yom Kippur War, were a peak period for Israel's military and security echelons. The actions—and inactions—of these "interwar" years would have an impact for many years to come.

Israel's military victory in the Six-Day War did not bring about the long-awaited political reward of having its neighbors recognize its legitimate existence as a Jewish state in the Middle East. Israel needed to make new security efforts, which incurred rising defense costs. During the War of Attrition in 1968–1970, Israel's defense spending soared to around 15 percent of GDP, almost double that of the period before the Six-Day War. In 1971–1973, following the end of the War of Attrition and amid social pressures (including from the Black Panthers movement), defense spending fell to about 11 percent of GDP, still higher than it had been before the Six-Day War. Military-defense spending accelerated Israel's exit from the recession of 1966–1967 and heralded a period of growth and high employment. Unemployment fell from 11 percent to around 3 percent in just two years. The maintenance of the Palestinian territories conquered during the Six-Day War entailed heavy ongoing costs, despite the relative peace that prevailed as a result of the shock of Israel's victory. In 1970, Palestinian workers were granted work permits, the first time that non-Israeli workers were active in the Israeli employment market. The development of Israel's defense industries grew apace, a result of the French embargo on arms sales to the country and boosted overall industrial and technological development. Even in this "interwar" period before the Yom Kippur War, Israel maintained its "Theory of Rounds" strategy of using the lull in hostilities to forge ahead with economic and social development. Yet worrying cracks emerged. The high rate of economic growth (around 11 percent per year) and full employment caused inflationary pressures, as housing and private consumption demands still outstripped supply, and an increase in public debt (both internal and external), and issues with the balance of payments. These were accompanied by social unrest arising from the gap between those benefiting from the growth and those left behind. This was a new aspect of Israel's socioeconomic existence, different from the formative, modest years between 1948–1967. Then, "Little Israel" had been confident it was on the right path toward realizing its vision of building a state amid fears of a "second round" of attacks from its neighbors.

The Yom Kippur War, which had come as a shock, was a watershed moment in Israel's short history. The year of the war, 1973–1974, sparked a crisis for Israel's economy. The war was costly. Despite emerging victorious, Israel lost its new-found self-confidence and was disappointed with its performance in this unexpected war. Its economic situation had been damaged and its deterrence eroded, as had the Israeli public's trust in their leadership. Skyrocketing defense spending burdened the economy and growth slowed. Per capita GDP grew by only around one percent a year over the next decade, about a quarter of the growth rate that Israel had experienced in its first 25 years. The slowdown now led to rapid inflation, which, driven by high energy and commodity costs, soared to about 40 percent per annum in 1974–1977, and at its peak in 1984–1985, reached over 400 percent per year. External public foreign currency debt reached 87 percent of GDP in 1984, and total public debt soared to 270 percent of GDP. Public expenditure on goods, which had stood at 45 percent in 1967–1972, rose to some 75 percent by 1984–1985.

Arab countries, through the cartel of the Organization of the Petroleum Exporting Countries (OPEC), increased the price of oil from a few dollars per barrel to ten times that during the Yom Kippur War. The Iranian Revolution of 1979, which saw the rise to power of a theocratic government led by Ayatollah Ruhollah Khomeini, sparked yet more oil price hikes. Soaring oil prices pushed the price of goods, food, and metals to rise by tens of percent. No doubt, these external factors played a part in bringing on the crisis. However, the intensity and duration of Israel's economic crisis were rooted in internal political and economic processes.

Yitzhak Rabin's first government (1974–1977), recognized the seriousness of Israel's economic crisis, and attempted to tackle it through a series of important reforms. The Ben Shahar Committee on Direct Taxation (1975) brought order and rationalization to direct taxation, while Israel's introduction in 1976 of an 8 percent VAT as its main indirect tax, not long after the first implementation of VAT in Western Europe, was an innovative and efficient move. The method of currency devaluation was amended to accommodate changes in the exchange rate, and in 1975 shifted from a rigid regime of currency devaluations at lengthy intervals to a monthly "creeping devaluation," pegged to the rate of rising inflation. However, these measures, even though they had been the correct ones to take, were not sufficient to address the challenges of the economic fallout caused by the Yom Kippur War or to meet the future needs of the Israeli economy. Israel's annual inflation rate, while around 40 percent in 1976–1977, was still under a semblance of control. It would have been possible to address the crisis with fiscal and monetary tools, had it not been for the economic upheaval of 1977.

The main weakness of the first Rabin government was its failure to adjust civilian public spending in light of increased defense spending. Instead, Rabin pushed ahead with social programs in education, health, welfare, and housing as they had been designed back in 1972–1973, before the watershed of the Yom Kippur War. However, at the same time, Israel reduced its investments in infrastructure. Thus, the delicate balance between defense and civilian spending was upset. This is the only period in Israel's history in which the principle of reinforcing the economy in the lull following a period of hostilities was ignored. The trauma of the "surprise" outbreak of the Yom Kippur War (the "failure", caused the government to overreact by excessively allocating funds to defense budgets and expanding the army, which had knock-on effects on economic performance). The increase in defense spending also increased the budget deficit, government debt, and interest expenses, while repressing much-needed investments in infrastructure.

The burden of defense spending in 1975–1985 reached an average of around 24 percent of GDP. In 1975–1976, defense spending reached a peak of around 30 percent of GDP and would remain high until the mid-1980s. Defense spending was also exacerbated by the First Lebanon War in 1982, and then by the fact that IDF remained in Lebanon until 1985. Meanwhile, it was becoming very clear that there was a limit to the economy's capacity to bear the burden of such high defense spending.

The positive economic trends of 1953–1973 ground to a halt, and even retreated. Growth stagnated, manufacturing productivity was curbed, the current account deficit in the balance of payments rose to crisis proportions, there were sharp increases in the prices of fuel and imported raw materials, government debt soared, and inflation had begun to spiral out of control. This was the "lost decade" of the Israeli economy.

## The Economic Upheaval

The loss of public trust in Israel's leadership that occurred in the wake of the Yom Kippur War led to a political upheaval in 1977. The right-wing Likud party, led by Menachem Begin, rose to power and began to lead the government, replacing the long-standing hegemony of the Labor Party and its allies that had been the status quo since 1948. The new government made critical errors in economic policy and monetary management, and exacerbated the crisis, not least because it lacked budgetary discipline and failed to address the structural problems plaguing the economy. The crisis had exposed the economy's weaknesses. Having experienced constant growth during Israel's first 25 years of statehood, the economy had difficulty coping with a combined external and internal crisis. Economists in Israel and elsewhere began to question whether the Israeli "economic miracle" was now over, and whether the Israeli economy was headed in a South American-style direction of recession and rampant inflation.

Following the Likud's rise to power, its first Minister of Finance, Simha Erlich, announced an "economic revolution," implementing an ideologically liberal policy of freeing the foreign currency market from state supervision and implementing a free foreign exchange market. Erlich's dream was to transform Israel into the "Switzerland of the Middle East." But for such a drastic move to be successful, ideological declarations were not enough. It required complex economic steps grounded in professional economic strategies. The new government was not equipped for such strategies.

The changes in the management of the foreign exchange market were not effective in dealing with the severe foreign exchange reserves crisis that

Israel was facing at the time. On the contrary, Likud's ideological "economic upheaval" failed miserably, plunging Israel into an even deeper crisis. Previously, Israel's price system had been anchored on a fixed exchange rate. Any changes in the exchange rate were calculated with care and discretion, via creeping devaluation, and took into account the foreign exchange deficit and the effects of the devaluation on prices and wages. The new government's economic upheaval, replacing state control over the exchange rate in favor of a free market and reduced supervision of foreign exchange transactions, was devastating to the inflationary process, which had previously been relatively controlled, albeit high, standing at around 40 percent in 1977. The government's lack of experience, combined with its populist policy of "for the good of the people," had created a real risk to Israel's economic stability.

Monetary policy in a free foreign exchange market is governed by the interest rate and control over the amount of cash in the market. This was not the case here. Israel's monetary policy was not effective in light of the public's transition to index and dollar-linked assets during a period of high inflation. The Bank of Israel printed money to finance the budget deficit and did not control the amount of cash in the economy. With its sharp and rapid "liberation" of the exchange rate, the government had let go of the reins of inflation. This example is an illustration of the holistic nature of economic policy, where taking an action in one area affects other areas of the economy. An economy is like a human body, whose systems are synergistically interconnected.

In 1978, inflation rose to 80 percent, and in 1979, it crossed the 100 percent line. Israel's ability to deal with the crisis using ordinary economic measures was greatly weakened. As the years passed, the government found it increasingly difficult to tackle the economic crisis and inflation using accepted economic tools, which were becoming more and more ineffective. Inflation had taken hold, and the public and businesses had adopted a "living with inflation" mindset. Inflationary expectations had been created and became firmly rooted in the consciousness and behavior of consumers and producers.

By this stage, Israel had entered a combined internal and external, fiscal-monetary crisis. The crisis had been precipitated by a large hike in government defense spending financed by the Bank of Israel printing money, and an increase in imports sparked by rising fuel and raw materials prices. All this was exacerbated by bad economic policies.

The crisis was dubbed the "lost decade." In the first half of the 1980s, budget deficits reached a peak of around 15 percent of GDP, government debt soared to 270 percent of GDP by the end of 1984, and inflation reached over 400 percent a year in 1984–1985. The economy was headed toward a threatening level of uncontrolled inflation. In the five years from 1980–1984, the cumulative rate of inflation reached 17,000 percent. Meanwhile, per capita GDP barely moved, and Israel's economic resilience took a hit. The balance between military growth and civilian economic resilience had been well and truly upset.

The crisis revealed the importance of professional and experienced economic leadership. The post of Minister of Finance is undoubtedly one of the most difficult and complex positions in any country, and in Israel even more so. In its early days, the Likud lacked experience in managing economic policy and was captive to the slogans and ideological clichés of its election campaigning. Effective economic policy requires strategic understanding and the ability to make tactical moves. To take a successful alternative path, one first needs to determine a policy that can set goals, and then choose policy tools and take the necessary steps to implement them to bring about the desired outcomes. While the Likud government led two important social projects—neighborhood rehabilitation and the law on free education through twelfth grade—these increased the already high government spending and the budget deficit, and further exacerbated the fiscal-monetary imbalance and the inflationary crisis.

Inflation in the 1970s and 1980s, experienced in Israel and internationally, was a different beast from the one the world had been used to. This was not only "classic" inflation, which arose from fiscal-monetary factors. This inflation was the result of an increase in oil and raw materials prices. This was a combination of classic factors and supply side factors. The term "stagflation," which was coined for this crisis, combined two problems—high inflation and weak growth—that should not occur at the same time. Stagflation had not been experienced anywhere, including in Israel, since the end of the Second World War. Attempts to manage the crisis exposed weaknesses in Israel's foremost economic institutions—the Bank of Israel and the Treasury. The academic sphere was also slow to understand and analyze the new reality and propose policies and measures to deal with the new challenges. In addition, the crisis also revealed fundamental weaknesses in the economy, among them labor market rigidity, a nationalized capital market, and a lack of openness toward the international market. After more than 30 years of Israeli statehood, changes were needed in the way its now-maturing economy was managed to meet the state's new needs. The crisis was a complex one, and economic policy management in these circumstances required professional and strong economic leadership and good economic understanding.

Israel had experienced a sudden reversal in fortune. From a country that the world had seen as an "economic miracle," it had deteriorated into a state experiencing a drawn-out, existential economic crisis. The economic prodigy had vanished, to be replaced by a problem child. The narrow line between security and the economy that Israel had to tread had become blurred after the Yom Kippur War, and the country's socioeconomic status was damaged. The First Lebanon War in 1982 also served to increase Israel's already sky-high defense spending. Unlike the Yom Kippur War, however, the First Lebanon War was seen as a "war of choice" and as such it did not gain legitimization from large sections of the public, even more so because of the perceived futility of remaining in Lebanon for such a long time. The second Lebanon War contributed to the further erosion of public trust in the security echelons, the government, and the leadership, a process that had been set in motion by the Yom Kippur War. There were public debates and questions regarding fundamental issues, such as the very concept of security and the size of the defense budget, as well as discussions on the economic situation and despair over the never-ending inflation. This situation became a cause for concern for the U.S. government, and in 1984, Washington held talks about it with the Israeli government. The Americans saw a risk to the economic stability and security of Israel, which played an important role in the Middle East during the Cold War. These concerns led to the United States' willingness to assist Israel financially.

## Leaving the "Mobilized Economy and Society" Behind

The economy had grown and developed to the point where it needed to be liberated from government control. Meanwhile, the Black Panther social protest movement reflected the hopes and dreams of the young immigrants who had arrived in the wake of Israel's declaration of independence, and who also wanted to enjoy the fruits of their new country's economic growth. The impressive success of Israel's economic policy and its impressive achievements in the years before the Yom Kippur War, had been first and foremost in public discourse. This success had masked the need for changes in economic policy and behavior to address new challenges arising from the size of the economy and global economic trends. Now, after the Yom Kippur War, preoccupied as it was with its deepening economic crisis, Israel was blind to the dramatic changes that were taking place in the global economy. While Israel was wrestling with its internal problems, new leaders—Margaret Thatcher, Ronald Reagan and Helmut Kohl—had come to power in the United Kingdom, the United States, and Germany. This new generation of leaders had changed their economies from over-reliance on state involvement, social safety nets, and the welfare state, and introduced drastic new policies of reduced government involvement, free market economics, and an increasing reliance on the private sector.

Israel, founded after the Second World War, built its economy and institutions around the concepts of the postwar world, with Europe as its closest reference point. In particular, Israel adopted a policy of large-scale state involvement in its economy, which suited the challenges faced by the nascent state. The new State of Israel was able to meet its national challenges not just because of its good security system and strong economy, but also—and even chiefly—by building a committed, mobilized society that was willing to pay a heavy personal cost to achieve national, collective goals. Israel was founded by a handful of pioneers who had managed to charge the larger population with a national enthusiasm that would endure for years after the birth of the state. But in the aftermath of the Yom Kippur War and the First Lebanon War, there was a certain level of fatigue among the public. Weary of the constant national tension, the Israeli public wanted to improve their living standards and achieve personal goals, not only the national ones The war proved, at least on an emotional level, that even the "great father" could be wrong. And if he was wrong about security, Israel's lifeblood, then it was possible that he was also wrong about economic and social issues. These cracks were exposed in the 1970s, and in the 1980s, Israel would see shocks and shifts in social values regarding the government and the military that reflected the beginning of the globalization process as well as political disagreements in Israel on key issues, especially the Israeli-Palestinian conflict. Israel's economic crisis proved that, even when it came to the economy, the government needed to make changes and try a different route, even if that path was unclear and unknown. While the rise to power of the Likud in 1977 did indeed lead to changes in economic policy, the results, at least initially, were devastating.

## Glints of Light

Even during this severe economic crisis, there were a few glints of light, economic bright spots that would serve as the basis for progress in the future. While Israel's macroeconomic policy was a failure, important strategic steps were nevertheless taken that did help to revive the market. Israel's free trade agreement with the European Common Market in 1975 was a strategic move to expose the market to imports and foreign competition. This was a big step toward abandoning protectionist policies toward the international market, as well as an important move toward integrating with globalization trends. In 1985, Israel signed a similar agreement with the United States. These steps created a special international agreement infrastructure. Indeed, for several years, Israel was unique in having signed two free trade agreements with two of the largest economic blocs in the world—the United States and the European Common Market—which benefitted foreign investors who could now enjoy tariff-free entry to these two blocs.

The development of Israel's high-tech industry, on the basis of R&D and innovation, was another significant achievement of this period. The creation and growth of an innovative R&D industry produced a number of successful high-tech enterprises and earned recognition from the business world and entrepreneurs that Israel was fertile ground for a new and promising high-tech growth engine. Two steps established Israel's sophisticated export industry. The first was the passing of the Research and Development Law in 1984. The law established binding and transparent legislation that would help Israel to build a cutting-edge, R&D-based technological industry that would maximize its comparative advantages. The second step was the encouragement and incentives that Israel gave to Intel for its Israeli operations. Intel, a leading global technology company, had established a development and production center in Jerusalem in 1981, thus positioning Israel as an important and worthwhile center for R&D with high-quality human capital. Intel's step sent a clear signal to global high-tech companies that they would benefit from entering the Israeli market and developing their businesses there.

# 13

# Tackling Inflation

## The Inflationary Process

There were a number of reasons for the rapid acceleration of inflation in Israel. The first was an increase in government spending and the budget deficit, and the decision to finance the deficit by the Bank of Israel printing money. The second was imported inflation due to a double-digit percentage leap in oil and commodity prices. To deal with inflation and protect the public from its effects, the government developed and honed numerous linkage mechanisms. In practice, however, rather than curbing the rise of inflation, the linkage mechanisms only served to exacerbate the inflationary flareup.

Defense mechanisms against inflation had existed since the British Mandatory period. Israel's price increase mechanism was built on an annual inflationary rate of around 10–20 percent. In 1972, inflation in Israel stood at 13 percent, and by 1973, it had risen to 20 percent. By 1975, inflation had almost doubled to around 39 percent. It was clear that these rates far exceeded the familiar patterns of the past.

During this period, inflation was a widespread global problem, a result of rising oil and commodity prices and the gradual abandonment of the gold standard worldwide. While there were no established defense mechanisms against this inflation, in most countries, it did decrease over time. However, most countries did not have such high budget deficits as Israel. Furthermore, unlike in Israel, rising inflation acted as its own stabilizing mechanism: when there are no mechanisms to protect against it, inflation erodes the value of financial assets and liabilities, as well as real wages and other incomes, thereby reducing purchasing power, which in turn curbs inflation. In this way, a structured solution is created against further increases in inflation. This was not the case in Israel, where official linkage mechanisms preserved the value of real wages, while tax laws were amended to address taxation under inflationary conditions. Further, the Bank of Israel Law of 1954 allowed the central bank to print money to finance the budget deficit, which also served to fuel rampant inflation, especially as there was no incentive for the government to take measures to reduce the deficit and stop printing money.

A sense of collective wisdom and an instinct for economic survival pushed the Israeli public to divert funds to help them maintain the value of their assets against the dollar. The dollar became a substitute for the Israeli lira, whose value was being steadily eroded by inflation every month. The Israeli public abandoned cash and current accounts in the local currency and switched to assets linked to a foreign currency or index. This behavior undermined the Bank of Israel's ability to operate, since it was not able to effectively tackle inflation by eroding public purchasing power. On the contrary, the government invested a great deal of effort into actually strengthening indexation mechanisms for wages and the capital market, with the goal of allowing the public to "live with inflation." In doing so, the government shot itself in the foot.

The government's lack of budgetary restraint, along with the loss of effectiveness of Israel's monetary policy, caused inflation to jump by 50 percent in 1978, over 100 percent in 1979, and 131 percent in 1980. Public lack of trust in the Israeli currency meant that many prices (including those of apartments, rent, consumer durables, and many services) began to be listed in dollars. However, the switch to listing prices in dollars did not solve the structural problems of the Israeli economy, which included a high increase in public spending of around 75 percent of GDP in 1984, an expansive monetary policy of printing money to finance the budget deficit, and a rise in public debt of around 270 percent of GDP by the end of 1984.

The government's approach of "living with inflation" via linkage mechanisms intended to make daily life easier—chiefly, reducing state subsidies of goods, increasing direct taxes, and fixed monthly devaluations—created an expectation among the public and businesses that inflation would simply continue. The government failed to adopt realistic (and painful) policies to address the real roots of inflation, such as slashing the soaring budget deficit and ceasing to finance the deficit through printing money. Instead, government policy only served to increase inflation because of its reliance on linkage index mechanisms. The country, waiting for a miracle to somehow occur, experienced a feeling of helplessness, embarrassment, and resigned fatalism.

Finance Minister Yigal Horowitz (in office 1979–1980), took partial fiscal measures by reducing government subsidies, but these failed to bring about the desired result of curbing inflation but actually exacerbated it. The public became increasingly convinced that these measures were not skillful or effective, and as a result, their implementation had no impact on public expectations regarding inflation. Indeed, as time went on, inflationary expectations took root, and became an inflationary factor in their own right.

In 1982, Horowitz's successor, Finance Minister Yoram Aridor (in office 1980–1983), implemented the so-called 5:5:5 program, with the aim of synchronizing the cost rate of the exchange rate, price increases, taxation rates, and subsidy reductions, in order to reduce inflation to a monthly rate of five percent. This was intended as an intermediate administrative measure to help Israel move toward lower inflation. Once again, however, this new plan did not even attempt to address the real root of Israel's inflation problem, i.e., its macroeconomic imbalance, and thus it did not succeed in lowering inflation. In 1983, Aridor proposed a dollarization plan meant to peg Israel's price system to an entity outside the government's control—the U.S. dollar. Aridor hoped that this technical move would stop the Bank of Israel from printing money and that inflation would stabilize to a Western inflation rate. Again, this was a complex and problematic plan that could never have been a substitute for realistic (and painful) economic measures including, tackling Israel's budget deficit, ceasing to print money, and abolishing the indexation mechanism. Instead, it would have simply created a demand for dollars, which would have required Israel to coordinate with the issuer of that currency, the United States. Unsurprisingly, Aridor's plan did not work.

Close and complex interrelationships had emerged between developments in cost prices, indexation mechanisms and inflationary expectations, as any government decision on raising indirect taxes or cutting food subsidies automatically resulted in increases in the consumer price index. Israel's inflationary spiral was persisting regardless of the level of total demand. Any external price shock quickly translated into price increases through Israel's complicated linkage mechanisms, thereby creating higher price levels due to inflationary expectations among producers and consumers. This vicious cycle caused frustration among both policymakers and the public. There was an increasing understanding that what was required was a shift in economic thinking, and the political ability to implement radically different policies. Inflation was seen as not just an economic problem. There was a sense of impending social and political collapse, and a recognition that Israel's economic system was simply not functioning. Rampant inflation was destroying public trust in money and in democratic market mechanisms. In this light, the establishment of the national unity government in the summer of 1984 was a crucial political, economic, and national moment in terms of preserving Israel's democratic system and tackling the problem of rampant inflation.

## The Package Deals, 1984–1985

By this time, many Israeli economists, including in government, academia, and the political community, had begun to recognize that the routine measures taken so far were not helping to curb Israel's hyperinflation and that reducing the budget deficit alone would not curb inflation. In November 1984, Israel's national unity government, which by then had been in power for just three months, made an unusual attempt to tackle inflation. The new government proposed a package deal with three partners—itself, the Histadrut, and industrialists. Each partner pledged to contribute to reducing price increases by renouncing their own sectoral interests in favor of the general good of fighting inflation. The deal included an agreement that emergency orders would be used to implement administrative price controls.

Shimon Peres, who led the unity government, made the fight against inflation the priority of his new administration. The September 1984 index, published on October 15, 1984, showed a startling jump in inflation of 21.4 percent, which served to accelerate the urgency of dealing with the problem. Fearing that inflation was on the verge of spiraling out of control and deteriorating into hyperinflation, Peres proposed the package deal as a "social contract," and convinced Finance Minister Yizhak Moda'i to join him. He also corralled Yisrael Kessar, general secretary of the Histadrut, and Eli Hurvitz, president of the Israel Manufacturers' Association, as partners in the deal.

Many had already recognized that reducing the budget deficit alone would not curb inflation. Professor Michael Bruno, one of Israel's leading economists, who would become Shimon Peres' economic advisor, and then Governor of the Bank of Israel, had already advocated drastic and comprehensive measures in cooperation with the Histadrut and industrialists. In a February 1981 newspaper article titled "A crushing and quick blow,"[1] Bruno called for a comprehensive, fast-working plan to curb inflation that would combine macroeconomic measures with agreements by the Histadrut and industrialists to neutralize the linkage mechanisms.

The first package deal, which began on November 4, 1984, and ran for three months, came as a surprise to the public. The government's contribution to the deal was to curb direct taxes and subsidies on certain basic goods, such as bread, dairy products, and cooking oil, the Histadrut waived wage increases, and industrialists agreed to price controls curbing the costs of goods and the prices of services. The government activated emergency orders to freeze and control prices, an unusual step designed to convince the public that the war on inflation was a high priority. Inspectors were recruited to enforce price controls, and the government used the media to explain to the public that it was serious about its intentions to tackle inflation. However, the package deal did not include any measures to reduce the budget deficit or to stop the Bank of Israel from printing, and as a result, it proved ineffective.

Having been personally involved in managing price controls under the package deals, I can attest to the fact that, in practice, the government did not completely freeze the prices of subsidized products. Furthermore, the government actually raised the prices of fuel and government bonds to avoid increasing the budget deficit. Neither the exchange rate nor the interest rate was included in the package deal, because of objections by the Bank of Israel (asserting its independence from government interference in their decisions).

Under the package deal, the exchange rate rose by around ten percent, and despite the neutralization of the cost-of-living allowance indexation and added costs, wages also went up. Manufacturers absorbed the increases in import costs and wages, and pressures were created to raise prices. The November inflation index rose by 19.5 percent, the December index by 3 percent, and the January 1985 index by 5.3 percent. Ostensibly, the package deal had been a success. However, producers and suppliers, who had absorbed the costs of devaluation, could not continue in this way for a long period of time. It was clear that administrative price controls could not curb inflation in the long term in the absence of any real macroeconomic measures. It would not be possible to slow inflation without also implementing a simultaneous, comprehensive treatment of all cost components, the most prominent of which was the exchange rate.

Despite the failure of the package deal, the partners did not despair. They continued with a second package with similar principles. However, the second deal was to prove worse than the first, because during it, prices were raised on a frequent basis, and, as a result, public trust was damaged, and public disdain for the failure of the government, suppliers, and sellers increased. Undaunted, the partners pushed ahead with a third package deal in May 1985. This time, the government really made a mess of things, taking two significant moves—increasing VAT by two percent and hiking gasoline prices—that further damaged its credibility with the public. This despite the clear and vital need for the government to gain the public's trust that prices would not be raised during the package deal. In the end, the government's lack of consistency around price rises contributed to the failure of the deals.

Administrative price controls were a new tool. They required the government to grapple with complex methodologies in order to freeze prices during a period of three-figure inflation. The price controls failed because they became a political, rather than an administrative and professional, issue when the government granted veto rights to each of the partners in the Exceptions Committee.[2] On the positive side, the price controls and related media information campaigns were successful in raising public awareness of the issues around price rises, which helped enforce the price controls. However, ultimately, this was simply not enough. The main lesson that the government learned from its first attempts to control the prices of tens of thousands of goods and services was that for these efforts to be effective, it needed to completely freeze all vital prices, including wages, the exchange rate, taxes, and subsidized products. Because the exchange rate was not part of the package deal, it was difficult to freeze prices, and there were built-in price distortions and potential for manufacturing disruptions. However, there was one positive outcome of the package deals—the government did gain administrative experience managing price controls. Ultimately, the lessons learned from these initial attempts at controlling prices as a measure to help curb inflation would succeed in creating a basis for the efficient implementation of further price controls a few years later, during the 1985 Economic Stabilization Plan.

## Notes

1. Michael Bruno, "A Crushing and Quick Blow," Migun, Feb 1981 (in Hebrew).
2. This was a special committee, comprised of representatives of the package deal's three partners, for granting requests for exceptions from the price control regulations.

# 14

# The 1985 Economic Stabilization Plan

## The Stages of the Plan

Undeterred by the failure of the package deals, the unity government, under the leadership of Shimon Peres, continued to be politically committed to the fight against inflation. The Finance Ministry's director general Emmanuel Sharon spearheaded preparations for a sweeping economic stabilization plan, with assistance from a team of economists from the Hebrew and Tel Aviv universities led by Professor Michael Bruno. Key lessons learned from the package deals were taken into account in the new plan. The 1985 Economic Stabilization Plan was born from the recognition that successful disinflation would require a comprehensive approach combining fiscal and monetary policy, addressing wages and the exchange rate, and including a fixed period of total administrative price controls.

By this time, it had become clear to the Ministry of Finance that there was simply no point in trying to implement partial measures. The looming threat of hyperinflation demanded a comprehensive and synchronized disinflation plan that addressed all aspects of the economy. Unlike the package deals, which were built on a partnership between the government, the Histadrut, and leading industrialists, the 1985 Economic Stabilization Plan was controlled entirely by the government, and the Histadrut and industrialists were given a reduced status. Preparations for the plan were kept secret and were discussed in detail in a lengthy cabinet meeting on June 30, 1985. The plan was implemented in one fell swoop on July 1, 1985. Although its participation was essential to the plan's success, the Histadrut originally opposed several elements of the plan, and refused to cooperate with it, unlike the industrialists. However, after Prime Minister Peres applied strong pressure on them for several days, the Histadrut agreed to the plan with some modifications.

The unity government provided a convenient political framework for the plan, because its broad political base of over 90 Knesset members made it easier to implement sweeping, complex, and painful measures. Moreover, such a drastic plan was now possible because of the safety net of a grant of $1.5 billion over two years from the United States, which was intended to avoid the risk of increasing Israel's current account deficit and a foreign exchange reserve shortage due to the exchange rate freeze. In short, United States aid was vital to the success of the plan, and the fact that Washington granted it is a reflection of its anxiety regarding the stability of the Israeli economy. It is also significant that the U.S. State Department advised the Israel government to seek professional advice from leading American economists Herbert Stein and Stanley Fischer.

The goal of the 1985 Economic Stabilization Plan was to reach zero percent inflation. This was an ambitious goal, simple to define, and understandable in its implementation. Defining a clear and ambitious goal was a smart move from both a political, professional, and public point of view. Tackling inflation required the use of fiscal and monetary policy tools that were both sharp and broad, along with a complete freeze of all prices, wages, and the exchange rate. The plan tackled all types of inflation—"demand" inflation, "cost" inflation, and "expectations" inflation—in a coordinated, simultaneous, and wide-ranging manner. It rested on three main elements. "Demand" inflation was addressed through fiscal and monetary measures designed to reduce the budget deficit and the amount of money in the market. "Cost" inflation was tackled by freezing prices, wages, and the exchange rate, and by suspending wage linkage cost-of-living allowance mechanisms. Combatting the inflationary expectations that had been firmly rooted in the minds of producers and consumers as a result of long-term inflation required the unorthodox step of total administrative price controls.

The plan included a balanced budget for the first time in years. Previously, the norm had been a budget deficit of about 13–15 percent of GDP, financed by loans from the Bank of Israel. To this, another key monetary measure was made in the form of an amendment to the Bank of Israel Law that completely prohibited the central bank from providing loans to the government to finance budgetary deficits (i.e., printing money). The Bank of Israel paid a very real high interest rate under the 1985 Economic Stabilization Plan. To stop the vicious cycle of spiraling prices, all of the main prices that affected the cost of products and services (the exchange rate, wages, and direct taxation rates) were frozen in one fell swoop, and price increase mechanisms were suspended. The price controls followed a substantial reduction and then freezing of subsidies for basic products, which was a central element of balancing the budget, but which had caused the prices of those key goods (including cooking oil and margarine) to rise sharply. The price controls were intended to prevent immediate price increases across the board following the sharp rise in price of these basic goods, and to buy time until the macroeconomic measures of budgetary and monetary restraint were able to modify demand-side inflation. The price controls were in force for three months under emergency regulations.

This was an unorthodox move, to say the least. It was never the intention that price controls alone would eradicate inflation. Rather, they were a necessary tool—a crutch, as it were—to be used for a limited period, to buy time for the budgetary cuts and monetary measures to take hold and break inflationary expectations. Without price controls, the other measures to balance the budget, including reducing subsidies, simply could not have curbed inflation. On the contrary, past experience had suggested that making sharp cuts to subsidies and increasing direct taxation without also introducing strict price controls led to large price increases as a result of the complex linkage mechanisms combined with inflationary expectations. Had price controls not been imposed, producers would simply have raised their prices, and consumers would have accepted this as a matter of course, as had been the case in the past. Indeed, economic research has shown that expectations play a decisive role in the level and persistence of inflation.

Furthermore, if Israel had simply reduced its budget deficit and exerted monetary restraint without price controls, the economy would have gone into recession as a result of price and wage rigidity. The economy would have paid a heavy price in terms of growth and unemployment, while prices rose (a program along these lines in Bolivia in 1985 resulted in 20 percent unemployment, and its achievements were limited).

The sweeping measures implemented under the economic stability plan were an appropriate response to all the causes underlying Israel's hyperinflation. The 1985 Economic Stabilization Plan was a watershed moment for Israel. It tackled (albeit belatedly) a major economic crisis that threatened Israel's economy and stability. While this creative and complex plan almost completely eradicated inflation, its impact went far beyond this. It represented a sea change in the trajectory of the development of Israel's economy. After the inflationary threat was removed, Israel began to make sweeping changes in the structure of its economy, which created profound shifts in how its markets operated and in the image of the economy changed in the international community and somewhat among Israelis.

## Price controls—an Unorthodox but Necessary Move

The architects of the 1985 Economic Stabilization Plan had given much thought to preventing the economy from falling into recession and sparking large-scale unemployment. Unemployment was a particularly sensitive issue in Israel. Had it risen sharply under the plan, it would have led to public resentment—even if it were the outcome of a dramatic drop in inflation. The price controls were a necessary step to circumvent the risk of high unemployment and its accompanying social damage and dissent. The unemployment rate in the first year of the economic stability plan was around 7 percent, an increase of less than 1.5 percent since the start of the plan. This was a relatively low rise, particularly in view of the large-scale measures that had produced the accompanying dramatic drop in inflation. The price controls severed the link between inflationary expectations and inflation, and indeed bought time for the drastic fiscal and monetary measures to take effect, almost without cost in terms of recession and unemployment, while bolstering public confidence in the government.

The only way to convince the public of the seriousness of the plan was to take administrative measures to cut the vicious cycle of inflationary expectations. The price controls prevented producers from raising prices through a combination of government orders and a system of price inspectors, information campaigns, and consumer monitoring. The subsidy cuts to basic goods were drastic. Cooking oil and margarine subsidies were completely abolished. For other basic goods, there were significant reductions in the size of the subsidies from around 90 to 20 percent. It is impossible to design such a wide abolition of subsidies on basic consumer goods without price controls, which helped break the cycle of inflationary expectations and rising prices at a tolerable social cost, including without causing high unemployment. The price controls created a short, narrow window that allowed the plan's macroeconomic measures to mature and take hold and for inflation to slow, helping curb skepticism from manufacturers and consumers, weary of yet more government pledges and plans to stop inflation.

## Implementing the Price Controls

To gain the public's trust and allow the plan's macroeconomic policy measures to mature, the government decided that the price freezes and controls would be implemented without compromise or exceptions. The price controls were successful largely because of the experience the government had gained over the eight months of the package deals, which meant it was now able to wield them as an efficient and effective economic, administrative, and legal tool. The same experience also helped the government to successfully enforce price controls, including through a public information campaign.

To gain public trust, the government took many steps to convey the message that this time, it was determined and resolute about beating inflation. It conducted bi-weekly consumer price indexes, made considerable efforts to enforce the set price levels, and published the results in the media. To reinforce the breaking of inflationary expectations and help build new expectations, the government undertook a public information campaign via television, radio, and print media. It printed and distributed pocket-sized price lists of about 400 products that the public could use; both to raise consumer awareness and "recruit" ordinary Israelis as voluntary price inspectors. Support for the plan grew, and new expectations regarding prices were created.

A rapid decrease from the three-figure inflation could have been problematic due to wide variations in the prices of unregulated goods and across the country. This can be compared to vehicles that are traveling down a road at different speeds and which are then all ordered to slow down to a complete stop at the same time. This creates traffic jams and accidents. In practice, however, there were almost no price distortions.

Price controls are an unconventional tool that liberal economists are averse to using. Free market economists view the markets as the most efficient method for regulating economic behavior and consider price controls to be an illegitimate and ineffective measure except in extreme situations of market failure, monopolies, and cartels. Indeed, some economists in the Bank of Israel and the Finance Ministry believed that it would have been possible to address inflation through strict budgetary measures and a restrictive monetary policy alone. Although the architects of Israel's 1985 Economic Stabilization Plan were economists from the mainstream current of liberal economic thought, they did not hesitate to use price controls because they understood that in this case—of market failure and a looming threat of hyperinflation—it was appropriate to intervene administratively in the market for a limited period. The economic stability plan made correct and effective use of price controls as a complementary tool to the plan's other macroeconomic measures. They enabled the government to freeze wages, taxes, subsidies, the exchange rate, and other prices simultaneously, which helped to stabilize prices quickly without creating unemployment. This was a brilliant plan in both its design and efficient execution.

## Interest Rates

The Bank of Israel had adopted a very restrictive monetary policy, with a sharp quantitative reduction in credit and high interest rates, with the goal of ensuring stability. However, even though stability was indeed achieved, interest rates remained very high for a long time, and the decline in interest rates was much more modest than that of prices. The very high real interest rates led to a sense of indignation in Israel's business sector, and questions were asked in government ministries as to whether such high interest rates were actually needed to stabilize prices. The annual real interest rate was about 100 percent, which caused difficulties for the business sector, and led to the collapse of companies and a slowdown in activity. It also raised the financing costs for businesses, which severely affected productivity, especially given the lack of equity, which had been eroded during the prolonged high inflation period. There was an impression that the Bank of Israel's high interest rates were a reflection of its skepticism and of its leaders' reservations regarding the economic stabilization plan. The lack of harmony between the central bank and the architects of the 1985 Economic Stabilization Plan violated the plan's basic principle that all of the economy's cost components, including the price of money, should be coordinated.

## The Return to Normalcy

Theoretically, it should have been a simple matter to remove the price controls after it had become clear that the 1985 Economic Stabilization Plan had been a success. In practice, a great deal of skill was required in moving the country from a regulated to a free market without introducing distortions after years of high inflation. In leaving the price control regime, both administrative and psychological considerations had to be taken into account. The price controls began to be lifted in January 1986, after economic analysis had confirmed that conditions were ripe for a return to normalcy. The beginning of the lifting of the price controls was clear evidence that the economic stability plan had been a success. It was also a basis for building new inflationary and economic expectations.

There were two options for lifting the price controls. The first was a quick, short exit from the price control regime over just a few months. This approach came with a risk of price increases due to uncertainty over whether inflation had indeed stabilized at such a low rate. In theory, in that case, the markets should simultaneously establish a new, stable equilibrium in relative and absolute prices. But there was a real risk that the complex linkage mechanisms would mean a return to the old inflationary expectations that were still fresh in the minds of producers and consumers, and cause prices to rise. The achievements of the plan were still all too fragile and delicate. Breaking inflationary expectations required engaging with human and social processes. It takes time to assimilate new patterns of behavior, ingrain new habits, and root out past behaviors. The second option was to gradually remove the price controls while monitoring and controlling every step, avoiding unnecessary risks out of recognition that such an enormous national effort had been invested in the stability plan that it was not worth jeopardizing its achievements. This strategy was based on the assumptions that there were no fundamental distortions in the price system or the production system, and that there was no suppressed inflation. It was just that a period of time was required to ensure that previous expectations had been shattered, and that new expectations had been created and had taken root in their stead.

Unsurprisingly, the government chose the second option, a gradual exit from the price control regime, which lasted until the summer of 1987. In January 1988, the proportion of goods subject to price controls stood at 26 percent, the same as on the eve of the package deals, which reflected the concentration of products in a small and closed economy characterized by little competition. Inflation had fallen in two stages. The first stage had reduced inflation from around 500 to 35 percent in the first half of 1986. The second stage had reduced inflation to around 18 percent, a level that was maintained for some six years. The hard core of inflation reflected price rigidity and linkage mechanisms. The move away from the high inflationary period increased public understanding that the decline in inflation was permanent.

Over the course of around a decade, the hard core of inflation was dismantled and dissolved, and at the end of the 1990s, the long-awaited goal of zero inflation became the status quo. The 1985 Economic Stabilization Plan succeeded in weakening the linkage mechanisms that had been integrated into the labor, financial, capital, and foreign exchange markets. The trade unions were also weakened. The large-scale immigration from the Soviet Union in the 1990s further helped to accelerate these processes. In reality, it took a full 15 years to fully eliminate inflation. Since 1992, the government has set inflation targets for the Bank of Israel of 1–3 percent per year. The 1985 Economic Stabilization Plan and the policies in the decade that followed changed the Israeli economy and the role to high real interest rate set by Bank of Israel created economic conditions that reduced the inflationary risk.

# 15

# The Consequences of the 1985 Economic Stabilization Plan

The success of the 1985 Economic Stabilization Plan, which was implemented without compromise, was a watershed, a "big bang" that changed the Israeli economy forever. It heralded a transition from a period of a mobilized, pioneering economy unique in its challenges and behavior, to a new period of a mature, serious state whose citizens sought a life of comfort and normalcy. Controlling inflation was not a substitute for the fundamental changes that the Israeli economy needed in order to compete and survive in a new era. In reality, there was no choice but to move away from the centralized, public administration of Israel's economy. It was no longer possible to continue on the same road, one that was well-suited for the initial period post-independence but was not appropriate for the new economic reality of the 1980s. The weight of the public sector and of the government's involvement in the economy were so great that they were hampering stable growth. Slashing government spending and moving away from state involvement in the ownership of companies and assets were fundamental conditions for recovery.

While Israel was in the throes of economic crisis, dramatic economic changes were unfolding in other countries. British Prime Minister Margaret Thatcher and United States President Ronald Reagan changed global economic trends in the 1980s by accelerating free market policies and reducing government involvement. This was a trend that quickly "spread to" other countries. Israel's national unity government, which was in power from 1984–1990, was comprised of the two major political blocs, Labor and the Likud. It recognized the need for fundamental changes in the structure of the economy and the way it was run. However, the Histadrut did not accept the new economic philosophy, advanced by experts in the government who espoused the conservative economic theories prevailing in the West. Over time, the Histadrut lost power, emerging from the economic crisis far weaker than it had been previously.

The first changes to come were fiscal and involved addressing the large budget deficit. Another key change was in the monetary policy, in the shape of the amendment to the Bank of Israel Law that banned Israel's central bank from giving loans to the government to finance the budget deficit. Controlling inflation was a first and necessary step toward revitalizing the economy, as a prelude to making deep and fundamental changes in the way it operated. These changes were spread over about 25 years in the form of numerous reforms. Managing a national economy is not like a laboratory where one can make controlled experiments and then examine the outcome of every economic step. Instead, Israel's recovery process continued by trial and error.

## Repercussions of the Persistent Crisis

The fact that the government had let the inflationary crisis drag on for so many years was due to incompetence and political and economic mistakes. A crisis must be dealt with "hard and fast." Procrastination is costly and causes long-lasting damage. The lengthy period of high inflation caused a great deal of harm to many industries and sectors. The financial system had difficulty functioning under persistent inflation. The costs of repairing all this damage would be very high.

At the beginning of 1983, the government bond market collapsed because of the increased risk of holding them—a reflection of the public's lack of trust in the government's ability to pay its debts. The 1983 bank stock crisis was one of the most significant events of the high inflation period. It was a direct result of the inflationary reality, which eroded the banks' equity capital. In attempting to tackle this problem, the banks resorted to illegally adjusting their stock prices amongst themselves, taking advantage of the weakness of the regulators. In doing so, they were able to raise the necessary capital from the public to issue credit. This came, to a large extent, at the expense of government bonds, which could not compete with the high yield generated from investments in bank stocks.

However, by mid-1983, the public had lost its faith in the bank stock bubble and began to sell their bank stocks and buy foreign currency instead. The banks had difficulty in rebuying the public's supply of stocks. On October 6, 1983, the banks completely lost their ability to absorb the large amount of bank stocks sold by the public, which would have bankrupted the banks' customers (because of the credit the banks did not have sufficient capital to repay) and the banks themselves (because the only credit guarantees they gave were their stocks). To prevent the collapse of the banks, which would have been a death blow to the Israeli economy, as it was already in the midst of a major economic crisis, the government had no option but to nationalize their stocks. To avoid a domino effect, all trading in the stocks of Israel's four largest banks was halted. Within two weeks, the Bank Stock Settlement was drawn up, under which the government assumed the obligation to redeem the stocks, at a certain discounted value, on the eve of the close of the Tel Aviv Stock Exchange on October 6, 1983. Control of the banks was transferred to the government. The value of the obligation assumed by the state treasury was estimated at the time to be 6.9 billion dollars. Nearly 20 years later, after the privatization of the bank stocks was finalized in 2014, the financial damage caused by the banking failure was re-estimated at 10 billion dollars.

The damage caused by inflation and the bank stocks crisis persisted for many years until the equity capital of the banks was rebuilt and they resumed their role as credit providers for businesses, households, deposit management, and public assets.

The economy had difficulty in catching up quickly after the prolonged crisis. The main fiscal problem was the huge amount of government debt, which at the close of 1985 stood at some 270 percent of GDP. It took around 25 years for this to fall to around 80 percent of GDP. Five more years were required for it to fall to 60 percent of GDP, a rate considered acceptable according to Maastricht Treaty guidelines for European Union members. The fact that it took such a long period for in government debt to fall to acceptable levels was a result of various challenges over the years, not least the Palestinian Intifadas and the large immigration from the former Soviet Union. The rate of interest payments from GDP was around 7 percent in the first decade after the 1985 Economic Stabilization Plan, and gradually decreased to about three percent in 2010–2019.

Another structural harm caused by the wider economic crisis was lower government investments in infrastructure projects, including transportation, water, sewage, drainage, communications, energy, and social projects. A gap was created in infrastructure investments, which failed to keep up with population growth, and what was worse, consumed the capital required to feed future growth. The present "ate" the future, and the economy has still not managed to close the gap even thirty years later.

The economic and financial crisis also hit the kibbutzim and moshavim. The drop in inflation exposed the precarious financial situation of Israel's communal settlement sector. Because of the political situation—the moshavim associated with the Likud, and the kibbutzim with Labor—the moshavim had much of their debt written off immediately, but the kibbutzim were left close to collapse. Only a government debt settlement toward the end of 1989, which included debt cancellations in exchange for the realization of kibbutz lands, managed to save them.

The kibbutzim debt settlement was the largest of such settlement in Israel and brought about a change in the lifestyles of the kibbutzim and an improvement in their economic and financial conduct. The mutual guarantees that existed between the kibbutzim, with wealthier kibbutzim guaranteeing debts of poorer ones, were cancelled, and each kibbutz became an independent financial unit. The arrangement was made possible because the government owned the banks following their nationalization in 1983 and were the main creditors. The kibbutzim debt settlement was conducted in stages over 25 years.

Most of the kibbutzim were streamlined and rehabilitated and came to set an example in terms of quality of life and diligence. After years of net migration away from the kibbutzim, they began to see positive immigration due to their privatization measures and improved economic situation, and in 2023, the kibbutzim made up around two percent of Israel's total population.

Another event that reflected the changes that had taken place in Israel's economy was the fate of ATA, the large textiles factory founded in the 1930s that was forced to close in the 1980s. ATA had a very strong brand and reputation in Israeli society and its economy and had become a symbol of Israeli industry, its products a kind of "national uniform" for Israelis for decades. ATA ran into difficulties at the height of the economic crisis, not only because of soaring inflation but also as a result of changes in Israel's competitiveness in the global textiles and clothing industries. This was an example for entire traditional sectors that could not compete in the globalized markets. However, this time, the government did not bail out the failing enterprise, a signal to the business sector it could no longer rely on the government to rescue them. The conduct of the government in 1984–1986 reflected a dramatic policy change, it no longer willing to insure the risks and management failures of the business sector, especially in an industry that was not able to compete globally. This represented a seismic shift in the government's approach. Previously, as Israel's main business insurer, the government had provided an economic, social, and occupational safety net to struggling enterprises. But now, it refused to provide blanket insurance to failed enterprises. Israel had shifted from its old collective, public approach to a new individualist, businesslike approach.

The year 1987 brought another defining event that reflected the sea changes in Israel's economy and society—the cancellation of IAI flagship project to construct an advanced fourth-generation Multirole jet fighter, the IAI Lavi. The IAI Lavi had turned out to be a hugely expensive project in relation to Israel's economic capabilities. The decision to cancel the IAI Lavi during its flight test phase in August 1987 came after heated debates among the government, the security establishment, the Israeli public, and even the United States government. This hugely controversial move would ultimately become a significant catalyst in the development of Israel's high-tech industry, as creative and skilled engineers who lost their jobs as a result of the cancellation moved into the burgeoning high-tech sector. At the time, it heralded the dawn of a new era. For the first time, economic and budgetary considerations had won out over security considerations. This reflected Israel's new, post-crisis reality, in which it sought to create an open economy, with economic and budgetary rules set according to the standards of an increasingly globalized world—a world to which Israel was keen to belong. These dramatic changes were consistent with Israel's old "Theory of the Rounds," in which the country strove to build economic resilience as a component of national security. Israel had recognized, once again, that security was about more than just its military, and that economic and social strength were also key. The IAI Lavi affair was, in essence, a test case for the new balance between Israel's civilian and military spending. It demonstrated the extent to which the 1985 Economic Stabilization Plan had sharpened fiscal thinking around budget limitations and national priorities.

The crisis had been costly. Israel was forced to slaughter some of its sacred cows, and some of its key institutions had fallen. The country had experienced nothing short of an economic earthquake. The economy had emerged strong, Israeli society a little less so. The old epicenters of economics and business had shifted. Values had changed; processes altered. In retrospect, Israel had experienced a "good," profound, and long crisis from which it had learned key lessons and made fundamental reforms and changes in the way in which its economy was structured and how it operated.

# PART FOUR

# A NEW ECONOMIC REGIME: 1986–2019

## 16

## Crises as Policy Correction

Economic crises have always served as catalysts for policy corrections and leaps forward. This was certainly the case with the economic crisis that dogged Israel's first years of statehood, and it was also true of the hyperinflation crisis of the early 1980s. Between these two major crises, Israel also underwent a series of minor crises, all of which gave rise to reforms and economic institution building. Facing these crises gave rise to new ways of thinking and made Israel's economic leaders aware of novel economic policy measures. At the same time, events in other parts of the world had an impact on other changes in the economy.

Israel experienced its first major economic crisis immediately after its establishment in 1948. Historically, this was indeed the worst crisis that the Israeli economy ever experienced. The enormous deficit in foreign currency reserves forced the government, lacking the right tools to deal with such a serious crisis, to adopt austerity and rationing policies. By 1952, the time had come for Israel's leaders to take stock and embark on a new approach.

Former Prime Minister of Israel, Levi Eshkol, built a professional Ministry of Finance and met the emergency situation by managing the country's cash flow. Eshkol developed a regular annual budget that, for the first time, set out specific priorities and devalued Israel's currency to reflect the economic reality caused by its foreign currency reserves shortage. The plan accelerated the development of Israel's economy and society, including by building institutions and infrastructure, investing in housing to accommodate the waves of mass immigration, and creating jobs through the development of import-substituting industries, a move that also helped to address the shortage in foreign currency reserve. Apartments were provided for most immigrants, central institutions were created, and national infrastructures were built. It was during these years that the foundations of Israel's modern economy were laid.

The second major crisis came after the Yom Kippur War. The 1985 Economic Stabilization Plan proved to be a major milestone in the creation of a new economic regime for Israel. The plan ushered in fundamental changes in Israel's economic policy, most of which occurred in the ten years following its implementation; and it continued to serve as the basis for the extensive changes that would occur in later years.

Israel moved away from its state-controlled, centralized, and nationalized economy in response to the hyperinflation crisis. The rampant inflation was partly the result of irresponsible policies of the Likud government's 1977 "economic revolution." However, it was also a byproduct of the previous Mapai government's economic approach, which had led to impressive achievements during Israel's first decades but was no longer suitable for the maturing economy of the 1980s. Israel's nationalized capital market, once understandable in the context of the 1950s and 1960s, was now impeding healthy economic development. In addition, Israel's complex system of linkage mechanisms, including heavy price subsidies on basic goods, may have made life tolerable for a limited amount of time under soaring inflation. However, these subsidies were also an obstacle that drove inflation even higher, exacerbating the crisis. It is almost impossible to manage a financial system under such conditions. In addition, Israel's budgetary management was problematic, with government spending reaching a peak of 75 percent of GDP, and public debt soaring to around 270 percent of GDP. The huge deficit in the balance of payments limited economic development and growth.

The stabilization plan was a "no other choice" plan. The long-term lessons of the crisis involved understanding the importance of budgetary discipline, reducing state involvement in the markets, promoting privatization, and encouraging competition by exposing domestic industry to imports. In effect, the 1985 Economic Stabilization Plan was the start of the construction of a modern Israeli economy, one that was open to international trade and the global economy. A decade after the stabilization plan, Israel could boast an independent central bank, a modern treasury, a new and functioning capital market, an advanced financial market, a modern and competitive export sector, and an openness to imports. Israel had transformed itself from a centralized economy to a free, modern, business-oriented market economy. The stabilization plan and its reforms led to economic policy changes in the government as a whole, and in the Ministry of Finance and the Bank of Israel. In implementing the stabilization plan, the Ministry of Finance demonstrated professionalism and firmness in the face of the political whims that arose from all sides of the political map. Prime Minister Shimon Peres, originally a Mapai stalwart and supporter of past policies, deserves praise for his realization that it was not possible for Israel to continue in its state of economic powerlessness.

## Macroeconomic Policy Shifts

In drawing lessons from the inflation crisis, Israel needed to first make changes in its macroeconomic policy, as a necessary condition for returning the economy to stable growth, as well as making sweeping reforms in various sectors of the economy.

***A new budgetary (fiscal) policy.*** Israel's fiscal parameters immediately before the implementation of the plan exceeded the "international comparison bar"[1] and could not continue for long, because they blocked stable and sustainable growth. The sharp cuts in subsidies reflected a shift in the government's approach, from subsidizing basic goods to subsidizing consumption. For years, the government had subsidized basic goods for all, even those sections of the population that were not in need. Now, it directed aid only to those in need, and, instead of a universal subsidy on basic groceries, transfer payments were distributed to the poorest citizens. In retrospect, these payments were not enough to compensate for the subsidy cuts.

Reducing budgetary commodities expenditure was a long journey, and it would take several years before a "normal" level of public spending and a "normal" deficit were reached. The hyperinflation crisis had forced the government to recognize that Israel had to adopt long-term fiscal discipline, something that would become synonymous with "correct" budgetary policy. There had been a shift in the fiscal paradigm, whereby a strict budgetary balance and low budget deficit were now maintained as a safe and stable way of reducing the ratio of public debt-to-GDP. Reducing public spending and maintaining a low budget deficit were essential for maintaining a level of taxation that would not be a burden on the business sector, and that would enable sustainable growth. This budgetary strategy was followed until a public expenditure rate of around 40 percent of GDP was reached in the 2010s.

Israel's strict fiscal policy was based on amendments to its Basic Law: The State Economy, according to which powers and tools are granted to the Minister and Ministry of Finance to ensure responsible fiscal conduct. The government later enacted two additional fiscal rules. The first was a limit on expenditure growth, while the second established that the permitted government deficit should not exceed around three percent of GDP, which would allow for a reduction in the GDP debt ratio.

Government spending fell from 75 percent of GDP in 1984–1985 to around 50 percent within a decade, and to around 40 percent after 25 years. Defense expenditure and interest payments decreased significantly over this period, while civil and infrastructure expenditure fell slightly as a percentage of GDP. As of 2015, Israel's rate of government spending to GDP of around 40 percent was lower than the average in OECD countries. Public debt, which reached about 270 percent of GDP percent in 1984, dropped to around 100 percent of GDP in the early 2000s, and to about 60 percent in 2015. These are long-term processes, the result of ongoing budgetary discipline even during the wave of new immigration in the 1990s (primarily from the former Soviet Union) along with continuing security incidents. In 2016, the government established a new fiscal "Numerator" rule as an additional control tool, which details the government's future spending commitments for a three-year forecast and warns of any future deficits exceeding the permitted ceiling for the coming years.

As Israel moved further away from the hyperinflation crisis of the 1980s, memories of these bad times faded and the temptation to increase spending and the deficit grew. Both the Minister and the Ministry of Finance were in constant battles with most of the other ministers.[2]

In coalition governments, the Prime Minister and the Ministry of Finance are responsible for formulating Israel's budgetary framework and economic policy.

The international gatekeepers that monitor Israel's economic policy—the international rating agencies, the International Monetary Fund, and the OECD—have reacted positively to Israel's fiscal policy following the 1985 Economic Stabilization Plan. Israel's first sovereign issuance, in December 1995,[3] was the first international expression of the improving status of Israel's economy in the global capital markets. The rating agencies have become important factors in evaluating economic policy and budgeting. Israel has taken their opinions into account when formulating economic policy, as their position is important in the international economic arena in terms of attracting foreign investments. Since Israel joined the OECD in 2010, the organization has become a regular participant in Israeli increasingly professional economic policy discussions, evaluating Israel's economy and society in the international arena. This was important for providing a measurement yardstick for measuring Israel's performance in all aspects of government policies and outcomes.

***Monetary policy.*** The economic crisis exposed the weakness of Israel's monetary policy. Ordering the Bank of Israel to print money to finance the budget deficit in the country's first decades was perhaps the government's most notable monetary policy failure, especially during the period of 1974–1985, when the Bank of Israel was pressured to print massive amounts. This meant that they did not control the amount of money in the economy. In 1985, Knesset approved an amendment to the Bank of Israel Law prohibiting the central bank from lending to the government. This gave the Bank of Israel an independent status, akin to that of central banks in other developed nations. Legislation enabling the Bank of Israel to be an effective central bank was now complete, giving birth to an independent and modern Bank of Israel after 30 years of statehood. The anchor price stability had shifted from the exchange rate to one based on interest rates and control over the amount of money in circulation. The importance lay in the public now believing that the Bank of Israel would stand up to any government demands to print money.

Strengthening the position of the central bank was integrated into reforms to denationalize Israel's capital and financial markets. After the stabilization plan, the targeted credit once given to preferred industries by the government and the Bank of Israel was abolished, and the foreign exchange markets were liberalized.

Starting in 1992, inflation targets were set by the government in consultation with the governor of the Bank of Israel. At first, these were rather high—14–15 percent in 1992, gradually decreasing to 7–10 percent in 1997–1998, and to 1–3 percent from 2003 onwards. Inflation targets influence inflationary expectations and monetary policy and are a signal to the financial and capital markets about the importance of maintaining price stability.

***Exchange rate policy.*** Until the mid-1970s, Israel's exchange rate policy had been based on a fixed exchange rate that was periodically amended by the government. Between these amendments, the government would introduce taxes on imports alongside incentives to boost exports. These moves created effective exchange rates that were higher than the nominal exchange rates. From the mid-1970s, in light of soaring inflation, the government introduced a "creeping exchange rate," whereby it devalued the currency by up to 2 percent every few weeks to prevent expectations of a high devaluation.

During the "economic revolution" of 1977, there was a major shift in how the exchange rate was set, when the newly elected Likud government introduced a free foreign exchange market, abolishing government control over the exchange rate. However, the macroeconomic conditions in the budget and the balance of payments were simply not ripe for such a drastic move. The result was an inflationary spiral.

From 1991, the exchange rate policy changed to the "diagonal" method, whereby the exchange rate moved within the limits of two diagonals set by the government and the Bank of Israel. The diagonal policy led to moderate adjustments to the exchange rate that reflected the rate of inflation and the health of the Israel's foreign currency reserves. From 1991–1998, the width of the diagonals and their angles were changed to increase exchange rate mobility, until they were completely abolished in 1998, when Israel transitioned to a completely free exchange rate.

Along with the diagonal reform, more and more restrictions and prohibitions in the supervision of foreign currency were abolished each year. The liberalization of the exchange rate accelerated when the private sector was allowed to invest abroad in real ventures at increasing rates. In fact, 1998 marked the year that the government ended most foreign exchange restrictions, other than those related to money laundering and terrorist financing, criminal activities not related to economic foreign currency controls. The New Israeli Shekel became a tradable currency outside of Israel.

This slow, gradual, and controlled foreign exchange reform process, which took less than a decade, was successful, not only because it was based on supportive macroeconomic moves, but also because price stability was strengthened, growth was renewed, and market reforms to open Israel's economy to international competition were accelerated. The exchange rate reforms also had important symbolic value, marking Israel's transition from a fixed, state-controlled exchange rate policy and a closely supervised foreign exchange rates to a free foreign exchange market centered on a floating exchange rate. The shekel became a convertible and tradable currency, and foreign exchange controls were removed. Israel's economy became integrated into globalization processes and became open to world trade. The transition to free trade in foreign currency was possible because of the considerable improvements to Israel's balance of payments situation that resulted from the country's improved economic performance.

The government's foreign currency debt decreased, and Israel became a lender country and not a (net) borrower of foreign currency. To demonstrate the magnitude of the change, in 1985, foreign exchange balances held by the Bank of Israel were less than $2 billion, while by the end of 2021, they amounted to $213 billion. Most of it was a reflection of the surplus in the CA of the BOP and also the purchases FX by the Bank of Israel. A major factor in this dramatic shift was the increase in the weight of Israel's high-tech sector in terms of exports and the sale of startups (exits) to foreign investors, which had a positive impact on the balance of payments. Foreign currency reserve surpluses caused the shekel to appreciate against most world currencies during 2010–2021.

***Sectoral and institutional arrangements.*** Following the stabilization plan, there was a broad understanding that now that inflation had rapidly declined, fundamental steps were now required to maintain stable and sustainable growth. As a result, Israel implemented dozens of market reforms, both large and small, that increased domestic and international competition, accelerated openness to globalization, and increased government efficiency.

The need for reforms, which required legislative changes, sparked the creation of a new tool, the Arrangements Law.[4]

First enacted in 1985, the Arrangements Law was used in the implementation of the 1985 Economic Stabilization Plan, which required swift amendments to a number of existing laws to allow extensive cuts to be made to the state budget. The Arrangements Law has been used by the government ever since as a tool to facilitate reforms and changes to legislation. A new Arrangements bill is submitted annually with the state budget, which guarantees that there will be a parliamentary majority to pass reforms. Knesset failing to pass a budget is a clear expression of distrust in the government and leads to its downfall. The Arrangements Law has been criticized because of the abbreviated process in which it is conducted and approved. While amendments have been made to it over the years, it remains an effective economic-legislative tool for the government in gaining Knesset approval for reforms.

Another key outcome of the stabilization plan was the weakening of the Histadrut, both as a trade union and as a commercial entity (through its Hevrat HaOvdim). Until the 1980s, the Histadrut had been a powerful and significant economic player. It had cooperated and competed with the government on numerous issues that went far beyond its nominal role as a trade union. The collapse of the Hevrat HaOvdim—the result of business and financial failures during the hyperinflation crisis—weakened the Histadrut. This development coincided with other political changes following the rise to power of the Likud, which eliminated some of the special privileges that the Histadrut had enjoyed under previous governments.

The Israeli economy was also affected by the technological revolution that began in the 1980s in the United States, which saw breakthroughs in computing and communications (the so-called "information society"), new materials, and molecular biology. The development of Israel's technology sector was boosted by a smart government policy of supporting research and development and creating innovative financing tools. The impact of the government policies by financing tools on the high-tech industry was supported also by the influx of highly educated immigrants from the Soviet Union, a migration from the defense industries to civilian industries, increased penetration of technologies from the military for civilian uses, and an increasing global demand for technology products. For many years, Israeli high-tech was based on hardware development, but the growth of the internet gave priority to software developments. This was a better expression of Israeli creativity and initiative, and, significantly, did not require large capital investment. The establishment of software development centers in Israel by international companies translated into exports and growth, and helped Israel gain its "startup nation" reputation.

The growth of Israeli high-tech coupled with the country's increasing openness to globalization helped it gain economic independence. Israel now has a surplus in its balance of payments, large foreign exchange balances, and has become a lender nation, with foreign entities owing it large debts. However, globalization took a social toll in terms of increasing social and economic inequalities that require changes to socioeconomic policy.

## An Economic Paradigm Shift

The hyperinflation crisis prompted a paradigm shift away from the ethos of the "mobilized society" and Zionist economy of Israel's first years of statehood. During that period, Israeli society had identified with the heroic Zionist mythos, embodied by the ideal of the "new Jew," a pioneer who realizes the Zionist vision of "muscular Judaism" both physically and spiritually. Over time, Israeli society drifted away from this ethos, gradually adopting the ethos and values of expanding globalization, free markets, and emphasis on for the private high-tech sector that characterized the West after the Cold War. Israel's post-heroic social climate also reflected its complex security reality. In terms of its markets, Israel had shifted from strong government involvement in the economy, with little reliance on market forces, to a more rational and privately based market economy, from a directed economy with protectionist policies around its manufacturing industries, to a competitive economy with a strong private sector. The old system of protectionism for domestic manufacturing was axed, the financial, foreign exchange, and capital markets were liberalized, state companies were privatized, and concentrated sectors were encouraged to introduce and increase competition.

Israel's long journey toward a modern, open economy was not without obstacles and roadblocks. However, Israel's leaders showed determination throughout the market reform process, which ultimately helped make the reforms a success. Israel is still on that journey. Its small economy is affected, to a considerable extent, by external factors over which economic policy has no control—the security situation, global business cycles, and waves of immigration.

Israel's extensive market reforms strengthened the market economy by boosting competition, encouraging privatization, and integrating the country into processes of globalization. The shift to a market economy glorified individualism and heralded the decline of Israel's old collective and public ethos. These processes dampened the elements of the old "mobilized" economy and society that had characterized the pre-state Zionist movement and the nascent State of Israel. However, this does not mean that Israelis' willingness and ability to meet Zionist challenges decreased. The large-scale waves of immigration of Jews from the former Soviet Union and from Ethiopia in the 1990s were met by an Israeli economy and society that had a successful absorption policy alongside a willingness to integrate these new immigrants, albeit within the constraints of the time.

Since the 1990s, Israel has adopted more and more neoliberal policies as neoliberal ideals infiltrated Israel, especially via Binyamin Netanyahu in his positions as Minister of Finance and Prime Minister. The main elements of this ideology include smaller government, labor cost flexibility, reduced "red tape," a reduced social security net, lower taxes, and privatization. In the United States, this ideology has resulted in widening socioeconomic disparities and increased budget deficits. In Israel, after nearly forty years of priding itself on upholding the value of equality, privatization intensified, public services reduced, taxes fell, welfare payments dropped—and socioeconomic inequalities widened.

The social justice protests that swept Israel in the summer of 2011 were a public expression of frustrations with the hardships that Israeli society continued to face in the name of forging a new, modern sense of "Israeliness." With the economy and society changing, individualism and consumerism were on the rise. In spite of the overall success of the 1985 Economic Stabilization Plan, the influx of a million, mostly highly educated, immigrants from the former Soviet Union, the high-tech revolution, and macroeconomic achievements, Israel has not advanced in the world rankings. The common index of per capita GDP indicates that, with respect to the rest of the world Israel has not improved its relative position vis-à-vis to other developed countries over the past four decades. As a small economy, Israel could have grown faster. Over the years 1975–2015, other small nations that previously had a lower per capita GDP than Israel, such as South Korea, Ireland, and the Czech Republic, have overtaken it.

In a number of areas, Israel shows suboptimal performance. It suffers from high levels of inequality, mediocre labor productivity, insufficient infrastructure, substandard civic public services, and relatively low internet connection speeds. Israel's achievements in education (as measured by the OECD's PISA tests[5]) are low, mainly because of poor performances in the Arab populations due to deficiencies in their education and prefrail secular Jews whose weight in the population are increasing. The reduction in civilian public spending without interest, to about 32 percent of GDP, is a positive achievement in terms of reducing the government budget deficit, but it also reflects a low level of spending on social services and infrastructure. Israel has also cut spending on employment training and retraining, which are prerequisites for increasing productivity, especially for unskilled workers. These weaknesses have prevented Israel from reaching the top of the league of developed economies. Economic growth is not only the result of pure economic processes, but is also influenced by a country's geopolitical environment, its internal political procedures, and social and demographic processes. Israel, in the 2020s, is in the throes of a profound demographic, economic, and social transition in an attempt to create a new ethos of a developed economy, social responsibility, and national struggle. The sense of tribalism that replaced the melting pot, alongside the Israeli-Palestinian conflict, deficiencies in political functioning, and increasing polarization in beliefs and values, are obstacles that hinder the development of the Israeli economy. However, the fact that Israel successfully survived three global economic crises—the dot-com crisis of 2002, the global financial crisis of 2008, and the coronavirus pandemic of 2020–2021 can certainly be considered an accomplishment.

## An Upheaval in the Kibbutz Movement

In Israel's first years of statehood, the kibbutzim symbolized and epitomized the "mobilized" Zionist economy. Kibbutzim were built on permanent, institutionalized frameworks, and the cooperative values they sought to implement were intended to meet the needs of a small, single-generational, under-resourced society. They were far less suited to large, established, multigenerational settlements. With the birth of the State, most of the goals they were designed to achieve gradually disappeared, and the conservative kibbutz leadership had difficulty in dealing with the new national goals that had emerged, such as absorbing the mass waves of immigrants. The kibbutzim's legitimacy and centrality as a "serving elite" gradually eroded. This loss of legitimacy intensified with Israel's shift to a market economy, which saw the strengthening of individualism and the adoption of anti-socialist models, and further reduced support for the kibbutzim's original ideals of sharing and equality.

In the 1960s, the kibbutzim underwent a process of industrialization, largely as a result of agriculture' reduced profitability. Water and land limitations, as well as increased mechanization, meant that agriculture could no longer provide sufficient employment for all the members of the kibbutzim. The rampant inflation of the 1980s, coupled with poor financial management on behalf of the kibbutz leaders, resulted in a financial crisis for the kibbutzim. The 1985 Economic Stabilization Plan exposed the magnitude of this crisis, not least the soaring debts that the kibbutzim owed to the banks. Despite the hostility of the new Likud-led government toward the traditionally Labor-associated kibbutzim, the rampant inflation, and the effects of the stabilization plan, the crisis was largely the result of economically irresponsible conduct on behalf of the kibbutz leadership. Most of the kibbutzim were able to emerge from the crisis thanks to a government recovery program that provided bailouts of billions of shekels, but which cost the kibbutzim their principles.

In the 1990s, the kibbutzim underwent significant changes. A large number of kibbutzim privatized various services, such as education and health. However, the real change was the shift away from the old concept of "from each according to his ability, to each according to his needs, according to the ability of the kibbutz," whereby kibbutz members had received an equal budget based on their needs, regardless of their position. This was replaced by a new model, in which each member received a differential salary depending on their position. This came in addition to the transfer of certain kibbutz assets to the private ownership of kibbutz members. Essentially, the kibbutzim, or certain aspects of them, underwent privatization.

Only about 20 percent remained as traditional cooperative kibbutzim (most of these were the economically strongest kibbutzim). The concept of the "revitalized kibbutz" was created, a collective settlement pattern that was nevertheless not fully based on the founding values of the original kibbutz movement. Some see as positive the ability of the kibbutzim to be flexible and adapt to a changing world, to find the right balance and maintain their old principles of equality and mutual aid, while responding to economic incentives. In the 2000s, the kibbutzim comprised some two percent of Israel's population. Despite the many changes they have undergone, Israel's kibbutzim remain one of the most interesting Israeli experiment a century.

## Notes

1. The budget deficit of 15 % in Israel was exceptional (the norm was 3%), as was the proportion of government expenditure to GDP of 75%, with the norm in the world being under 50%.).
2. My personal testimony as State Budget Director and Director General of the Ministry of Finance from 1991–1997.
3. It was my honor to lead the issuance as part of my role as Director General of the Ministry of Finance.
4. Also known as The Omnibus Law of Arrangements Economic Policy Law or The Economic Recuperation.
5. PISA is a test administered internationally measuring 15-year-olds' reading, mathematics, and science knowledge and skills.

# 17

## Sectoral Reforms

The economy had emerged from the hyperinflation crisis rigid and inflexible, and struggled with both internal and external competition. In the decade following the 1985 Economic Stabilization Plan, Israel undertook sweeping economic reforms, some maturing even beyond the decade. The intense activity around these reforms stemmed from the recognition that they were essential to ensure stable and sustainable economic growth and help Israel adapt to international trends toward globalization. The trauma of the hyperinflation crisis, still fresh in the public and politicians' memory, provided fertile ground for making far-reaching market reforms. The first wave of reforms, tackling macroeconomic functioning, the foreign currency market, and the exchange rate, involved a wave of privatizations. These measures indeed helped Israel integrate into the global economy. At the same time, aiming to improve competitiveness, Israel embarked on a series of sweeping sectoral reforms and streamlined its public sector. Undoubtedly, the 1985 Economic Stabilization Plan and the reforms it sparked shaped the 1980s into a fruitful and formative decade for Israel's economy.

By the 1990s, the pace of market reforms began to slow, possibly due to a sense of fatigue from the effects of the reforms of the previous decade. Nevertheless, Israel continued to recognize that more reforms were needed to create a flexible economy that could withstand internal and external crises. The Second Intifada (the second Palestinian uprising of September 2000–February 2005) sparked fresh market reforms. In addition, the new challenges of the 21st century—changes in globalization, rising inequalities, population aging, and more—intensified the need for additional reforms to support sustainable economic growth, including cultivating and employing the human potential within Israel's most disadvantaged populations—Arabs, ultra-Orthodox Jews, and the disabled. Reforms were also needed to address the growth of the Arab and ultra-Orthodox populations, as well as the aging of the general population. Housing shortages and rising real estate prices were also serious issues that generated considerable public and government attention. Israel's acute housing problem demanded a clear and comprehensive strategy to help incentivize local authorities to build infrastructure that could be integrated along with economic development in the north and south of the country. Meanwhile, although Israel (like the rest of the world) has undergone a "digital revolution," major infrastructure improvements are still needed, including building a fiber broadband network, strengthening existing digital networks, and expanding 5G services. This is especially important in light of the rise of work-from-home and online learning.

## Foreign Trade Liberalization

The creation of the European Economic Community (Common Market) in 1957 presented an immense challenge for Israel's existing and potential exporters. Believing that future exports to Europe would drive economic growth and employment, Israel signed a limited trade agreement with the Common Market in the mid-1960s, followed by a preferential free trade agreement in 1975. These developments heralded the opening of Israel's manufacturing industry to imports, a process that was fully finalized in 1989. In 1985, Israel signed a free trade agreement with the United States, with additional agreements entered into in the 1990s. Israel completed its foreign trade liberalization with a unilateral lowering of tariffs for third countries not party to its bilateral agreements in 1991, a process completed in 2000.

Over the course of a lengthy process spanning three decades, Israel succeeded in realizing its export strategy. This has been a key driver of economic growth and has helped integrate Israel into the global economy. While this strategy has completely changed the status and development of Israel's economy, it has nonetheless met with determined opposition from vested interests, and successive Israeli governments have been required to stand firm, alongside other interested parties, in order to make it happen. The weight of imports and exports in Israel's economy has always been high, at around 80 percent. Exposure to imports and openness to foreign trade has improved consumer choice and improved manufacturing efficiency. It has shifted Israel away from its strategy of attempting to produce everything domestically to a modern manufacturing policy focused on comparative advantage and specialization. As a country lacking in natural resources, Israel has come to concentrate on sectors reliant on skilled human capital, technological manpower, innovation, creativity, and entrepreneurship. Since the 1990s, Israel has made a complete transition from a closed market to one that is open to trade, capital movements, and foreign investments. Exports have led growth and have evolved from basic goods to knowledge-intensive products and services.

## Credit Rating

In the 1990s, Israel's policy of encouraging market openness, which had been focused on developing foreign trade, shifted its focus to the capital and financial markets. The government and business sector understood that in order to turn to the international capital markets for investment, Israel needed to have a healthy international credit rating—an assessment of the level of risk to lenders regarding a its ability to repay its debts.

Israel never defaulted on a debt, not even in the midst of the hyperinflation crisis of the 1980s or during the Second Intifada. The high payment culture has demonstrated its effectiveness, even in the days when Israel was not rated by the rating agencies.

Israel received its first credit rating from the leading international credit rating agencies Fitch and Moody's in 1995, ahead of its first global sovereign bonds issuance in the United States in November of that year.[11]

Israel was rated as A-, a respectable score for a country that had only just entered the club of international issuers (which at that time consisted of some 30 nations). The macroeconomic changes that have occurred since the 1985 Economic Stabilization Plan set Israel on a path of sound economic policy management by maintaining a tight budgetary framework and responsible monetary policy, and by improving its current account. As Israel's debt-to-GDP ratio reached approximately 60 percent in 2018, its credit rating rose to AA-.

Beyond the positive benefits inherent in the opportunity to raise government capital at a low interest rate, the improved credit rating was a signal to international companies to invest in Israel—effectively, a vote of confidence of the international capital markets in Israel. The credit ranking expresses, in a single score, factors that affect the solvency of the country. In reality, every trading day, the financial world "rates" Israel's credit risk in terms of the rates of its bonds in the international markets. In Israel, the rating companies are viewed as an international panel of judges who give a score to the country and its government with regard to the success of their economic policy management. It is significant that the coronavirus pandemic of 2020–2021 did not damage Israel's credit rating, despite increases in its budget deficit and public debt (in line with trends in most countries of the world), because of the high trust in Israel's basic economic data. However, the government's judicial reform plans introduced in 2023 did cause concern among the rating companies regarding the willingness of investors to continue investing in Israeli companies. Nonetheless, Israel retains a high and stable credit rating. During the Gaza war in 2024 there was a significant downgrade.

## Labor Market Flexibility

The growth of the market economy, increasing international openness, the wave of privatizations, and the effects of globalization, all impacted Israel's traditional labor relations. Until the 1990s, government bodies and the public sector had played a major role in Israel's economy, and most workers were represented by the Histadrut. However, the wave of privatizations forced many of the old state- and Histadrut-owned companies to change. The Histadrut had already been weakened as a result of the rise to power of the Likud in 1977.

A growing public sense of disgust with the business and politics of the Histadrut was also a factor in its decline and in that of other trade unions. The large-scale immigration from the former Soviet Union also played a large role in reducing the power of the Histadrut, which the Soviet immigrants viewed with suspicion and antipathy, seeing it as similar to the widely despised trade unions that had flourished under Soviet rule.

The new wave of Soviet immigrants was willing to work in worse conditions than established Israelis without seeking protection from the Histadrut. In doing so *en masse*, they helped create a more flexible labor market. The development of Israel's high-tech industry, whose labor relations were vastly different from the old collective agreements of Israel's traditional industries, also helped weaken the trade unions and boost labor market flexibility. Beyond high-tech, the wave of privatizations and increasing globalization had changed how Israeli workers were employed. There was an increase in contract workers, and outsourcing expanded. The entry of foreign and Palestinian workers (both legally and illegally) into Israel's labor market created competition with Israeli workers. This mainly affected low-educated and lower-skilled workers who were less protected by the Histadrut, which had often preferentially protected larger workers' committees dominated by higher-skilled employees.

Israel's increased labor market flexibility boosted the competitiveness of the domestic market. The trade unions refocused their efforts on uncompetitive public sector organizations but were limited in influence over the growing private sector, such as the high-tech industry, which operate in competitive markets.

## Competitiveness in the Essential Infrastructure Sector

Following the 1985 Economic Stabilization Plan, important structural reforms were also implemented in Israel's essential infrastructure sectors (transportation, electricity, telecommunications and postal services, energy, water, and sewage). They are essential for growth, as they link different parts of the economy, both within Israel—connecting various regions to employment centers—and beyond its borders to international markets. The infrastructure industries on which the economy is so dependent possess notable advantages in terms of their size and capital appeal, and because they are natural supply monopolies (of fuel, water, electricity and others). However, competition can and should be encouraged in the production of utilities such as electricity, water, and fuel distillates.

The reforms included a restructuring of Israel's infrastructure sectors, changing the rules governing their activities, increasing competition, consolidating companies, regulation and deregulation, and privatization. The telecommunications industry in particular, which had been operated under the state-owned Bezeq telecommunications company, underwent rapid changes following reforms introduced in the decade between 1986–1996. Meanwhile, the transportation infrastructure sector—roads, railways, seaports, and airports—was far slower to change. The energy sector, which encompassed the Israel Electric Corporation, oil refineries, gas and oil exploration companies, and gas and oil pipelines, all underwent fundamental changes in terms of their function and activity. Meanwhile, decades of water shortages led to reforms in industrial and potable water production, sewage, and in how water is transported to the local authorities that supply households, all of which required new service concepts and technologies.

The monopolistic structure and external advantages inherent in the essential infrastructure sectors necessitated government regulation. Infrastructure is one area in which government investment is justified, since the return to the investor is lower than the return to the economy ("external benefits"); therefore, there is no incentive for private investors to invest sufficient funds. Before privatization could proceed, the government had to establish clear, competitive rules that would determine how the industry and the newly privatized essential infrastructure companies would operate

Where it is impossible to create competition, regulation is the only effective way to protect consumer interests, by setting rules for the functioning and competitiveness of the sector. To this end, the government adopted the approach that regulation for creating competition or regulating the monopolistic company must precede privatization. Privatization and regulation of these companies was accompanied by political struggles with their workers' committees that in effect controlled the "on-off switch" of essential utilities and could shut them down over any labor dispute. During the process of privatizing these infrastructure companies, there were protests by workers and sometimes even by management, who did not want to relinquish their special positions and interests, and who enjoyed good and rewarding working conditions thanks to the companies' monopolistic power.

The difficulties of public financing forced the government to assist the private sector with financing investments in infrastructure through build-operate-transfer (BOT) and private finance initiative (PFI) programs combining public and private capital. Some utilities (transportation, energy, and more) were completely privatized, while in other cases, private entrepreneurs invested in infrastructure.

***Telecommunications:*** Until the 1980s, Israel's telecommunications industry had been characterized by low competitiveness and poor service standards.

Starting in 1994, Israel's telecommunications industry underwent rapid liberalization, shifting from a state-run national monopoly dominated by analog technology to a new free market regime with competition. The breaking of the national monopoly was made possible by rapidly accelerating technological changes and by the recognition that the state's role is to design policy and regulation, not provide operational services. Advanced telecommunications technologies and the development of new regulations amounted to a "revolution," which arrived late in Israel. Communications rapidly shifted from a mechanical, analog world to an electronic and digital age that offered expanded possibilities for large-scale, fast information transfer via optical fibers as well as for reducing the amount of investment needed to create a particular output. The new technologies enabled improvements in consumer services and new business opportunities. They lowered the investment threshold, making it easy for more players to enter the market, which increased competition. These changes were rapid, and encompassed all areas of the telecoms industry, increasing its scope exponentially.

The telecommunication revolution in Israel was dramatic. Previously, home telephone services were rare, and consumers faced years-long waitlists for telephone installation. Now, telephone services were available immediately, and the market was fiercely competitive. New cellphone and cable services emerged. Competition in international calls in the 1990s began when new operators were granted licenses to enter the market, which reduced prices dramatically. There was competition in cable and satellite television broadcasting after the granting of licenses to new operators in 1989 and again in 1999. Another giant leap forward was the internet revolution, that expanded communications into new areas, completely altering the world of content creation and public influence. The expansion of the internet and the rise of social networking in the 2000s has created new challenges for the global community, including Israel, regarding regulating giant corporations, in particular Google and Meta. In addition, Israel's state-run public broadcasting service also underwent reforms, with the granting of licenses to commercial channels in 1993 and 2002.

Industry reforms are a complex process that involves a great deal more than simply professional programs to improve the functioning of a particular sector. Rather, reforms are a political act, involving numerous processes with a multitude of different interests. Israel's telecommunications reforms shed light on the connections between technology, the economy, and business, and politics and policymaking. The country's telecommunications industry evolved from a collection of state-owned monopolies to a competitive market. The state assumed a critical role in ensuring competition and the continued modernization of the country's communications infrastructure in order to advance economic development. Even liberal policies require government regulation, both in the event of market failure, and to prevent market forces from gaining complete license to control public infrastructure (for example, in determining the number of broadcasting frequencies). Without government regulation and intervention in infrastructure, cable TV broadcasts would not be available to all the country's residents, and fiber optical networks would not be installed in the country's peripheral regions.

***Postal services.*** The state-run Israel Postal Authority became a government company, the Israel Postal Company Ltd. in 2006. In contrast with the telecommunications industry, where an explosion of new technologies opened the doors for competition in service provision, there has been no such technological revolution in postal services. As a result, it has only been possible to open Israel Post to limited competition. "Snail mail" post is essentially a direct mail monopoly that needs to provide services to the entire nation. The government faces a dilemma regarding how to ensure flexibility in setting postal rates and reducing requirements for universal distribution all over the country, while increasing competition for small letters similar to the private solutions that already exist for larger parcels and bulk mail.

***Water.*** Water is a sensitive issue for Israel, not least because of its inherent water shortages and the historical government and public support for agriculture. Israel has three natural water sources—the Sea of Galilee, the coastal aquifer, and the mountain aquifer—which are interconnected by the National Water Carrier of Israel. The management of Israel's water supplies has become a complex subject in view of increasing demand due to population growth, and the decrease in Israel's natural water supply as a result of its semi-desert climate conditions and short rainy seasons. Already by the 1990s, Israel had begun to exceed the government's red lines for exploiting natural water resources. In response, the government severely rationed the water supply to agriculture. Since then, Israel has taken additional steps to reduce safe water consumption, including through schemes to educate the public in domestic water conservation, increasing prices, and improving agricultural irrigation via drip irrigation systems. However, domestic water consumption barely changed since the elasticity of the demand for water in relation to its price is very low. The cumulative deficit in water reached its peak in the early 2000s. The government realized that, in view of upward population growth trends, the only real solution was to increase the supply of usable water. In 2002, a program of building desalination plants began. By 2023, Israel had five operational desalination plants, all of which use the reverse osmosis method, and which supply around 85 percent of the country's usable water through desalination of seawater and brackish water.

Mekorot, Israel's state-owned water company (founded in 1937), has historically been responsible for the production and supply of water to various consumers, but has not been involved in desalination

Since Israel's founding in 1948, its domestic and commercial water systems have been managed by local authorities. There have been claims that these systems have been managed inefficiently, and that many local authorities have not allocated sufficient resources to upgrade infrastructure, causing repeated breakdowns, leaks, and the loss of valuable water. In 2001, as part of efforts to privatize and streamline the management of Israel's water network, Knesset enacted the Water and Sewage Corporations Law, which transferred the management of Israel's water sector from local authorities to municipal water corporations. Among the main goals of the law was creating a mechanism for upgrading Israel's water and sewage networks, and preventing funds allocated to water and sewage services from "leaking" into local authorities' general budgets.

Another major change occurred at the start of 2007, with the establishment of the Government Water and Sewage Authority (the Water Authority) as a single government body.

Most of Israel's treated wastewater is designated for agricultural irrigation, industry, and public parks, and has become a vital part of Israel's water resource management, especially for agriculture. Israel has around 100 wastewater treatment plants (the largest being the Shafdan facility near Tel Aviv) which supply treated wastewater, mainly for agriculture. Thanks to these plants, Israel has the highest rate of treated wastewater recovery in the world (around 90 percent of the country's wastewater is reused).

***Seaports.*** Prior to 2003, Israel had three international seaports that were managed under a single entity, the Israel Ports Authority. The fact that a single body controlled all the import and export resources for Israel's seaports was highly significant given that some 98 percent of Israel's foreign trade is conducted by ship and passes through the country's ports. While each seaport had its own workers' committee (known as port committees), these were unified under a single large committee, and so a strike at one port shut down all Israel's ports. The lack of competition also had negative consequences for foreign trade, including comparatively high costs and low yields, long wait times for loading and unloading, frequent disruptions, and tariffs that, because of political pressures, did not reflect the real costs of goods.

In 2003, Israel began to implement a program of structural changes to its seaports with the goal of increasing competition among them. In February 2005, the Israel Port Authority (originally established in 1961) was disbanded. The Haifa, Ashdod, and Eilat ports were reorganized into three separate, independent government companies which were intended for privatization in the future. At the same time, a regulatory authority in the Ministry of Transport was established—The Ports Authority— with the responsibility for long-term planning and regulation of Israel's seaports. However, the 2005 reform establishing port companies and a regulatory authority largely failed.

In 2013, efforts to complete the reform of Israel's seaports continued with the preparation of breakwaters for new private terminals. To increase competition among the ports, the Ministry of Transport issued two tenders for competing deep water seaports. These were intended for operation by private concessions, under a BOT scheme. The HaDarom (the South) Port Terminal was established in Ashdod to compete with Ashdod Port, and the HaMifratz Port (known as Bayport) in Haifa to compete with Haifa Port. China's Pan Mediterranean Engineering Company (PMEC), a unit of China Harbour, won the tender to complete the construction of the Hadarom Port Terminal in Ashdod, while Dutch company Terminal

Investment Limited won the operating concession. Israel's Ashtrom Group and Shapir Engineering won the concession to construct Haifa Bayport, while China's state-owned Shanghai International Port Group won the operating tender. Both terminals began operating in 2021, advancing the much hoped-for competition. Meanwhile, in 2022, a consortium of India's Adani Ports and SEZ Ltd., and Israel's Gadot Group won the tender to privatize Haifa Port.

***Aviation.*** Since the establishment of the State, Israel's state-run aviation company El Al has been a major player in Israeli air transport. From the mid-1990s, gradual changes began to be made to Israel's international passenger and cargo flight industries. In December 1999, a second carrier, CAL Cargo Airlines, was granted a government license to operate cargo flights using its own aircraft, alongside El Al. Licenses were also granted for passenger charter flights on a large number of routes that were already covered by El Al's scheduled flight services. In addition, in 1999 Israeli charter airline Israir was awarded a scheduled operator license on a number of international routes that were not operated by El Al, while in 2007 Arkia, another Israeli domestic airline, was awarded a scheduled operator license for a number of routes not covered by El Al.

El Al was privatized in 2005, with the aim of giving it the necessary tools to contend with increasing competition in the industry and respond to challenging business conditions. In April 2013, the government approved an "open skies" agreement that brought many low-cost airlines from abroad into the Israeli market, significantly reducing the prices of scheduled flights to destinations in Europe and increasing the number of passengers flying to new destinations.

***Land transportation.*** Israel has traditionally had a high demand for public and private travel by road and train, coupled with a severe lack of infrastructure. From the 1990s, the planning restrictions and bureaucratic red tape that had hindered road and rail planning were gradually scrapped. Infrastructure budgets for land transport increased to around two percent of GDP. However, these improvements did not last.

In 2003, the Public Works Department ("Ma'atz"), the government company responsible for the development and maintenance of Israel's intercity road network, became a government corporation, the National Roads Company of Israel . The National Roads Company is responsible for the planning, construction, and maintenance of Israel's road infrastructure. The company makes extensive use of outsourcing, with road surfacing undertaken by private companies either with government funding or private finance via BOT and PFI schemes.

***Buses.*** Israel's transit bus industry, which had been controlled by the Egged and Dan transport cooperatives in the pre-State Yishuv, was opened to competition in the late 1990s. Privatization led to a drop in prices, reductions in government subsidies, and a partial improvement in the frequency of bus routes. The new transit bus operators have increased the number of passengers using public transport, but this is still not enough to provide adequate service to the public. The government has continued to issue tenders for additional bus lines, and every few years holds a tender for lines run by existing operators, which creates competition to improve bus services, reduce government subsidies, and introduce new management methods.

***Rail.*** The origins of Israel's rail network lie in infrastructure developments from the Ottoman and British Mandatory periods, starting from the laying of the Jaffa to Jerusalem railway at the end of the 19th century. In 1988, management of Israel's rail networks was transferred to the Ports and Railways Authority. In 2003, a government company, Israel Railways Ltd, was formed as a business entity for operating Israel's passenger and freight transport, as well as for planning and development the country's rail infrastructure.

The government heavily subsidizes Israel Railways because of the advantages of mass transit in reducing congestion from private vehicle traffic. From the second decade of the 21st century, the government recognized the railways as a basic infrastructure and directed considerable resources to developing Israel's rail network in the small, densely populated country, where most of its residents live in urban settlements, thereby make a rail network advantageous.

***Mass transit.*** In the 1990s, there was a growing recognition that Israel's road congestion problem, a result of the large number of private vehicles on the roads, needed a systemic solution. This solution was mass transit systems—a metro (underground) and a light rail system in the Gush Dan metropolitan area, light trains in Jerusalem and Tel Aviv, and heavy trains for intercity connections. Jerusalem's light rail system began operating in 2010 and served as a model for Israel's planned mass transit solution for urban and suburban transport.

Light rail systems are easier and less costly to build than metro systems. Light trains can be integrated into pedestrian streets, are able to handle gradients and sharp turns, offer fast, convenient, and low pollution travel within cities. By giving pedestrians priority in the traffic light system, light rails are convenient for pedestrians and facilitate fast and safe intra-urban travel.

***Electricity.*** The Israel Electric Corporation long had a monopoly in the production, transmission, and distribution of electricity. In the mid-1990s, the Israeli government announced a reform program to open the market to privatization and competition. However, this was not carried out until 2018, when the government adopted a decision to reform and partially dismantle the electricity production monopoly by agreeing to sell five gas power plants owned by the Israel Electric Corporation. Prior to 2015, Israel Electric Corporation controlled 95 percent of electricity production, which was reduced to less than 50 percent by 2023.

The main benefits of the reform have been the dismantling of part of the Israel Electric Corporation's vertical monopoly in electricity production, and the transfer of network management, planning, and development from the IEC to another government company, Noga—The Israel Independent System Operator Ltd. Noga serves as the "brain" of the electricity supply network, determining which power plants will supply electricity and setting priorities for the privately owned gas power plants, allowing independence from the IEC. The IEC retained its monopoly on transmission and distribution to consumers.

Alongside these structural changes, there have been shifts in the sources of electricity production. Oil and coal are disappearing. Natural gas has become a major source of electricity generation in Israel, although work is being done to develop renewable energy sources, in light of climate change and Israel's announcement in 2021 that it had committed to reducing its net carbon emissions by at least 85 percent from 2015 levels by 2050.

***Agriculture.*** Israeli agriculture has not undergone significant competitive reforms. This is rooted in the way that agriculture functions, in particular because produce prices usually fluctuate according to a cobweb model, where farmers plant and harvest the next year's crops in response to the previous year's prices. To avoid the alternating scarcity and abundance that this produces, the Israeli government guarantees farmers a minimum price for crops, to allow them to increase production for the next year. Prices are set via the Plant Council which was founded in the 1950s to regulate the prices of agricultural produce. This system was critical in Israel's early years of statehood, when agriculture formed a large part of the economy, and was responsible for producing all the country's fresh food crops, regardless of relative advantage. Today, agriculture has shrunk to just one percent of Israel's GDP.

Agricultural protectionism relies on high import tariffs and quotas to disincentivize the import of produce, even when domestic fruit and vegetable prices are high and in seasons when import would be welcome because there is no domestic production of a particular crop. Agriculture in Israel is an example of the struggle between public perception and that of the market. Public perception advocates protecting Israel's agriculture to preserve green spaces, to encourage rural settlement, and to ensure food security. In the dairy and egg production sectors, centralized planning and lack of competition have caused the prices of these products to be very high by international standards, which impacts the cost of living. Due to high tariffs on agricultural products and policy preventing agricultural imports into Israel, in 2010–2022 agricultural output was static, and productivity decreased, despite a population increase of over 25 percent. The closures to imports harm consumers, and pose a risk to food security. The historical policy that domestic agriculture should provide all of Israel's fresh produce does not meet the test of national security when it come in the import of basic need like rice, grains, sugar and vegetable oil.

To ensure the preservation of Israel's agricultural industry and food security, import tariffs should be reduced and direct subsidies given to farmers (differential by industry). Opening the market to imports will increase competition and reduce price inequality. In recent years, partial steps have been taken to open the market and reduce tariffs on imported fish, seafood, chilled meats, and olive oil. Reforms were also made to the poultry industry in 2022, the results of which should be realized over the coming years.

Opening Israel's fresh produce market to competition from abroad needs to be done gradually. The government should invest in research and development of technologies such as greenhouse growing, the efficient use of irrigation systems, climate control, and digital sensors that could help Israel establish a relative advantage in a number of crops under its prevailing conditions of water and agricultural land shortages.

In Israel, as throughout the world, agricultural reforms are inevitably accompanied by conflicts between the interests of farmers and those of consumers. In 2022, the government began moves to reform Israeli fruit and vegetable farming by partially lowering import tariffs. The intention was that farmers would be supported directly through grants and investments rather than via protectionist import tariffs and quotas. The overall goal was to make Israeli agriculture more efficient, increase competition and consumer choice by developing imports, encourage a shift to larger farms, and reduce fruit and vegetable prices to help ease the cost of living. However, political pressures have held these reforms back.

Market reform is a complex, ongoing process with many challenges and obstacles. Changing the status quo requires a determined government policy. Advancing reforms involves a constant struggle in the face of strong opposition from the status quo and inaction or indifference from those who stand to benefit. Those fearing injury become well-organized, while the benefitting consumers are scattered. Because reforms offer consumers a relatively smaller benefit compared to dramatically adversely affected stakeholders, the government finds it difficult to fight the far stronger stakeholders and power holders. Furthermore, experience shows that market reforms take about ten years on average to be completed and come to fruition. Politicians often have few incentives to wait so long for political reward, especially when they are met with public anger for spearheading painful changes. In addition, reforms must undergo periodic adjustments to keep pace with a changing reality. While Israeli reform efforts have tackled many sectors of the economy, far-reaching reforms are still needed in areas such as agriculture and local services.

## Notes

1. This issuance, which I led together with the accountant general, was delayed for three weeks following the assassination of Prime Minister Yitzhak Rabin in Tel Aviv on November 4, 1995.

# 18

# Financial Reform

Until the 1980s, the government was fully involved in every aspect of Israel's financial and capital markets, including raising and allocating capital, and setting rates of return and imposing discriminatory tax rates. This exceptional government involvement in the capital market had begun during Israel's first decades of statehood, when the government needed to finance its budget deficit and direct private investments amid a dearth of capital and investors. As a result, the lion's share of public savings was directed to the government and the Bank of Israel, via government bonds and high liquidity rates on savings plans, deposits, provident fund assets, and pension funds.

The traditional function of financial intermediation is to link individual savers and borrowers (the public) with investors (businesses). State involvement in Israel's capital market reduced sources of private investment, distorted the relative yields of various assets and liabilities, and prevented public assets from being allocated as efficiently as possible.

Government involvement in the financial and capital markets actually increased during the hyperinflation crisis of the 1980s, when government spending soared to around 75 percent of GDP, the budget deficit to 15 percent of GDP, and government debt hit a record high of 270 percent of GDP. Reduction in the government deficit in the wake of the 1985 Economic Stabilization Plan was a cornerstone of financial reform.

Reform of Israel's capital market began in 1987, when the government took two important steps. First, licenses were granted to nonfinancial companies and mortgage banks allowing them to issue private bonds. The government also reduced the pension funds' obligation to invest in non-tradable government bonds and granted them a license to invest in private bonds.

Most of the later significant financial reforms came about due to the work of professionals within the Ministry of Finance, setting in motion a process of reform that would last for two decades. One of the manifestations of their efforts was the 1995 Brodet Committee that recommended reforms that would separate non-financial and financial corporations, a process that was also referred to by the Anti-Concentration Committee some 17 years later. Reforms to taxation on income from financial instruments eliminated tax discrimination between different financial assets. In 1994, the Fogel Committee on Pension Reform reduced government involvement in the capital market by closing the Histadrut pension funds and opening new pension funds run by institutional investors. The Bachar Committee (2004) focused on reducing centralization in financial intermediation, reducing the power of the banks, strengthening institutional investors, and developing sources of non-bank credit.

All of these reforms were driven by a shift in macroeconomic perspectives following the 1985 Economic Stabilization Plan that aimed to reduce government involvement in the economy and open it up to the global economy. This led to increased competition and a more streamlined capital market to improve resource allocation within the economy. As a result, the number of participants in the capital market increased and competition in financial intermediation improved. Due to these reforms, the number and power of institutional investors managing long-term savings has increased dramatically, and banks have mainly become providers of traditional banking services only. With the stock market reforms, the development of Israel's capital market as a tool for the efficient allocation of public resources was completed. Now, the amount of credit available to businesses has increased through the issuance of public and private bonds.

In the 2010s, technological developments led to dramatic changes in the financial system, some of which proved even more significant than the reforms themselves. The rise of the smartphone has sparked an information revolution, which, among other things, has dramatically changed the relationship between banks and their customers. The new technology also accelerated the development of small, agile financial entities, fintech companies, and payment apps, which challenged the existing financial system. The establishment of a credit pool benefitted non-banking credit companies and "open banking."

## Milestones

The following are a number of key milestones, some mentioned above, in the reform of Israel's capital and financial markets that occurred as part of its transition to a free capital market.

***The Brodet Committee (1995)***[1] discussed abolishing bank investment in non-financial corporations, similar to the Banking Act of 1933 in the

United States (the Glass-Steagall Act), which effectively separated commercial banking from investment banking. The Committee's report was the first governmental attempt to address a fundamental financial issue as part of building a modern Israeli economy and transitioning from a public, centralized market to a private, commercial, open, and competitive economy.

The report outlines a new structure for business costs and heralded a new approach to the relationship between financial and nonfinancial companies and to potential conflicts of interest. The banks held significant shares in domestic corporations and were used as underwriters in issuances, which created conflicts of interest between the banks and savers.

The Committee recommended that banks be limited to holding 20 percent of nonfinancial corporations, and that banks should not have such control that would enable them to influence such companies' activities and make business decisions. Applying the Committee's recommendations, changes were made that were highly beneficial for the economy, and that created a completely new playing field for Israel's business and financial sector. There is no question that the Brodet Committee's recommendations served as a turning point for Israel's business and banking system.

Following the Committee's report, there was an increase in the number of private business players in the Israeli economy, with the acceleration of the privatization of government and union-owned companies and the development of the high-tech sector, new private businesspeople and companies.

***The Bachar Committee (2004)***[2] discussed reducing centralized holdings and conflicts of interest in the banking system in the capital market, as well as the development of a non-bank credit market. Previously, most financial intermediation was controlled by the banks, which had vertical control over most capital market activities fund management, underwriting, credit provision, and portfolio management. However, what was needed was a competitive, multi-broker market that would reduce brokerage discrimination and optimize business activity. The Committee recommended decentralizing the ownership of the management of existing investment channels, developing a non-bank credit market, and exposing the public to alternative investment funds beyond the existing banking channels.

By 2022, credit provided by non-banking entities constituted over 50 percent of business credit, compared to just a few percent in the early 2000s (i.e., before the reform). The growth in Israel's non-banking capital market was fueled by pension savings, insurance, and provident funds managed by institutional investors, and a diversified and decentralized competitive market was created for the public's savings accounts. In 2022, 10 institutional corporations managed around 90 percent of consumer financial assets, while Israel's three largest pension funds accounted for some 75 percent of the market. The risk of concentration has now shifted from the banks to institutional investors, characterized by the institutional "group thinking" of a small number of financial managers who are responsible for managing enormous financial investments. This situation requires fresh regulation.

***The Committee for Increasing Competitiveness in the Economy (Shani Committee, 2010).***[3] The Committee's recommendations addressed three areas: the conditions for the allocation of public assets, tackling the pyramid holding structure[4] within Israel's public companies, and separating financial and nonfinancial holdings. It soon became clear that some 20 business groups controlled around two-thirds of the market value of Israel's public companies, mainly through pyramidal holding structures that created a significant gap between the controlling owner's equity capital holdings and its percentage of voting rights holdings, thus enabling a single shareholder to exercise control over a company while retaining only a small fraction of the equity claims on the company's cash flows. This situation was a clear violation of competition and stability, as well as an inefficient allocation of public assets. It concentrated considerable power in the hands of just a few individuals, ultimately harming the investing public. The Competition Law provides a remedy by separating major nonfinancial and financial corporations so that a controlling stakeholder in a major nonfinancial entity cannot also hold a major financial entity. The purpose is to avoid an inefficient allocation of public assets as a result of any conflict of interest that may arise between a controlling stakeholder's nonfinancial and financial activities, since this would harm the interests of members of the public who had invested in the financial corporation.

To prevent pyramidal structures whereby a second-layer company controls a third-layer company, the Centralization Law stipulated that a public company or company that is publicly traded cannot control a pyramidal structure of more than two layers. As a result of the legislation, eight of the largest business groups on the Tel Aviv Stock Exchange were dismantled, and the pyramids disappeared.

As with many economic issues, solving one problem only creates another problem in a different area. Over the last decade, the number of large institutional investors has shrunk from 15 to just 10 entities, which together control 90 percent of the market. The institutional investors have grown from representing 25 percent of the amount floating on the stock market to 36 percent, and in 2021 managed 2.8 trillion NIS of public money (about 200 percent of Israel's GDP), which has raised fresh fears about economy-wide concentration and competition.

***The Strum Committee (2016)***[5] focused on competition in retail banking (public companies and small and medium businesses). The Committee recommended increasing competition by introducing non-banking companies, which would exert competitive pressure and reduce the price of banking services for private consumers and small businesses and firms. The available competitors were the credit card companies, which the Committee recommended should be separated from the ownership of credit card companies from the banks and turned into independent bodies with an infrastructure for providing credit and information about consumers.

## Pensions

Israel's pension sector underwent significant reform between 1995 and 2003, in terms of both pension funds and the budgetary pension. The "old" Histadrut pension funds had been responsible for managing the public's pension savings. In 1995, the then-Finance Minister Baiga Shochat and the Histadrut agreed that in face of their large deficits, the "old" pension schemes would be closed to new members. Instead, balanced "new" pension funds were established, which had less favorable conditions for new members. The reforms reduced the actuarial deficits of the "old" pension funds and reduced the government's involvement in the capital market.

In 2003, the "old" pension funds were nationalized, and a special manager from the Ministry of Finance was appointed to oversee them. The government undertook to cover the actuarial deficits, which became based on direct contributions (DC) at the fund level. The actuarial balance was achieved by reducing members' rights, raising the pension age, increasing contributions, and requiring pensioners to pay management fees for their pension payments.

In 1999, another major reform was carried out, this time to the budgetary pension of state employees. Under a collective agreement between the Histadrut and the government, the budgetary pension was closed for new employees, who were directed to the "new" pension funds. In 2008, a mandatory pension scheme was introduced, requiring all employers to pay into a pension fund for all staff, which boosted the size of the funds managed by Israel's institutional investors. In 2016, the Mandatory Pensions Law was expanded to include the self-employed and stipulating that the long-term savings instruments of pension funds, life insurance policies, and provident funds will pay an annuity upon retirement, while changing the nature of the provident funds, which now would be used for retirement savings only, and not for encouraging long-term savings, as they had in the past.

In 2022, Israel's pension bodies (pension funds, provident funds, and life insurance) managed about 2.2 trillion NIS, about 25 percent more than Israel's total GDP, an amount that has doubled within a decade. These funds are now an important source of financing infrastructure and business investments. After the extensive changes made to the pensions system over the past 20 years, a good and stable system has been created that benefits both the individual and the economy, and which is considered one of the best pension systems in the world in terms of sharing risks between the individual and the government. A pension in Israel today is based on real, transparent, and supervised financial assets that guarantee a return and take into account life expectancy. The distortion of the imbalance in retirement age between men and women was mostly corrected in 2021.

## Summary

After a decades' long journey of reform, Israel's once nationalized, feeble, and limited financial and capital markets are now efficient and competitive, resembling those in other developed countries and without government involvement in the capital markets. The reduction of the government deficit and state involvement in the capital market, as well as improved economic growth and the move to mandatory pension contributions for all those in employment from 2008, have helped to significantly increase the scope of the assets controlled by Israel's institutional investors.

As a result, the financial center of gravity has shifted from banks to the institutional investors. Past concerns about increasing centralization in the banking system have been replaced by similar fears about the institutional investors, whose power has increased considerably, as that of the banks has shrunk. The power of Israel's institutional investors is expected to grow, in view of the increase in long-term savings as a result of population growth and economic expansion. Meanwhile, a high level of concentration has also developed in the pension fund industry.

Since the beginning of the 1990s, Israel's capital market has managed to withstand global and local financial crises. Market reform has successfully created a secure, competitive, and stable capital market. The importance of institutional investors in the capital market and as gatekeepers in public companies has increased. Since the early 2000s, the volume of foreign assets as a proportion of the total assets managed by institutional investors has increased from zero to around 25 percent by 2022. In recent years, Israel's capital market has been defined as a "developed market" and not an "emerging market," which indicates optimal channeling of capital sources for utilization, a condition necessary for economic growth.

In summary, since the mid-1980s, the financial markets have undergone dramatic changes, evolving from a nationalized market to a modern and global financial market serving the modern needs of the Israeli economy.

## Notes

1. Report of the Committee for Examining the Aspects of Bank Holdings in Nonfinancial Corporations, December 1995 (Brodet Committee).
2. Report of the inter-ministerial team regarding capital market reform, September 2004 (Bachar Committee).
3. The Committee for Increasing Competitiveness in the Economy (Centralization Committee), March 2012.
4. A pyramid structure refers to a business entity composed of a number of smaller companies, where there is a top-down chain of control in the ownership structure. See Report of the Committee for Increasing Market Competitiveness (Chaim Shany, Centralisation Committee), Mar 2012 (in Hebrew).
5. The Committee for Increasing Competition in Banking and Financial Services, September 2016 (Strum Committee).

# 19

## Globalization

For almost four decades following its independence, Israel's markets were closed to foreign trade. This was a strategic decision, intended to give the new state a chance to develop its economy by protecting domestic manufacturing from international competition. During 1960s and 1970s, Israel began to take slow, cautious steps toward opening its economy. By the 1990s, this process had accelerated, and Israel had begun to make consistent progress in integrating into the global economy.

In the wake of the 1985 Economic Stabilization Plan, Israel adopted a clear policy of international openness, which included transitioning to a market economy and implementing measures to increase internal and external competition. Reducing defense spending to a level more commensurate with that throughout the world became an element of the 1985 Stabilization Plan. While it took some time to accomplish this, from the mid-1980s economic growth helped Israel achieve a steady decrease in defense spending as a proportion of GDP, albeit alongside an increase in absolute security spending. As these processes unfolded, there was a shift away from the old "mobilized" society to a civilian society. This was an ideological transformation, representing the slow and steady decline of Israel's past collective ethos and the rise of a more individualistic culture. The pressures for economic and social normalization were expressed in public calls to increase living standards and improve social services. As the effects of globalization increased, Israel experienced growing conflicts with the traditions and behaviors that had developed over its short history. Meanwhile, Israel's strong technological and global capacity helped transform it into a regional power with international ties. Tensions between the relative power of the individual and the state are a reality in Israel and the wider world.

Meanwhile, the coronavirus pandemic of 2020–2021 disrupted global supply chains and globalization processes, and global opinion began to recognize the important role of the state in aiding their citizens and safeguarding strategic national assets for public health and security. During the pandemic, many Israelis learned to work remotely and recognize that in some respects the world was getting smaller due to greater connectivity. Israel enjoyed comparative advantages in innovation, entrepreneurship, creativity, and the presence of international companies' development centers. Israel has derived a considerable benefit from globalization and has no intention of withdrawing from a process that has helped its economy. However, because of the worldwide trend of weakening globalization, Israel, as a small economy in a big world, will be required to adapt to the new trends.

## The Growth of Globalization in Israel

Three key factors combined to facilitate the growth of globalization in Israel: ironically, its very particular Jewish tradition and heritage, geopolitical reality, and economic advantages.

***Jewish tradition.*** Historical circumstances forced the Jews to be a people in exile, scattered across the globe for many centuries. This strengthened the global culture among the world's Jewish communities, and ultimately helped facilitate Israel's organic integration into the international community. Strong Jewish communities in most of the world's key economic centers are able to help support Israel, whether it be financially or politically. Although Zionism advocated the denial of the Diaspora and called for the Jews to congregate in the Land of Israel and discard their traditional Diaspora occupations, traditions that have developed over hundreds of years do not change in just a few generations. Globalization and a sense of belonging to a worldwide community are part of the natural reality of the so-called "wandering Jew," even when living in their own country. Israelis' integration into globalization processes was a collective expression of their aspirations for education, entrepreneurship, and innovation, responding to a global demand for knowledge-rich products, and reflecting their long tradition of openness to the world.

***Geopolitical reality.*** From its inception, Israel was isolated from its neighbors with no formal ties to any country in the region. Politically, this prompted a need to establish international ties with nations outside the Middle East. Economically, the Arab boycott motivated Israel to look for markets in other regions. Already in the 1960s, Israel had established ties with the European Common Market that resulted in a free trade agreement in 1975. From the mid-1980s, relations with other countries expanded, culminating in a free trade agreement with the United States in 1985. Israel's peace efforts first bore fruit in the late 1970s in the form of an agreement with Egypt, and then again in the 1990s with the Oslo Accords with the Palestinians and the 1994 peace treaty with Jordan. These agreements gave impetus to the expansion of Israel's international ties and access to new markets, improving Israel's position in the international economic community.

In 1991, Israel continued its efforts to integrate into the global economy and boost bilateral trade by unilaterally lowering tariffs. In the 1990s, Israel signed free trade agreements with Turkey and some South American countries. Israel's burgeoning high-tech industry and technological prowess helped accelerate its integration into the international economy and capital markets, and foreign investors and leading technology companies began to open development centers in Israel.

Significant recognition of the success of Israel's economy came in 2010, when it was accepted into the Organization for Economic Co-operation and Development (often dubbed "a club of rich countries."[1]) This was an important milestone in Israel's integration into the global economy and its compliance with international standards. The Abraham Accords with the United Arab Emirates, Bahrain, Morocco, and Sudan in 2020 gave an additional impetus to Israel's economy globally and regionally.

***Economic Advantages***. In the 1990s, Israel adopted the economic norms of the developed international economic community, including fiscal discipline and an independent central bank, and adhered to the principles of the Maastricht Treaty[2] and the Washington Consensus[3] in its economic management. In this spirit, Israel carried out reforms to its foreign exchange policy that made its currency tradable on the international market. A modern capital market was created. Fiscal reform, including reducing the public sector as a percentage of GDP, cutting government spending,[4] and privatizing state-owned enterprises have all served to strengthen the efficiency of the economy and make it attractive to international investors. Israel's high-tech industry has become a significant engine of growth that has helped attract investment from venture capitalists.

An important, substantial, and strategic move was Israel's entry into the international credit rating regime in 1995, reflecting the willingness of the government and the business sector to be exposed to the judgment of international credit agencies and leading global investment bodies.

## Israel and Globalization

Israel integrated quickly and relatively seamlessly into the globalization process. These processes began at a strategic time, allowing Israel to take advantage of the historical opportunity provided by a unique convergence of social, economic, and political developments. Key among these were Israel's exit from the hyperinflation crisis of the 1980s, the rapid development of its technological industries, an injection of skilled human capital in the form of mass immigration from the former Soviet Union and the young men and women who had been discharged from the IDF. Other factors included good institutions of higher education, a strategic relationship with the United States, increased global demand for products that Israel had a comparative advantage in producing, and the opening of new international markets as a result of improvements in Israel's political status.

Israel's integration into the global economy coincided with its recovery from the severe economic crisis of the early 1980s, the 1985 Economic Stabilization Plan, and the major market reforms that were implemented in the following decade, all of which improved internal and external competitiveness. The reforms strengthened Israel's ability to compete globally, including by helping it exploit its comparative advantages. Some industries took off (high-tech), while others collapsed (notably, the textiles industry). The reform period passed without any major economic shocks, largely thanks to growth and healthy employment figures.

As a small country with no natural resources, Israel has successfully exploited the potential inherent in globalization and openness to large international markets. Israel's economy is relatively small—a fact that is not, *per se*, a disadvantage in a globalized economy. High-tech products, with their high added value based on knowledge, technology, and innovation, are greatly prized in the global marketplace. Technology, knowledge, skilled human resources, and entrepreneurship have become key components of the "wealth of nations" and an engine for stable and rewarding growth.

Israel entered the process of globalization in December 1995 with its first issuance, in New York, of a sovereign bond without the backing of the United States Treasury. The bonds (known as Yankee bonds), the first backed only by Israel, raised $250 million. Additional issuances took place in Europe in 1996, and in Japan in 1997. Israel now has a presence on the global stock exchanges and other global capital market sites. The many positive outcomes of globalization include the maturation of its foreign currency liberalization, a flexible exchange rate that is not subject to foreign exchange controls, openness to international capital markets, increasing foreign investments in Israel and Israeli investments overseas. In 2022, Israel had become a nett foreign lender (to the tune of over $200 billion), in contrast to previous years.

Israel has retained some of the social consciousness of its original "mobilized" society, but globalizing processes have weakened its traditional foundations. Israel is still engaged in the historical process of establishing its individual society and economy, a national process that is in conflict with globalization, which contradict its traditional and mobilized foundations. Its new market economy is very different from its old, government-controlled economy. Israel's high defense spending stands in stark contrast to that of the developed countries against which it has to compete in the global markets. Israel's conservative, ultra-Orthodox, and Arab populations, often very insular, must face an increasingly open world. In contrast, the country's skilled workforce is tempted by global opportunities outside Israel, in particular for high-tech workers. The challenge for Israel is to integrate into the global and regional spheres while maintaining an ethos of "a nation shall dwell alone," as well continuing to face its ongoing national conflict.

Israel, which seeks to be integrated both globally and regionally, is embroiled in an ongoing national conflict and has an ingrained mentality of "a people that shall dwell alone" (Numbers, 23:9). The challenge is— how can Israel be part of global processes? Despite the 2020 Abraham Accords, Israel's integration in the Middle East remains incomplete due to resistance in some parts of the Arab world. The region finds itself caught in the vortex of a struggle between Sunni and Shia factions and non-Arab powers (Iran and Turkey), as well as internal battles between traditional, non-global regimes and the desire to reap the benefits of globalization. As a result, Israel is still very much governed by its old "theory of rounds" in which it seeks to build a state in the lulls between periodic bouts of violence.

The structure of industry in Israel is another area in Israel which has undergone significant change due to globalization. High tech is thriving while non-globalized industries, including many services, traditional industries, construction, and agriculture, which, as in other developed countries, remain outside of the rising arc of globalization. Exports are of great importance in the globalization process, especially technology exports. As the "startup nation" of high-tech entrepreneurship, Israel has tended to prefer the startup exit route—starting a company with the end goal of cashing out, usually to an international buyer—over the creation of local, scale-up companies. The number of technological ventures that actually take root in Israel, as opposed to being sold to international companies, is small—but a new trend is emerging of creating local companies. Many international technology companies have opened development centers in Israel (there were 360 such centers as of 2022), where the majority of Israeli development engineers work. As well as the startups that have achieved successful exits, Israel does have a handful of companies that have developed into global corporations—notably Teva Pharmaceuticals, Keter Group (a consumer plastics manufacturer), and Amdocs. International companies operate in Israel in production, such as Intel, and others have bought out or entered into partnerships with Israeli companies like Osem, Tnuva, and Strauss (Israel's leading food conglomerates). Globalization has brought large international chains to Israel in food, fashion, furniture, and leisure that influence local consumption, as has been the case in many other countries.

Globalization is not only about trade, investments, and capital movements. It is also the adoption of international accounting rules and standards, global standardization, and participation in international organizations. The major accounting firms in Israel have joined the "Big 4" global accounting firms, and similar trends have occurred in law and advertising. This is another reflection of Israel's increasing integration into a globalized world.

## Israel and Superpower Rivalries

Israel's leadership has long understood that its survival in the region requires more than just a skilled and strong military. Israel also needs a strong economy and robust society with an essential global component. While Israel has not formally aligned itself to any of the economic and political blocs that have emerged in the globalized world, it does enjoy special and extensive ties with the United States as a patron and key political, military, and economically. Unsurprisingly, Washington has thus viewed Israel's developing ties with Beijing with concern, a situation that has created difficult dilemmas for Israel.

As tensions between Beijing and Washington continue, Israel is facing an unprecedented economic and political challenge. Its ties with the United States are extensive and long-standing, while its relationship with China is new, having developed only since the turn of the millennium. Already, Chinese infrastructure companies have made an important contribution to Israel, to the value of tens of billions of NIS, thanks to its low prices. But there are global as well as internal and/or security risks arising from dependence on investments from these companies. More recently, Washington's concerns over Israel's growing ties with Beijing have shifted to Chinese activity in Israeli infrastructure and technology. Israel has a vested interest in not harming American security interests and in maintaining U.S. military and financial support. In this context, the struggle between China and the United States poses difficult political and economic dilemmas. Israel is walking a tightrope that requires close monitoring and keen insights into the political and economic moves and sensitivities of each power, and above all a good understanding of China, which is different from the West.

As an open country and economy that seeks to be part of the globalized world, Israel must maintain economic relations with all the major economic blocs, through exports and investments. Indeed, economic growth relies on being able to export to all blocs, regardless of their economic affiliation.

## Israel's Membership in the OECD

Its economic success paved the way for it to join the OECD in 2010, a move that sharpened the implications of its adopting the economic standards of the developed Western world. Alongside the prestige of joining the so-called "club of rich countries," Israel has been given the opportunity to align itself with the economic standards and norms of the developed world. In joining the OECD, Israel has exposed itself to a continuous, long-term process of comparison with the socioeconomic performance of other OECD nations and with international standards and benchmarks and can directly see how it measures up vis-à-vis the countries it has always wanted to resemble. The public transparency of the OECD's comparative data (which included information on some 38 countries in 2022) has occasionally exposed Israel to some unpleasant truths, which can serve as an impetus for improvement. Israel has also chosen to adopt the economic standards and norms of the developed world, accepting the international economic parameters of the International Monetary Fund, the European Union (the Maastricht Treaty), and the international credit rating agencies. Since 2010, Israel has also followed the norms of the OECD countries in terms of its public spending to GDP and national debt ratio (40–50 percent).

## The Challenges of Globalization

Israel has been able to successfully exploit the trends of globalization by focusing on exports with a relative advantage and high added value and taking advantage of a growing global demand for technology products. However, it is torn between the desire to continue to benefit from globalization and the need to respond to its unique problems as a country fighting for its existence.

Globalization has fundamentally changed the absolute and relative values of education and entrepreneurship. Those with a greater level of education and skills earn far more than the uneducated and unskilled. Wages and income gaps have widened as a result of globalization. The global world favors the skilled and educated, while the unskilled and uneducated are left behind. Israel, with its dual economy and society, is torn between the success of its high-tech sector and the struggles of its less-educated populations of Arabs, ultra-Orthodox Jews, and other groups on the social and geographical periphery. This situation has produced increasing socioeconomic disparities and poverty and poses a threat to Israel's social and economic stability. The ultra-Orthodox and Arab populations are having a hard time dealing with globalization. Unless Israel can increase these groups' participation in the labor market and improve their education, it will not be possible to increase economic growth and reduce the socioeconomic and income disparities that are undermining social cohesion and increasing the sense of alienation and abandonment. The government should tailor education programs and professional training for each of these demographics, in order to help them become more productive, especially the ultra-orthodox male category who object to receiving a core curriculum.

Globalization and the development of Israel's high-tech industry has increased the mobility of workers and entrepreneurs with technological skills, who are in demand in the most advanced development centers in the world, i.e., in the United States and Europe. Large global corporations and companies are just waiting to swallow up successful tech startup companies and attract talented Israelis who do not intend to develop themselves or their products in Israel but prefer to try to operate in the largest and most developed markets in the world. A relatively large number of startups have developed in Israel in relation to its output. The developed world, which encourages the immigration of educated, skilled, and entrepreneurial workers, offers lucrative rewards to those with entrepreneurial skills, who are in great demand in the globalized world. Israel has a relative abundance of such people, whose emigration would constitute a great loss of human capital to its economy and society. The phenomenon of Israelis temporary relocating abroad for work is expanding, as is the risk of those Israelis choosing to make their relocations permanent.

In a competitive global market with vast possibilities, Israel needs to be an attractive location for business and investments in order to strengthen its position. A policy for global comparison (benchmarking) is needed to help attract foreign business investment and expand businesses that are already in Israel. In particular, a country that seeks to integrate into the global space must improve the quality of the transportation infrastructures connecting its economy to the international markets, which is an important factor influencing foreign currency.

## Notes

1. https://www.economist.com/the-economist-explains/2017/07/05/what-is-the-oecd.
2. https://www.europarl.europa.eu/about-parliament/en/in-the-past/the-parliament-and-the-treaties/maastricht-treaty.
3. The Washington Consensus, developed by Washington, D.D-based institutions, such as the World Bank and the U.S. Department of the Treasure, contains a "standard" package of ten economic reform steps for developing countries in crisis. See https://en.wikipedia.org/wiki/Washington_Consensus#cite_note-piie.com-1.
4. According to reports published annually by Israel's Central Bureau of Statistics.

# 20

# Privatization

## Public Ownership

From its inception, Israel enjoyed a rich legacy of public economic activity, the foundations of which are rooted in a socialist ideology. These pioneers helped establish a set of economic, social, and political institutions that served as an infrastructure for the Yishuv and later for the State of Israel. The country's collective heritage and centralized economic management began with the establishment in 1920 of the Histadrut, which quickly became a significant factor in the Yishuv's economy. A decade later, the creation of the Jewish Agency, which represented the entire Jewish community in its national struggle until Israel's declaration of independence, further bolstered the Yishuv's public and collective ethos. These two institutions provided the organizational infrastructure that supported the political and economic fulfillment of the Zionist movement's vision, including by building the Yishuv's financial institutions and its industrial, manufacturing, agriculture, and construction sectors. Significantly, they also helped nurture a small but thriving private sector, predominantly of traditional crafts, small businesses, trade, and services, thereby creating a division of labor and helping reinforce the economy of the Yishuv and later of Israel.

The British Mandatory government bequeathed the nascent State of Israel its infrastructure, mainly in the form of transportation (roads and railways), communications (telecommunications and mail), energy (the electricity company, refineries, transport pipelines), water (wells and pipelines), and planning and administration systems. Confronted by the challenges the new country faced—in particular, the huge waves of indigent and vulnerable immigrants, security threats, and the need to build an economy—Israel's first government, led by the Mapai party, continued to heavily intervene in the economy. The Jewish Agency and Histadrut also played an active role in initiating, financing, and implementing the great projects of "building the nation and the state" by helping absorb immigrants, construct infrastructure, and invest in employment. It is impossible to describe the evolution of Israel's economy without noting the important contribution of the Histadrut and Jewish Agency as entrepreneurs and implementers in response to the state's early needs.

Not once during its first five years in power did Israel's first government precisely define its preferred economic regime. While some powerful voices (the left-wing Mapam party) called for the adoption of a strict socialist regime, others (the more centrist Mapai party) took a more practical approach to dealing with the immediate challenges facing the new state. Opposing them were the General Zionists party that advocated a private, liberal economic regime. These political struggles formed part of a broader debate over Israel's political orientation, which intensified during the Cold War between the United States and the Soviet Union. In the early 1950s, in the light of the reversal of initial Soviet support, the government, headed by Ben-Gurion, conceded to those calling for a Western-oriented political regime, and Israel turned to the United States and Western Europe.

While Israel's first government did openly advocate a broadly social democratic ideology, it never went so far as calling for nationalization, nor did it outlaw the private sector. Instead, Ben-Gurion's government adopted a pragmatic, state-run economy that allowed the private sector to engage in commerce, hotels, personal services, and similar activities. In fact, the government actively encouraged the private sector, including by providing various incentives to help it develop.

## Economic Crisis and Privatization

Israel's first government established dedicated state-run enterprises to carry out specific tasks in various areas of the economy. They benefited from the ability to obtain capital easily and from their proximity to the government decision-making centers. It was convenient for the government to act through these enterprises, which were managed by people loyal to it. Many of them lost money, and the government stepped in to support them from the national budget in various ways. It is clear that this web of state-owned infrastructure and security enterprises was essential at the time, and that similarly, it was natural for them to be under government control (indeed, this approach prevailed in Europe). However, this situation was not an effective long-term strategy for commercial enterprises, which are usually privately run.

The economic crisis of the 1980s was a turning point for Israel, bringing with it the recognition that the economy was in need of serious reform, including privatization, a concept that first emerged in the 1980s.

For years, the government had worn several hats—policymaker, owner of significant assets (the state-run enterprises, land, and infrastructure) and of products and services (security and health), and a regulator that set the rules for overseeing its business operations. These multiple roles placed the government in several fundamental conflicts of interest, where it effectively stood above the rules that it had put in place to regulate itself and to which it claimed to be committed. Its multiple conflicting roles created the potential for inefficiency and a lack of transparency, and, as the economy grew and became more complex, these risks increased.

As noted, the extensive involvement of the government in the economy during Israel's first years of statehood was the appropriate response to major market failure caused by mass unplanned immigration, a complex security situation, and a critical lack of resources. Although the economy benefitted from state intervention, the government had become invested in preserving the status quo and was in no rush to relinquish its central role, due to considerations of economic and political power and socialist ideology.

The 1985 Economic Stabilization Plan was a watershed. Successive national unity governments between 1984–1990 adopted privatization and market economics as the basis for deciding how to allocate tradeable goods and services. The involvement of the United States in the 1985 Economic Stability Plan and the dialogue with the American government that grew out of the U.S.-Israel Joint Economic Development Group (JDEG)[1] forum in 1985, as well as pressure from private stakeholders, hastened the adoption of market ideas and privatization.

The move toward privatization was reflected in the prevailing atmosphere around the world in the late 1980s. At the end of the Cold War, there was a widespread sense that the United States had won a history-ending economic victory over the Soviet Union, and that the ideology of the free market and globalization had triumphed over the public, centralized regimes of the communist Soviet bloc.

This convergence of historical events boosted pro-market and pro-competitiveness currents in Israel. The move to privatize Israel's state-run enterprises that began after the 1985 Economic Stabilization Plan would continue for years. The privatizations ultimately helped Israel construct a new economy by empowering its private and commercial sector.

From the beginning of the 1990s, privatization began to have an enormous impact on Israel's economy and society. The market share and power of the private and third sectors grew at the expense of the state and public sector. This dramatic change corresponded with a shift away from Israel's old collective mentality toward one of greater individualism.

In the period between 1986–1996, the assets of the Jewish Agency and the Histadrut were also sold. These privatizations boosted Israel's private sector, changing the face of the Israeli economy by introducing new private controlling owners (mostly Israelis, along with a few foreigners). These companies were initially sold to private parties and not through the capital market, which at the time was not sufficiently developed. Foreign parties were mostly not interested in buying these companies, as the dark shadow of the hyperinflation crisis still loomed over the economy. Ideas for privatization through the capital market, such as options plans,[2] were developed in the 1990s.

## The Jewish Agency and the Histadrut

In the second half of the 1980s, the business holdings of the Jewish Agency were the first entities to be privatized. The Agency's American leaders, who needed to extricate themselves from the financial crisis in which the Agency had become embroiled, were heavily influenced by the politics of Ronald Reagan in the United States and Margaret Thatcher in the United Kingdom, who both advocated a neoliberal worldview, small government, and a free market.

The hyperinflation crisis severely hit the Histadrut, especially its Clalit health fund and its economic arm Hevrat HaOvdim (Society of Workers), whose severe financial problems were exposed by the 1985 Economic Stabilization Plan. Hevrat HaOvdim could not service its debts to financial institutions, and nor could it rely on the unsympathetic Likud government to help bail it out. The resulting privatizations, which came in the 1990s, were rapid, as most of the Histadrut's assets were commercial companies operating in competitive markets,

Semi-public privatization occurred following the Brodet Committee report in 1995, which advocated that the control by the banks (nationalized in 1983) of nonfinancial corporations should be abolished. As a result, many companies controlled by Bank Hapoalim and Bank Leumi were sold to private owners.

## The government's role in privatization.

In the early 1990s, Israel had 159 state-owned enterprises. By 2023, in the wake of privatization, this number had shrunk to 70, most of them non-commercial. Most of the state-run enterprises that were not sold off were small and unsuitable for privatization. A number of large state-owned enterprises still remain, among them Israel Aerospace Industries, Israel Electric Corporation, Rafael Advanced Defense Systems, Mekorot, and Israel Post, some of which will be privatized in the future.

However, it was not easy to persuade the government to relinquish its commercial and political power and influence. The privatizations were a complex process, and required financial and corporate maturity, as well as agreements with employees, security officials, regulators, and the Securities Authority.

The privatization of the government's state-run enterprises did not result from any immediate and pressing financial problems, as was the case with the Jewish Agency and Histadrut. Rather, the privatizations were part of a greater ideological shift. Israel had come to the conclusion that governments were not suited to owning and managing commercial companies and should limit themselves to policy and regulatory oversight.

The new reality that emerged after the 1985 Economic Stabilization Plan introduced new economic concepts into the dictionary of economic discourse—among them "privatization," "sectoral reform," "regulation," and "deregulation," as well an old concept that gained new life— "competition." Privatization was a tangible expression of the shift that had occurred in Israel's economic regime, from the collective-public ideal to an individual-business worldview, from state intervention to private ownership.

Today, after some three decades of privatization, there is no thought of changing course, despite the doubts that have arisen about the viability of "privatization at any cost," as part of a wider debate about the role of the state in the economy.

The privatizations to date have been accomplished mainly by selling control of state-owned commercial enterprises to private owners, and by strengthening the capital market by issuing shares, including controlling interests, on the stock exchange. The time it took to sell a particular company depended on how easy it was to regulate the industry in which it operated. The more complex the regulation of a particular industry and market, the longer the privatization process took—in some cases, as long as 30 years.

Privatization also included the establishment of mechanisms for building public infrastructures and their management by private concessionaires, whereby the concessionaire builds the infrastructure and operates for a fixed period, after which the infrastructure reverts to the state, "BOT model. Route 6—the Trans-Israel Highway"—was one of the first such BOT infrastructure projects.

In later years, privatization expanded to include granting licenses to private operators to operate services in new areas (e.g., cable and satellite television), or to allow private companies to operate alongside public entities (e.g., by granting licenses to private schools).

In special cases, the government has preserved key national interests by holding golden shares, which give the holder veto powers over any changes to the company's charter, or entering into agreements to protect vital interests, measures used in the privatizations of Zim Integrated Shipping Services Ltd., Bezeq, El Al, and Israel Chemicals Ltd.

## The Stages of Privatization

There were four stages in the government's privatization process:

> (A) "Simple" privatization—i.e., the privatization of state-owned commercial enterprises operating in competitive markets.
> (B) "Complex" privatization—i.e., the privatization of monopolistic state-owned infrastructure enterprises, which first required comprehensive sectoral reform (communications, transportation, energy, and water). The government adopted a rule of "regulation before privatization" in order to prevent state-owned monopolies being sold off "as is" to a private buyer, which would have simply transformed them into private monopolies and made it difficult to implement sectoral reform.
> (C) Privatization by outsourcing.
> (D) Privatization of social services.

## "Simple" Privatization

In the late 1980s, the government, which had little experience with privatization, hired an international investment house to advise it on how to go about implementing this new and unfamiliar process. The government started with "simple" privatizations, i.e., privatizing state-owned enterprises operating in competitive markets. In these cases, transferring control to a private buyer did not require broad sectoral reform and fundamental changes to how the industry operated.

## "Complex" Privatization—Regulation before Privatization

"Complex" privatizations involved the sale of state-owned monopolies, where simply transferring control from the state to a private owner would have meant transforming a public monopoly into a private monopoly. The privatization of state-owned communications, transportation, water, and energy enterprises required extensive reforms, which enabled the privatization of Bezeq, the oil refineries, El Al and Zim.

In addition to necessary reforms, privatization relies on extensive regulation, and, in special cases where national interests need to be protected, special agreements or golden shares, as mentioned above. These regulations also allowed for the privatization of oil refineries, as well as the sale of power plants, the granting of concessions to desalination companies, and the privatization of public transport lines.

The regulations implemented prior to privatization were designed to prevent the creation of private monopolies, whose prices would remain artificially high, and whose streamlining would enrich the private owner and not the consumer. If these industry sectors had not been regulated prior to privatization, the new private owners would have opposed regulation, on the grounds that it would violate the property rights they had purchased.

Regulation entails organizing the sector for competition or for a combination of competition and supervision. The goal is to create order with clear rules anchored in legislation and regulations which allow the government to supervise the company. The new owners of a privatized company need to know what the laws and regulations will be in the industry in which they are operating, so that privatization can benefit the economy and the consumer. Good regulation safeguards consumer interests and helps maintain cheap, good quality goods and services, or inputs for businesses competing with manufacturers in Israel or abroad.

A natural monopoly is a situation where there is no economic viability for a competitor to enter the market, due to high threshold levels (e.g., electricity transmission). In these cases, the correct order of action was determined to be first industry sector regulation, then establishing regulatory rules, and then and only then, privatization.

Privatization is not intended to achieve a high return for governments seeking to maximize their assets. Rather, governments need to ensure that markets operate properly and that consumers receive services at a reasonable price and under appropriate conditions.

## Outsourcing

Outsourcing is a form of privatization where private contractors are hired to carry out tasks on behalf of the government, at a cheaper cost than if the government had undertaken the work itself. Under this form of privatization, there is no transfer of state authority to a private entity. Since the 1990s, Israel's government ministries and offices have outsourced various jobs, such as cleaning, security guarding and other security services, as well as professional consulting activities that used cheaper contract staff instead of employing staff directly. In some cases, the outsourced workers' employment terms and conditions were compromised, and the power of workers' organizations was weakened. This practice has harmed wages and job security for a number of employees, some of whom are from disadvantaged backgrounds, thus provoking economic and moral debate.

Fierce debate has also developed over whether to outsource public services in coercive settings, such as prisons. In the early 2000s, the state issued a tender for the construction of a private prison. The issue reached Israel's Supreme Court, in 2009, which ruled that incarceration was a sovereign duty that must remain the sole responsibility of the state. Clearly, prisons are coercive settings that are directly responsible for the well-being of prisoners.

Another form of outsourcing involves special privatization mechanisms that were created for infrastructure. Concessions were granted under a (BOT) model in cases like Highway 6 and Highway 23 (the "Carmel Tunnels"), or under a private financing initiative PFI model, as in the case of Route 431 or the fast lane to Tel Aviv, where the government pays the concessionaire for the use of the road according to an agreed-upon formula. This model has also been used to fund desalination facilities, power plants, and in the privatization of the Israel Air Force's flight school, as well as other services that do not involve the transfer of state authority.

## Privatizing Social and Welfare Services

Israel's wave of privatizations began from an assumption that governments are not best suited to run commercial enterprises. Later, this assumption expanded and shifted to incorporate the idea that governments are also not best suited to run social services. Thus, government social services were transferred to the third sector and, in some cases, even to the private sector. Supporters of these moves argued that there was no advantage to having the state-run social services, and that it was more appropriate for the state to focus on policy, budgeting, and supervision, and leave service provision to charities and companies that specialize in this kind of work. However, since ultimate responsibility for these services still rests with the government, transparent regulation was required (which in hindsight proved to be poor, due to a lack of personnel, budget, and oversight.

The privatization of welfare services began in the late 1990s, when the state began to outsource this work to the third sector. Hundreds of social welfare charities began to run services ranging from elderly care to care for at-risk youth. This privatization trend increased during the 2010s, when the government began also outsourcing social services commercial companies providing comparable services. These companies were seeking to expand into new fields and finding social service provision on the grounds that welfare, education, social services provision—welfare, education, and increasingly costly healthcare—represents a market worth billions of shekels and offers lucrative opportunities for commercial activity.

There are two opposing schools of thought as to whether the privatizations preceded and helped create Israel's strong third sector, or whether it was the existing presence of a strong third sector that allowed the privatizations to happen. Some argue that the first scenario is true—i.e., that the third sector developed and became stronger as a result of the privatization of government services. That is, when the state stopped providing particular services, the third sector had to expand to fill the vacuum this created. Opposing this is the argument that social service privatization was only possible in the first place due to the existence of a robust and thriving third sector, which, after first gaining legitimacy as an alternative service provider, then encouraged the state to privatize social services. Whatever the case, there is no doubt that the shrinking of the welfare state has increased the power of Israel's third sector.

In terms of education provision, a lack of state budget has resulted in the growth of a "grey" education sector, in which parents' organizations and private companies began to sell private education services. Opponents of private education have argued that the wealthier and more powerful local authorities (mainly in Israel's richer coastal plain) benefit more from this development than the poorer, less powerful local authorities of the country's geographical periphery. In terms of healthcare, private medicine has expanded with the establishment of private hospitals alongside a "shadow economy" in which patients make under-the-table payments to doctors in public hospitals for private services.

One dilemma of privatization concerns the cost of government services, which are often more expensive than private ones and usually of better quality. This is a complex issue to measure, but central to the quality of service to consumers and the significance of privatization.

## Summary

Privatization is an ideological process stemming from a neoliberal worldview. The debate between the proponents of privatization in Israel and those who oppose it has been going on for many years.

Those who support privatization believe that it increases economic efficiency, since the free market is a more efficient business mechanism than the state. Private businesses can carry out reforms relatively easily, since they are not limited by staffing policies. They argue that the government is constrained by powerful labor committees and political interests, while privatization allows private companies to compete, instead of state monopolies, and competition encourages price reduction. Further, they contend that private companies generally provide better and cheaper services, since improving services increases demand and thus generates more profit, and that privatization reduces government spending, which in turn lowers the budget deficit and enables tax cuts. According to proponents of privatization, a modern state cannot afford to have welfare systems and state-run enterprises as they did in the past, since globalization increases international competition and makes it harder for state-run enterprises, which in the past enjoyed government protections at the expense of higher taxation, to operate efficiently.

The supporters of privatization also claim that government involvement in the economy harms democracy, violates civil rights, and makes individuals passive and dependent. Reducing state intervention encourages individuals to act for themselves and cooperate with others, and encourages volunteerism and civil society, contributing to democracy and freedom.

On the other hand, the opponents of privatization argue that it harms service provision, in particular to disadvantaged populations that cannot afford to pay for high-quality social services. To its opponents, privatization risks concentrating capital and ownership of infrastructure in the hands of a few individuals. They argue that privatization harms employment and working conditions as a result of efficiency and cost-cutting processes, which include layoffs, and because of the reduction in the power of workers' committees and the transition to "individual contracts." According to privatization's detractors, privatization exacerbates economic disparities because of layoffs, the increase in cost of social services, and the damage it causes to the working and lower middle classes. The wealthier classes, on the other hand, enjoy the fruits of the development of the capital market, tax cuts, and the ability to receive good, paid-for services. Furthermore, they argue that privatization harms national security interests by selling natural resources and infrastructure (electricity, transport networks, and communications) to foreign companies. They also believe that privatization erodes desirable values and norms, including social solidarity and cohesion, encourages egoism and individualism, and increases the power of a small number of wealthy capitalists, who are not elected by the public and are not obligated to it. It harms the civil rights of the poor, because it prevents them from receiving social services to which they are entitled, and harms democracy.

While it may not be clear which, if either approach, is completely right, the story of the history of Israel's economy over the past four decades is instructive. Undoubtedly, the country has thrived economically, and people's standard of living has risen dramatically.

However, the government has not been an effective regular and supervisor of social services, and many of those services were poor quality, harming the weakest links in society.

## Notes

1. As a member of the Forum in its early years, I can personally testify to how important privatization was to the Americans.
2. See: The Committee for Examining the Implementation and Consequences of Introducing a System for the Mass Distribution of Government-Owned Shares to the Public (the Options Plan), February 1995 (Brodet Committee).

# 21

# Market Regulation

The story of regulation in Israel is relatively new, as regulation rather than intervention started characterizing the government's economic approach only following the 1985 Stabilization Plan. Regulations gradually took on greater importance in the 1990s in Israel, as reforms expanded and privatization grew. In the early 21st century, some began to think that perhaps regulation itself had become an impediment to Israel's economy. As important as regulation is for the economy, it can also impose burdens, and a healthy balance must always be sought.

Throughout the world, market regulation involves the control and oversight of certain market activities by government bodies. It includes both legislative activity (undertaken by the legislative authority) and executive activity (undertaken by the administrative authorities), which, together, regulate and supervise specific activities by means of intervention and sanctions. Regulations and laws are essential to the operation of free markets, since without them, free markets cannot really operate effectively, as recognized as far back as Adam Smith in the 18th century.

Market regulation involves limiting the freedoms of individuals and organizations. It both serves and is evaluated in accordance with the goals it seeks to achieve through defined processes. Therefore, regulation should constantly be evaluated to ascertain whether it is beneficial and efficient, and whether the regulator is aware of the costs imposed on the regulated.

The main obstacles facing market regulation in every country where it is introduced are powerful special interest groups in the private and public sectors. Since market regulation is intended to serve the public interest, it needs to be transparent, high-quality, and fair. The aim of good regulation is to protect consumers, workers, and taxpayers by preventing abuses of economic power by the commercial sector and harm to free competition. Pro-market regulation ensures fair competition, as well as public health, safety, welfare, and well-being. Nonetheless, in democracies, economic policy and regulation face pressure from powerful groups. Regulating the market is an ongoing struggle that necessitates the appointment of qualified people and regular monitoring of the regulators' work.

In general, there are several situations in which government intervention in the market is justified:

***Market failure.*** While the aspiration is that free markets are self-regulating and will result in optimal output (the so-called "invisible hand" of the market), there are situations in which this is not the case. Even free market loyalists, who advocate minimal or zero state intervention in the market, recognize the need to regulate economic activity in situations where there is no free competition—i.e., market failure. In such cases, regulation is designed to prevent the formation of monopolies, where a single company controls such a large market share that it harms fair competition and causes lower output than a competitive market situation. Similarly, regulation is intended to prevent cartels, where a group of companies coordinate prices or tactics among themselves such as to discriminate against other companies or consumers. Regulation does not always result in the dismantling of unnatural monopolies but is sometimes content with merely supervising them.

***Asymmetric information.*** Asymmetric information occurs when one party to a transaction has greater material knowledge than another. In certain cases, this can be harmful, such as if manufacturers conceal information about their products, consumers have no fair way to compare prices and ensure free competition. The capital market is very sensitive to asymmetric information. In healthcare, for example, asymmetry stems from disparities in medical knowledge between service providers (doctors) and clients (patients). For this reason, regulation is required in professions where the seller has far greater expertise than the buyer to ensure that consumers can trust their providers. Therefore, there is licensing in professions such as medicine, law, accounting, and engineering.

***Externalities.*** Externalities arise in situations where it is difficult to attribute the outcome to those who are performing the activity and to measure their part in it. For example, if car drivers had to pay for the air pollution their cars created, car usage might change, or car manufacturers might change how cars are built.

Externalities can be positive. Research and development indirectly boost the whole economy, and therefore direct budgetary support for R&D is beneficial. The government intervenes because it views this as "distributive justice"—transferring money from one set of citizens to another for social reasons.

***Labor market intervention.*** In Israel, the Minimum Wage Law guarantees a minimum income for employees. The Working Hours Law is designed to protect employees' well-being. Restrictions on the employment of foreign workers are intended to protect the interests of local workers.

***Paternalistic regulation***, for example, can be found when the state stipulates that motorcycle riders must wear a helmet because it believes that citizens do not assess risk properly.

***Public good.*** This involves ensuring the provision of public services that are used by an entire society, such as security and the establishment and operation of public parks, roads, and more. Regulation of cellular telephony is intended to ensure cooperation between competing companies, to create uniform rates for dialing between cellular networks at connectivity rates (transferring the service provider between the cellular companies).

***Price controls.*** These are a means of controlling monopolies, based on the idea of fair profit at a price that allows the monopoly to profit but not to exploit its power and charge exorbitant prices to make excessive gains.

## Regulatory Dilemmas

A regulation is positive only if its costs are less than the those of its implementation; similarly, a regulation is negative when the regulator serves a certain political interest or target audience (such as protecting farmers or industrialists). Sometimes the intention of a regulation is good, but the bureaucracy involved causes damage.

Strict regulation of a particular market or industry does not necessarily result in an efficient outcome, or an outcome that is in the best interests of the consumer. There are cases where partial competition in a market is preferable to arbitrary regulatory rulings. Regulatory capture—the tendency of regulatory agencies to come to be dominated by the special interests they regulate, rather than public interest—reduces the effectiveness of the regulatory activity. Regulators are not necessarily aware that they are biased in favor of the industry or interests they are charged with regulating and believe that they are serving the public good. For such reasons, in 2021, Israel decided to appoint a "super regulator" to oversee the regulators, prevent regulatory capture, and assess the impact of regulation.

Businesses do not like regulation that prevents them from maximizing their profits. It is sometimes necessary to examine whether a regulation established in the past is still relevant today, or whether it will remain relevant in the future. A distinction must be made between regulation and bureaucracy. Because regulation is essential it must not be carried out negligently, which would lead to the dangerous conclusion that regulations are ineffective and that the market would be better off without them.

Regulation supervises the rules of the market out of concern for public well-being and safety. However, regulation is steeped in countless laws, procedures, and notices, some of which are difficult to understand. This bureaucracy must be reduced if we are to ensure that the benefits of regulation outweigh the costs. Regulation should be well-defined, and any bureaucracy around it should be examined to avoid creating unnecessary burdens.

Entrepreneurs and businesses look for ways to meet consumer demand and make a profit. The market is "cruel" like nature, and any business that fails to meet consumer demand will be devoured by a successful competitor that offers a better and cheaper product. According to this worldview, artificially intervening in the market therefore has consequences, the price of which is sometimes hidden or unpredictable, and "payment" is sometimes delayed. Regulation can sometimes lead to over-zealous and excessively rigorous supervision, arising from a lack of faith in market forces and the desire to protect consumers or investors. However, this can undermine the normal functioning of the market and competition. Indeed, excessive government action can often prove to be a prescription for failure. There are also cases where politicians use regulation to show the public that they are "doing something." All this harms the smooth operation of the market and competition. The opponents of regulation also argue that the role of the state is to remove barriers and ensure competition in the commercial sector, and that governments should focus on providing high-quality, low-cost public services—education, security, welfare, health, energy, water, and communications.

Proper regulation must balance the interests of the consumer with those of the industry or market being regulated, by striking a balance between the consumer, who wants to pay as little as possible, and businesses, that want to make as much profit as possible. Regulation that neutralizes incentives for private investment is ineffective and harmful, in the same way that state intervention that protects failed businesses and saves their owners from bankruptcy is harmful. Risk and chance are the lifeblood of a market economy. Regulation cannot replace them, but rather correct the market when they fail.

## Regulation since the 1990s

Regulation is an aid to competition and must be high-quality, proportionate, effective, and transparent, while exercising sufficient enforcement to be a deterrent. As regulatory activity increased in Israel, opposition to it also grew. Opponents of regulation have argued that it is not a cure-all for commercial and economic failure, but that it is actually the disease. According to them, markets have a natural equilibrium, and the market forces that dictate the everyday decisions of billions of consumers worldwide are governed by natural economic laws.

Regulation in Israel developed alongside privatization, as the country transitioned from a centralized, public economy to a competitive free market that operated both locally and globally. Regulation was designed to address three issues—to impose price controls in areas where competition was not possible (natural monopolies or complex industry structure), to maintain the stability of industry, and protect the consumer in terms of safety, public health, and the environment.

When establishing regulation, there is a built-in tension inherent between lowering prices for the public and maintaining the stability of a company or industry. In finance—banking, insurance, and pensions—regulation limits "wild" competition that would harm stability. The wave of market reforms and privatizations that began in Israel during the 1990s saw an increase in regulation. New governmental authorities were established to regulate market sectors and existing bodies were strengthened and the laws under which they operated were updated.

In 2022, Israel had 209 regulatory bodies spread over many areas, employing a large number of staff in government authorities and supervised entities. A large industry has developed around regulation. The competitive and regulatory reforms that were introduced following the 1985 Economic Stabilization Plan improved how the markets operated, and reduced the areas of the market that were governed by monopolies. Regulation has become professional and meticulous. The government has adhered to its policy of "regulating industry before privatizing."

The debate in Israel over regulation is complex and has raged over the last few decades in the wake of the introduction of new legislation in the 1990s. Those who support reducing regulation in Israel have argued that, due to the size of the Israeli economy, it is not possible to create competition or multiple players in every industry, and it is better to allow competition between just a handful of companies, even if the scale of this competition is very small compared to other countries.

In 2016, an OECD report found that Israel has an excess of regulation that hampers growth, and that the lack of coordination between regulators burdens businesses. At the same time, the government violates the basic principles of proper regulation, namely clarity, simplicity, and stability over time. Following the 2016 OECD report, Israel established a five-year plan tasking government ministry with reducing the burden of bureaucracy by 25 percent. The government pledged to streamline regulation by using the OECD's Regulatory Impact Assessment (RIA), which uses a systemic approach to critically assess the positive and negative effects of proposed and existing regulations. Under this evidence-based approach, the government must examine the need for intervention, evaluate non-regulatory alternatives, and estimate costs. The financial regulators were excluded from this process.

In 2018, a regulatory branch was established in which government ministries committed to assessing the impact of regulation using the RIA approach for each new regulation. There has been slow progress in assimilating the RIA culture.

In 2022, the "super regulator" unit was established, with which government ministries are expected to consult regarding regulation, and which will check that business needs are set according to consumer need and regulatory transparency, and that bureaucratic costs will be based on the standards of other OECD countries.

Israel, which has made a shaky transition from intense government intervention to a free market, remains embroiled in a political and ideological debate between the proponents of government regulation, and neoliberal currents that oppose it. Those supporting regulation believe that it is required to ensure the functioning of the market, since market failures necessitate regulation in order to benefit the consumer. Adherents of a free market, especially neoliberals, decry intervention as being harmful to the market, arguing that market regulation harms consumers. They reject regulation just as they oppose the welfare state and are in favor of widespread privatization.

According to their "revealed preference," the majority of the Israeli public wants to live in a country with a (controlled) government system and a welfare state. During the coronavirus pandemic, the public called for government intervention, some of which remained in place even after the crisis. The debate is not over.

# 22

# The Markets after the 1985 Economic Stabilization Plan

## 1986–1996

Compared to the "lost decade" preceding the 1985 Economic Stabilization Plan, the period from 1986–1996 saw far-reaching market and economic reforms that greatly changed the way Israel's economy functioned. The hyperinflation crisis was still fresh in public memory, and the unity governments of 1984–1990 gave political backing to economic reform. The reforms continued during Yitzhak Shamir's premiership (1990–1992) and gathered steam under Yitzhak Rabin's second government (1992–1995), which was resolute in making economic and social changes in order to boost the development of a market economy, accelerate privatization and Israel's participation in globalization, expand the welfare state, and advance the peace process.

While still recovering from the hyperinflation crisis, Israel absorbed two large waves of immigration from the former Soviet Union and Ethiopia, built a high-tech industry, coped with the First Intifada, and made regional political agreements with the Palestinians and Jordan that served as leverage to reopen the economic ties with Eastern Europe, Asia, and Africa that had been severed following the Yom Kippur War. The events of this formative period would influence Israel economically and socially for many years to come. It was during this time that Israel enacted a number of key market reforms that helped it transition toward a competitive economy. In particular, the exposure of the domestic market to competing imports was completed, the foreign exchange market was reformed, and the financial and capital markets were liberated after four decades of nationalization. A free market developed, as the reforms bolstered the private and commercial sectors. Significantly, it was during this period that Israel's high-tech industry developed.

These crucial years also saw significant reforms of Israel's higher education system, with the establishment of new colleges that made higher education accessible to a wider cross-section of the population. A state health law was enacted that created a stable financial and competitive infrastructure for the healthcare system. These and other reforms, together with the injection of educated immigrants from the former Soviet Union, enriched Israel with skilled human capital, which had a positive effect on the country's economy and society.

Macroeconomic, fiscal, and monetary policy shifts brought Israel closer to the standards accepted in developed Western economies. The most prominent expression of the processes and changes that the economy had undergone was the A- rating given to Israel by the international rating agencies in November 1995, reflecting Israel's strength in the international capital market.

The cancellation of the IAI Lavi fighter jet project in 1987 was an important test of budget rationalization in the area of defense. Another important event came in 1991, with Israel's unilateral decision to lower import tariffs across the board. The government, on the initiative of the Ministry of Finance, opened the economy to imports from countries with which Israel did not have free trade agreements, including China. Import tariffs dropped by dozens of percentage points to around 8–12 percent. This move streamlined Israeli industry and opened the door to inexpensive imported goods, which benefitted consumers.

The exposure of Israel's manufacturing industry and markets to imports was spread over an entire decade, and allowed factories time to organize, train, and retrain laid-off workers. The fact that the economy grew in the 1990s helped smooth the successful implementation of this move and paved the way for a new economic structure centered on high tech and business services. Factories producing textiles and clothing, simple electronic goods, and plastics ceased to operate in the face of competition from Asia.

Toward the end of the 1980s, the economy experienced another change in the form of an influx of foreign workers into the labor market in need of inexpensive workers. Their numbers swelled in the wake of the 1993 Oslo Accords due to an increase in terrorism that prevented Palestinians from working in Israel.

## 1997–2009

The first government of Binyamin Netanyahu (1996–1999) continued the reforms set in motion by the previous administrations. The Ehud Barak administration (1999–2001) was predominantly concerned with political matters, rather than economic policy. However, in 2001–2003, Israel was catapulted into an acute economic crisis as a result of the outbreak of Second Intifada and the wave of severe violence that followed the breakdown of the Camp David talks. The crisis sparked a significant slowdown in economic growth and capital flight, exacerbated by the dot-com crisis. Unemployment rose to 10.2 percent' while per capita GDP decreased in real terms—a rare phenomenon in Israel.

In 2001–2005, two successive governments of Ariel Sharon addressed this general crisis with an economic policy dubbed "Economic Defensive Shield." The policy was first implemented by Minister of Finance Silvan Shalom in 2002 and continued by his successor. The sudden economic crisis had reawakened an old bogeyman—the foreign exchange reserve deficit—forcing Israel to turn to the United States for guarantees of $9 billion to shore up its foreign currency reserves and prevent shocks and capital flight. Netanyahu, pursued a neoliberal capitalist policy that aimed to change the very essence and structure of Israel's economy and society. It accelerated Israel's transition from a public to a market economy, provoking considerable public debate. Netanyahu's policy was based on the arguments that "high taxes are not good for the economy," "big government is a problem,". Israel's welfare state shrank as child benefits, unemployment benefits, and income support were slashed, with the aim of encouraging welfare recipients to join the workforce. The policy also shrunk the public sector, with Netanyahu often referring to the parable of the thin man (the private sector) carrying the fat man (the public sector). Taxes were cut on the assumption that they would "finance themselves" and accelerate growth. This despite the fact that studies have shown that there is no connection between tax cuts and growth. Pension rights under the old pension fund schemes were reduced and the government raised the retirement age from 65 to 67 for men and from 60 to 62 for women. The so-called Israeli "Wisconsin plan"—a welfare-to-work scheme based on an American program of the same name—was put in place with the aim of integrating people on a guaranteed minimum income into the workforce.

This period saw two more political and security events that impacted on Israel's economy: the disengagement from Gaza in 2005, and the Second Lebanon War of 2006, which, like the Second Intifada, damaged the lives of Israeli civilians due to the firing of rockets at population centers. The disengagement from Gaza did not bring peace to the region, and after the rise of Hamas in 2007, Gaza became a hostile and aggressive entity that threatened the lives of residents of the south and later the center of the country.

The Second Intifada increased the need to replace the cheap labor of Palestinian workers with foreign workers. In the mid-2000s, over half a million non-Israelis (including Palestinians) worked in Israel, about half of them illegally (i.e. without a permit)—a record number, which harmed poorer and disadvantaged Israeli populations.

## 2010–2019

Israel's increasingly strong economy meant that it was hardly affected by the global financial crisis of 2008–2009 and passed through this turbulent period relatively unscathed. The financial system remained stable due to its conservatism and effective regulation, and because it was able to draw on the lessons learned from previous crises. There was little effect on Israeli exports, largely due to the strength of Israeli high-tech.

In 2010, Israel joined the OECD, an achievement made possible by the results of the economic efforts and improvements made in the quarter century since the 1985 Economic Stabilization Plan. Israel now had a developed economy that maintained fiscal discipline and international openness, with a positive balance of payments, price stability, and a solid financial system. However, there were growing social disparities and inequalities. In July 2011, a cost-of-living crisis that impacted the middle classes sparked widespread public protests calling for "social justice" and "a new set of social and economic priorities." The protests were short-lived, ending when the government responded to a number of issues.

However, Israel had a per capita GDP (23rd place in the world) similar to that of the 1980s, in spite of the fact that the GDP per capita rose substantially due to a very significant increase in labor force participation because of moderate increase in productivity of about 11 percent. Meanwhile the GDP to national debt ratio shrunk from 75 percent at the start of the decade to around 60 percent in 2019, a result of economic policy and budgetary discipline.

The rise in social awareness and the needs of an innovative economy shone a light onto Israel's education system, which was struggling to provide an appropriate education that would enable children and young people to meet the demands of the changing economy. Meanwhile, housing was proving to be the Achilles heel of the economy, due to a 75 percent rise in house prices over this period.

During this period, Israel completed its shift to a post-industrial service economy. Exports of software services soared and there was an increase in foreign investments in the high-tech sector. The government initiated offshore natural gas programs, first the Mari B/Yam Tethys reservoir and later the Leviathan and Tamar gas fields, which cut imports of coal and oil by billions of dollars and reduced air pollution and greenhouse gas emissions. The balance of payments improved as a result of the discovery of natural gas and because of foreign investments in high tech. The doubling of Israel's high-tech exports created a permanent surplus in the balance of payments and increased foreign currency reserves. Israel shifted from being a net borrower to a net lender.

The period also saw several important reforms, among them the Centralization Law, the reforms proposed by the Sheshinski Committee, which was formed to advise on what tax the government should levy on companies producing natural gas, and Resolution 922, a five-year roadmap to accelerate the economic inclusion of the Arab population, which had a budget of NIS 15 billion. However, these reforms did not generate enough momentum to allow the Israeli economy to take a leap forward on the international stage. Inequality remains a key issue that demands thorough attention, mainly in the ultra-Orthodox and Arab communities, in particular because the ultra-Orthodox are a rapidly growing population.

## Economic Outcomes

The changes in macroeconomic policy and reforms since the mid-1980s have resulted in an improvement in the performance of the Israeli economy. Openness to the world has advanced Israel's economic position in the international marketplace. The economic recovery that began the 1990s took place amid the enormous challenge of the mass immigration from the former Soviet Union (over a million immigrants), two Intifadas, the Gulf War, the Second Lebanon War, the disengagement from Gaza and military operations in Gaza, and significant changes in Israeli society.

Israeli companies have integrated into international capital markets and are traded on leading stock exchanges around the world. High tech has become an important engine of growth and has strengthened the economy with significant achievements in technological innovation, R&D, the proportion of people employed in high tech industries, and the number of patents registered by Israelis. In 2004, the rapid growth in high tech exports allowed Israel's current account balance to come out of the red for the first time in its history, and to have a surplus by 2006. The shift in external debt as a percentage of GDP from a net of 87 percent in 1984 to about 45 percent in 2021, is testament to the enormous improvements in the external state of the economy.

Israel's accession to the OECD confirmed its place among the top of the world's developed nations. Yet alongside its economic achievements, the shadows of Israel's social problems are threats looming over its society and economy. Since the 2000s, there has been a trend toward unbalanced growth that has created a dual economy. While there has been rapid growth and high productivity in the high-tech industry, where the economy has a relative advantage, there has also been a fall-off and low productivity in traditional industries. Israel's knowledge-intensive industries benefitted greatly from globalization—their sales spread to expanding markets hungry for high tech products and services. Simultaneously with the expansion of Israel's export markets, companies exploited new avenues to purchase inexpensive inputs from imports that increased the competitiveness of producers. At the same time, however, Israel's traditional industries were harmed by globalization. Some were unable to retain their export markets and were not equipped to deal with competing imports and lost the local markets as well. The key to creating competitive advantages in a global market lies in increasing productivity and creating innovation in processes or products.

The dual economy points to two serious problems. First, low growth in traditional industries has left Israel languishing among the bottom rankings of OECD countries and has hampered the country from producing sufficient output to raise living standards, provide adequate public social services, and finance security needs in line with the country's existential problems. Second, income disparities have deepened. Although Israel had previously been one of the most egalitarian countries in the world, it now has one of the highest levels of income disparity of all the OECD countries.

Inequalities create social unrest, harm the delicate fabric of belonging and social cohesion, and have a negative impact on growth. There is a huge disparity between the macroeconomic strength of Israel's economy and household inequalities in terms of early years education, housing, transportation, and health. Improving the growth and productivity of Israel's traditional industries would prevent the polarization of the dual economy and help reduce disparities by increasing the incomes of the poorest members of society through employment rather than taxation and state benefits.

# PART FIVE

# TOWARDS A CIVILIAN ECONOMY

## 23

## The Soviet Aliyah

The Soviet Aliyah began with the opening of the borders of the Soviet Union in the last quarter of 1989, as a result of Soviet President Mikhail Gorbachev's policies of *glasnost* and *perestroika*. While the exodus of the Soviet Union's Jews had begun back in the 1970s and 1980s, only a minority of those who left during those years had chosen to immigrate to Israel, with most preferring the United States or Western Europe. Jews began to immigrate en masse to Israel in the 1990s a result of a request made by Yitzhak Shamir's government to the United States in 1987 that Washington refuse to grant free entry of Soviet Jews into the United States. Israel accepted Soviet immigrants willingly and without conditions, despite the immediate difficulties inherent in absorbing them. By that time, around 200,000 Jews from the Soviet Union had already immigrated to the United States. Germany was also open to Soviet Jews, even in the 1990s, but by that time, most preferred to immigrate to Israel.

The first, during 1989–1999, saw around 825,000 former Soviet citizens immigrate to Israel. The second wave, from 2000–2009, consisted of around 165,000 immigrants, with 200,000 more arriving in the third wave in 2010–2022. In comparison, some 150,000 Soviet Jews had immigrated to Israel during the 1970s and 1980s. The immigrants who arrived in the first wave had a distinct Soviet mentality, conditioned by decades of Communist rule, whereas by the time of the third wave, the newcomers were already much more liberal and westernized. In the short term, the increase in Israel's population caused by the Soviet Aliyah gave rise to a number of difficulties, but in the longer term, the mass immigration was positive both for the newcomers and Israeli society in general.

The Soviet and post-Soviet immigrants arrived in Israel with ambitions, motivation, and a willingness to work. These immigrants were notable for their high levels of participation in Israel's workforce, and for the fact that around a third of adult immigrants were highly educated. As a result, Israel's workforce became the most educated in the world. The Soviet Aliyah created opportunities for Israel's economy, society, culture, politics, and government-religious relations.

When the Soviet Aliyah began, Israel had just emerged from a major economic crisis, which had had a severe impact on the functioning of its markets. It was in the midst of a recovery process that would transform it into a modern market economy, open to international trade. The Soviet Aliyah would provide the fuel for the flourishing of the burgeoning Israeli high-tech industry. The Soviet immigrants, including those who arrived in Israel as children or young people, acquired good Hebrew-language skills, integrating well into the labor market and higher education system. The Soviet immigrants gained a reputation of having a high work ethic and a resilient character. The Soviet Aliyah brought an influx of doctors, engineers, scientists, and musicians, who, realizing that they would have difficulty integrating into Israel's professional job market due to age and language barriers, were willing to find work as street cleaners and security guards. On the whole, Soviet doctors and engineers found work relatively easily, because there was a demand for those professions. And despite attempts by the government to change how it absorbed immigrants and to invest more resources in their successful integration, many older Soviet immigrants in particular, who did not speak Hebrew and who found themselves in a country very different from the one in which they had lived all their lives, did struggle with integration.

Soviet immigrants had to contend with trying to obtain suitable employment and housing, secure nursing care for the elderly, and find financial solutions for those past retirement age who had not accrued pension rights in Israel.

The sudden population jump of some 20 percent meant that, beyond the challenges of providing these immigrants with housing and employment, the government also had to increase its investments in economic and social infrastructure, in particular in health and education. This came after years of stagnating investments in infrastructure and social services as a result of the hyperinflation crisis. Unsurprisingly, it posed a considerable economic and budgetary challenge. It was no small effort to absorb an additional population of this size, many of whom had arrived in Israel with very little money or property within just a decade. For comparison, the reunification of Germany, which was occurring at the same period, required no investment in language teaching or housing. Nonetheless, it yet encountered considerable difficulties and proved relatively more costly than Israel's absorption of Soviet Jews (and arguably, the unification of West and East Germany has not yet been fully completed).

Despite the recognition at the time that the Soviet Aliyah was a key event in Israel's history, there were nevertheless fears that the large expenditures required to absorb these immigrants, in particular given the precarious state of Israel's balance of payments, would lead to an economic backslide, one that loomed ominously in light of the fresh scars left by the recent economic crisis. The large upfront costs required to absorb the Soviet immigrants did not cause any backsliding from the achievements of the 1985 Economic Stabilization Plan and Israel's subsequent economic recovery. Moreover, the economy derived economic benefits from the immigrants, while the economic reforms were able to continue apace.

The fact that a large proportion of the Soviet immigrants had a higher education increased the number of skilled and educated workers in Israel's labor market. The demand for higher education overall increased, and, among other things, accelerated the reform of Israel's academic colleges that took place in 1993–1994. The value of the Soviet immigrants' human capital was estimated at around $25 billion, which boosted the economy, particularly the high-tech industry, which was growing apace. The combination of Israel's western academic education system with the new immigrants' Soviet academic background served as a power-multiplier that created technological advantages, particularly in terms of creativity and entrepreneurship. This combination of Western and Soviet technology and Israeli entrepreneurship helped revolutionize the country's nascent high-tech sector.

The government encouraged Israel's young high-tech industry to employ more Soviet immigrants with higher education, including by establishing the Yozma Fund to encourage venture capital funds, and tech incubators to give the immigrants experience in a Western and Israeli scientific and business environment. Israel's healthcare system benefitted from the influx of Soviet doctors, and the country's cultural life was enriched by an injection of classically trained musicians and other artists.

The first wave of Soviet immigrants proved yet again that Israel's economy ultimately flourishes with a large population infusion, which serves as an engine for economic growth and development. In Israel, the positive effect from the population growth came despite the fact that the Soviet Aliyah was not selective. The immigrants included older adults and people with disabilities, a phenomenon that is not seen in countries that restrict immigration based on age, health, education, and income. After several years, the Soviet immigrants had integrated effectively into the labor market.

## Immigrant Benefits—The "Absorption Basket"[1]

The enormous scale of the Soviet Aliyah required government intervention—something that ostensibly went against the grain of the policy of government withdrawal from economic interference in the wake of the 1985 Economic Stabilization Plan. Accommodating the Soviet Aliyah called for government intervention in the short term for it to then build the economy on new, long-term foundations.

It is important to note that, in 1988, there had been a shift in government policy regarding immigrant absorption. Previously, the government had maintained a policy of "direct absorption," which had included the provision of state services to new immigrants for a defined period following their arrival in Israel. This consisted, first and foremost, of providing new immigrants with accommodation in "absorption centers" (temporary living quarters designed especially for new arrivals). In 1988, this policy was amended in favor of providing all new immigrants with a "*sal klita*" ("absorption basket")—a package of financial benefits. The "absorption basket" policy was designed to provide new immigrants with a sum of money in their initial period in Israel, and then leave it to their discretion to determine their priorities according to their personal needs and wishes. This was a policy designed around individualism, rather than paternalism or collectivism. On its surface, this policy appeared not be suited to the Soviet immigrants, who had come from a Communist regime with a command economy. Most of them did not own property, had no experience of market economies or of a Western-style economic system.

In retrospect, however, the "absorption basket" turned out to be a great success, since it addressed the main issue facing both the government and the immigrants—housing. Nevertheless, the "absorption basket" system allowed them to purchase or rent housing on the free market. Some chose to use the money to secure housing for several households in the same apartment. The decision to defer to the immigrants' own preferences regarding how to use their "absorption basket" benefits helped solve the troubling issue of how to provide accommodation for large numbers of immigrants amid a housing shortage, by allowing them access to the market and find practicable solutions.

## The Labor Market

According to data published by Israel's Central Bureau of Statistics, the percentage of Soviet immigrants with a higher education was greater than that of Israel's general population, and a greater proportion of Soviet immigrants held advanced degrees (masters' degrees or doctorates) than did native-born Israelis. From 1981–1990, among all Israelis who had gone on to acquire a higher education, 77% of all graduates during this period achieved a bachelor's degree, 20 percent a master's degree, and 3 percent a doctorate. Among all Soviet immigrants who had achieved a higher education before immigrating, around 26 percent had obtained a bachelor's degree, 68 percent a master's degree, and 6 percent a doctorate, many in engineering and medicine.

The process of helping the Soviet immigrants acclimatize to the Israeli labor market so that they could find suitable employment took time. Employment difficulties among Soviet immigrants stemmed from several factors, including the inability of some to fully transfer their academic professional skills to Israel, language difficulties (in English as well as Hebrew), and the fact that they had to learn to adapt to Israeli working processes and methods. The immigrants needed a period of time for adaptation and adjustment in order to learn Hebrew, and they also had to possess a certain degree of willingness to accept work in jobs outside of their areas of expertise. As a result, some 66 percent of Soviet immigrants who held a higher degree managed to find work in their professions within the first three years of their immigration. The professional and occupational integration of Soviet immigrants began to stabilize after their first five years or so in Israel, and the process was considered successful, in that they achieved a sense that they were needed by their new society, which was important in helping to foster a sense of belonging.

Before the Soviet Aliyah, Israel's labor market had been in a state of equilibrium, with a relatively high level of employment. The large influx of new immigrants caused unemployment to rise to about 12 percent in 1992–1993, and this was accompanied by a drop in salaries. Meanwhile, the Soviet immigrants, who were disillusioned with communism, loathed anything that even slightly resembled this ideology, including membership in trade unions and labor strikes. The influx of these immigrants into the Israeli labor market weakened the trade unions, not least because most of these newcomers were content to work for lower wages than their Israeli counterparts, including in occupations outside of their professional fields.

However, the number of immigrants from the former Soviet Union who subsequently left Israel to live in other countries is high. Estimates suggest as of 2022, around, 150,000 had left, mostly young people who had immigrated to Israel to try to establish themselves there after facing economic and social difficulties in their home countries.

## American Loan Guarantees

Absorbing the Soviet immigration was an extremely costly exercise, and there was a real fear that Israel would encounter fresh fiscal problems just as it was emerging from a major economic crisis. Regardless, Israel did not hesitate to come to the aid of the Soviet immigrants, considering this to be one of the *raisons d'être* of the Jewish state. The Ministry of Finance debated the optimal way to absorb the first wave of Soviet immigrants while avoiding a crisis, drawing on lessons learned from the past. The key concern, beyond the fears of precipitating a fiscal crisis, was that Israel would experience a major problem with its balance of payments.

However, Israel knew that, beyond the immediate financial difficulties, there were many long-term economic benefits to the Soviet Aliyah, not least the import of a highly educated workforce that would contribute to economic growth and exports. But in the short-term, absorbing these immigrants came with high budgetary costs, and would only exacerbate Israel's foreign currency reserves problem. The government estimated that the foreign currency reserves deficit in the years following the Soviet Aliyah would amount to at least $25 billion. Israel believed that world Jewry would mobilize, as they had in the past, to help absorb the Soviet immigrants by contributing 10 billion dollars over five to ten years. However, there were also fears that these efforts would not be enough to offset the large amounts of foreign currency that the economy would need. The government concluded that the only way to bridge the short and longer-term deficits was with an injection of a large amount of foreign aid.

The government conducted its economic analysis of how to absorb the Soviet Aliyah as if it were any other economic project. It reasoned that, with the Aliyah, Israel would import human capital of great economic value, which would generate income by increasing exports and replacing imports in the long-term. Therefore, the reasoning went, the Aliyah could be financed with a loan that would pay for itself after some 15 or 20 years. The key question was, who would be willing to grant Israel such a large amount of credit?

Israel was still not able to raise large sums in the international capital market. It remained in the throes of recovering from a major economic crisis and had a high external debt of about 75 percent of GDP. The government's calculations showed that, above and beyond any assistance it might receive from the international Jewish community, it would need at least $10 billion in aid. Collateral for such a loan would be the growth of the economy based on the Soviet immigrants' human capital.

However, the foreign debt situation worried the Israeli government. The considerable assistance that Washington had already extended to Israel naturally led the Jewish state to turn to its American partner again to help with the challenges of Soviet Aliyah. The dilemma was whether Israel ought to ask for a grant, or for guarantees for issuing bonds on the capital market.

For economic and political reasons, Israel, then led by Prime Minister Yitzhak Shamir, chose to ask Washington to provide it with loan guarantees. Israel submitted a plan that estimated the foreign currency expenses required to absorb the Soviet Aliyah at $25 billion and requested guarantees for a loan of $10 billion. However, Israel's relations with the United States encountered difficulties as a result of the lack of a political process with the Palestinians and Israel's ongoing settlement activities in territories captured after the Six-Day War. President George H. W. Bush, and U.S. Secretary of State James Baker were willing to grant Israel loan guarantees only when it made political progress with the Palestinians.

In this regard, I had a personal, one might even say dramatic, experience. As head of Budget Department in the Ministry of Finance, I was tasked with promoting the program to absorb Soviet Aliyah and presenting the need for the guarantees before Congress. In September 1991, I traveled to Washington to present an economic analysis to Congress demonstrating the cost-benefit to Israel of absorbing the Soviet Aliyah without falling into a foreign currency reserves crisis. In one-on-one and group meetings with members of Congress and Senators, I set out Israel's strategy for absorbing the Aliyah, as well as the need for loan guarantees from the United States. However, to my misfortune, I found myself caught up in a stormy political battle. President George H. W. Bush was determined to link the loan guarantees that Israel was requesting with the political arrangements he wanted to establish in the wake of the U.S. victory in the First Gulf War. Bush sought to convene a conference with Israel and the Arab states in the Middle East to restart the Israeli-Palestinian peace process. After some time, the Israeli government, under Yitzhak Shamir, begrudgingly agreed to participate in the Madrid Conference co-sponsored by the United States and the Soviet Union in the fall of 1991. However, this did not help Israel receive the loan guarantees, which were only finally agreed on by President Bush in July 1992, with Yitzhak Rabin, who had been elected Prime Minister of Israel earlier that same year. Loan guarantees totaling $10 billion were eventually received in 1993 and helped Israel get through the 1990s without experiencing difficulties in its balance of payments. They also helped Israel absorb about a million Soviet immigrants overall, who fulfilled the expectations that their integration would allow Israel to grow and successfully repay its loans.

## Planning and Construction, Center and Periphery

When this wave of immigration began, there was no planned inventory of land or approved urban construction plans in Israel's cities. Although the "absorption basket" policy created temporary solutions, it was obvious that a permanent housing and infrastructure solution was needed.

Ariel Sharon, as housing minister, sought to take advantage of the Soviet Aliyah and increase residential construction in towns, strengthen Israel's peripheral regions, and change the demographic ratio between the center and the periphery. Construction in the development towns was easy and inexpensive, because of the availability of land and because approvals for construction programs could be obtained quickly. However, most employment opportunities were in Israel's central coastal plain. There was tension and debate among Israel's planners and the immigrants. The "absorption basket" provided the government with a short breathing space to plan residential construction, since the immigrants found accommodations in existing housing in the central coastal plain. The immigrants preferred employment in the central region and overcrowded accommodation over life in the peripheral areas, which offered better living conditions but no work. The immigrants, mostly small families, often rented a single apartment for several families and shared the rent between them.

The government's prodigious efforts to provide housing for the immigrants was successful, but mistakes were made, including in construction—which is evident on the ground. In 1990, the Ministry of Construction and Housing, led by Ariel Sharon, amended planning and construction procedures and sped up construction to meet was the burning challenge of the day. In doing so, they bypassed the procedures and strict planning processes typical of a modern, "normal" country in order to free up tens of thousands of dunams of agricultural land for residential construction.

Sharon's steps reflected the planning and construction principles that had characterized the 1950s, including population dispersion and Judaization of the land. And just as with these efforts in the 1950s, the outcomes of these new planning and construction projects also required corrections in later years. Despite attempts to act at the regional level, irreversible damage was caused by the approval of immature plans, the result of pressure at the time to address the housing problem.

Tensions arose between professional planners, who preferred to build in existing settlements (for reasons of employment opportunities for residents and the efficient use of existing infrastructure), versus those who advocated building in new settlements that were very distant from centers of employment, and which required the rapid construction of new infrastructure. In essence, this was a conflict between the aspiration to achieve national population dispersal goals versus the need to maintain sound planning considerations and high-quality construction.

The Soviet immigrants did not fully go along with the government's preferences regarding where they should settle. Some did move to peripheral areas, because the housing shortage offered them no other choice. Some of these immigrants would later move to towns and cities in the central coastal plain, where they were able to find employment opportunities that better matched their skills, improving their housing standards as they became more financially established. These trends created, among other things, a demand for housing over time (as people moved up the housing ladder), which affected housing demand and drove up prices in 2010–2019.

Those who continued to live in the development towns were mainly in areas close to big cities and employment centers. As a result, the Soviet Aliyah benefitted a small number of development towns that are located reasonably close to the central coastal plain. As these towns grew, they developed a critical mass of population that sparked the improvement of urban services and raised their socioeconomic status. However, in the dilemma between choosing employment or better housing, employment won, and even the enormous size of the Soviet Aliyah failed to produce any lasting significant change in the overall socioeconomic status of Israel's peripheral regions compared to the central coastal plain.

## Note

1. Israel's absorption basket refers to a package of benefits, resources, services, and other assistance the Israeli government provides to immigrants to Israel to help them integrate into the country.

# 24

# From Traditional Industry to High Tech

## The Dynamic Changes of Israeli Industry

Prior to Israeli statehood, industrial plants had been built in British Mandatory Palestine, but widespread industrialization really took place only in the 1950s, after the Israeli government created a broad import-substituting, labor- and capital-intensive industrial sector based on simple technologies.

Rapid industrialization meant that in the 1960s and 1970s, a quarter of Israel's workforce were employed in manufacturing. In the 1970s and 1980s, Israel adopted the technologies and principles of the Third Industrial Revolution (also known as the Digital Revolution), first in its defense industries and later in its civilian industries. Modern equipment, the latest machinery, and advanced working methods meant that Israeli industry was able to compete in the domestic market even after its exposure to imports and the expansion of industrial exports in the 1980s. From the 1990s, with Israel's free trade agreements with the European Union and United States reflecting a new policy of increased openness to foreign trade, Israeli industry became more efficient, focusing on areas where it enjoyed a comparative advantage.

At the start of the 21st century, Israel underwent the Fourth Industrial Revolution, also known as Industry 4.0, at the same time as other developed countries. This dramatic change saw the introduction of robotics and sophisticated information production processes. Meanwhile, since the turn of the 21st century, many of the industries that were built in the 1950s have been disappearing. The most prominent and symbolic of these is the textile industry. At the forefront of Israeli manufacturing in the 1950s–1970s, as time went on, the textile industry found itself simply unable to compete with Asia—a story that has played out in many developed countries.

The decline of traditional industries in Israel was partly the result of the composition and quality of the workforce, now best suited for export-oriented industries with high earning power. In particular, knowledge and technology-rich industries, which have benefitted from government aid in the form of R&D grants, venture capital funds, and the development of technology incubators for immigrants from the former Soviet Union, became engines for economic growth.

## The Growth of Israeli High Tech

The growth of Israel's high-tech sector and Israeli innovation was sparked by the recommendations of the Katzir Committee for the formulation of a national science policy in 1971, which called for government ministries to each appoint a chief scientist. Following this recommendation, in 1974, Minister of Trade and Industry and former IDF Chief of General Staff Haim Bar Lev appointed Yitzhak Ya'akov, the IDF's head of defense R&D, as chief scientist at the Ministry of Trade and Industry. In his new role, Ya'akov worked to implement R&D in Israel's civilian industries. Lagging behind Israel's defense industries, these were slow to introduce computers and electronics, let alone incorporate R&D or innovation into their work practices.

By this time, Israel's defense, were already involved in advanced R&D. These activities had intensified after the 1967 Six-Day War, in response to the French embargo on the supply of offensive weapons to Israel[1], a move that would accelerate the development of Israel's knowledge-rich defense industries. At the same time, individual private entrepreneurs developed a number of R&D-based companies, a trend that also helped establish new knowledge-based industries in Israel, alongside independent and original R&D. The Discount Investment Corporation[2], founded in 1961, was the first private investment company to invest in Israeli entrepreneurs.

In the 1970s, Electronic Industries, Elbit Systems, Scitex and Elscint became the first Israelis companies to adopt R&D as a pioneering pursuit for the civilian sector. In 1971, Elscint became the first Israeli company to have its shares issued on NASDAQ, an early signal of Israel's strong technological prowess and a vital link to the American capital market and venture capital funds.

In 1982, the international chip giant Intel, which had already founded a development center in Israel in 1974, became the first foreign company to establish a manufacturing center in Jerusalem. The center, F8, was created with support from the Israeli government. Later joined by other similar centers established by other multinational tech firms, F8 -trained Israeli managers and engineers, many of whom would later become entrepreneurs and found their own start-up companies. Meanwhile, in

1977, the United States and Israeli governments established BIRD, the Israel-U.S. Binational Industrial Research and Development, the aim of which was to stimulate, promote, and support industrial R&D to benefit both the United States and Israel. BIRD was instrumental in establishing Israeli high tech.

The Israeli government's decision to provide financial backing for R&D in civilian high tech in the 1970s was an astute response to market failure—an inefficient allocation of resources—in this area. The considerable risks inherent in funding entrepreneurship and development mean that the overall economic benefits to the economy of Israel of funding R&D are far greater than any potential financial return to individual investors. Government funding for R&D reduced the risk for private entrepreneurs and investors to a level where it was feasible for them to support and realize initiatives. Government support for civilian R&D is not designed to enable every private entrepreneur to succeed—indeed, such an outcome would be impossible and illogical. Rather, by providing assistance to all entrepreneurs who meet the criteria, with the understanding that many will fail, the government can ensure that the overall return on investment to the high-tech sector will be sufficient to make up for individual failures.

While in the 1970s and 1980s, the government was an important source of financing to high-tech ventures, by the 1990s, the government began encouraging the creation of VC funds. Since then, VC funds have come to be the primary source of funding for high-tech ventures, with the government continuing to assist the riskiest and smaller startups with seed funding. By solving the problem of market failure by supporting the development of VC funds in Israel's knowledge industries, the government has been able to promote growth and widescale employment. The private sector determined which innovations would be developed, while the state supported innovation, absorbed part of the risk, facilitated large projects, and seeded new industries. Through this policy, the Israeli government has been, and continues to be able to successfully influence the integration of innovations into the economy.

The Soviet Aliyah of the 1990s brought tens of thousands of scientists, engineers, and technicians to Israel, who helped boost the growth of the high-tech sector. In response, the Israeli government expanded its incentives for the high-tech sector, including through the establishment of Yozma, a government initiative that helped encourage venture capital funds by building an infrastructure for them as a financial source for ventures based on commercial R&D. Thus, within just a few years, Yozma, as a government company,[3] succeeded in establishing an extensive venture capital market. This helped in launching startups that were successful in initial public offerings (IPOs) on the New York Stock Exchange and the NASDAQ and in obtaining investments from international corporations. Israel also established technology incubators for Soviet immigrants designed to help facilitate their integration into the civilian high-tech sector. In the 1990s, a creative and innovative ecosystem developed, which saw the establishment of a critical mass of R&D-based high-tech companies that helped catapult the Israeli economy to the top of global innovation. Meanwhile, in 2016, the Israel Innovation Authority (IIA) replaced the Office of the Chief Scientist, expanding the concept of innovation beyond the high-tech sector to the entire economy, including the public sector. Undoubtedly, the government has been a major player in shaping Israel's high-tech development.

Israel joined the high-tech revolution at an auspicious time. From the 1990s, high tech became an important engine of growth for the Israeli economy. A successful combination of Israel's entrepreneurial character, boldness and creativity, and its high number of technologically trained workers (including university and college graduates and veterans from the IDF's technological units, as well as highly-qualified and trained Soviet immigrants), made it possible to break through to the forefront of the global information and communications technology (ICT) industry. The decade between 2010 and 2019 saw a global leap forward in cyber tech, and by 2021, Israel accounted for about 10 percent of global cyber sales.

High tech is an almost unregulated industry in Israel that relies more on global demands and developments and less on domestic market needs. Israel's high-tech success has been documented by Dan Senor and Saul Singer in their well-known 2009 book *Startup Nation*.[4] Israel's "Startup Nation" brand, which was born in the 2000s, has since been challenged by other countries that also promote technological initiatives under the same concept. Israel has had to compete with these rivals for money, human resources, markets, and innovations.

By the 1990s, Israel had already experienced high-tech success in terms of IPOs and exits. This boosted the self-confidence of its young, entrepreneurial community, and served as a model for other entrepreneurs to follow. The emergence of the internet at the beginning of the decade changed the rules of the game, leaving traditional media behind in culture and tourism (one of the first sectors affected by the growth of the internet) as well as many areas of personal, social, and economic life. Israeli high tech was able to integrate successfully into this brave new world, with the chat software firm ICQ being Israel's first major tech exit in 1997.

The weight of high tech in Israel's economy is increasing. In 2000, high-tech products represented about four percent of GDP. By 2022, this figure had grown to about 17 percent of GDP, around 20 percent of business products, and 45 percent of export. The number of Israelis employed in high tech reached 11 percent of the total workforce in 2022 (compared to 5 percent in the United States). High-tech service exports amounted to about $42 billion in 2021, more than double that of 2014, and in that same year, high-tech companies represented some 40 percent of the value of all the companies on the TA-35 Index (a stock market index that tracks the performance of 35 large companies listed on Israeli stock exchanges). In 2021, the aggregate value of the 85 Israeli high-tech companies traded on the New York Stock Exchange and NASDAQ amounted to the same value as the 507 companies traded on the Tel Aviv Stock Exchange ($300 billion, or around 75 percent of Israel's total GDP). Before the coronavirus pandemic, the value of publicly traded Israeli high-tech companies listed on stock exchanges in the United States amounted to some $70 billion. StartupBlink, a startup ecosystem map and research center based in Haifa, has ranked Israel's high-tech ecosystem third after the United States and United Kingdom, its high position standing in stark contrast to the low score that Israel has received for its business environment.

Between 2010–2022, an annual average of around 6,000 high-tech ventures operated in Israel. Of these, some 100 companies obtained loans from venture capital funds, and 220 were public companies listed on national and international stock exchanges. Currently, there are 1,600 Israeli high-tech companies operating in the United States and 300 in the United Kingdom. As of 2021, over 9,000 technology companies, 500 multinationals, and 450 incubators operated in Israel. Israel has the highest number of startups per capita in the world. Between 2010 and 2019, Israel saw around 800 exits, with a combined value of some $45 billion. Every year, Israeli startups are sold to international companies (mergers and acquisitions), and there are issuances of Israeli companies on global stock exchanges.

Israel has also become a global export hub for computing services. It is a powerful growth engine for software and computing services for its 360 international corporate R&D centers, which are not dependent on ports, supply chains, or transportation rates. Israel also has a number of what StartupBlink has dubbed "Pantheon companies," (that is, current and former "unicorns," or privately held startup companies that have reached a valuation of $1 billion without being listed on the stock market) that have made a large impact on a global level, among them Waze, Mobileye,

Checkpoint, and ICQ. Since the 2010s, Israel has been ranked high on innovation indices, including those of Bloomberg and the World Economic Forum (WEF) in Davos, which reflects its capabilities in innovation and its position as a growth and prosperity leader. It is no mean feat to be ranked highly in these indices, not least because of competition from other countries that also invest considerable resources in innovation. In addition, to maintain its position, Israel must also constantly reinvest in innovation.

Israel's transition from startup nation to high-tech state took shape following the establishment of 360 international development centers and a new wave of innovative technology companies. In addition, companies and world-renowned products and brands have been developed in Israel. Israeli high tech has matured, and over the past decade, rather than making quick exits, investors are choosing a path of pursuing long-term local growth, with an uptick in the number of fundraising rounds for early-stage Israeli startups in no rush to be sold to international companies. Israeli entrepreneurs have learned to develop products that solve real-world problems. The number of startups producing significant business and employment in Israel, and which are not being sold off in their early stages (as happened in the past) has increased. The number of Israeli "unicorns" (companies worth over $1 billion without being floated on the stock market) has also grown. In 2010, Israel did not have a single "unicorn," but by 2021, there were 60—the result of maturity and a positive capital market with the ability to grow large companies with high valuations. Some of these firms have already given birth to the next generation of companies and to hundreds of new startups.

If in 2001 high tech was about creating products, then by 2022, it was mostly about services (software). Some 75 percent of Israel's high-tech sector is based in Tel Aviv and the central coastal plain, a fact that has created yet another disconnect between the country's central and peripheral regions. Indeed, high tech has widened Israel's economic and social disparities. However, Israel's growing high-tech sector has also suffered from a shortage of skilled human resources. This dearth of skilled human resources has meant that in 2021, some 27 percent of Israeli high-tech companies employed around 11,000 staff in overseas countries, including Ukraine and India (in a process known as offshoring).

There has been a year-on-year decrease in the number of new high-tech ventures that have opened, from a peak of 1,400 in 2014 to 500 in 2021–2022. The lack of skilled human resources available domestically has pushed Israeli companies to open development centers abroad. This has caused a shift in Israel's branding, from "startup nation" to "scale-up nation."

These changes have also led to high levels of recruitment in the United States and the development of large-scale marketing systems. Israel's high-tech sector has acquired startups in the United States to enable it to expand its product portfolio, increase its customer pool, and obtain access to skilled human resources. In 2011, the number of acquisitions made by Israeli companies was just 5, rising to 45 in 2021. Israeli high tech has become an integral part of the world's leading technology and recruitment centers, and its capital-raising is now well-integrated into Silicon's Valley's business climate. Most funding for Israeli high tech comes from overseas sources, mainly the United States. A typical venture ownership structure for an Israeli startup is 30 percent entrepreneurs, 20 percent employees, and 50 percent foreign investors.

Somewhat counterintuitively, the coronavirus pandemic of 2020–2021 was a prosperous time for Israeli high tech, helping to speed up processes that were then able to mature and meet new needs. From 2010–2019, Israeli high-tech IPOs in the United States and mergers with U.S. companies were worth about $10 billion. In 2020, this figure rose to $15 billion. The year 2020 (during the coronavirus pandemic) proved an exceptional one for Israeli high tech in terms of exits, IPOs, mergers, and VC fundraising abroad and domestically, amounting to some $84 billion in just a single year, around the same as in the entire decade from 2011–2020.

In 2022, the high-tech market in Israel and globally experienced disillusionment, and a sector-wide slowdown began. However, this development has not harmed Israeli high tech because of its decentralized maturity across a number of areas, including cyber, fintech, life sciences, and organizational solutions. This decentralization has provided the sector with resilience in times of crisis. Israeli high tech has been able to use the slowdown to increase efficiency, cleanse itself of "toxins" acquired during the peak period, and burst some of the bubbles in which these arose. However, Israeli high tech still faces risks, including, the domestic risks that arose in 2023, the independence of Israel's judiciary and Gaza war. These developments in the country have damaged the confidence of foreign investors, that has been built up over the past 50 years, prompting a drop in investments, and sparking fears of a brain drain, and of Israeli companies registering or relocating abroad.

## International Development Centers

In 2021, 360 development centers run by world-leading high-tech multinationals operated in Israel, compared with just 10 such centers in

2000. These centers employed some 68,000 staff, or about 2 percent of Israel's total workforce. Israel has gained the reputation of being a leading global development hub, with optimal conditions for innovation, creativity, and entrepreneurship. Israel's national expenditure on civilian R&D in 2021 was 5.6 percent of GDP, the highest of all OECD countries, the result of its high concentration of multinational development centers.

The international development centers based in Israel are subject to decision-making from their headquarters abroad. The centers are owned by leading companies, which are at the forefront of global knowledge and boast sophisticated marketing and distribution channels. The centers bring Israel important knowledge, collaborations, and acquisitions, and boost the country's native high-tech sector. While the centers benefit from Israel's technological, creative, and innovative human resources, they also serve as an important source of cross-fertilization and inspiration for smaller Israeli firms that enjoy advantages in conducting R&D for new products.

The R&D centers represent a leap forward for high tech and help develop high-quality subcontractors that benefit the entire sector. While they attract the brightest minds and offer young talent rewarding salaries and working conditions, they also reduce the total pool of available skilled human resources, meaning a scarcity of skilled workers available for Israeli startups. As a result, since 2017, there has been a decrease in the number of new startups—a trend that, if it continues, could have a negative impact on the Israeli high-tech sector. At the moment, the international development centers are all located in Israel's developed and prosperous central coastal plain, around 40 percent of them employ up to 50 members of staff, and most have no ongoing economic activity in Israel outside of their development centers. A key question in all this is how Israel can harness the power of international corporations to drive processes to boost the underdeveloped regions outside of the central coastal plain.

## Introducing Technology to Traditional Industries

Around 60 percent of all Israelis who work in industry are employed in traditional (non-high-tech) industries. The very low levels of R&D in Israel's traditional industry affect worker productivity and leads to low wages. Therefore, it is vital to introduce innovation to traditional industries outside of the high-tech sector. The introduction of new technologies and innovation is essential if Israel is to increase the productivity and competitiveness of its workforce both domestically and internationally, which will boost wages and living standards. It is only fitting that the high-tech revolution, which is based on information, should extend to all branches of Israel's economy.

A "bi-polar economy" has developed in Israel. Israel's innovation and R&D industries, which lead Israel's growth and exports, boast a high GDP per worker, in line with the rest of the developed world. In Israel's traditional industries, however, GDP per worker is low—about half that of the United States in 2021. R&D spending in Israel's traditional industries is also low compared to other developed countries. Exposing Israel's traditional industries to the advantages of high tech and innovation will increase their productivity as well as their competitiveness in export markets. Studies show that the marginal return for investing in R&D in traditional industries is ten times higher than that of investing in physical capital.

Israel's traditional industries face two major barriers to encouraging innovation and investment in R&D. The first is low technological awareness among most factory managers, which is largely due to a lack of knowledge about how technology can help increase productivity. The second is the lack of government support for the adoption of technologies, innovation, and advanced management methods and knowledge. Government aid can be justifiable because of the external benefits of upgrading traditional industries and exposing them to R&D and innovation and changing their conservative organizational cultures. Strategic evidence is needed about the relationship between R&D and innovation, competitiveness, and growth in all sectors of the economy. There is no high tech without traditional industry, just as there is no traditional industry without high tech.

## Dilemmas for the Future

The development of Israel's high-tech sector has been impressive. However, one must be careful not to fall into the trap of idealization and complacency. Israel needs continuous innovation, as it has no other comparative advantage with which it can face challenges to its future. Furthermore, a scarcity of appropriately skilled human resources may hamper the expansion of Israel's high-tech sector. Ultra-Orthodox Jews, Arab citizens of Israel, women, and residents of Israel's less developed and less prosperous regions outside of the central coastal plain remain under-represented in Israeli high tech. Many countries and cities around the world are attracting Israelis to emigrate, and there is a real danger of a large-scale brain drain if current economic, social and political trends, including fears of political instability, continue.

Major questions that have arisen include: Will there be sufficient human resources to sustain Israel's high-tech sector, let alone expand it? Is the large workforce currently employed in international development centers in Israel being used to benefit Israel's own economy, given that the products these centers develop are produced and marketed abroad? Is the startup "exit" model beneficial for Israel's economy? How can Israel produce more startups that develop into mature companies based on local R&D that do not only employ developers, but a diverse Israeli workforce?

In practice, Israel has created a (unique) economic sector from selling innovation in tech and high-tech startups, and this has generated considerable revenue. Early sales of startups benefit entrepreneurs, not only because of the lure of a tempting financial reward, but also because of their recognized management weakness after the startup phase. Support is required, mainly in terms of funding, to encourage entrepreneurs to choose a direction of travel that produces large, mature companies that provide employment for a wide range of local staff.

In 2021, high-tech workers accounted for about 11 percent of Israel's total workforce (of whom 70 percent worked in the service sector and 30 percent in industry). These employees have a disproportionate impact on the economy and society, including through exports and tax payments. Meanwhile, the groups that are under-represented in Israeli high tech—ultra-Orthodox Jews, Arabs, women, and residents of the less developed towns and cities outside the wealthy central coastal plain—need government intervention in education and training if Israel is to expand and diversify its economy and reduce social disparities.

High tech is an engine that competes for talented employees and harms productivity in other sectors of the economy. Israel's shortage of skilled high-tech workers has created intense competition and driven up wages in the high-tech sector.

According to the OECD's Survey of Adult Skills (the PIAAC test), which examines the labor market skills of adults, Israel is languishing among the bottom tier of OECD countries. This is largely due to Israelis' lack of English skills and appropriate scientific knowledge. The high-tech sector has exacerbated social and economic inequalities and created disparities between the sector and Israel's traditional economy. These developments could lead to social unrest if they are not addressed. In the final analysis, the role of Israel's high-tech sector is not just economic—it can also be mobilized to help reduce social disparities.

Israel's high-tech sector needs a robust, modern infrastructure, in particular high-speed internet and a large-scale fiber optic network. High-quality internet services are a prerequisite for high productivity as well as a precondition for the development of modern smart homes, smart cities, and autonomous transport systems. High-speed internet is also a gateway to the world of smartphone app development, and a precondition for innovation. Studies have pointed to the relationship between growth and productivity and broadband infrastructure. The Israeli government has left the deployment of broadband infrastructure to the private sector, and has been content to serve in a regulatory role. However, this has not produced good results. Only in 2021 did the government begin to make efforts to close the gaps in fiber optic deployment and improve internet speeds.

The government's civilian R&D policy has always been characterized by "neutrality," that is, establishing criteria for uniform support across all branches of industry without favoring one over another. However, Israel's high-tech sector has been biased toward ICT because of the security context. Israel must continue its neutral R&D policy and consider, from time to time, investing in industries with notable external advantages, such as cyber, where government investment has helped create a critical mass for Israeli companies on a global level. Such a policy requires a mechanism for identifying external advantages. For applied R&D to flourish and grow, it is imperative that Israel increase its basic science research budgets.

## Notes

1. France had maintained a close relationship with Israel in the 1950s and early 1960s, serving as its main arms supplier. Prior to the outbreak of the 1967 war, France, led by President Charles de Gaulle, declared neutrality and placed an embargo on all offensive weapons to the region, a move that primarily affected Israel.
2. The Discount Investment Corporation is a holding company founded by the Recanati family, founders and then owners of the Israel Discount Bank.
3. I was the State Budget Director during the establishment of Yozma.
4. Dan Senor and Saul Singer. (2009). Start-Up Nation: The Story of Israel's Economic Miracle. New York: Twelve, 2009.

# 25

# Israel's Labor Market

## Labor Market Participation Rates

Israel's economy is based on human capital, not natural resources. As a result, the government needs to develop policies for extracting as much human potential as possible from the labor market. A country's labor market is a function of its population size, age distribution, education, and specific work practices that affect labor force participation. As more and more people participate in the labor force, more products and services (outputs) can be produced, and private and public living standards will rise. Undoubtedly, participating in the labor force and earning a wage are central to the everyday lives of citizens and families. Labor force participation rate is affected by its specific age distribution, demographics, cultural and religious practices, education and professional training, and labor relations.

Until the 1990s, Israel's labor force participation rate had been low relative to that of developed countries. From the 1950s through the 1980s, there were changes in the labor force participation rate among different population groups in the country. As a general trend, men's labor force participation rates decreased while women's increased.

In terms of its labor force participation rate, Israel stands out in comparison to other developed countries because of its security situation. Israel prides itself on its "people's army model," that is, the compulsory conscription of all high school graduates (at the age of 18) to the IDF. For many years, conscription rates were very high, and most young Jews, young men and women, aged 18–22 did not participate in the civilian workforce, unlike in Western countries, which do not have mandatory conscription. Conscripts and career soldiers were not included in Israeli labor market statistics until 2012, when Israel joined the OECD and began to be measured alongside other OECD countries, which added about two percent to Israel's labor force participation rate.

Since the 1990s, there has been a rise in Israel's labor force participation rate as a result of the Soviet Aliyah and the ongoing rise in the number of

Israeli Jewish women working outside the home. However, Israel's labor force participation rates remain lower, because of the low numbers of ultra-Orthodox men and Arab women who are active in the workforce but in 2023 exceed the average OECD rates (ages 25-64 that are relevant for international comparisons).

In the 1950s and 1960s, labor force participation rates among both Jewish and Arab women in Israel were lower than in other countries, and lower than the labor force participation rates among Israeli men. In the 1990s, labor force participation rates among non-ultra-Orthodox Jewish women in Israel reached levels similar to those among women in developed countries, while labor force participation rates among ultra-Orthodox women in Israel caught up only in the 2020s. Labor force participation rates among Arab women in Israel remained lower than those of Jewish women in 2023, even though there has been a continuous increase in Arab women working outside the home since the 1990s, a result of changes in their education and increased openness within this community to women seeking paid employment.

Between 1980–2000, there was a drop of about 6 percent in the labor force participation rate among men in Israel. This can be attributable to increases in the numbers of students in higher education, yeshiva students, pensioners, and discouraged workers—those who have given up looking for employment—and who receive social allowances. The latter two groups have low levels of mainstream education. Disadvantaged groups, with less socioeconomic or political power, or less education and fewer skills, have been unable to cope with the entry of Palestinian and migrant workers into the labor market on the one hand, or with the demands of Israel's modern, competitive economy on the other. In the 2000s, Israel took steps that pushed up employment rates, including making cuts to child benefit and income support, which led to labor force increases among Arab women, ultra-Orthodox, and other groups with lower levels of mainstream education. When benefits rose again between 2010–2019, the labor force participation rate among ultra-Orthodox men shrank.

Until 2022, the retirement age for women in Israel was five years younger than that for men. Women's life expectancy in Israel is two years higher than men, meaning that overall, women have less time to save for more years of retirement. A gradual correction to the retirement age for women began in 2021, as a result of which women will eventually retire with almost as much in pension savings as men. Further, because women usually work both inside and outside the home, they are more likely to work part-time jobs and for less than full salaries. Even women who work full-time are paid less than men on average, both because women are more likely to be in lower-paid occupations, such as teaching or nursing, and because of gender pay gaps, whereby men are paid more than women for equivalent roles.

## Disadvantaged Groups

Israel's low labor market participation rates are largely a reflection of low employment rates among two groups—ultra-Orthodox men and Arab women. The high fertility rates of the ultra-Orthodox community, their low levels of mainstream education in core curriculum subjects, and their employment patterns, all pose a real threat to the future of Israel's economy and society. There is resistance within Israel's ultra-Orthodox community, mainly for religious and cultural reasons, toward acquiring a mainstream education that would allow them to train for more skilled work.

Labor force participation rates among ultra-Orthodox men are affected by the "Torah Umunato" ("Torah is his job") agreement that the government made with ultra-Orthodox community leaders at the time of Israel's independence. Under this agreement, the government set a quota for the number of young ultra-Orthodox yeshiva (religious seminary) students allowed to defer compulsory military service until they completed their yeshiva studies (in practice, most were never conscripted). In 1977, Menachem Begin's newly elected Likud government agreed to abolish the quota. In 2023, this figure stood at around 165,000 yeshiva students, a large part of whom do not work at all. The phenomenon whereby elementary school education for Israel's ultra-Orthodox communities does not include, or severely limits, core curriculum ("secular") subjects like science and English has negatively affected labor market participation rates among this demographic. Ultra-Orthodox men wishing to seek work face barriers because of their lack of job skills. Aware that they can secure only low-paying jobs, many prefer to continue to receive benefits and income support from the government and their own community. The Torah Umunato agreement, coupled with generous increases to child benefit in the 1990s, have meant that a significant part of the income of Israel's ultra-Orthodox households has come from state benefits rather than employment.

In 1980, labor force participation rates among ultra-Orthodox men aged 25–64 was 63 percent, but by 2003, this had plummeted to 36 percent. Once the government slashed welfare payments in 2003, there was a rise in labor market participation rates among ultra-Orthodox men, as the loss of benefits pushed them into seeking paid work. Their labor force participation ultimate reached a record high of 54 percent in 2014–2015. However, in 2016, when state benefits were raised almost to earlier levels, labor force participation rates in this demographic began to fall and stood at 52 percent in 2022. Already in 2020, the government had failed to meet its target of 63 percent for the labor force participation rate among ultra-Orthodox men.

There is evidence that labor force participation rates among young ultra-Orthodox men in Israel depends on whether they receive financial support in the form of welfare and other incentives that allow them to avoid work. Due to Israel's political system, the ultra-Orthodox parties wield immense political power, holding the key to coalitions in governments, which then provide these incentives that enable men to remain in yeshivas and to shun a basic mainstream education.

Until 2004, the increase in labor market participation rates among ultra-Orthodox women was lower than that for non-ultra-Orthodox Jewish women. The gap between these two groups increased from about 8 percentage points in 1980 to 20 in 2004. After 2004, the gap began to close as women became the main breadwinners in ultra-Orthodox households. In 2022, the gap between ultra-Orthodox and non-ultra-Orthodox women in terms of labor force participation was just 2 percentage points. However, average salaries for ultra-Orthodox women are about 30 percent lower than for non-ultra-Orthodox Jewish women, largely because more ultra-Orthodox women than non-ultra-Orthodox women tend to work part-time. The increase in the labor force participation rate among ultra-Orthodox women has occurred almost without any decrease in average family size, unlike the patterns often seen among other population groups.

In the 1970s, labor force participation rates among Arab men in Israel were about 75 percent, higher than among Jewish men, reflecting the fact that Arab citizens of Israel tended to join the workforce at a younger age than Jewish men, and unlike Jewish men, were not conscripted into the IDF. Also, fewer Arab men than Jewish men went onto higher education. After the 1970s, the rate of Arab men's labor force participation began to drop. It began to rise again at beginning of the millennium, reaching 77 percent in 2022, but is still lower than among Jewish men. The drop in the labor force participation rate in 2022 was greater among Arab men aged over 50 due to early retirement, reflecting the high number of manual laborers in this demographic.

Despite the growing number of Arab women in employment, as of 2022, the labor force participation rate among this group was about 42 percent, far lower than among Jewish women (82 percent). The increased number of Arab women into the labor market has been accompanied by a drop in the average number of children per family in the Arab sector. The percentage of married Arab women with three or more live births fell from 40 percent in 2002 to less than 30 percent in 2020. This reduction in birth rate has prompted an increase in the labor force participation rate among Arab women, which in turn reduced their fertility rates. The rise in younger Arab women in the labor market is a result of increased numbers of this demographic attaining a mainstream education, and a rise in women's empowerment within this community. The government target for 2020 for Arab women in employment was 41 percent, which was achieved. Arab women still lag behind their Jewish counterparts in terms of salaries and rewarding employment opportunities.

## Employment Sectors

Until the 1980s, around 50 percent of the Israeli workforce worked in productive branches of industry—manufacturing, agriculture, and construction. Indeed, Israel boasted that it had sparked a revolution that had changed the status of the Jewish Diaspora and made the Jewish people productive. From the 1980s, there was a continuous fall in the proportion of industrial, construction, and agricultural laborers in Israel's workforce, and by 2022, these sectors comprised just 20 percent of the total labor market. In the second half of the 1950s, about 18 percent of Israel's total workforce was employed in agriculture. By 2022, this had dropped to just a single percent. The proportion of the workforce employed in manufacturing and construction was 35 percent in the 1960s, but just 19 percent in 2022. In the 2000s, Israel transitioned into a post-industrial economy. By 2022, only 17 percent of the workforce was employed in manufacturing.

Changing the structure of the so-called "inverted pyramid" of Jewish society had been a central tenet of early labor Zionism, whose vision was for Diaspora Jews to abandon the commerce and service industries for "productive" work in a Zionist state. However, this change was short-lived. Over time, Jews in Israel returned to their traditional and historic sources of employment in service professions, as Israel transitioned into a "normal" economy. The high-tech, finance, and service sectors became a modern expression of creativity and entrepreneurship that served the needs of the state. International openness and globalization have transformed Israel into a post-industrial economy where employment is concentrated in high tech and services. The proportion of high-tech workers in Israel's workforce in 2022 was 11 percent, the highest in the world, and their contribution in terms of GDP, productivity, and salaries is higher than in most other employment sectors.

In 2022, about 80 percent of Israel's workforce were employed in service jobs, compared to an OECD average of 73 percent. Most of Israel's service workers are at the bottom of the salary, education, and productivity ladders. Clearly, Israel's employment sectors have become polarized, as the country developed a "dual economy" split between competitive high-tech jobs with a high GDP per worker and high productivity, and services and traditional industries, whose workers have a low level of education and productivity, and which are protected from imports and non-competitive.

## Employment and Education

In the 1960s, after Israel had absorbed the mass influx of immigrants that arrived post-1948, the importance of education and skills to economic growth began to rise. Israel's rapid transition from a country with a low per capita GDP to a modern state with membership in the "club of developed nations" was to a great extent the result of educating its workforce. Human capital relies on the education and higher education system, professional training and retraining, and reflects a desire to secure equal opportunities in the labor market.

In the 1990s, Israel's high-tech sector was bolstered by an educated and skilled workforce—a result of the increase in homegrown university graduates and the influx of highly educated Soviet immigrants. In Israel's first decades of statehood, its higher education institutions were unable to supply all the educated human resources the developing nation required, and immigrants were therefore a much needed and important source of human capital. Since the 2000s, however, the Israeli academy has become the main source of educated human resources for the economy and society. In 2022, about half of Israel's working-age population had a post-secondary or higher education. The average income of Israelis with a post-secondary or higher education is 60 percent higher than those with no further or higher education, and labor force participation rates among the more educated group are also higher.

The increasing weight of Arab and ultra-Orthodox citizens in Israel's population requires targeted steps to improve their education and boost their occupational diversity. This helps cultivate a wide range of opinions and cultures, which fosters increased creativity, innovation, productivity, and profitability. There is a growing need for digital literacy to be taught as a necessary skill for disadvantaged and less affluent populations, in particular the ultra-Orthodox and Arab populations, in order to boost their labor force participation and incomes. Meanwhile, a considerable proportion of Israeli schoolchildren are failing to acquire the digital skills they need to successfully integrate into the labor market. Israel needs to make changes in its education system and emphasize the teaching of critical thinking, problem-solving, self-study, and teamwork skills.

## Productivity and Professional Training

The productivity gap between Israel and the developed world has remained almost static for about 40 years. A precondition for improving Israel's productivity rates is the integration of its disadvantaged and less affluent population groups into the labor market. To do this, Israel must improve and strengthen the human capital of its ultra-Orthodox and Arab communities, and that of its geographic and social peripheries, not least because these demographics are expected to grow significantly. Education from a young age is needed in the country, along with continuous professional development and retraining for those in the workforce. The latter is required to ensure that workers can obtain and maintain up-to-date skills, in particular in view of rapid changes in technology.

Working hours for workers in Israel are about 10 percent higher than in other OECD and EU countries and over 25 percent higher than in the more developed nations in Europe. Despite their generally longer working hours, Israeli workers produce less than in developed countries, which indicates low productivity rates (there has been little improvement in this area since 2015).

Over the last few decades, Israel has failed to create a high-quality professional training system, despite technology's emerging dominance in the workplace. Developing employees' skills throughout their working lives is a necessary condition for achieving high productivity and work outputs. Europe actively invests in its workers via professional training schemes that allow employees to continue working without their incomes being affected. According to the OECD, the disparity between the investments that Israel and Europe make in their respective workforces explains disparities in skills between adults in Israel and those in other OECD countries. In the 2000s, Israel spent an annual average of just 0.16 percent of its GDP on an active labor market policy (ALMP) compared with the OECD average of 1 percent. Vocational training and retraining are of particular importance for

Arab citizens of Israel, ultra-Orthodox Jews, Ethiopian Jews, and older adults who are facing redundancy due to industry and technological changes.

In a comprehensive survey[1] of adults aged 16–65, the OECD found that Israelis scored poorly in terms of the basic skills needed to participate successfully in the economy and society. This is a worrying indication of the poor state of Israel's education and professional training systems. Improving workforce skills requires effective use of technology and big data in partnerships between government, academia, employers, and recruitment agencies. The standard system in place around the world is that governments are responsible for providing education services from kindergarten through elementary, middle, and high school, and later in further education institutions (or in some cases, the military). Once people graduate from this system and enter the labor market, it is the employers' responsibility to ensure continued training and education. Israel today is in need of a new partnership between the government and employers to maintain and develop workers' skills.

The 21st century labor market is changing swiftly, as the rapid development of new technologies is rendering certain professions obsolete. This is a worldwide phenomenon, and Israel is not immune to its effects. While the emergence of new technologies has caused job obsolescence in the past, they have also created new opportunities, albeit in a painful process of change that not all workers have emerged from successfully. The advent of robotics and the artificial intelligence (AI) revolution are expected to wipe out certain jobs and create fewer new opportunities, which will transform the world of work and create a new challenge for humanity. Studies indicate demand for workers in professions that robotics and AI cannot replace, and there will be a continual need for relevant skills training that will enable workers to stay in their jobs.

The coronavirus pandemic hit Israel's job market and businesses hard. At the height of the first lockdown in Israel in 2020, unemployment soared to 27 percent. However, the end of the lockdowns showed that the labor market was flexible. Unemployment fell to four percent in 2022, similar to pre-pandemic levels. The main damage was to disadvantaged, low-skilled communities in the geographic and social. Unfortunately, the pandemic period was not used to retrain the tens of thousands left unemployed. Some of these hard-hit individuals now work in the gig economy, which is based on part-time and temporary work from contractors, without direct employment relationships or long-term commitment on either side, and which offers zero-hour contracts with no pension provisions, vacation days, social rights, or safety net. This represents negative employment flexibility without social rights that may increase the burden on society.

## Implications

According to demographic trends[2] for Israel's three main population groups (non-ultra-Orthodox Jews, ultra-Orthodox Jews, and Arabs), the proportion of Arabs and ultra-Orthodox Jews will reach about 50 percent of the total population by 2060 (compared with around 33 percent in 2022). If these two groups (but mainly ultra-Orthodox Jews) continue to avoid acquiring a mainstream education that can prepare them for the world of work, Israel will see a drop in its overall employment rates, and the percentage of educational minorities (groups with educational goals distinct from those of the majority, whether as the result of language or cultural differences and budget discrimination, or out of ideological choice, as with the ultra-Orthodox), and those who do not possess relevant skills for work will increase. This trend, combined with the overall aging of Israel's population, will result in a drop in labor market participation. In light of the fact that most of Israel's taxation revenue is generated from those with average and above average salaries (the three highest deciles), the government will need to considerably increase the tax burden on these workers to finance public spending, including for welfare payments to those who avoid participating in the labor market.

In setting taxation rates and generating revenue from their citizens, governments are not acting in a vacuum. Thus, if Israel increases the taxation burden on its educated and successful citizens in order to finance those who avoid work and/or who refuse to obtain a mainstream education that prepares them for work, young Israelis with in-demand skills and high earning capacities will emigrate to countries with lower taxation rates. The resulting erosion of human capital will harm economic growth, and Israel can expect to see a retreat from its achievements of the past decades. To prevent this development, the government must cease budgetary support for educational institutions that do not provide a mainstream education or relevant job skills.

In terms of Arab citizens of Israel, efforts will be required to increase their absorption into the labor force. This can be done by strengthening and expanding the nascent Arab middle class through improving the education system for this population, and by reducing the number of migrant workers in Israel, who usually replace Arab workers in the labor force, especially in construction. Maximizing the economic capabilities of

Israel's Arab population will greatly contribute to improving their sense of belonging to the country, and to the growth of its economy.

## Non-Israeli Workers

Israel's labor market was officially opened to Palestinian workers in September 1970, a move that included arrangements for social rights. In a short period of time, there was a big shift in the Palestinian employment structure. A significant part of the Palestinian Authority's national income began to be derived from work in Israel, where salaries were comparatively high compared with the Palestinian Authority. In the early 1970s Israel's move to provide work permits to Palestinians stemmed from a demand for laborers and a sense of responsibility and concern for neighbors under Israeli control.

Prior to the Oslo Accords in 1993, including during the First Intifada that began on December 8, 1987 and lasted until September 13, 1993, the movement of Palestinian workers in Israel was almost unrestricted. Most returned to their homes in the Occupied Territories at night, although a minority remained illegally in Israel. At its peak, about a third of the Palestinian workforce was employed in Israel. Wage receipts accounted for 35–40 percent of the Palestinian Authority's GDP. Until the terrorist acts of the 1990s, the Palestinians were considered a reliable workforce, whose availability and hard work could be trusted. When the terrorist incidents began, Palestinians began to be seen as untrustworthy and unreliable, because of closures that prevented them from traveling to jobs in Israel, and security considerations came to dominate decisions about employing them.

Meanwhile, the need for labor for construction projects, in particular amid the influx of Soviet immigrants, and the labor demands of Israel's agriculture industry, pushed employers to pressure the government to grant permits for migrant workers. Prior to 1994, some 20,000 migrant workers were employed in Israel without a valid permit. After that date, the government allowed employers to legally employ tens of thousands of migrant workers, a socialist and administrative policy that was ultimately considered completely inadequate and which resulted in serious difficulties and problems that grew worse as time went on. In response, the government hiked unemployment and income support benefits able to hire cheap migrant labor, Israeli employers had less of an incentive to invest in technology, especially in Israel's construction industry, where productivity was already low.

Following a relative period of calm, in 1998–2000, around 130,000 Palestinians worked in Israel, both with and without permits, as well as a similar number of migrant workers, half of whom were legal. On the eve of the Second Intifada in 2000, the number of Palestinian and migrant workers in Israel reached over a quarter of a million, or about 13 percent of the workforce, a higher rate than in European countries. The Second Intifada (2000–2004) saw a reduction in the number of Palestinian workers in Israel and an increase in the number of migrant workers. In 2005, around 25,000 Palestinians worked in Israel.

In 2019–2022, the number of Palestinians from the West Bank working in Israel was around 12 percent of the Palestinian workforce, and their share in the Palestinian GDP was around 20 percent. The Palestinians see the ability to work in Israel as a central component of their economy. Thus, in every negotiation with Israel, they strenuously demanded that the labor market be completely open to them, regardless of any future trade agreement. The 1994 Protocol on Economic Relations (the so-called Paris Protocol)[3] between Israel and the Palestinian Liberation Organization, allowed for the "normal movement" of Palestinian workers and the right of Israel to limit their number for security or labor market reasons.

The fluctuations in the number of Palestinian workers in the 2000s demonstrated the need for a comprehensive policy toward them. In 2011, the Eckstein Committee[4] recommended gradually reducing the number of Palestinians working in Israel and weakening the link between the two economies. The wage gap of at least 100 percent between the two economies had created a fundamental ambivalence within the Palestinian labor market. Even under conditions of political conflict and security tensions, the laws of economics continue operating. With the Israeli market offering greater rewards than the Palestinian market, skilled Palestinian workers prefer work in Israel over work in the Palestinian Authority, which, as a result, loses quality human resources to Israel.

In the medium and long-term, it is essential to develop the Palestinian economy and create jobs through entrepreneurship and public and private investments. Most international aid to the Palestinians has been used to fund the public sector, rather than economic development. This situation has posed a political and economic dilemma for Israel. High employment and economic prosperity in the West Bank, which are basic preconditions for economic and political stability, rely on economic development. Hence, the number of Palestinian workers in Israel needs to be limited in order to create jobs in the West Bank, as at the moment, it is easier for the Palestinian

Authority to send its population to work in Israel rather than create jobs within its territory.

Their cheap labor has pushed unskilled Israeli workers out of the workforce and turned them into welfare recipients without the ability to return to the labor market. Among these welfare recipients are Arab citizens of Israel who can no longer find work in the construction industry. It is in Israel's interest to reduce the number of migrant and Palestinian workers in the labor market, and, at the same time, to encourage Israeli citizens to seek work by raising low wages. Israel's minimum wage, high by Palestinian standards, has created an incentive for Palestinians to come to Israel for work. At the same time, it has encouraged migrant workers to migrate and remain in Israel, even illegally. Palestinian and migrant workers have harmed Israel's productivity. Without their cheap labor, employers would have had to invest capital in labor-saving technological improvements to compensate for the shortage of labor. An "addiction" to cheap labor and technological backwardness has created a situation where employers hire the same type of workers who are content with low wages, while traditional technology is never upgraded, and productivity remains low.

Economic migration to Israel is not just an economic issue, but also a demographic and social one, demanding that the government formulate an effective immigration policy. One major question concerns the fate of the children of migrant workers without a legal work permit. There is a large community of migrant workers in Israel, which at its peak included around 100,000 individuals without a valid work permit who had overstayed in Israel and risked deportation. This group was boosted by tens of thousands of undocumented immigrants from Africa (mostly from Eritrea, Sudan, Ethiopia, Ivory Coast, and Nigeria), and individuals who entered Israel on tourist visas, then overstayed and sought political asylum and work in Israel. The Israeli government finally realized the extent of the problem, and established an immigration police and took action to reduce the number of migrant workers from about 300,000 in 2010 to less than 200,000 in 2022. These include around 150,000 legal and 20,000 migrant workers without a valid work permit, 30,000 economic migrants, and about 30,000 tourists working without a valid permit in Israel, in addition to some 160,000 Palestinian workers, including those with a work permit and those without. In total, in 2022, there were about 350,000 non-Israelis working in Israel—about 7.5 percent of the total workforce, a very high figure compared to other countries. Currently, the demand for migrant workers is mainly in private nursing and personal care services for the elderly, a result of the aging of Israel's population. Businesses that make a profit from brokerage fees from employers seeking cheap labor will continue to import Palestinian and migrant workers.

From an economic perspective, the low cost of Palestinian and migrant labor has benefitted Israel's middle classes and those with high incomes by stemming increases in production costs in agriculture and construction (albeit while also delaying the introduction of technological advances). However, the use of cheap migrant labor has harmed low-skilled, low-paid Israeli manual laborers, who have been pushed into unemployment and poverty. These workers had previously lost manufacturing jobs as a result of globalization, when the industries employing them were exposed to competing imports from countries whose relative advantage is cheap labor. It was natural for these workers to then switch to jobs in industries whose outputs are not exposed to international competition, either because their products cannot be transported from one country to another (such as the construction industry or personal services), or because of a high level of protection against imports (such as agriculture). A combination of lobbying by employers seeking cheap labor and ineffective government enforcement of work permits has robbed the lowest paid Israeli workers of a significant number of the jobs that had been available to them. The resulting rise in social inequalities and income disparities has forced the government to bear the burden of increased unemployment and income support benefits.

Clearly, the Israeli labor market reflects Israel's unique socio-demographic structure, ultra-Orthodox and Arabs, as well as the political reality of Israel's control over the Palestinians and dependence on foreign workers.

## Notes

1. The survey included 200,000 people in 32 countries as part of the OECD's Program for the International Assessment of Adult Competencies (PIAAC).
2. Central Bureau of Statistics, Population Forecast for Israel, February 2019.
3. The economic agreement between Israel and the Palestinians following the Oslo Accords. As Budget Director in the Ministry of Finance, I led the Israeli delegation to the Paris Accords' economic negotiations on behalf of Israel in 1993–1994.
4. Report of the Committee for the Supervision and Enforcement of the Employment of Palestinian Workers in Israel, May 2011 (Eckstein Committee).

# 26

# Demographics and Social Structure

## From the melting pot to the tribe

Israel is unique in that its economic growth and per capita GDP are typical of a developed nation, while its rate of natural increase is more like that of a developing one. In Israel, the population is growing; at the same time, living standards and quality of life are also rising. Will these processes continue? There is no way to know, since past statistics are no guarantee of what will happen in the future.

Israel is a dynamic society. Because it has absorbed a huge number of immigrants from all over the world (3.5 million immigrants between 1948, when there were few than one million people in the country, and 2022), it has an extremely heterogeneous population with a wide range of ethnic groups and a diverse cultural-religious and demographic profile. For Israel's first prime minister, David Ben-Gurion, a key function of the new state was to create a new, shared national identity in which all the diverse groups of Jews would feel a sense of belonging. Ben-Gurion imposed a melting pot model, which, even with all its advantages and disadvantages, would help achieve sovereignty and forge a coherent and cohesive society out of an assortment of "seventy Diasporas," which, in turn, would mobilize to create a functioning economy and model society. The melting pot would generate a new sense of 'Israeliness' that would supplant the disparate identities of the heterogeneous mass of Jewish immigrants. Implementing the melting pot was not an easy task, and at times felt cruel, but it was necessary for building a functioning society and economy. Nevertheless, the melting pot paradigm took its toll on successive waves of immigrants, requiring these very different communities to compromise on values that were socially and culturally important to their identities. Israeli society never fully embraced the melting pot concept, and opposing forces have fought to maintain a multicultural society in which each community retains its values and traditions.

However, identity politics also emerged from Israel's multicultural society, whereby political alliances have developed along ethnic and social, rather than along ideological or broad party politics lines. The social polarization and alienation that has resulted from this trend have been exacerbated and leveraged by various groups seeking government intervention and dependence on the government. Indeed, a fundamental conflict—between those who believe in universal values, human rights, and liberal democracy, and those who advocate an authoritarian democracy based on more restrictive, insular ethnic and religious principles— is now diluting any broad shared sense of being "Israeli."

In what has become known as his "Four Tribes Speech," in 2014, Israeli President Reuven Rivlin set out the changes that had taken place in Israeli society and called for a new domestic national order. This was no futuristic apocalyptic prophecy, but the reality of Israel in the 21st century. Israel had shifted from a society with a clear majority and minority and a shared vision, where most of the population had trust in government and a sense of partnership in building government institutions, into a country marred by tribal schisms. As Rivlin described, Israeli society now broadly consists of four equally-sized sectors or tribes—secular (non-religious) Jews, national-religious (religious-Zionist) Jews,[1] ultra-Orthodox Jews,[2] and Arab citizens of Israel. Each tribe is divided ideologically and socially, and isolates itself from the others while demanding intragroup loyalty. Tribal values are generated within each of these groups and are used by political actors who seek to leverage a particular tribe to mobilize support for themselves. No single tribe gets everything it wants, each has to live with the rest, and all have partially differing visions for Israel's present and future. As a result, all of the tribes are dissatisfied, while the main tenets of the core national vision shared by all have weakened. This has harmed Israel's core vision of statehood and governance, once highly valued and enjoying a broad national consensus. Israel's heterogeneous society has deeply affected the balance of power among its various ethnoreligious groups. This has affected its economy, culture, and politics, and will continue to do so in the future.

Tribal struggles for resources, power, and prestige affect the economy. Tribal politics seeks to maximize the gains for the individual tribe, without taking into consideration the common good. The splitting of Israeli society into tribes poses a risk to the country's future and can undermine the economy and give rise to political complications. The political sociologist Prof. Baruch Kimmerling described Israeli society as a "society of struggle, characterized by struggles between groups over shaping the image of the state and the 'rules of the game' within it, under cultural control (hegemony)."[3]

Between 1948–1977, Israel's secular (non-religious) middle classes, made up of the so-called "veteran immigrants" generation (the mostly Ashkenazi secular Jews who had lived in the country for a long time, including since the British Mandatory period), filled most jobs in the public administration, the economy, the security echelons, the media, art, law, science, and academia. The hegemonic power of this group began to weaken with the rise to power of the Likud government in 1977, and by the 2000s, the cracks in its hegemonic position had become very evident. The once powerful secular Ashkenazi middle classes had shifted from being a role model for other social groups to being just one of many interest groups in Israeli society. This secular and traditional, but not religious tribe, that had once carried the weight of creating the Israeli state, had been downgraded from its position as an elite with a strong sense of service and mission, the very flagbearers of Israeli statehood, to a mere defensive minority.

The decline of the power of the labor movement from the 1970s, together with the struggle of those advocating for an Israeli state based on Orthodox Jewish law against Israel's once powerful liberal and secular groups, also helped transform Israeli society into today's tribalistic status quo. There is a growing distance between each of Israel's four main tribes and the state. This struggle is a zero-sum game. Any influence, resources, or power gained by one tribe comes at the expense of another, while no one tribe can accept even the smallest of concessions, lest this be seen as an achievement for a rival tribe.

On the fringes of each tribe are pockets of extremism that harm the functioning of the state and threaten its governance and economy. The coronavirus pandemic of 2020–2021 exposed a number of significant fault lines in Israeli society, such as the refusal of Israel's ultra-Orthodox population to comply with government coronavirus guidelines, which affected morbidity and mortality in the ultra-Orthodox tribe. Another example can be found in Israel's 2005 disengagement from Gaza, which revealed the autonomy to which Israel's national-religious (religious-Zionist) tribe aspires, placing their belief in God's law above the law of the land. Arab citizens of Israel demanded autonomy in the wake of the October 2000 killings of 13 Arab demonstrators by police in Arab villages in the north of Israel, and after the May 2021 riots that broke out across Israel during the IDF's Operation Guardian of the Walls in Gaza. The Negev Bedouin community also wants to preserve its traditional ways of life. The secular Jewish tribe, which, as noted, has seen a decline in its once high status, is experiencing tensions between its expectations from the state and its sense of its own importance in terms of its contribution to the economy and society, as reflected in the mass social protests of 2023. All of these crises among so many ethnic and religious groups pose a challenge to Israeli statehood. From the 2000s, Israel's secular Jewish majority suffered a loss in status, as society realigned itself into tribes that have gained in status and power. This created problems with authority and enforcement, which in turn affects economic performance.

Israel's division into tribes is not only an economic problem. Indeed, it is inextricably intertwined with questions regarding the foundations of Israeli society, the relationship between religion and state, the Israeli-Palestinian conflict, and the legal and justice system. The tribes each demand separate "contracts" with the state in terms of budgetary support, military conscription, education, housing, public transport, and employment. However, it is notable that there has been positive progress regarding the long-standing disparities between Israel's Ashkenazi and Mizrahi (Sephardic) communities. A Mizrahi middle class developed that has integrated into business, the army, politics, and the development towns. They have also exercised impressive social leadership that has seen a reduction in economic disparities, which has served as a springboard for progress in other areas.

The coronavirus pandemic was undoubtedly an extreme event. Social solidarity—the ability and desire to act in a mutually beneficial way, including toward social groups with which one has no affiliation or even consensus. In demanding that the Israeli public demonstrate personal discipline, make sacrifices, and show concern for others, the pandemic exposed Israel's social fault lines when specific tribes acted in their own self-interest and in contravention of government directives, with, for example, the ultra-Orthodox refusing to close schools and members of the Arab sector not heeding restrictions on movement and gatherings. The resulting inter-tribal struggles exacerbated existing disparities, weakened national resilience, and endangered the country's ability to overcome security and economic challenges. At the start of 2023, this state of affairs found expression in legislative proposals designed to change the very foundations of governance in Israel.

At least two tribes—the ultra-Orthodox and Arab citizens of Israel—have quite distinct socioeconomic characteristics. Their influence on the economy will dictate Israel's place within the global marketplace in the future. Israel's multicultural community has created a dynamic of identity politics and disparate, disconnected communities. Instead of a cohesive society and economy, a shared economic vision, and a functioning civil society with internal solidarity, Israel's new-found tribalism has generated a perfect storm of powerful forces that are tearing society apart and ripping up the roots of its shared national vision. This has already exacted a significant macroeconomic cost.

## Indications of tribal fragmentation

Understanding the fertility rates of each tribe is critical to understanding how each of these populations will affect Israel's economy in the future. The table below shows the fertility rates (mean number of live births per woman) for each tribe in 2022:

| **Subgroup category** | **Fertility rate (mean number of live births per woman)** |
|---|---|
| Ultra-Orthodox Jewish | 6.5 |
| National-Religious (Religious-Zionist/Non-ultra-Orthodox) | 4.2 |
| Traditional Religious | 3 |
| Arab Citizens | 3 |
| Traditional Non-religious/ Secular | 2.1 |

Higher fertility rates correlate with lower labor productivity. According to population growth projections, by the middle of the 21st century, it is expected that over a quarter of Israel's population will be ultra-Orthodox Jews, a quarter national-religious (religious-Zionist) Jews, a quarter Arab, and a quarter secular (non-religious Jews). These are only future projections, but the processes and recognition of future consequences exist today and are already affecting Israel's daily life and economy. The question is not which tribe will have hegemonic power in the future. Rather, we should ask what the practical results of this power will look like, since these are what will affect Israel's national security and economic strength, in particular employment rates, types of occupation, incomes for breadwinners and households, public services for each tribe, and tax revenues.

The separate education systems that have been developed by and for Israel's tribes are among the most prominent manifestations of social fragmentation that the country is experiencing. A nation's education system teaches its young people about the values of society and induces them to uphold its ideals. The sociocultural identity of the education system to which children are exposed is thus a crucial factor in determining what they are actually taught, and how they will subsequently integrate into the labor market and the economy. The education that each of Israel's tribes receives, and how each tribe adapts to the needs of the labor market, will ultimately determine the strength of the economy.

"Israel 2008,"[4] pointed to the country's economic disparities as a central problem for Israeli society. The report defined Israel as a dual economy, in which social inequalities were generated by low employment rates mainly among ultra-Orthodox men and Arab women, and by the relative lack of relevant job-related knowledge, education, and skills among ultra-Orthodox Jews and residents of Israel's social periphery. The "Israel 2028" report warned that this problem will negatively affect the long-term performance of Israel's economy. Meanwhile, the OECD's 2018 Economic Survey of Israel[5] also warned of the dangers posed by the country's low social cohesion, in particular to its long-term economic output. The OECD found evidence of economic inequality between Israel's population subgroups and noted that overall levels of inequality are high. The number of working people living below the poverty rate has increased, particularly among Arab and ultra-Orthodox citizens, who are often trapped in low-skill jobs with low wages. As of 2022, three-quarters of Israel's low wage earners were ultra-Orthodox and Arab citizens. It is forecast that these two groups will make up half of Israel's population by 2060.[66]

Welfare policy is limited in terms of how it can address such large economic disparities. In Israel, there are disparities in the rights, duties, and compliance of its various tribes, and in the sources of authority that these tribes follow. There are also stark differences between Israel's various socioreligious groups in terms of their adaptation to a modern lifestyle. The shift in Israel's security ethos toward a civilian agenda, and the evolution from a mobilized society to a globalized economy, has created challenges for maintaining solidarity between Israel's very different communities. Values of personal fulfillment, openness to the world, and a global outlook have become prominent. Other principles that had previously been very important to Israeli society have also changed. The pioneering society of Israel's early years of statehood, which had enjoyed broad equality with most living at a relatively modest economic level, and with a mostly state-run economy, has disappeared, replaced by a private and individualistic nation, with a free-market economy open to international economies, but suffering from ever-growing socioeconomic gaps fueled by globalization and education, and that undermine the national's solidarity. Meanwhile, opposition from the ultra-Orthodox and national-religious (religious-Zionist) Jewish publics toward liberal economic policies and worldviews has intensified. The public sector is facing a quandary, since a developed welfare state is not possible without broad social solidarity, but Israel's sectarian and tribalistic welfare policies, where different tribes are treated differently, have eroded the solidarity and consensus that underpin a welfare state. Meanwhile, the most prominent demographic trends of recent years—including the rapid growth of the ultra-Orthodox population, social changes within the Arab population, increasing population density, and an aging population—will continue to significantly affect Israel's economy and society in the future.

## Demographics and birthrate

Israel has one of the highest rates of live births per woman in the developed world. The OECD average for live births per woman is 1.6, while in Israel this figure is 3.1. Even the non-ultra-Orthodox Jewish population in Israel has a higher number of live births per woman (2.2) than the OECD average. Unsurprisingly, therefore, Israel's natural rate of increase is the highest in the OECD. The average fertility rate in Israel in the 2000s is one full live birth per woman, more than that of any other OECD country. Meanwhile, birth rates are falling worldwide. Demographics affect a country's socioeconomic health, including its population density and the burden on its healthcare, education, transportation, housing, welfare, ecology, recreation, and leisure systems. Population growth requires government intervention in the form of investments in education, infrastructure, environment, health, and housing. The idea that "unbridled" population growth is a recipe for disaster has been attributed to Thomas Malthus, who warned in his *Essay on the Principle of Population* in 1798 that over time, populations would grow until there was not enough food to support them, and only the fittest individuals would survive. Others see natural population growth as a source of renewal and creativity by increasing the proportion of young people, who also provide a pension hedge against population aging, provided that they receive a proper education and can participate in the labor market.

In the 1950s and 1960s, Israel considered encouraging childbirth among its Jewish citizens as a national goal. Families received (modest) government support to encourage them to have large families as a way to maintain the Jewish majority, as was expressed in the discussions around these policies, which were completely changed in the 2000s. Israel's population has grown on average by about 2 percent year-on-year as a result of policies that encouraged families to have more children and reducing the economic burden of children mainly among ultra-Orthodox Jews and

Bedouin Arabs, who tend to have large families, low employment rates, and make low contributions to the GDP. In 2004–2015, when child benefits were reduced, especially for families with four or more children, there was a decrease in the birth rate among ultra-Orthodox Jews, proving that economic incentives do impact on the number of children families choose to have.

## The middle classes

In developed countries, the middle class is considered the basis on which the economy and society functions. The accepted definition of the middle class is those whose income is between 75 and 200 percent of net median per capita income. The middle classes are the mainstay of society, and their health determines a country's social, economic, and political stability, which in turn creates public trust in society's laws and institutions. The middle classes sustain the economy by consuming products and services, acquiring an education, and providing the backbone of the labor force. Taken together, these form the core of economic growth.

In the 1980s, Israel's middle class constituted around 59 percent of the population, the result of economic growth in the 1960s and 1970s. The entry into the economy of Palestinian workers in the 1970s and foreign workers in the 1990s had weakened the position of the middle class, which, by the time of the social justice protests that swept the country in 2011, had shrunk to about 48 percent of the population. The hike in the minimum wage that occurred in response to the protests was an important step for revitalizing Israel's lower middle class. By 2019, the middle class had grown to 53 percent of the population, the highest level since the 1990s, but still smaller than it was in the 1980s.

A dual economy has emerged in Israel, a result of the growth of the high tech industry, which rewards entrepreneurship, innovation, and creativity in contrast to the low employment rates and incomes of the ultra-Orthodox and Arab populations. This has increased income disparities, exacerbated polarization, and reduced the middle class. In any event, Israel's middle class is not spread evenly among all the country's population groups. About 60 percent of Israeli Jews belong to the middle class, compared with just 27 percent of Israel's Arab citizens. The Arab middle class is comprised of professionals and the self-employed, and began gaining in number and in socioeconomic strength around 2010, with the reduction of the birth rates within this population, the increase in education, employment rates among Arab women, and the integration of this population into mainstream Israeli society. In contrast, a middle class has begun to develop only very recently among Israel's ultra-Orthodox community, and still only constitutes around a quarter of this population.

Among OECD countries, the middle class makes up between 50 and 70 percent of the population, with an OECD average of around 61 percent. Over the past two decades, the middle class has declined across OECD countries in line as nonprofessional jobs have declined, including those replaced by technology and robotics. The demand for workers with a technological education has caused social disparities to rise and the middle class to shrink. Technology poses a threat to the middle class, and Israel is not immune to this global trend. Indeed, this threat may intensify in the coming years, leading to social unrest and threatening political stability.

## Population density and overcrowding

Israel has one of the highest population densities in the world. In 2017, Israel was the third most densely populated OECD country in terms of number of people per square kilometer. If current trends continue, by 2035 Israel should top the list of OECD nations in terms of population density. Unsurprisingly, in recent decades, questions regarding Israel's high rate of natural increase and growing population density have received more attention on the national agenda. The types of problems that affect overcrowded countries are on the rise in Israel—rising housing prices, traffic congestion on urban and intercity roads, infrastructure expansion, long waiting lists in hospitals and law courts, congested beaches, overcrowded classrooms, shrinking green and open spaces, and air, water, and soil pollution. Tackling these challenges requires a considerable investment of money and other resources.

Israel's high rate of natural increase means that it will have to double its number of housing units within the next 30 years, a rate unprecedented in any other developed nation. Israel's population density is highest in its central Mediterranean coastal plain, where most housing demand is expected to be met by building tower blocks. These high-rise blocks will not only change the existing urban landscape but will also alter the fabric of residents' daily lives. Meanwhile, road congestion in the Tel Aviv metropolitan area and the rest of the central Mediterranean coastal plain is already among the highest in the developed world. Overcrowding in Israel's classrooms, hospitals, and emergency rooms is also among the worst in the world. These pressures are only set to increase as Israel's population continues to grow. Maintaining public infrastructure and quality of life is becoming increasingly complex and expensive. Quality of life will deteriorate if the development of key infrastructure is not increased in line with rising demand. However, to date, the pace of investment in infrastructure has not caught up with demand, and gaps between supply and demand in infrastructure, especially transportation, roads, and more, are widening, exacerbating the effects of overcrowding in various areas of everyday life.

From a land that had been considered sparsely populated with a great deal of open space, a situation that had once encouraged rural settlement, Israel has become one of the world's most densely populated nations. Land shortages will shape the way of life of its population and will demand considerable financial investment on top of innovative urban and land use planning. Israel is a distinctly urban society, and its urbanization is growing steadily. In 2022, some 93 percent of the country's residents lived in urban settlements, while rural living had become a rarity. Meanwhile, Israel's urban landscape has started to shift away from low-rise buildings toward high-rise apartment blocks. This trend marks not just a change in the urban landscape, but in the lifestyles of city dwellers as well. In the past, a city neighborhood was a community based on a sense of local belonging and the fulfillment of physical and social needs. Social connections in tower blocks are rather different from the way of life familiar to residents of traditional low-rise city apartment blocks. Israel's central Mediterranean coastal plain is likely to be dense with high-rise blocks, akin to Hong Kong and Singapore. However, families in Hong Kong and Singapore do not tend to have large numbers of children, unlike those in Israel. Raising children in tower blocks will likely be problematic. Will there be a correlation between the number of children in a household, and the quality of life of families living in tower blocks?

High population density will require Israel to formulate strict land management policies, in particular in its central Mediterranean coastal plain, which will involve increased urban renewal planning and infrastructure development. There will also be growing demands for vacant land for construction at the expense of agriculture and recreation. The importance of good urban planning will increase in light of rising population density. Israel is already experiencing the reality of what it is like to be an overcrowded country. The accelerating pace of urbanization raises the question of how to determine development policies for Israel's metropolitan areas. Does Israel need three (or even four) large metropolitan areas, or should the government concentrate on improving the existing Tel Aviv metropolitan area and constructing a high-speed train network, which will allow people to live in remoter areas and commute to the central coastal plain? The main solution will involve building more densely populated cities and ensuring efficient urban development, all while preserving nature.

## Population aging

The increased life expectancy of men and women in many countries is a significant human achievement that is allowing more people to live longer lives. Some 80 percent of Israel's older population are independent and relatively healthy, with many working past retirement age, deriving personal meaning from the productive and interesting activities in their lives. Studies have shown that after retirement, people lose a significant part of their daily routines, and the loss of day-to-day social interaction can accelerate the onset of problems associated with aging. Continuing to work contributes to health and daily functioning, while the added productivity benefits both the individual and society.

In 1950, only 4 percent of Israel's population was over the age of 65. Today, however, the population is aging, as life expectancy is increasing. In 2022, Israel had 1.2 million citizens over the age of 65, about 12.5 percent of the total population. There has also been a jump in the number of Israelis aged 75 and over, to around 4.5 percent. Around 50,000 Israelis are now aged 90 and over, about half a percent of the total population. In 2022, the number of older Jewish citizens of Israel stood at 13 percent of the total population, with the number of older Arab citizens of Israel standing at about 5 percent of the total population. The high proportion of older people among Israel's Jewish population is due to the long life expectancy of this population group and waves of immigration that had a higher percentage of older immigrants than usually seen in countries like the United States, Canada, Australia and New Zealand, which limit the number of older immigrants. According to population projections, by 2040 the proportion of older people in Israel is set to rise to 18 percent, or approximately 2.5 million people, and the demand for more nurse caregivers (both Israeli and migrant workers) to look after its elderly citizens will also grow.

The proportion of people in Israel's total population aged 65 and over is relatively low compared to other developed countries, because Israel has a much higher percentage of children aged under 14. In 2022, approximately 12 percent of Israeli citizens aged 70 and over participated in the labor force. There is a positive relationship between education levels and employment rate, with higher levels of employment correlating with higher levels of education.

Two issues must be addressed as a result. First, healthcare services for older people should be improved; and second, this must occur while maintaining high standards of care for the rest of the population. This will require the expansion of specialist healthcare for older people, including geriatric medical teams, and improved care in the community and the home. The aging of the population has implications on various aspects of life, including social security, healthcare, nursing homes, nursing care, housing, pensions, and leisure. Healthcare services for the over-75s are different from those needed by younger age groups, and this will demand that a balance be found between care in the community, institutions, and hospitals.

The dependency ratio is an economic term indicating the ratio between working-age citizens—the economically productive population—and the economically unproductive population (the sum of the population aged under 15 plus those aged over 65). In 2022, about 11 percent of Israel's population was of retirement age (i.e., 67 and older), while about 54 percent was of working age. This ratio is expected to change. In 2060, it is expected that 17 percent of Israel's population will be of pension age, while fewer than 50 percent of Israelis will be of working age. This shift towards an aging population will slow down growth and affect pension and social security systems. In this scenario, Israel's high natural increase is considered positive, on the assumption that younger people can and will work and provide for older retirees.

Israel's pension fund reforms of 1995 were a response to the crisis faced by its old, underfunded pension funds. The reforms involved the creation of new, balanced pension funds, which have increased individual risk arising from concerns about a reduction in retirement benefits due to low returns on the capital market and/or fund due to management failures. Nonetheless, the new policies will meet the challenges of ensuring the financial stability of the pension funds. The early retirement age for women in Israel has had a negative effect on women's ability to accumulate pension savings. This, together with the fact that women's life expectancy in Israel is higher than men's, has meant that women receive relatively low pension benefits. Additional pension reforms that began in 2021 are designed to gradually increase the official retirement age for women in Israel from 62 to 65 and will correct most of this distortion. The state should allow older people to live with dignity in order to reduce the gap between life expectancy and years of good health.

The coronavirus pandemic highlighted the realities of the lives of Israel's older population, and the particular risks they face. The concept of societal resilience defines the ability of a social system, starting with the individual citizen, through social groups, organizations, communities, and eventually the entire nation, to cope with a persistent or severe disruption, maintain reasonable functional continuity, and recover quickly from the crisis to function at its previous level. The key factors affecting social resilience are the intensity of the disruption, and the severity of its consequences on the affected social system. Societies with high levels of social resilience are able to deal with severe disruptions while maintaining a reasonable level of functioning. Social resilience in Israel was severely tested during the coronavirus pandemic. The older population suffered more, but by fulfilling their necessary functions during the state of emergency, they were able to bounce back and make a quick recovery. For the most part, Israel's older population managed to demonstrate social resilience, even though the pandemic caused high morbidity and mortality among this age group.

As discussed here, Israel has grappled with a wide range of evolving social issues in its over 75 years of existence, including demographic changes, inequality and an aging population. While it has sought to address many of them, the challenges anticipated in these areas for the future call for comprehensive policies and substantial resources.

## Notes

1. The Religious Zionist movement is an Orthodox faction within the Zionist movement combines a belief in the importance of establishing a Jewish state in the Land of Israel and following a religious way of life, in contrast to both secular Zionism and Haredi Orthodox, non-Zionist movements.
2. Orthodox Judaism that are characterized by their strict adherence to halakha (Jewish law) and traditions, in opposition to modern values and practices.
3. Baruch Kimmerling (2001). The End of Ashkenazi Hegemony. Jerusalem, Keter.
4. D. Brodet, (2008), Israel 2028: Vision and Strategy for the Economy and Society in a Global World. Presented by a Public Committee Chaired by Eli Horvitz. US-Israel Science and Technology Foundation.
5. 2018 OECD Economic Survey of Israel: Towards a More Inclusive Society. Jerusalem, March 11, 2018. https://www.oecd.org/economy/surveys/Towards-a-more-inclusive-society-OECD-economic-survey-Israel-2018.pdf.
6. Israel Central Bureau of Statistics, Population Forecast for Israel through 2065, May, 2017.

# 27

# Israel's Arab and Ultra-Orthodox Populations

Two of Israel's main population subgroups, its Arab and ultra-Orthodox citizens, have a special status within the country's demographic, social, religious, cultural, political, and economic structures. From the outset of Israeli statehood, neither population has been part of mainstream Israeli society. Rather, each has developed its own separate community structures with discrete systems of internal autonomy and economic conduct.

While these two populations share some similarities, in other ways they are very different. Their similarities include large families, poor-quality education systems that do not adequately prepare children and young people for jobs in Israel's free market economy, nonparticipation in military service, and low employment rates. However, while increasing numbers of Israel's Arab citizens have sought to integrate into the economy in recent years, the majority of the ultra-Orthodox population still wish to remain segregated. In Israel's first years of statehood, both populations wielded far less social and economic influence than they do today since their demographic weight and economic contribution were low. In recent decades, however, both communities have grown substantially larger, and their demographic weight in the population is projected to increase even further especially the ultra-Orthodox. Their economic behavior will thus be increasingly significant for Israel's economy. Indeed, these two population subgroups contain Israel's economic growth reserve.

In 2020–2021, as a result of the coronavirus pandemic and the widespread protests sparked by Israel's Operation Guardian of the Walls operation in Gaza, both populations attracted a great deal of media exposure regarding the risks posed by their autonomous conduct. Both are collectivist societies, where the interests of the community carry more weight than the rights of the individual. While dissimilar in the amount of political power they wield, they resemble each other in their autonomous conduct. In addition, the contribution of both to the economy is low compared with other population subgroups. Further, both populations feel that they are overlooked by the state. Most of Israel's Arab and ultra-Orthodox citizens want an autonomy that will allow them to preserve their sociocultural and religious identities and their differing economic approaches. The ultra-Orthodox community wishes to maintain its segregated societal structure, including the tradition of men studying full-time in yeshivot rather than seeking employment. Within this structure, Israel's ultra-Orthodox population only makes a limited contribution to the country's economic productivity, but still enjoys the benefits of Israel's economic achievements, including access to the same level of public services as the rest of Israeli society. Meanwhile, most of Israel's Arab population want to integrate into the economy and enjoy the benefits of a modern, mainstream education, public services, and economic rights.

From the 2000s, policies began to be developed to expand their access to education and the labor and capital markets. Nonetheless, labor force participation rates among this population remain low to today. About half of Israel's poorest citizens are concentrated within its Arab population. In 2022, 45 percent of Israel's Arab population, and 40 percent of its ultra-Orthodox population, were living below the poverty threshold (for comparison, in that same year, 13 percent of Israel's non-ultra-Orthodox Jewish population of one million people were living under the poverty threshold). In view of the projected growth of both populations, especially the ultra-Orthodox, the government needs to take urgent action to help them integrate into the economy.

In a special report published in 2010,[1] the OECD warned of the socioeconomic disparities between Israel's Arab and ultra-Orthodox communities on the one hand and its non-ultra-Orthodox Jewish population on the other, claiming that this situation threatens the country's stability, resilience, and even its future. Further, in light of forecasts by the Israeli Central Bureau of Statistics predicting that ultra-Orthodox and Arab citizens will comprise around half the population by 2059, Israel does not have the luxury of leaving these populations to their fate. Indeed, the very future of the country depends on their successful integration. The government needs to invest around one percent of GDP (around USD100 billion) per year in education and professional training for both populations over the next 20 years if they are to be integrated properly into the economy.

The Bank of Israel[2] has found that young ultra-Orthodox Jewish men face more difficulties than ultra-Orthodox adults in terms of their participation in further education and the workforce, and that their earning power is lower. Among the Arab population, the situation is the opposite—

young people are more involved in further education, and income disparities are shrinking. The rapid expansion of the number of ultra-Orthodox men engaged solely in yeshiva study, coupled with the fact that an entire generation of ultra-Orthodox Israelis have been raised without a basic mainstream education, has severely damaged the ability of this population to find adequately paid work. Meanwhile, the government's decision to pay generous benefits to ultra-Orthodox yeshivot and kollelim (yeshivot for adult married men only) has only served to further distance Israel's ultra-Orthodox population from the labor market.

## Arab Citizens of Israel

Israel's Arab minority is conflicted over how to live in a state that is at war with its people. Until 1966, Israel's Arab population was subject to martial law, which restricted their movement and freedom of occupation. On March 30, 1976 Arab citizens of Israel called a general strike and held marches in Arab towns and cities across Israel in protest at land expropriations of some 20,000 dunams in Sakhnin, Arabba, and Deir Hanna. This was a defining movement for the Arab population of Israel, and a symbol of their political consciousness (March 30 is now commemorated each year as Land Day ("Yawm Al-Ard" in Arabic) by Arab citizens of Israel and Palestinians).

In 1992, the second Rabin government (1992–1995) was the first to approve a plan to bridge the gaps between Israel's Jewish and Arab populations, although later administrations did not provide many more resources. In the 1990s, steps were taken to eliminate discrimination, such as providing Arabs with the same level of child benefits as Jews and integrating them into the public sector. The October 2000 protests in Arab villages in Israel, some of which turned violent, posed a temporary setback for Arab integration, as Arabs turned their backs on Israeli society, amid fears of Israeli Jews moving into Arab areas.

Israel's Arab population has been characterized by insularity and a desire to safeguard its traditions in the face of the increased westernization and openness of Israeli Jewish society. Nonetheless, from a small, defeated, and frightened minority, Israel's Arabs have become a vibrant population with the potential to be a modern society. They have opened up and built a social and cultural identity, civil society organizations, and a national-Palestinian leadership, which has concerned itself less with local civil issues. Israel's Arab population comprises about 20 percent of the total population and has potential for economic growth. Awareness of the importance of

Israel's Arab population and its needs has increased in recent years, in particular with regard to their full integration into the economy. This involves a commitment to material equality, budget allocation, land distribution, and equal opportunities for Israel's Arab population. The integration of the Arab minority is also in the best interests of Israel's economy, since future growth will be severely hampered if a fifth of the population—a significant minority—is economically unproductive. In-depth surveys have identified significant trends of change over the last decade, with some 70 percent of Arab citizens of Israel seeking to integrate into the economy and decision-making, expand the discourse, take part in civil political life, becoming full participants in the country's economy and society. If Israel wants to be an economic leader, it cannot afford to neglect a fifth of its inhabitants.

In Israel's 2021 elections, the United Arab List political party (usually referred to by its Hebrew acronym Ra'am, which means thunder), led by Mansour Abbas, tipped the scales in the formation of Israel's government by signing a coalition agreement with opposition leader Yair Lapid. This move made Ra'am the first independent Arab party to join a ruling coalition. Abbas has openly stated that his party wishes to integrate into Israeli society and to promote equality and a civil agenda for Arab society in Israel. This move reflects a growing recognition among Israel's Arab population that their traditional approach of isolating themselves from Israeli state institutions is economically and socially detrimental. Ra'am has broken a long-standing taboo in Arab politics, which had preferred neutrality over integration into the "Zionist" government, a situation that had only served to exclude Arab citizens of Israel from the decision-making table and prevented them from having a say in the distribution of national resources. Abbas' decision was a sea change and left the old Arab politics behind in favor of a new, flexible, and practical approach. Ra'am represents a public that wants to address civil problems, including tackling crime and violence, rather than political issues, including the Palestinian issue.

## Processes of Change

Much like in the West, birth rates among Arab citizens of Israel are falling, reflecting a trend unfolding in other Islamic countries. These are the result of modernization processes, including a massive population shift from the countryside to the city, the expansion of women's education and employment, a shift to marrying at a later age and a consequent reduction in childbearing years, and the increasing availability and use of contraception and family planning. While the mean number of live births per woman has fallen in recent years among Arab citizens of Israel, the Arab public still lags behind Israel's Jewish population in terms of economic performance, with the exception of the ultra-Orthodox community. Crime and violence sparked by this housing crisis is on the rise, including because Arab citizens of Israel are turning to grey market lenders as a substitute for mainstream bank credit and mortgages, which will not give them credit without guarantees.

An important step for the advancement of Israel's Arab population was taken at the end of 2015, when the fourth Netanyahu government approved Government Decision 922, a five-year plan drafted by the Ministry of Finance for the integration of Arabs into the economy. Government Decision 922, along with parallel plans for the Druze and Bedouin populations, were significant moves towards integrating Arabs into Israeli society. Budgets were allocated for areas where there are large disparities between Israel's Arab and Jewish populations—chiefly, education, infrastructure, employment, Hebrew language acquisition, developing industrial zones, and public transportation. Government Decision 922 aimed to reduce budgeting disparities between Israel's Jewish and Arab population, allocating some NIS 10 billion for developing services for Arab communities, and around NIS 5 billion for improving education. A comprehensive plan with a critical mass for changes in Arab society, Government Decision 922 was implemented slowly and only partially, as a result of issues with the interface between central government and local authorities. These issues were mainly a result of shortages of public lands, problems around planning and construction, and a lack of matching funds, which made it difficult to implement budgets for building community centers, sports and cultural facilities, and welfare facilities.

The most important step is improving education through more funding, increased classroom space, and better teachers. Training is a key condition for helping Israel's Arab citizens integrate into the economy. The existing education system for Israel's Arab community does not prepare children properly for integration into the economy. With inadequate teaching staffs, young people do not have sufficient knowledge or command of the Hebrew language, let alone English, to allow them to fit into Jewish workplaces, and often lack basic job skills. Informal education is almost nonexistent, due to the poor state of Arab local authorities and a lack of awareness among Arab families. Arabic-speaking high school students in Israel score poorly on the OECD's PISA tests (which measure the ability of 15-year-olds to use their reading, science, and mathematics knowledge to meet real-world challenges). There are disparities in teacher training and budgeting for students between Israel's Arab and Jewish schools. It should be noted that among the OECD nations, Israel has the largest gap between its highest performing schools and lowest performing ones.

Government Decision 922 was important not just from a budgetary perspective but also declaratively: with it, the government admitted that there was discrimination against Arab citizens of Israel, and that it was working to reduce this. Even though the Decision was slow to be implemented, there have been several important successes. Almost all Arab towns and villages have now been connected to Israel's sewage system. The number of Arabs in higher education reached 18 percent in 2022, exceeding the government target of 17 percent. The number of Arab women in employment rose to 42 percent in 2022, the number of trips by public transport increased, the number of Arab high school students eligible to graduate with a diploma rose, as did the number of Arab children benefitting from after-school classes. Nineteen more Arab local authorities were ranked in Israel's higher socioeconomic clusters in 2019 compared to 2017.

The difficulties facing the Arab population in Israel include land shortages, a lack of planning, and the absence of comprehensive planning and zoning programs for Arab settlements, without which it is impossible to prepare detailed plans and obtain building permits. A shortage of private land has led to high-density building in Arab towns and villages and construction without a permit. The demand for industrial and commercial areas and public buildings has increased. One of the great achievements that has come out of Government Decision 922 has been that 95 percent of Israel's larger Arab towns have been provided with improved planning and zoning plans. The Arab population is still faced with the need to regulate land registration via the official land registry deed system (known as the Tabu) and develop infrastructure, moves that will facilitate integration into national planning trends around land shortages and overcrowding.

The number of Arab students in higher education increased between 2010–2020, marking the first generation of Arab citizens of Israel to obtain a post-secondary education. The Arab elite have tended to gravitate toward health professions, and the Arab community is well-represented in medical professions in Israel. The healthcare professions are free professions, such as physicians and more, favored by many minorities in countries around the world because they meet a global demand and allow for independence. Nonetheless, in Israel, the number of Arabs studying computer science has also increased, indicating a desire among young people to join Israel's growing high-tech sector—the result of encouraging young Arabs to enter these professions. The number of Arab undergraduates studying computer science, mathematics, computer engineering, and electronics in 2022 was 12 percent, double that of 2017. In 2022, Arab citizens of Israel make up just 2 percent of the high-tech industry. The real challenge for this population will be in acquiring soft skills (non-technical skills regarding how one works), Hebrew language proficiency, and life skills. Israel's Arab entrepreneurs lack experience and knowledge regarding how to write CVs and an understanding of the organizational culture. Another reason they experience difficulties in entering the labor market and joining Israeli Jewish high-tech ventures is because, unlike Jews, they do not undertake compulsory army service in the IDF, which is where young Israelis are able to develop connections and experience for future employment.

The second five-year plan, drawn up by the Bennett-Lapid government in 2021 as a continuation of Government Decision 922, amounted to NIS 30 billion. It was intended to reduce disparities among Israel's Druze, Circassian, and Bedouin communities in terms of education, housing, employment, and infrastructure. In addition, the government allocated around NIS 2 billion for infrastructure, and about NIS 2.5 billion for police and law enforcement to tackle violence and crime among Arab citizens of Israel, which is currently a heavy burden on the population's economy. A budget of NIS 20 billion was also earmarked for 2022–2030 for a strategic plan to improve urban transportation in Arab towns and villages.

The coronavirus pandemic exposed an array of weaknesses in Israel's Arab population— economic, social, and civic—that harmed the employment of those with low levels of educational attainment, leaving households without a safety net. Arab communities were less organized more vulnerable economically and socially, and less compliant with government instruction and law enforcement. Furthermore, Arab schoolchildren and students found it difficult to access remote learning, largely due to a lack of infrastructure in their schools to support remote learning. The negative impact on employment within this population created a large group of young people who neither study nor work, due also to a lack of job-related skills and an increase in the number of migrant workers. Some of these youths have been driven into violence and crime. High crime rates among Israel's Arab population, which are among some of the highest in the country, are tearing apart Arab society in the Galilee, the "Triangle" (the concentration of Arab towns and villages along the Green Line in the center of the country), and among the Bedouin community in the south. During Israel's Operation "Guardians of the Walls" in Gaza in May 2021, Arab criminal gangs of young people who had degenerated into crime also participated in demonstrations, many of which turned violent, rolling back the achievements of the Arab population in Israel's economy and society and jeopardizing the Arab population and the country as a whole. This is a national problem, and not just a sectarian one.

Israel's Arab community is not homogeneous, and consists of a mosaic of identities, religions, and denominations. Like any society, it faces significant challenges, yet inherent within it are many opportunities. There are social tensions with Jews, and pressure from residents of the West Bank to form a shared national and religious identity (the political leadership strongly expresses this). The events of May 2021 during Operation "Guardian of the Walls" in Gaza damaged Jewish-Arab relations but did not change the desire to integrate into the economy. The processes taking place are slow and include a transition from a collective to a private society, increasing employment rates among women, and rising numbers of businesspeople, academics, scientists, doctors, and high-tech workers. The Arab population is a young society, with the majority (74 percent) under 40. Many spend time on social networks and are connected to the internet. Expanding women's employment will provide families with two bread-winners, which will positively affect living standards, savings, and long-term planning of families' needs.

Natural increase has resulted in the growth of new Arab cities built upon old village structures without any urban planning. In the past, only Nazareth was a large Arab city, but by 2022, there were several Arab cities with over 40,000 inhabitants: Rahat (75,000), Umm al-Fahm (60,000), Nazareth (60,000), and Taibeh (50,000). There are also dozens of rural settlements that grew and urbanized, including Tamra, Sakhnin, Baqa al-Gharbiyya, Tira, and Shafaram. These towns suffer from poor infrastructure, low quality of life, and poor local government services. The Bedouin diaspora in the Negev are a special group, who numbered around 300,000 in 2022. Some of the Bedouin live in towns (including Rahat, Kuseife, and Hura), while a large number reside in unrecognized villages scattered between Beersheba and Arad and maintain their own autonomy with inferior services and little enforcement. Because of their feelings of deprivation and neglect, they threaten public order in the Negev alongside a serious crime problem, proving harmful to themselves and their surroundings.

Israel's Arab population also includes residents of East Jerusalem, who numbered around 375,000 in 2023. This population was annexed to Israel in June 1967 following the Six-Day War as residents, not citizens, and do not have the right to vote in national elections (that is, to elect representatives to Israel's Knesset). They suffer from a lack of government and municipal services, and a high percentage are living under the poverty rate and/or on low incomes. In 2013, the huge disparities between the east and west of the city in terms of municipal and government services led the government to allocate, for the first time since 1967, dedicated measures and budgets to improve the situation of East Jerusalem residents. Government Decision, agreed in June 2014, allocated NIS 200 million over 5 years for civil and economic issues, with a further NIS 100 million for security. This was followed by Government Decision in May 2017, which allocated NIS 177 million to reduce disparities through economic development, treating environmental hazards in sewage, waste removal, and environmental awareness education. The culmination of the process was Government Decision 3790 in May 2018, whose goals were to "reduce social and economic disparities and economic development in East Jerusalem for the purpose of strengthening residents' ability to integrate into society and the economy, and strengthening the economic and social resilience of Jerusalem as a whole."[3] The scope of the investment for 2018–2023 is about NIS 2.1 billion, and is intended to improve the economic and social status of the residents of East Jerusalem, a third of whom live beyond the separation barrier that was built following the Second Intifada. The motivation for the program is multidimensional—security, politics, sovereignty, governance, and economic improvement. This is government recognition of the neglect and large disparities that exist between the two parts of the city, exacerbated by the construction of the separation barrier, which drove the younger generation to turn to Western Jerusalem for education, higher education, and employment. The Arabs of East Jerusalem now make up about 38 percent of the residents of Jerusalem, the capital of Israel, which is the largest Arab city in Israel, the largest ultra-Orthodox city, and simply the largest city in Israel.

## Israel's ultra-Orthodox Community

Israel's ultra-Orthodox community has grown from 4 percent of the population in 1980 to around 13 percent in 2023, reflecting an annual growth rate of around 4 percent compared with just 1.4 percent among the secular (non-religious) Jewish population. There are high levels of poverty among Israel's ultra-Orthodox community, where men prefer to devote themselves to unpaid Torah study rather than to paid employment. The community is "poor but wise," with an organized community life based around mutual aid and guarantees. By leveraging its advantages of size and scale, the ultra-Orthodox community has created an effective economic system that has been able to extract a relatively high real purchasing power from a nominal income. Israel's ultra-Orthodox population is dependent on government support, and its community, spiritual, and political leaders work to obtain resources from the state by leveraging their political power and participating in the coalition government. The ultra-Orthodox population has segregated and isolated itself from the rest of Israeli society. Ultra-Orthodox towns, cities, and neighborhoods maintain unique community resources and services, such as mikvehs (special baths used in Judaism for immersion to achieve ritual purity), Talmud Torahs (elementary schools for boys from modest backgrounds), yeshivot, and kosher businesses, as central components of their communal and economic lifestyle. Within this society, a limited number of rabbis—and not individuals—make the decisions.

Between 2010–2019, around 40 percent of Israel's ultra-Orthodox population were living below the poverty rate. However, these statistics do not imply a low level of welfare or an experience of poverty, and the ultra-Orthodox community do not perceive themselves as being in economic distress. The ultra-Orthodox score highly on the Israeli Central Bureau of Statistics' happiness index, considering themselves as happy families. Their community has high levels of solidarity, mutual aid, charity organizations, and *gemachim* (Jewish free-loan funds that are interest free and usually set up with easy repayment terms). Most of Israel's ultra-Orthodox Jews need government assistance, without which they would find it hard to maintain their lifestyle. In this sense, the ultra-Orthodox community has embraced a socialist-style ideology with government intervention and a welfare state. Their increasing weight in the population has pushed up government spending on welfare and income support.

## The "Learners' Society"

The ultra-Orthodox community holds in high esteem its "*chevrat halomdim*" ("learners' society"),[4] in which most ultra-Orthodox men dedicate their lives to studying in kollelim within the Torah Umunato system ("Torah Study is his job," the special framework that exempts ultra-Orthodox men who study in yeshivot from compulsory military service), which distinguishes them from men in other communities in Israel who go out to work. This arrangement was made possible politically through state support for almost free education for the ultra-Orthodox sector over the age of 18, various allowances and benefits, and the avoidance of compulsory military service. Beyond child benefits and health insurance, state benefits for Israel's ultra-Orthodox community include stipends for married yeshiva students, income support, daycare subsidies, housing assistance, and property tax discounts. These benefits make going to work simply unprofitable for ultra-Orthodox men, who would lose a large portion of their incomes as a result of the loss in benefits and discounts to which they are entitled as long as they remain unemployed. During periods when the government has cut some benefits, the number of ultra-Orthodox men in employment increased—demonstrating that the ultra-Orthodox community responds to economic incentives just like other populations. In 2023, the Netanyahu government increased state support for yeshiva students, established funding for ultra-Orthodox education without requiring them to teach core curriculum subjects, which has reduced the incentive for ultra-Orthodox men to go out to work.

With the rise to power of the Begin government in 1977, the quota for yeshiva students (the restrictions on the number of ultra-Orthodox young men allowed to defer their compulsory military service until they complete their yeshiva studies) were abolished completely. In the 1950s, the quota had applied to about 400 yeshiva students. By the 1960s, the number of yeshiva students had risen to a few thousand. In 2022, Israel had around 155,000 yeshiva students (around 70,000 of whom were exempt from compulsory military service). The "learners' society" of the 2020s are the third generation of ultra-Orthodox families without a breadwinner. This status quo is a concern to ultra-Orthodox parents and their offspring alike, since most of these families have exhausted any intergenerational capital they may have had to use to buy apartments for their adult children. Furthermore, the older ultra-Orthodox generation is facing a looming pension crisis that will render them dependent on the government forever. Children will not have any means to support their elderly parents financially, while life expectancy is increasing. As a result, Israel's ultra-Orthodox community will have no choice but to continue to rely on the state to provide them with a living, and to use their political power to secure state benefits.

The Israeli ultra-Orthodox ethos, which demands that men dedicate their lives to becoming Torah scholars by studying in yeshivot and kollelim is an expression of the prestige and loyalty that yeshiva students enjoy in this community. Studying in the higher yeshivot (as some 165,000 ultra-Orthodox Israeli men did in 2023)[5] has created an exclusive "club"[6] of Torah scholars, whose members benefit from the special prestige conferred by membership in a select, elitist ingroup. The members of this elite are perceived by the rest of the ultra-Orthodox community as making significant material and personal sacrifices in order to devote themselves to learning Torah. Within ultra-Orthodox society, group loyalty is often at odds with loyalty to the state and is sometimes even stronger than loyalty to the individual and the family. A high proportion of Israel's ultra-Orthodox population simply do not consider state institutions as relevant, and those who do choose to integrate into the state do so for practical reasons to position themselves to leverage government benefits and connections. This situation has given rise to a complex struggle between Israel's ultra-Orthodox society and the state over who is the source of authority for Israel's ultra-Orthodox population. The rabbis and *admorim* (Hassidic spiritual leaders) are far more important within the ultra-Orthodox hierarchy than the prime minister and state institutions. The ultra-Orthodox community has put its "learners' community" on a pedestal, seeing its members as more valuable and important than those of mainstream, secular Israeli society. The extent and depth of the struggle between the state and ultra-Orthodox community leaders for authority was exposed most recently during the coronavirus pandemic of 2020–2021, and during the Mount Meron "disaster" in 2021 on the Jewish Lag BaOmer holiday.[7]

There is a question mark over the extent to which Israel's mainstream society can, or would even be willing to, finance the ultra-Orthodox community's unsustainable lifestyle, which threatens to undermine the economic stability and living standards of the working public. The state has deliberately not interfered in the affairs of Israel's ultra-Orthodox population and has frequently given in to pressure from ultra-Orthodox leaders in exchange for their political acquiescence on various issues. It is convenient for the ultra-Orthodox leadership to maintain the status quo whereby their community is poor and uneducated. This situation cannot even be described as ultra-Orthodox autonomy, since in a democracy, autonomy is determined by those in power and by the government that is in charge of setting the rules. In practice, within the ultra-Orthodox community, the rules are set by the ultra-Orthodox leadership, that is, by its rabbis and *admorim*. Israel's ultra-Orthodox population is already a large tribe and not a small minority with a seat at the majority table. The political power of Israel's ultra-Orthodox community, due to their political parties' key role in creating parliamentary coalitions, allows it to extract financial benefits from the government, enabling it to support large families without needing to work. Meanwhile, the ultra-Orthodox community's growing demographic weight is strengthening its political power. It is clear that, unchecked, this vicious cycle will lead to an economic crisis.

The reality is that Israel's ultra-Orthodox population cannot survive without the support of Israel's secular-liberal society. The per capita GDP of an ultra-Orthodox man in Israel is about a third of that of his non-ultra-Orthodox fellow citizen. Rather than striving to create a segregated population outside of, but financially supported by, mainstream society, the ultra-Orthodox community must take responsibility for its own future, which can occur only within the framework of the state and its liberal order. Israel's ultra-Orthodox population must find ways to integrate into their country's modern and technological labor market, without losing their integrity. Israel cannot continue to abdicate responsibility for the fate of young ultra-Orthodox people, who need to be able to make a living. Nor can Israel risk its own future and continued existence by allowing yet another generation of ultra-Orthodox families to become dependent on welfare. The return of authority from ultra-Orthodox rabbis to the government can happen only if there is a change in the ultra-Orthodox education system, which currently operates as if it is completely independent from the state.

Israel is facing a dilemma regarding its young ultra-Orthodox population. Either it can enforce ultra-Orthodox conscription into the IDF, so that young ultra-Orthodox men and women can share the burden of military service more equally with the rest of the country's young people, or it can encourage them to participate in the workforce instead of conscription. In the latter case, Israel's non-ultra-Orthodox population would continue to unfairly bear the lion's share of military service. In the name of the principle of equality, believing that yeshiva students are bearing the burden of studying Torah on behalf of all of Israel's Jews, many young ultra-Orthodox men remain in their yeshivot, preferring to maintain the Torah Umunato arrangement and avoid work. The main barrier for young ultra-Orthodox men to entering Israel's labor market is not their lack of compulsory military service, but rather their lack of skills and professional training as a result of poor mainstream education in core curricula. The increase in benefits granted to the ultra-Orthodox community in January 2023 by the sixth Netanyahu government only serves to perpetuate the situation of ultra-Orthodox men avoiding work. The ultra-Orthodox, rabbinic, and political establishments are not interested in lowering the age of exemption from military conscription for yeshiva students, preferring to confine young ultra-Orthodox men to religious seminaries where they can maintain their control and supervision over them.

## Ultra-Orthodox Education

As mentioned,up until the 1980s, the fertility rate among Israel's ultra-Orthodox community was about 5 live births per woman. In the 1980s, the fertility rate increased to 6 live births per woman, peaking at 7.5 live births per woman in the early 2000s. By 2022, the fertility rate had dropped again to 6.5 live births per woman. In 2023, about a quarter of children in Israel aged 0-4 years were ultra-Orthodox. By 2065, this figure is predicted to reach around 50 percent. Torah education is a top priority among the ultra-Orthodox population, where the ideal is that young men will go on to study in kollelim. The ultra-Orthodox education system creates a large number of jobs within the community to serve the community—47 percent of ultra-Orthodox women (compared to 21 percent of non-ultra-Orthodox women) and 23 percent of ultra-Orthodox men (compared with 3.5 percent of non-ultra-Orthodox men). Many of their skills are suitable for the community and not for the general labor force.

Israel's Free Compulsory Education Law is intended to create national and personal human capital that will ensure high productivity and equal opportunities in the labor market. The compulsory core curriculum subjects taught in Israel's public-school systems (state-secular, state-religious, ultra-Orthodox, and Arab) are designed to enable children to acquire an education that will enable them to go on to get jobs. Ultra-Orthodox education is mostly privately-run and does not accept the values and core curriculum ("secular") subjects taught in the public school system. The ultra-Orthodox education system does not care about integration into the job market and enlisting in the IDF in the same way that the majority of Israelis do. The ultra-Orthodox have created their own education system (for boys) that is almost devoid of secular core curriculum subjects.

The legal status of Israel's ultra-Orthodox elementary education institutions is unique and is reflected in their state budget allocations and the scope of the core curriculum subjects that each education network is obliged to teach. Two education networks operate in Israel's ultra-Orthodox elementary education system. They receive equivalent budgets to those allocated to regular Israeli public schools (secular and national-religious). Pupils at these schools make up 51 percent of all ultra-Orthodox elementary students. Their schools must commit to teaching 100 percent of Israel's mainstream core subjects. Ultra-Orthodox schools that are designated as "exempt" institutions are independently run. They receive 55 percent of the budgets allocated to regular public schools and are required to teach 55 percent of core curriculum subjects. Their pupils make up 23 percent of all ultra-Orthodox elementary students. "Recognized but unofficial" schools teach about 12 percent of Israeli ultra-Orthodox elementary pupils, receive 75 percent of the budgets allocated to state schools, and are required to teach 75 percent of the core curriculum subjects. Ultra-Orthodox public schools teach 5 percent of all ultra-Orthodox elementary pupils, receive the same budgets as regular public schools (secular and national-religious), and must devote the same number of hours as regular public schools to teaching core subjects.

Most ultra-Orthodox students are not given the tools they need to integrate into the labor market and into rewarding occupations, despite ultra-Orthodox schools being allocated budgets from the government. The government's oversight supervision of the teaching of core curriculum subjects in ultra-Orthodox schools is poor, and pupils' achievements in standardized tests ("Meitzav") are also poor.

The creation of a public ultra-Orthodox education system in 2014, which teaches full core curriculum ("secular") subjects alongside Torah education, is a bright spot that offers great hope for the future.

## The Labor Market

The lack of a mainstream education and labor market skills among Israel's ultra-Orthodox population will result in the loss of Israel's growth potential in years to come. The growth of the ultra-Orthodox population, which does not contribute its relative share to the labor market, has created a year-on-year gap between supply and demand, and increases labor shortages in Israel.[8] The Israeli Institute for Democracy has estimated that the loss of GDP as a result of low employment rates and low wages among ultra-Orthodox men was NIS 29 billion (1.5 percent of GDP) in 2021, and could reach as much as NIS 80 billion (3 percent of GDP) by 2050. The growth of the ultra-Orthodox population will cause a decrease in labor market participation rates. If ultra-Orthodox children are not given the right tools to help them integrate into the modern labor market, they will inevitably end up in low-wage jobs and poverty, which will impose a heavy burden on Israel's growth.

According to estimates, many ultra-Orthodox men work in the shadow economy and do not pay tax. This is because ultra-Orthodox men who receive an exemption from compulsory military service on the grounds that they are studying in yeshivot are then prohibited from taking up paid employment. Ultra-Orthodox men who work in the shadow economy are either self-employed but do not declare their income to the tax authorities or are employees whose employers pay them "off the books." Between 2015–2019, the average income of an ultra-Orthodox Israeli man was only 55 percent of the income of a non-ultra-Orthodox counterpart.

The number of ultra-Orthodox students studying in academic institutions (that is, not yeshivot or kollelim) increased from about 4,000 in 2000 to 10,000 in 2022. On the face of it, this is an impressive increase, but the proportion of ultra-Orthodox Israelis in academia is still only 4 percent of the total student population. Around 70 percent of ultra-Orthodox students are women, with relatively far fewer men, around 3000, undertaking academic studies. The subjects that ultra-Orthodox men choose to study often do not help them go on to find work. A high percentage choose to study law, but overall dropout rates are high, often because ultra-Orthodox men do not have the required grounding in core curriculum studies. They also have difficulties in earning a living, especially in professions that require mathematics and science. Further, ultra-Orthodox men who leave the yeshiva to take up academic studies lose income and benefits, which makes it harder for them to make a successful transition to a non-religious, academic education. Only 3 percent of ultra-Orthodox men in Israel are employed in the high-tech industry, which is perhaps unsurprising given that integrating into the high-tech sector requires a significant investment in academic studies.

One bright spot is the successful integration of ultra-Orthodox women into work and higher education. Their entry into the labor market is a direct result of ultra-Orthodox men avoiding employment. The wife is often the main breadwinner in the ultra-Orthodox Israeli family, and her professional education is often much higher than that of her husband. Labor market participation rates among Israeli ultra-Orthodox women has risen from 51 percent in 2022 to 80 percent in 2022 (the labor market participation rate among non-ultra-Orthodox Israeli women is 84 percent). The improvement in employment rates among ultra-Orthodox women has resulted from their studying computing, programming, and other academic subjects.

## Living Conditions

Until the 1990s, most of Israel's ultra-Orthodox population was concentrated in Jerusalem and Bnei Brak (an ultra-Orthodox city in Israel's central Mediterranean coastal plain, and the fifth most densely populated city in the world), with smaller populations in other cities. Population growth has led to the creation of new ultra-Orthodox towns and cities, which have been specially designed to preserve the ultra-Orthodox community and lifestyle by segregating this population from mainstream Israeli society. This has helped make it possible for ultra-Orthodox families to buy inexpensive apartments adapted to their specific needs, such as educational institutions, rituals baths, glatt kosher food, quiet neighborhoods without bars and nightclubs, and more, in various towns and cities, including Modi'in Illit, Beitar Illit, and Elad, as well as large, segregated ultra-Orthodox neighborhoods in Ashdod, Beit Shemesh, Kiryat Gat, and Arad. The considerations of the ultra-Orthodox Israeli public when choosing a place to live are less about history and a connection to holiness, and more about the ability to sustain their unique lifestyle.

Israel's ultra-Orthodox leadership have pushed for the construction of new, segregated ultra-Orthodox-only settlements and neighborhoods, with cheap housing and specific ultra-Orthodox institutions, but without any infrastructure for employment. Experience has shown that the growth of the ultra-Orthodox population has led to segregated ultra-Orthodox neighborhoods in various towns and cities, as well as ultra-Orthodox only towns. These towns and neighborhoods are disconnected from the labor market and perpetuate poverty within the ultra-Orthodox population. Israel's ultra-Orthodox population must be integrated into existing cities and into Israel's heterogeneous urban life. Modern cities must have diverse, mixed populations, which helps create a healthy society.

The coronavirus pandemic, during which the ultra-Orthodox and— the Arab community— did not always comply with government instructions, both exposed and increased two opposing trends within Israel's autonomous ultra-Orthodox population. The first involves ultra-Orthodox distrust in the government and science, refusal to accept or abide by the laws of the land, defiance in the face of government instructions and advice, and alarming signs of a retreat in the process of "Israelification," which makes it difficult for ultra-Orthodox Jews to integrate into mainstream Israeli society and into the labor market. Second, and counteracting the prevailing trend toward increased segregation from mainstream Israeli society, is the increased exposure of ultra-Orthodox Israelis to the internet, including through remote learning and working, and a recognition among some segments of the ultra-Orthodox population of the need to adjust to a new reality. This trend may lead to the integration of at least some of Israel's ultra-Orthodox population into mainstream society. The pandemic exposed the terrible price of ultra-Orthodox isolationism and separatism. If Israel wants to survive, it must act to stem the tide of this autonomous and isolationist trend, by creating a series of incentives and disincentives that will boost the teaching of core curriculum subjects in ultra-Orthodox schools, encourage ultra-Orthodox men to work, and encourage ultra-Orthodox families to live in mixed cities rather than in segregated communities. However, major change can occur only if the ultra-Orthodox population and its leadership consider themselves partners with the rest of Israeli society in taking responsibility for their country's future. The more liberal among the ultra-Orthodox population, who manage to work and maintain their ultra-Orthodox values by adopting elements of a more general Israeli identity, can be used as role models for others to follow. In particular, the ultra-Orthodox public education stream that does teach the full core curriculum subjects should be promoted as an example for the rest of the ultra-Orthodox education system, showing the community a way to combine their Torah studies with a general education and thereby become prepared for better employment leading to an improved economic situation.

The Israeli middle class already feels strongly that it is being made to (literally) pay for the ultra-Orthodox to maintain their lifestyles and avoid work, and will push for the development of positive and negative incentives to effect a change in the economic behavior of the ultra-Orthodox population (the first signs of this were seen in the mass protests in 2023 that deepened the conflict between secular and ultra-Orthodox society). The impacts of changes to child benefit for ultra-Orthodox yeshiva students over the years have already demonstrated that the behavior of ultra-Orthodox families is affected by financial incentives and disincentives. It is of immense strategic and economic importance to change the status quo quickly, and to help Israel's ultra-Orthodox population to become economically productive citizens. This will prove difficult, however. The sheer size of the ultra-Orthodox population has given it political power, which has enabled it to obtain special budgets and allowances as concessions from the government, which encourage ultra-Orthodox men to avoid work. This situation is a significant barrier to change.

The general public should be aware that ultra-Orthodox Israelis who integrate into mainstream education and employment experience psychological and social barriers, from their experience of being "the Other," and because they are unaccustomed to being in spaces that are not set up to meet the needs of their unique lifestyles. Israel's ultra-Orthodox Jews fear that integrating into mainstream Israeli society will indirectly harm the way of life of their esteemed yeshiva students, and thus prefer to continue to segregate themselves. However, experience has shown that when learning frameworks are adapted to the ultra-Orthodox environment, the ultra-Orthodox community do not perceive them as a threat. Israel must create a suitable sociocultural learning framework that can support the efforts of the ultra-Orthodox community to integrate into mainstream society. This includes being sensitive to encouraging ultra-Orthodox men and women and reassuring them that their lifestyles will not have to change. Incentives must be created for their integration into the labor market, with study scholarships and assistance in professional training in an ultra-Orthodox orientation and environment, with an emphasis on study content adapted to their lifestyle. The ultra-Orthodox population needs to find its own balance between modernity and tradition. In essence, the conflict between Israel's ultra-Orthodox and secular populations is just the latest chapter in the historical struggle of the Jewish enlightenment and modernity with conservatism and orthodoxy, a story that began in 19th century Europe.

## Notes

1. "Israel: A divided society. Results of a review of labor-market and social policy." OECD, 2010. https://www.oecd.org/social/family/44394444.pdf.
2. Report of the Bank of Israel, 2022 (Hebrew).
3. Reduction of Economic and Social Disparities and development in East Jerusalem, Government Decision 3790, May 13, 2018.
4. A term coined by Prof. Menachem Friedman, a scholar of ultra-Orthodox society in the 1980s. 89. The Yearbook of Ultra-Orthodox Society in Israel 2021, Israeli Institute for Democracy.
5. See: Berman, E. (1999). Subsidized sacrifice: State support of religion in Israel. Contemporary Jewry 20, 167–200 (1999). https://link.springer.com/article/10.1007/BF02967964; and Berman, E. (2000). Sect, subsidy, and sacrifice: An economist's view of ultra-Orthodox Jews. The Quarterly Journal of Economics. 115(3), 905–953.
6. Ultra-Orthodox leaders had ignored safety warnings from local council leaders, the state comptroller, and the police chief, while no government agency took on the task of enforcing safety rules. In the deadly crush, 45 ultra-Orthodox men and boys were killed and another 150 injured in what was one of the deadliest peacetime tragedies in Israel's history.
7. The Israeli Institute for Democracy, 2022.

# 28

# Welfare

During the first years of Israeli statehood, welfare payments to its needier residents were limited. As a relatively poor country, Israel did not have the luxury of introducing a generous welfare policy. At the same time, however, Israel's government understood that its citizens had a right to welfare, even in light of the difficult conditions that the fledgling state was facing. Benefit payments were provided to Jewish citizens who had been injured in the War of Independence, and the government introduced a rationing and austerity policy that allowed every citizen to buy basic food products at the same fixed price. Income disparities and poverty rates were low. After the austerity period ended, the main tools of Israel's nascent welfare policy were generous subsidies on basic food products, public transport, and water. Meanwhile, the state assisted unemployed citizens through self-initiated work schemes, based on the principle that labor should be the main source of household income. Israel's National Insurance Institute was established as a social security body only in 1954, and its activities were limited at first. The state did devote resources to developing education, health, and professional training systems, assisted by the Histadrut, which provided a range of social services via its various institutions. The Histadrut's network of day care centers, small discount supermarkets, libraries, and sports clubs, which had been established during the British Mandatory period.

The riots that broke out in Wadi Salib in Haifa in 1959 in reaction to the shooting of a Moroccan Jewish immigrant by Ashkenazi police officers sparked social welfare thinking for the first time. Some years later, in 1971, the Black Panthers protests by second-generation Jewish immigrants from North Africa and the Middle East accelerated the process of building a welfare state. In the wake of the Black Panthers demonstrations, Prime Minister Golda Meir appointed the "Prime Minister's Committee for Children and Youth in Need," (1972), which recommended regulating universal allowances and increasing social services in education, housing and employment security. The ensuing changes marked Israel's adoption of the principles of a European-style "welfare state," albeit within the constraints of Israel's economic situation.

When the first Rabin government came to power in June 1974, it pushed forward with these social policies, despite the rise in defense spending that had increased the budget deficit. When Menachem Begin's Likud party came to power in June 1977 and replaced the Rabin government, it failed to adjust social spending to fiscal limits. As a result, the budget deficit soared. It was clear that it would not be possible to maintain a high defense budget alongside soaring spending on subsidies and social security.

The 1985 Economic Stabilization Plan curbed Israel's rampant inflation but had a negative impact on social spending, including subsidies on basic commodities, education, welfare, and health. The decision to end food subsidies, a politically sensitive move, was possible thanks to the unity government's broad consensus that Israel needed to change its priorities. In short, the government realized that economic recovery was more important than social services.

In the first decade following the 1985 Economic Stabilization Plan (until 1996), social inequalities in Israel largely remained unchanged, despite budget cuts. In 2003, after the economic crisis had abated, then-Finance Minister Binyamin Netanyahu introduced his Economic Protective Wall financial plan. Netanyahu took a neoliberal approach, slashing child and unemployment benefits and income security ("work allowances"), and reducing government spending on education, health, and welfare under the slogan of feeding the "thin man" (the private sector) by slimming down the "fat man" (the public sector).

Since the 2000s, social inequalities in Israel have widened as gaps in income distribution have grown (as reflected in the OECD's Gini coefficient measure of income inequality). This is a result of privatization, the globalization of Israel's economy, cuts in welfare budgets, the weakening of trade unions, large rises in managerial salaries, and increases in remuneration for high-tech entrepreneurship and financial and legal knowledge. The increasing reliance on contract and migrant workers has harmed Israel's lowest paid employees. A new generation of businesspeople and entrepreneurs emerged who knew how to take advantage of the opportunities afforded by the globalization of Israel's economy. In contrast, the large swathes of the workforce who had not been partners in these globalization processes and could not adapt to Israel's competitive market economy were left behind. Social inequalities have deepened as a result of Israel's transition from a public to a capitalist economy. This has had marked effects on its very diverse population, large sections of which—in particular its Arab and ultra-Orthodox citizens—have not benefitted from the globalization of the economy. The growth in social inequalities is reflected in Israel's Gini coefficient scores, which rose from 0.33 in the 1990s to 0.392 in 2006, the peak year for inequality. The Gini coefficient started going down in delayed reaction to the "welfare to work strategy' that increased the employment rates among the poor. Initially the Gini of labor income started to decline and a few years later also that of net (disposable) income.

Social spending is broadly divided into social investment and social protection. Social investment includes schemes to boost the skills of individuals and promote leadership, education, and early years care, while social protection involves providing benefits for those in financial difficulties (such as older people and people with disabilities). An examination of social spending in relation to GDP in various countries reveals a considerable gap between Israel and Europe. Since the 2000s, Israel's welfare policy has been torn between two conflicting trends: Western Europe's welfare state model, which provides state benefits and generous social services, versus the neoliberal approach taken by the United States, which is based on low social welfare expenditures. Israel has fluctuated between reducing its welfare budgets and expanding them (in particular after the wave of social justice protests that erupted across the country in 2011). In short, Israel does not have a consensus about its welfare policy.

In the 2000s, social spending amounted to only 15 percent of Israel's per capita GDP compared to the OECD average of 21 percent. Data from Israel's Taub Institute, which specializes in social economics, indicate that between 2016–2018, Scandinavian countries spent an average of over 11 percent of GDP on social investment schemes, compared with just 7–8 percent in Israel. Meanwhile, in the same period, Israel spent just 4 percent of per capita GDP on social investment schemes for working-age individuals, similar to rates in the lowest-ranked OECD countries. Further, Israel spends only 8 percent of its per capita GDP on education and early years' care for children aged 0–4 years, compared to about 27 percent in the leading welfare states. Studies indicate that the main beneficiaries of social investment in Israel are the middle classes, and not less advantaged and less affluent population groups. Of the 41 percent of children in Israel who attend supervised daycare centers, around 24 percent are from middle class families and just 17 percent from less affluent and less advantaged groups. The beneficiaries of higher education (all subsidized) in Israel are overwhelmingly non-ultra-Orthodox Jewish Israelis from medium to high socioeconomic backgrounds. In terms of public expenditure on pensions, in 2021 Israel spent about 4.7 percent of GDP, below the more developed OECD countries' average of 7.8 percent.

The World Economic Forum has noted that in the United Kingdom, it takes an average of five generations for a low-income family to attain an average income. In Denmark it takes just two generations. Israel is in the middle of these two extremes. The gap between Israel and other welfare states is growing, according to data examining spending in social protection programs. Since 2009, Israel has earmarked a smaller percentage of its GDP on social spending than any other OECD country. In terms of social mobility, Israel ranks 33 out of 82 countries in the world, according to data from and WEF survey. Israelis who work in the high-tech industry tend to improve their socioeconomic situation. However, Israel's ultra-Orthodox and Arab populations, who make up about 5 percent of the labor force, and young people who live in less affluent peripheral regions, and citizens from other less advantaged populations, are relatively underrepresented in the high-tech industry.

## Income Inequality

The Gini coefficient is an accepted measurement of a country's income inequality. It is based on the comparison of cumulative proportions of a population against cumulative proportions of income they receive, and ranges between 0 (perfect equality) and 1 (perfect inequality). The Gini coefficient relates to wage-earners and not to the owners of capital, and it is clear that the main source of income inequality is concentrated in the accumulation of capital. The Gini coefficient measures disparities in financial income and does not take into account the value of social services, some of which were provided for free in the past. Since the 2000s, these services have become more expensive as a result of privatization, which has exacerbated inequalities. There are two measures of income inequality: gross income inequality, which refers to inequality arising from economic income before state intervention in the form of direct taxation and benefits, and net income inequality, which measures inequality after state intervention in the form of direct taxation and state benefits. The net Gini coefficient tells the story of Israel's social disparities. When it was first calculated in 1979, Israel had a reasonable net Gini coefficient score of 0.3, which placed it squarely in the middle of the other OECD countries. In the 1980s, Israel's net Gini coefficient score had risen to 0.32, and by the 1990s, it reached 0.33–0.35. From the beginning of the 2000s, the net Gini coefficient score began to rise again, reaching a peak in 2006 of 0.392. After the social justice protests of 2011 and the government's corrective measures, Israel's net Gini coefficient score fell. By 2019, it was 0.35, rising slightly in 2021 to 0.375 (for comparison, the OECD average for 2021 was 0.31). Meanwhile, in 2019, the disposable income share ratio of Israel's top decile was 25.4 percent, the highest of all the OECD countries, and the difference in the income quintile share ratio between Israel's ninth decile and its bottom decile was 4.8, lower only than that in the United States, indicating high levels of inequality.[1]

The increase in net income inequality in the 2000s was partly attributable to the government's policy of cutting allowances (so-called "work allowances") and cutting direct taxation rates, which had a negative effect on income disparities. The cuts to work allowances mainly affected the two lowest deciles, while tax cuts benefited the upper decile, who saw their disposable incomes rise. A type of "scissors effect" was created, whereby the income gap increased significantly, with the lower deciles becoming less well-off and the upper deciles growing richer, thus increasing net inequality. In the 2000s, Israel scored the highest among OECD countries in terms of inequalities. Unlike in most OECD countries where governments managed to reduce inequalities through direct taxation and benefits, Israel did nothing to change this situation.

In the 2000s, the government faced a difficult situation. Labor force participation, especially among ultra-Orthodox men and Arab women, was low—a phenomenon that was attributed to high benefit payments. The "work allowances" policy increased the labor force participation rate and economic income and reduced gross inequality. The following developments unfolded in this period: the labor market participation rate among Arab and ultra-Orthodox citizens increased, the process of absorbing Soviet immigrants in professions that matched their education and skills was completed, and the number of migrant workers granted permits to work in Israel was reduced, which had a positive impact on Israel's Arab citizens who had been hard hit by the widespread employment of Palestinian and migrant workers.

Between 2001–2003, as the global economic recovered and Israel's security situation improved after the end of the Second Intifada, Israel's economy began to emerge from recession and gross inequality fell. However, net inequality rose as a result of the government's program of tax cuts for the upper deciles and benefit cuts for the lower deciles. This development was one of the root causes of the social justice protests that erupted across Israel in the summer of 2011, as a result of which the government was pushed to end its direct tax cuts, raise the minimum wage and a number of benefits, and introduce a negative income tax. Even after these measures, Israel, albeit with higher defense spending than other European countries, still scored poorly in terms of net inequality compared with other OECD countries. The World Inequality Report 2021 noted that, in terms of purchasing power parity, the average income in Israel was higher than in many countries in Western Europe but lower than the United States, while inequality in Israel was high compared to Western Europe, but similar to the United States. Israel also scores highly on the OECD's poverty index, which defines a household as poor if its disposable monetary income (not including income in kind, i.e., income other than money income, such as employee benefits) is less than half of the median income. This definition uses a relative measurement of poverty, unlike that used in the United States, where poverty is measured by comparing a person's or family's income to the value of a pre-determined basket of basic needs updated annually People whose income falls under the threshold are considered poor.

The Israel National Insurance Institute's regular poverty reports[2] has indicated that in the 1980s and 1990s, the proportion of Israeli families living under the poverty threshold was fewer than 20 percent of the total number of families. From the mid-2000s, the proportion of poor families in Israel jumped to 20.6 percent, a comparatively high rate when compared to other countries throughout the world. This figure dropped to 18 percent in the wake of measures to address inequalities in response to the 2011 social justice protests but crossed the 20 percent threshold again in 2017. Meanwhile, in 2022, the proportions of ultra-Orthodox and Arab families living under the poverty threshold were 36 percent and 39 percent, respectively. Among Israel's secular (non-religious) population, the number of people living under the poverty threshold is about 16 percent (compared with the OECD average of 11.5 percent for a comparable population). From the mid-1990s, the average rate of return on labor fell, while the rate of return on capital increased, another expression of the rise of inequality in Israel.

Studies by Israel's Taub Institute have found that academic achievement helps Jewish Israelis to reach the top deciles, while engaging in an independent occupation requiring an academic education helps Israel's Arab population to do so. Research by Prof. Momi Dahan[3] has indicated that since the 2000s, income gaps between Israel's Ashkenazi and Mizrahi (Sephardic) Jewish communities have narrowed, and the proportion of Mizrahi Jews in the top deciles has increased, as a result of reducing disparities in education and effective integration into the government and business.

## Social Security

After the Second World War, social security institutions began to be established as part of the welfare state, mainly in Western Europe. Israel's National Insurance Institute (NII) was not established until 1954, in the aftermath of the tumultuous period prompted by the mass waves of immigration that followed Israel's declaration of independence in 1948. Social security systems are designed to prevent a sharp drop in consumption and quality of life as a result of old age, disability, decreased cognitive ability, bereavement, orphanhood, or unemployment. There are two main schools of thought regarding national insurance. The first holds that national insurance should operate as an insurance company, albeit not a fully commercial one, and that a country's national insurance institute should accumulate reserves (using an actuarial approach) to fulfill its obligations. The second maintains that the state does not need to accumulate full reserves in order to meet its obligations. Israel's NII was founded according to the first approach. However, from the 1980s onwards, the Israeli government effectively adopted the second approach, according to which welfare is just one aspect of a government's priorities, like education, health, or other social services.

In the early years of Israel's national insurance system, there were only four categories of national insurance programs—old age, disability, bankruptcy, and maternity. The risk assumed by the NII, then trying to base its system on the actuarial method, was not reflected fully in its payments to the insured, although actuarial calculations were made to ensure the NII's financial stability. From the 1980s, the concept evolved, and the NII became a government payment agent for welfare matters, with a weak connection to actuarial accounting. This was a result of the dynamics of the NII's arrangements and relations with the Ministry of Finance, and also a practical political result of the government's prioritization of its current needs regarding the various welfare issues that had emerged over the years.

The NII gradually became a clearinghouse for the payment of a wide variety of welfare benefits (such as alimony and child support). For some years now, Israel's national insurance funding has relied not solely on contributions from citizens, but from ongoing budgetary support as well. The state is required by law to pay old age, disability, and unemployment benefits regardless of the NII's formal independence.

Another dilemma faced by national insurance institutes is whether benefits ought to be means-tested, with only the poorest entitled to them, or universal, and paid to everyone regardless of income. The current view in Israel is that some benefits should be universal and others means-tested. Israel's middle classes feel that they do not receive adequate compensation for their social security contributions (e.g., in terms of pensions), and are less inclined to publicly support assistance when they do not see anything in return. In 1980, the government passed the Income Support Law, which provided a safety net in the form of benefits for people who found it hard to find work. In 2003, these benefits were eroded by the government, under the guise of a welfare-to-work scheme that aimed to push unemployed (including discouraged, long-term unemployed) people into work. The question of welfare payments versus labor market participation is one that most developed countries face. Each country must determine its own balance point. In the 2000s, Israel chose to pursue an aggressive policy of work over welfare.

## Healthcare Services

Healthcare services are, in essence, an investment in the well-being of a country's human capital and also an ongoing cost for the health of its residents. Healthcare services are significantly different from other goods and services. Healthcare is a public benefit that suffers from the inherent market failure in the imbalance in medical knowledge and information between manufacturers and suppliers (the doctors) and the insured (the patients). This requires government intervention. Basing healthcare services on market forces produces poor outcomes for consumers in terms of social justice and equality, and especially in terms of cost. Private healthcare systems are biased towards profit. They create unnecessary work, push up prices, and are expensive (the most prominent example is the United States, where national expenditure on health is about 17 percent of GDP, and healthcare provision and spending are not equally distributed among the population). A public healthcare system confers advantages on large organizations (such as Israel's health maintenance organizations) that can operate as a single buyer and manage negotiations with service providers to benefit their service users.

Israel's healthcare system was developed in the Jewish Yishuv in British Mandatory Palestine, before the establishment of the State of Israel. Its leaders were aware of the market failure inherent in healthcare provision and responded to these challenges by providing low-cost, readily available services to the general public of the Jewish pre-state Yishuv. This fledgling national healthcare system was based on the Clalit health maintenance organization (HMO), which was commonly known as Kupat Holim Clalit in Hebrew. Clalit started in 1911 as a socialist cooperative, and officially became the Clalit HMO under the rubric of the Histadrut in 1920, providing low-cost and equitable services to its policyholders (in the same way as do Israel's well-baby clinics, which provide a service for all that includes vaccinations and healthcare monitoring for babies and preschool children). Over time, other HMOs were founded alongside Clalit. As these grew, they were able to operate on the same principles, that is, as large providers that could leverage their purchasing power to buy healthcare services (doctors, nurses, hospitals, drugs, medical equipment, and other professional services) relatively inexpensively, and provide low-cost and equitable healthcare insurance for all. Israel's HMOs provide both community healthcare services and a hospital referral system and have had a positive impact on life expectancy and infant mortality rates.

In their dual roles as both healthcare provider and insurer, Israel's HMOs have proven that a combination of public financing (private participation), independent management, a competitive structure, and proper regulation can work extremely well. There are very few examples of such healthcare models worldwide, but in Israel this structure has proved successful. Past weaknesses in the structure of Israel's HMOs have been largely political, especially in the case of Clalit.

The State Health Insurance Law 1995 separated Israel's HMOs from political bodies and transformed them into nonprofit and competitive entities. Israel's healthcare system, which had originally taken a socialist approach, underwent competitive and operational changes over the decades, while always remaining a nonprofit system that provides. It has maintained a balance between providing a relatively efficient community healthcare and hospitalization system while remaining low-cost, universally available, equitable, and unbiased. Israel's HMOs compete with each other under strict government regulation and are financed by a special tax collected by the NII and redistributed among the funds according to a formula that calculates the profiles of the insured. The State Health Insurance Law 1995 made Israel's healthcare system competitive by providing a "basket" of healthcare services to every citizen, with incentives for efficiency and improvements. The Law enshrined the rights of every Israeli to receive medical services of a reasonable quality, within a short waiting time and at a reasonable distance from their places of residence. The HMOs operate as nonprofit organizations and nonprofit insurance companies. Today, Clalit Health Services is the largest single healthcare insurer-provider in Israel and among the largest in the world.

Israel's HMOs excel in terms of their advanced information systems for patient medical data. In the age of artificial intelligence, this is an important resource for medical research and treatment follow-up, which benefits patients and helps in delivering preventative therapies. This data can also be used in research to help develop new technologies and drugs. A unique national strategic asset, it consists of raw and aggregated patient data that does not violate patient privacy. One of the reasons for Pfizer's willingness to develop coronavirus vaccines quickly was the special structure of Israel's HMOs, which allowed their patient databases to be used for follow-up and research.

While there is much to praise about Israel's health system, we should not turn a blind eye to its problems, weaknesses, or difficulties, or indeed to any changes that need to be made now or in the future. Israel's national expenditure on healthcare as a percentage of its GDP is lower than the OECD average (about 7.5 percent compared with the OECD average of 9 percent), and the number of nurses, doctors, and hospital beds per capita in Israel are among the lowest in the OECD. Israel's healthcare system relies heavily on already trained new immigrants and students studying abroad. Some 60 percent of Israel's newly qualified doctors studied medicine at foreign universities, a high rate compared to other countries.

Israel's public health system is relatively efficient, with public expenditure in this area standing at only around 4.5 percent of GDP (out of a total national expenditure of 7.5 percent). However, public health funding is lower now compared with the past. The healthcare system has been pushed to the very limit of its capacity and has few backup processes. Hospital budgeting is carried out according to ownership (by either the government, Clalit, a public-private partnership, or purely private) rather than according to performance or objective measures, and this needs to change. Two healthcare systems have been created in Israel—a private, expensive system for the wealthy, and a good public system that also offers private services not accessible to some parts of the public.

In the coming years, Israel's aging population will pose new challenges for its healthcare system. This, alongside an increasing number of Israelis aged over 75, the rising cost of innovative drugs, and pressures for salary increases for medical staff, may erode the efficiency of Israel's healthcare system. Moreover, Israel's healthcare system is currently weak in terms of its provision of mental health and geriatric medicine services. Addressing these issues requires increased health spending, the expansion of existing mental health and geriatric medicine services and departments, and more healthcare professionals, notwithstanding the shift to home hospitalization and care in the community.

Israel's healthcare system, which suffered from shortages of PPE and intensive care beds during the coronavirus pandemic, nevertheless proved that it was able to adapt and operate quickly, efficiently, and professionally in a crisis. In opening coronavirus wards and treating patients, the system as a whole demonstrated a high level of flexibility and agility. Lessons from the pandemic have pointed to the need to improve doctor-patient communications, increase the number of hospital beds, and promote and improve home hospitalization services and remote patient care.

## Social Protests

The seeds of the social protests that swept across Israel in the summer of 2011 had been sown in the previous decade. The government's neglect of less advantaged and less affluent population groups had caused existing social inequalities to deepen. Basic structural problems were not addressed. The first ten years of the new millennium were a "lost social decade," and the resulting social problems did not disappear, but came back to bite the government in the form of mass social protests. Israel's social disparities were exacerbated by the government's Economic Defensive Shield program of 2003, which had slashed welfare and social services. Years of suppressed public discontent and anger finally erupted in mass demonstrations in July 2011.

The 2011 social justice protests—which were variously dubbed the "cottage cheese protests" the "tent protests" and the "stroller marches" shone a light on the gap between Israel's macroeconomic achievements and its social realities, including the soaring cost of living, a housing crisis, and crumbling social services. The 2011 protests were initiated by Israel's middle classes, who felt hard-hit financially. They complained that even though many middle-class households had two breadwinners, they were struggling to make ends meet. Discontented with the status quo, they were worried about their economic future. Although the middle class had benefitted more than Israel's poorer residents from the country's welfare policies, they were well aware that their country's welfare state had been effectively dismantled. The cost of public services had skyrocketed, and the financial burden on young middle-class couples had increased. Initiated by young people, the protests focused on rising housing costs and the soaring cost of living.

This was a public expression of economic frustration. The protesters were not Israel's poorest residents from its less affluent peripheral regions, but young middle-class people from the wealthier central Mediterranean coastal plain, who felt that Israel's social services had been crippled and the social safety net weakened as a result of government economic policy in the 2000s. They were mostly protesting against the skyrocketing house prices that made buying an apartment almost impossible for most young, educated, working families. Many were angry at spiraling costs of preschool education and extra charges in compulsory, otherwise free education for older children, and harbored a deep sense of dissatisfaction with the government's taxation and benefits policies. The protests, which began in Tel Aviv and other cities in Israel's central coastal plain under the slogan "the people demand social justice," quickly spread throughout the country. Large swathes of the Israeli public went out into the streets to demonstrate against cuts to benefits and social services. However, the protests did not manage to become a sustained movement, mostly because their leaders had no political action plan. Indeed, the demonstrations petered out following the recommendations of the government-appointed Trachtenberg Committee, some of which were actually implemented.

Since the 2011 protests, Israel has seen a rise in public involvement in, and knowledge of, socioeconomic problems. Public bodies have been established to monitor and research socioeconomic issues, competition, and regulatory reforms. The protests affected the public, political, and media agendas, and brought about changes in how the government conducts itself, as well as increased awareness of the problem of private sector interest groups. Among the tangible achievements that came out of the protests were the introduction of free preschool education from the age of three, an increase to the minimum wage, tax credits for those with low incomes (a negative income tax), an increase in teachers' salaries, and an expansion of preschool services. These developments did manage to somewhat blunt the negative trends that Israel had been experiencing. However, there were few achievements in terms of curbing housing costs, in spite of various plans sketched out by the government. The Economic Concentration Committee was established to reform economic concentration in certain economic sectors and fight the monopolies that caused higher prices. In addition, an Open Skies agreement with the European Union was ratified in April 2013, and cellular pricing reforms, reducing very high mobile phone costs and immobility, were implemented. The 2011 social justice protests contributed to increased business regulation and increased competitiveness. There were changes in taxation and regulation in real estate, food regulations were amended, and a salary cap was introduced for senior officials in the financial system. Inequalities fell in the decade after the protests, as reflected in the Gini index, which dropped from its peak of 0.39 to 0.355 in 2019.

## The Third Sector

Among the many changes to Israel's economy and society has been the development of a thriving third sector and civil society. This evolved from two processes: economic—a drop in public spending and a reduction in state involvement in social service provision; and social—public awareness of social services and social rights has grown. Meanwhile, from a political point of view, the development of Israel's third sector and the growth of civil society has increased citizens' exposure to advocacy issues within a democratic society. Civil society organizations have value in creating programs and ideas that the political system cannot, but which the state can adopt. Israel's nonprofit social organizations have focused on service provision, while advocacy groups have become involved in issues arising from privatization, market liberalization, the globalization of the economy, the reduction of the welfare state, the rise of individualism at the expense of collective ideas, the expanding market economy, and widening socioeconomic disparities. Nonprofit organizations have been granted broad operational leeway to carry out certain government functions, which has meant that the government has been able to step back from operating in a number of social fields.

The growth of advocacy organizations has been an important part of the development of Israel's civil society. It has led to an expansion of public discourse on rights, an increased desire for pluralism, and an understanding of the importance of environmental quality.

Israel's third sector has carved out a respectable niche for itself alongside the first sector (the government) and the second sector (the commercial sector). Between 2015–2019, the scope of their activity, in a broad sense (including the large corporations operating in education and health) was estimated at about 10–11 percent of GDP. The third sector continues to grow and expand. Some 400,000 people work in it, alongside another 250,000 volunteers. In terms of funding, third sector activities and operations receive around 55 percent from government support, about 30 percent from sales of services, and 15 percent from donations, mostly from abroad. The government's relationship with nonprofits and private associations is complex. A significant part (some 45 percent) of the activities of these organizations is funded by the state and municipalities, prompting the question of why the government prefers this way of working. There are several explanations. By outsourcing work to the third sector, the government can reduce its commitments, make cost savings, improve employer-employee relationships, bring in private money as an addition to government funding, and create operational flexibility in social service provision, in contrast with the relative rigidity of government-provided services.

The third sector benefits significantly from the activities of businesses and households. Philanthropy is a significant part of the business community, which prefers organizations that make proper use of the funds available to them, both in routine times and in crisis situations. There are around 1,000 philanthropic organizations in Israel whose worth totals some NIS 10 billion, which is very low in comparison to other countries. In addition to the income, they receive for providing services to the government and the public, Israel's nonprofits are also funded by donations from private individuals and foundations in Israel and abroad. They have a vision, strategic goals, a work plan, and a realistic budget. When economic crises occur, there is a slowdown in donations or payments from the government, and internal organizational thinking increases. Social financial entrepreneurship has developed the concept of impact, which is measured in terms of a combination of economic and social-environmental profit that creates lasting social change.

## Notes

1. Each quintile represents 10 percent of the population in terms of national income, Perfect equality is achieved when each 10 percent receives 10 percent of the national income, in which case the Gini coefficient is 0. In a case of full inequality, 1 person receives all the national income, resulting in a Gini coefficient of -1. Thus, when there is a reduction in the Gini index from 0.375 to .35, there improving equality.
2. National Insurance Institute Poverty Reports, 2000–2022.
3. Momi Dahan. Income inequality in Israel: Developments and recommendations. (2021). In: In A. Ben-Bassat, R. Gronau, & A. Zussman (Eds.), The Israeli Economy, 1995–2017: Light and Shadow in a Market Economy (pp. V–Vii). Cambridge: Cambridge University Press.

# 29

## Living Standards in a Privatized Society

The 1985 Economic Stabilization Plan dramatically changed living standards and quality of life in Israel. From a closed and largely ascetic nation, Israel became an open, pluralistic, democratic, and consumerist society, with a free-market economy and consumption patterns similar to those in the developed world. While its first leaders' vision was of a "melting pot" creating a model society for Jews from all over the world, Israel has evolved into a divided nation with no consensus on major sociopolitical issues, and where tribal politics continuously recreate and reinforce socioreligious differences and factionalism. The collectivist society of Israel's early years has been replaced by an individualistic, dynamic, creative, and entrepreneurial ethos.

There is still social and optimistic solidarity in Israel, reflected in its high ranking in the World Happiness Report:[1] Between 2018–2021, Israel placed between ninth and twelfth out of 149 countries, even jumping to fourth place in 2022. While some of our understanding of human happiness is provided by psychologists and philosophers, the rise of behavioral and happiness economics has brought this concept to the attention of economists, who have developed indices for measuring quality of life and happiness as part of wider economic estimates. Polls by Israel's Central Bureau of Statistics have also shown that residents of Israel are happy. How can we explain these results, given the complex reality of life in a country which has an ongoing and occasionally violent conflict with the Palestinians, deep religious and sectarian rifts, discord between Jews and Arabs, poverty, and social inequalities?

There is a common assumption that a rise in per capita GDP results in better quality of life. In practice, however, economists found that happiness does not only depend on an increase in GDP. In 1974, the economist Richard Easterlin showed that an increase in the financial income of a population does not necessarily contribute to an increase in happiness over time (a phenomenon that has been dubbed the Easterlin paradox).[2] While GDP is mainly a measure of market-related activities, there are other human endeavors that do not involve the market, but have an impact on society and the environment, including volunteering, work in the home (about 20 percent of GDP), and activities related to sustainability and environmental protection. These activities generate benefits that are not measured in terms of GDP. A country's per capita GDP is a reflection of its living standards, productivity, and wealth. Some of the answers to why Israelis score high on happiness economics indices can be attributed to a continuing sense of community solidarity, a strong sense of a national pride, full employment, job satisfaction, financial security, and fulfilling and creative work. Happiness in Israel stems from the meaning of life found in aspects of life of Israel—including the value of living in the country, building a new nation and society, identifying with traditional and evolving forms of Judaism, and more. Israel's small size makes physical travel around the country easier, which helps maintain the family unit. Each community experiences the meaning of life in Israel in its own way, despite inequality, poverty, religion, corruption, and violence.

"How's Life" indicators offer insights into the well-being and happiness of OECD citizens. In 2015, Israel performed relatively well in just three of these indicators: health, social relations, and happiness. Israel also ranks highly in terms of higher education (the number of citizens with an undergraduate degree or higher), investment in technological innovation and civilian R&D spending, and life expectancy. In measures relating to employment, Israel's scores are close to the OECD average. However, Israel scores poorly on all other indicators: housing, education, environmental quality, level of earnings, social disparities, work-life balance, personal security, social skills, civic involvement, governance, inequality, and in education in terms of student achievements. Education is critical because it provides inherent benefits for the long-term health of the economy and society. In terms of public health, Israel is considered to have an efficient healthcare system that functions well.

All these data, with their different trends, reflect the complexity of life in Israel, including the phenomenon of its heterogeneous population, which is manifested in the wide range of Israel's scores across the various quality of life indices. Although Israel scores highly on happiness indicators and its GDP and per capita consumption have risen, it is also important to note the phenomenon of "yordim,"[3]—Israeli Jews who emigrate from Israel to other countries—whose numbers range from 0.15–0.2 percent of the population per year. Some consider emigration from Israel a form of silent protest that reflects the dissatisfaction of the emigrants, among whom are "olim" who had once made their lives in Israel. In Israel, it is often assumed that Jews who choose to emigrate attach less significance to living in Israel than do the majority of the Israeli Jewish population.

Israel sees itself as part of the Western world, and Israelis seek to maintain a standard of living similar to that in other developed countries. This was also true in the past, even when Israel's per capita GDP was low. This was reflected in private consumption and in Israel's good level of civil public services (its welfare state). In recent years, increasing importance has been given to the concept of inclusive growth in Israel—a long-term increase in GDP that is distributed fairly across society and that creates good employment opportunities for all while maintaining environmental sustainability and reducing poverty. Increases in GDP that create or exacerbate socioeconomic inequalities, poverty, and social polarization, are inherently unstable and unhealthy from both an economic and a social perspective. Inclusive growth includes investing in less developed and less affluent social groups and geographical regions, promoting equal opportunities and occupational diversity in the labor market, and building an efficient and responsive public sector that will boost economic growth and reduce disparities. Economic inequalities have a negative impact on longer-term growth.

An increase in GDP, while necessary for translating economic growth into increased quality of life across an entire population, is not enough on its own. In Israel, some have argued that since the 2000s, growth has been inequitable—in particular among those population subgroups that already suffer from the effects of the country's high levels of inequality. The resulting unequal growth has deepened the socioeconomic disparities between Israel's wealthier central Mediterranean coastal and more peripheral, less affluent regions. There are inequalities in Israel's taxation system, and also disparities in social rights and the economic and social integration of minorities. Maintaining inclusive and balanced growth across so many parameters is a very complex task. However, rising awareness of the importance of inclusive growth has produced positive changes in Israeli government policy.

## Cost of Living

According to OECD data, the cost of living in Israel is among the highest in the OECD. This is partly due to the appreciation of the Israeli shekel against other currencies, coupled with low productivity in Israel. The cost of living for a foreign tourist in Israel, who pays for local goods and services by exchanging foreign currency into shekels, is higher over time than for a local whose income is paid in shekels—since one U.S. dollar buys less in Israel than in it does in the United States. The appreciation of the shekel against foreign currencies, including the dollar, between 2011 and 2020 has resulted in the foreign currency price of goods rising over that period compared with the price of the same goods in shekels. Among the reasons for the high costs in Israel are the appreciation of the shekel against foreign currencies, Israel's low levels of competition, and high market concentration of manufacturers and suppliers. The fact that the shekel price of goods and services in shekels have not risen a great deal over this decade does not contradict the fact that the cost of living in Israel is high in international comparison, or that Israel suffers from high market concentration and low competition. In terms of purchasing power, Israel is an expensive place to live.

In this same period, 2011–2020, Israel has also witnessed contradictory developments in the prices of non-tradable services. The cost of healthcare services has increased by about 19 percent, mainly due to the rising costs of private healthcare. Home prices rose by about 100 percent. Meanwhile, despite being non-tradable services, education and higher education costs have barely increased at all because they are state funded. The prices of communications and tradable products have fallen, thanks to cuts to import taxes for goods coming from Asia, in particular China, a development that has seen the Israeli market flooded with all manner of industrial and consumer goods, from toys and clothing to advanced electronics. Since 2000, clothing and footwear prices in Israel have fallen by over 30 percent, improving consumer purchasing power. Meanwhile, food prices in Israel are higher than the OECD average, a result of low competition in the food industry and costs associated with kosher supervision and certification. According to the World Trade Organization, Israel's tariffs on agricultural produce are among the highest in the world. The nine largest manufacturers and importers in Israel's food industry and consumer goods—Tnuva, Strauss, Osem, the Central Bottling Company, Diplomat, Neto, S. Schestowitz, Leiman Schlussel, and Kimberly-Clark—enjoy a high market share. The aggregate market power and concentration of these large companies has allowed them to dominate Israel's food chains and suppress smaller suppliers.

In an open and global economy, there is a constant dilemma and tension between domestic production and imports. Israel has adopted a policy of producing a range of basic goods domestically, and importing products for which it has no comparative advantage and whose quality is better than domestically made equivalents. Israel imports some 95 percent of grains and grain products and most of its fish and beef. Meanwhile, Israel's deeply-ingrained agricultural ethos has—so far—protected its fresh fruit and vegetable growers from competition from imports. In today's geopolitical reality, food security—guaranteeing that all a country's residents have constant access to nutritious, healthy, and high-quality food based on domestic production—is extremely important. Agriculture and industry are essential strategic infrastructures for ensuring food supply, but Israel still needs to find a balance between domestic production and the ability to import high quality, cheap produce.

Israel's high food prices are a result of its high market sector and inter-sector concentration, which results in low levels of competition. Other factors involved in pushing up food prices include import barriers in some sectors, exclusive importers (brand monopolies) for some products, a failed system of regulation, non-tariff barriers (regulatory), and the high cost of security and kosher supervision. Imports play a role in generating competition (because of reducing import taxes) and in reducing the power of big importers whose exclusive deals with foreign suppliers shield them from competition with other importers (parallel imports). To drive prices down, Israel needs to regulate cartels in certain agricultural markets (notably, eggs and milk), improve enforcement by the Israel Competition Authority, and open up the market to imports.

Public sensitivity toward the cost of living was one of the flashpoints that sparked the 2011 social justice protests. In the wake of those protests, the government introduced a series of reforms intended to lower prices in certain industries, including cellular communications and airline travel. The government also introduced free state education for all children from the age of 3, and a VAT exemption on personal imports up to a value of $75. These reforms did go some way toward easing the cost of living, with increased competition helping to drive down prices. However, comprehensive reform is still needed to address the soaring cost of Israelis' biggest household expense—that is, housing. Such reforms should mainly target government practices (particularly land allocation), which are responsible for most of the cost components that affect house prices in Israel.

## Tax Burden and Public Expenditure

Prior to the 1985 Economic Stabilization Plan, Israel's tax burden was relatively high. Today, at about 32 percent of GDP, Israel's tax burden is relatively low in comparison with other OECD countries. Direct taxation in Israel is particularly progressive: those on the lowest incomes pay little or no tax, while its highest income tax bands are comparable to those in other OECD countries. Most of the state's direct tax revenues thus come from a relatively small number of taxpayers—the two upper deciles. The weight of indirect taxation (primarily VAT and excise duties) is relatively high in terms of total taxation: over 40 percent, compared to the OECD average of 35 percent. Indirect taxes are easier to collect than direct taxes.

A low tax burden is considered positive, because it encourages growth and reduces incentives for tax evasion. Reliance on indirect taxation also indicates a less cohesive society, since citizens in countries with low social solidarity are likely to be more resistant to contributing to the common good through direct taxation. Further, a low taxation burden results in low public expenditure. Leaving aside Israel's relatively high defense spending, we can see that civilian public spending in Israel is the lowest in the OECD on education, health, welfare, infrastructure, and public transport. In other words, Israel collects fewer taxes and provides fewer public services than other OECD countries. Israelis are forced to either pay the shortfall from their disposable incomes or settle for fewer public services. In the two decades between 2000–2019, civilian public spending in Israel was on average around 35 percent of GDP, compared with the OECD average of 47 percent of GDP. In comparison, the countries with the highest levels of public spending earmarked around 55 percent of GDP for this purpose. Israel's high defense budget provides only a partial explanation for its low public service provision. The main reason stems from Israel's perception during the 2000s that a small government and a low tax burden were needed.

Despite rising levels of investment in infrastructure between 2010–2019, the gap between Israel and most other OECD countries remains high, especially in road space and in mass transit systems. In terms of environmental quality, Israel scores poorly in most international indices. The achievements of Israel's education system are comparatively low compared to other OECD countries, as measured by performance in standardized tests. There needs to be a major shakeup of the education systems for Israel's ultra-Orthodox and Arab populations, particularly in light of the fact that these two populations are growing larger.

Poverty and net inequality in Israel are among the highest in the world, even after the measures the government put in place to tackle these issues in response to the 2011 social justice protests. Israel also scores poorly on international welfare spending indices. While Israel's health system is considered efficient, with life expectancy, and low infant mortality, the country ranks lower than the OECD average in terms of health expenditure indicators, e.g., the number of hospital beds, nurses, and MRI machines per capita.

In some cases, decisions regarding the allocation of public resources have a cost in human lives and cannot be calculated solely in terms of economic value. These include decisions to restrict medical benefits, allocate public funds to purchase protective equipment for soldiers, pay for proper surfacing for roads with a higher-than-average number of traffic accidents, make investments in nursing care for elderly people and in nonprofit welfare organizations or charities that work with vulnerable young people, or fund initiatives to combat air, soil, and water pollution. The coronavirus pandemic exposed the need for efficient public services. Israel's education system had difficulty functioning during the pandemic, for example, because of overcrowded classrooms, and its professional training system was negatively affected by limited services.

## Innovation

Ironically, although their country has been dubbed "the Startup Nation," Israelis do not feel that they live in a technologically developed country. High tech contributes directly to the living standards of the approximately 11 percent of Israelis who work in the high-tech sector. Meanwhile, Israel's transport, commerce, education, and public sectors all lag behind the rest of the developed world in terms of digital service provision. Part of this technological disconnect stems from Israel's geopolitical situation as an "island state" located far from global supply chains. Israel's small size and geographic isolation affects its competitiveness in non-tradable industries that are not exposed to imports, such as construction, communications, finance, and commerce, where investments in innovation and technology have been relatively low. As the globalization of Israel's economy intensified, the Israeli public began to demand Western-level rail transport, mail services, and other infrastructure services. Innovation and technology are not evenly distributed across Israel, and there are considerable gaps between the more affluent central coastal plain and more peripheral regions. The central Mediterranean coastal plain is well-developed, with a high concentration of high-tech industries, and its residents mostly enjoy a high standard of living equivalent to that of other countries where high-tech centers influence innovation in metropolitan areas.

## Finance and Personal Wealth

In the wake of the 1985 Economic Stabilization Plan, the government carried out a number of financial reforms. One key reform was the privatization of Israel's previously nationalized capital market. Also notable were a series of pension reforms, which resulted in a good pension system that provides reasonably priced pension services to the entire population. The privatization of financial responsibility, where citizens act for their own benefit, has been good for the economy. Pension savings were diverted to the newly competitive capital market and managed by institutional investors. The level of personal savings in Israel is one of the highest in the OECD, and since 2000, the Israeli public has grown wealthier. In 2021, the public portfolio of financial assets (including life insurance, pension funds, provident funds, advanced study funds, and securities) reached over 5 trillion NIS (three times the GDP), compared to around 2.5 trillion NIS in 2010. The mean value of the financial assets of an Israeli household in 2021 was USD150,000 per capita, higher than the OECD average, and household debt in 2023 stood at around 43 percent of GDP, most of it in mortgages.

Credit Suisse's Global Wealth Reports (2021–2022) has indicated that Israel is among the countries that have shown a rapid increase in average financial capital per person.[4] Israelis' financial capital increased from $465 billion in 2000 to $1.2 trillion in 2010, comprising about 0.3 percent of global capital, while Israel constitutes around 0.13 percent of the world's population and produces about 0.3 percent of global GDP. Credit Suisse estimated that in 2021, Israel had approximately 180,000 millionaires (individuals whose financial wealth was worth over one million U.S. dollars), with an average value of USD3.3 million, the result of multiple exits and issuances by high-tech entrepreneurs. Over 1,000 Israelis had a fortune of over $50 million, with 50 having amassed over $500 million. This is a new phenomenon for a society that had accumulated almost no private wealth until the 2000s. Israeli Hebrew-language business daily *The Marker* estimated that in 2021, Israel had 71 billionaires (although not all permanently reside in Israel), placing Israel in second place globally in terms of the number of billionaires per capita. In April 2022, American business magazine Forbes reported that there were 31 Israeli billionaires in 2021. The concentration of capital in the hands of a small group of billionaire and millionaire capitalists is a symptom of the growing phenomenon of inequality in Israeli society, where a significant part of the general public still does not benefit from the fruits of high-tech development and innovation.

## Notes

1. The World Happiness Report has been calculated annually since 2012, by a team of economists led by Professor Jeffrey Sachs.
2. Richard A. Easterlin, (1974). Does Economic Growth Improve the Human Lot? Some Empirical Evidence. In: Paul A. David & Melvin W. Reder (eds.). Nations and Households in Economic Growth: Essays in Honor of Moses Abramovitz. Cambridge, Mass. Academic Press. pp. 89–125.
3. In Hebrew, Jewish immigration to Israel is referred to as Aliyah ("ascending" to Israel), and Jewish immigrants are known as olim ("those who ascend"). Jewish emigration from Israel is known as Yeridah ("descending" from Israel), and Jews who emigrate are referred to (sometimes derogatorily) as yordim ("those who descend"). Aliyah is considered to be positive, while Yeridah has negative connotations, although less so than in the past, when yordim were considered almost as traitors.
4. See Credit Suisse: Average wealth in Israel rose 17.6% in 2021, Globes, September 20, 2022.

# 30

# Housing and Planning

Housing demand is influenced by a combination of investment and consumption, human psychology, and perceptions of housing market trends. Buyers' desires and expectations play an important role in determining the price that they are willing to pay for a home.

The acute housing shortages that periodically ensued in the wake of mass waves of immigrants arriving on Israel's shores pushed up real estate prices. However, there have also been times when home prices in Israel have fallen.[1] From the end of the 1960s through 2020, home prices in Israel rose by a real annual average of 2.7 percent—a reasonable rate in light of the country's increasing population and economic growth. Studies have shown that home prices display similar levels of volatility to stock market prices. And like the stock market, the housing market also suffers from occasional bubbles even though real estate is an illiquid and immovable asset. Israelis tend to assume that home prices will always rise, given that Israel has a limited amount of land while its population is constantly growing.

Alongside Israel's high rate of natural increase, other trends—including rising per capita incomes and living standards, increasing average age of marriage, rising divorce rates, and increased life expectancy—all help push up demand. Israel has a high proportion of homeowners, about 65 percent of households. The remainder of the population prefer to rent—or in some cases, they simply have no choice. Israel's rental market is less developed than that of many OECD countries. Israel's sales and rental markets, while not always in perfect equilibrium, are usually coordinated and together determine developments in the overall housing market.

In Israel's first decades of statehood, the government was responsible for the construction of housing, through its state-owned companies and firms owned by the Histadrut. Building new homes both in established cities and development towns was seen as an effective method of balancing population dispersal to hold land throughout the country, including in agricultural and rural areas. As Israel began privatizing its state-owned companies amid a shift to a market economy in the wake of the 1985 Economic Stabilization Plan, the government bowed out of the construction industry, leaving new projects to private developers. In the 1980s, however, the government began an urban renewal drive to rehabilitate decaying, modest inner-city neighborhoods that had been built quickly in the 1950s and 1960s to meet the urgent need for new homes. Later, in the 2000s, land shortages in Israel's cities pushed the government to launch two more housing improvement schemes, respectively dubbed Urban Renewal ("Hithadshut Ironit") and Vacate and Build ("Panui-VeBanui"). These schemes had a dual goal. First, the government wanted to replace poor-quality, rundown apartment blocks, some of which had deteriorated into slums, thereby improving residents' quality of life and environment. Second, it sought to increase the supply of available housing.

The wave of Soviet Aliyah from the end of 1989 generated a huge jump in housing construction. Between 1996–2007, after the Soviet Aliyah had dwindled, there was a lull in residential construction and apartment prices fell. This volatility in housing starts (which are a measure of residential construction) meant that the long-term needs of Israel's housing market were not met, and between 2011 and 2022, home prices rose by over 50 percent in real terms, prompting more limited government involvement in the housing market. Even so, home prices have continued to rise.

One metric for gauging the severity of Israel's housing crisis is the number of monthly salaries that are needed to purchase an apartment. In Israel, this metric is higher than the OECD average. In 2022, the number of monthly salaries needed to purchase an apartment in Israel was 151,[2] higher than most OECD countries, and a threshold that is difficult for many people to meet in light of current mortgage conditions. This situation drives up social inequalities and makes it hard for the lower deciles to purchase a home. In the 1960s, only around 40 monthly salaries were needed to buy a home. This figure jumped to around 55 by the mid-1970s, and by the 1980s, had reached about 90 monthly salaries. This type of price rise is socially risky. It creates a discrepancy between the sense of prosperity felt by homeowners compared to the distress of those who do not own a home.

Israel's rising living standards are also reflected in terms of average apartment size. In the 1950s and 1960s, the average apartment size in Israel was about 60 square meters. Apartments were constructed from basic materials according to modest and even ascetic specifications. In the 1970s, the average urban apartment size had jumped slightly to about 70 square meters. By the 2000s, this figure had increased much more significantly to 110 square meters, and apartments were being built to high-quality specifications, with far more attention paid than in the past to details of design and even luxury. Some of Israel's rise in house prices can be attributed to changes in construction standards and materials costs, including for elevators, lobbies, and communal gardens.

## Structural Issues in Residential Construction

The construction industry in Israel is characterized by heavy government involvement, even with the government no longer involved in construction. This is because the government controls 92 percent of Israel's land, and is responsible for infrastructure development, planning and licensing processes, and for issuing permits to Palestinian and migrant construction workers. Residential construction in Israel has suffered from volatility and has been plagued by various crises, not least the sudden and unplanned large influx of Soviet immigrants in the 1990s. Yet other crises have arisen as a result of failures in government functioning, in particular the lack of joint strategic thinking among the responsible government bodies. The housing crisis and measures taken to correct it have led to volatility in the housing market. The government has found itself in a position of having to contend simultaneously with all aspects of residential construction, including planning, land allocation, licensing, and issuing permits for construction workers.

Israel's high natural increase demands that the government ensure a long-term, continuous supply of land for residential construction. Urban renewal schemes are also essential if Israel is to address the problem of land shortages in its densely populated central coastal plain.

The housing crisis of the 2000s was a result of a combination of planning failures, insufficient allocation of land for residential construction, and low interest rates, which together pushed up house prices. In turn, rising house prices were one of the triggers for the cost-of-living protests that erupted across Israel in the summer of 2011, as an entire generation of Israelis, the middle classes and the less affluent alike, saw their dream of buying a reasonably priced home evaporate. In many ways, the housing crisis was a planning crisis. In the early 2000s, the government made a conscious decision to allocate less land in the central coastal plain for residential development, as part of a plan to try to encourage people to move to less expensive, less densely populated, more peripheral regions. The housing crisis dragged on into the 2010s, as the government continued to fail to designate sufficient amounts of land for residential construction to meet the continuing and growing demand for land in the central region.

During the housing crises, the government deepened its involvement in the housing market through planning, infrastructure development, urban renewal programs, and subsidies for development and land costs, such as through the Buyer's Price scheme (which ran from 2016–2018), and the Target Price scheme (which ran from 2020–2022). The aim of government involvement in the housing market has been twofold: first, to help less affluent households purchase an apartment; and second, to try to disperse the population. However, in both these areas, the government has only been partially successful. It has found it difficult to curb house prices and has largely failed to prevent the central coastal plain from becoming ever more densely populated and expensive. Neither has the government had much success in dispersing the population, including immigrants from the former Soviet Union. Repeated attempts to encourage people to settle in more peripheral regions away from the central coastal plain have not worked, and population density and housing costs have continued to rise in that region.

In attempting to deal with Israel's housing crises, the government has frequently chosen to bypass local and district planning processes. Sprawling new residential areas, which are often disconnected from older and more established neighborhoods, have sprung up in various towns and cities across Israel. In many cases, government intervention in local urban planning processes and land subsidy allocation has ignored new approaches to infrastructure and public transport development, land use, and population density, and failed to take into account local authority plans and projects.

The scheme offered discounted land to eligible buyers, creating a shortage of available housing on the free market that pushed up apartment resale prices. In hindsight, to meet demand, the government would have been better advised to release more land to the private sector throughout the country rather than the course it took of releasing land only to specific developers and in specific areas. Instead, the Buyer's Price scheme enabled wealthier buyers to buy expensive apartments in the central coastal plain at a higher effective discount, a situation that has only served to exacerbate existing socioeconomic disparities.

As one solution to the housing crisis, the government has approved the development of new residential neighborhoods on agricultural land. This wasteful approach to land use has already had negative economic consequences, including reducing the amount of open space available for future generations. The rushed, often slipshod construction of apartment blocks on agricultural land has meant that flood prevention measures, needed to mitigate the effects of heavy rainfalls, and which have become increasingly important due to climate change, have not been implemented in these areas. Without floodplains to absorb rainwater overflow from existing watercourses, these new residential areas are at risk of periodic flooding.

Israel's housing market continues to be a source of tension between local and central government. In recent years, local authorities have begun to insist that central government work in partnership with them when developing new neighborhoods, since these require costly investments in infrastructure. Israel's local authorities prefer high-quality and more expensive housing to smaller and cheaper apartment blocks. New residential neighborhoods bring an influx of new families, who demand new schools, kindergartens, and public institutions, all of which are expensive to build and maintain. In the main, local authorities prefer to build office blocks and commercial zones, as these are a source of revenue in the form of high property taxes, and at the same time consume fewer public services. Meanwhile, the Israeli public want reasonably priced homes within a convenient distance from centers of employment and business. By developing efficient public transport from Israel's more peripheral areas to employment and business centers in the central coastal plain, the government can help ease demand for housing in that overcrowded region.

## Notes

1. Yossi Yakhin and Inon Gamrasni. Analysis of the housing market in Israel: Long-term relationships and short-term dynamics. Bank of Israel Research Division, June 2021.
2. This calculation is made by dividing the mean national apartment price published by the Israel Central Bureau of Statistics by the mean salary as published by the Israel Central Bureau of Statistics.

# PART SIX

# THE FOUNDATIONS OF THE "KINGDOM"

## 31

## Institutions and Government

### Administration and governance

In Israel's first years of statehood, its government bodies developed from a combination of these pre-state Yishuv institutions and those of the British Mandatory government, with some new entities established to meet the needs of the nascent state. These government bodies largely developed organically and gradually, albeit sometimes as a result of the demands of current events. They contributed to the democratic stability and successful economic functioning of the fledgling state, and, over time, helped it gain international recognition for its economic status. However, this process was not simple in a country where the issue of the relationship between religion and the state has always been subject to intense public and government debate. In Israel's first years of statehood, its leaders managed to create a solid economic administration, with government ministries, a state prosecutor's office, a system of courts that enforced contracts and property rights, and a universal taxation system as opposed to one based on individual status. Dedicated government companies and state authorities were also developed to serve the public. Israel's "constitutional" regime is not based on a written constitution. Instead, the country has 14 "Basic Laws" with quasi-constitutional status, setting forth the basic guiding principles of the government and the liberties of the citizens. There is an effective division of state authorities—legislative (the Knesset), executive (the government), and judicial (led by the Supreme Court), as well as the State Comptroller's office and the Bank of Israel.

The quality and stability of a professional civil service is important in Israel, whose political system is based on ever-shifting coalitions. Over the years, its economy has shifted from a centralized, public regime to a market economy with a private sector and system of professional regulation that can oversee the efficient functioning of the markets in case of failures. The 1985 Economic Stabilization Plan reinforced Israel's macroeconomic system and led to the development of rules for the efficient functioning of the various branches of the economy.

In Israel's first 40 years of statehood, its regulatory institutions were weak, and the economy was dominated and controlled by a network of monopolistic government bodies. Among the most pressing objectives of Israeli policy in 1985 was improving competitiveness and creating a program of privatization. The increased regulation of state monopolies led to the creation of dozens of supervisory bodies in various economic sectors that operated according to legislation as well as a number of independent, specialized regulatory institutions.

Studies have shown that "good" institutions design rules that allow the public to realize economic opportunities regardless of individual or group identity. They guarantee personal security, the enforcement of contracts, and the preservation of property rights and equality. The institutions themselves are more important than the individuals who lead them. Well-run financial institutions and regulatory bodies, and—above all—an independent judiciary all have a positive effect on growth and economic prosperity, including by preventing corruption and safeguarding individual freedoms, entrepreneurship, and creativity.

Israel's institutions have played a critical role in its economic growth and stability, especially following its transition to a market economy and its integration into the global economy and competitive international markets. Israel, which aspires to be a global leader, needs to have an outstanding government and institutions, and cannot be complacent in the face of government corruption or the noncompliance of officials with the rule of law. The politicization that had characterized the Israeli administration in its early years was gradually replaced by a politically-appointed professional public service, which, together with the political echelons, were able to make fundamental changes in governance and *mamlachtiut*—meaning, in this case, appointing a skilled and professional civil service to serve the needs of the country and not any partisan or sectarian interest. An efficient and fair government ensures law and order, prevents violence and corruption, and guarantees equitable regulation as preconditions for sustainable growth and achieving social goals.

Israel's acceptance into the OECD represented recognition that it belonged in the so-called club of developed nations. Like its fellow members, Israel needed to demonstrate compliance with legislation and rules of conduct, in particular in combatting bribery and corruption, avoiding conflicts of interest between the public and elected officials to ensure public trust in government, preventing public sector nepotism, and reducing political appointments in public bodies. Citizens' quality of life, and their trust in democracy, is maintained not only through regular elections, but also by the way in which state institutions conduct themselves in the periods between elections. At the heart of a healthy democracy is the rule of law based on judicial independence and efficiency, the timely issuing of judgments, and effective law enforcement.

Studies in institutional economics have indicated that strong state institutions[1] with comprehensive powers in their spheres of authority, including the Knesset, government ministries and regulatory authorities, the courts and the legal system, and the Bank of Israel, are key to ensuring competitiveness and efficiency, helping people establish businesses, and improving competition for goods and services. They are also fundamental to preventing excessive economic and political privileges. Together, these functions encourage the values of freedom and critical thinking. Good institutions help engender processes of democratization that, in turn, foster economic growth and ensure government responsibility toward citizens.

A complete institutional ecosystem combines a good financing system, the protection of intellectual property rights, a culture of entrepreneurship, a high-quality education system, and an efficient labor market, which together boost productivity and reduce social disparities. Israel developed and grew due to a combination of human capital, democratic principles, innovation, and good institutions. Its independent legal system helped establish international trust in doing business in Israel and reduced the risk premium for investors, which is reflected in Israel's credit rating. An independent court system has helped foster growth by safeguarding contractual and proprietary rights and ensuring the fair resolution of disputes between citizens, companies, and government bodies, even over the course of frequent policy changes.

For years, a phenomenon of autonomy and sectarianism has been on the rise in Israel and is posing a threat to the rule of law. The state cannot relinquish its authority and responsibility vis-à-vis determined minority groups. This need for maintaining the authority of the state was starkly clear with respect to the refusal of some ultra-Orthodox and Arab citizens during the coronavirus pandemic to comply with government guidelines, and during the tragic crowd crush at Mount Meron during the annual ultra-Orthodox pilgrimage to the tomb of Rabbi Shimon bar Yochai on the Jewish Lag BaOmer holiday in 2021.[2] These developments are also reflected in the poor levels of governance among the Bedouin residents of the Negev, rising crime in Arab towns and villages, and the lawlessness of the hardline "hilltop youth" in the West Bank. The return of governance is essential for the country and the economy, even if it causes friction.

Since 2016, a number of fault lines have emerged in Israel's government, alongside a rise in authoritarian and anti-elitist populism. These developments should be seen as warning signs of the erosion of Israel's democracy. There has been a drop in the quality and legitimacy of public services, while the balance between the government's executive branch and the legislative and judicial authorities has been violated. Decentralizing power among the various branches of government is an essential foundation of a democratic regime and a free society. It serves as the most important source of power for the state, alongside the existence of a strong civil society that can serve as a check on that power.

Quasi-professional and quasi-political appointments are more dangerous than overt ones. They pose a threat to the status of the judicial system, the police service, the state comptroller's office, and the budget, which may harm economic stability and achievements. Damage to state institutions also damages the quality of economic policy, taxation and transfer payments, regulation, and competition. A populist regime defined by protectionism, sectarianism, and fiscal irresponsibility, together with the weakening of state institutions, all serve to harm growth. Studies have shown that there is a correlation between the corruption index, economic performance, and rising inequalities in OECD countries.

Israel's governance problems peaked in 2019–2022, with the country holding five general elections. Israel was left with no approved budget during this period, which included the coronavirus pandemic of 2020–2021. The failure to approve a budget was a serious problem that impaired political governance and economic stability and made it difficult for government ministries to formulate long-term plans or undertake detailed reforms. The governments that were formed in May 2020, June 2021, and December 2022, each of which had 30 or more ministers, highlighted Israel's governance problems, and saw various divisions being transferred from one ministry to another, rising sectarianism, and the weakening of bureaucrats and gatekeepers, all of which have harmed government efficiency. The pandemic exposed serious gaps in the government's ability to function. The difficulties it faced in creating and implementing policies for Israel's ultra-Orthodox and Arab populations threatened their health and socioeconomic conditions and led to gross disobedience. The administrative legislation proposed in 2023, which is intended to harm Israel's independent judiciary, will have a negative impact on the economy by increasing uncertainty.

## Public Service

Israel inherited the British tradition of a public administration, with fixed professional ranks (a civil service) appointed by the government on the basis of their skill and abilities (indeed, many early members of Israel's civil service had served in the British Mandate government). This differs from the system in the United States, where the highest ranked civil servants are political appointees. In other words, in Israel, civil servants are public servants, whereas in the United States they are the long arm of the incumbent president. The status quo in Israel is threatened by the adoption of an American-style model, including the neoliberal concept whereby the upper tier of civil servants is replaced with each change of government. The American model is rooted in a two-party political system and a stable constitution, which is completely different from Israel's multiparty parliamentary coalition system. Indeed, any comparison between Israel and the United States in this regard is almost entirely irrelevant.

The effectiveness of national policy relies on the professional, high-quality, and objective work of public servants, who essentially form an infrastructure that accumulates expertise and anticipates long-term consequences. Indeed, there is a close connection between the economic success of a country and the quality and professional skill of the public administrators who serve it. This is all the more so in Israel, where the government must plan and implement constant economic and social changes, throughout the education system and in physical infrastructure, and undertake reforms in many different areas amid the uncertainty of a shifting international environment and constant security pressure. Politicians cannot afford to dismiss the expertise of public administrators when to comes to matters on which they are professionally qualified to input or hold investigative processes to correct.

Successful public policy depends on the quality of a country's public service, the professional expertise and knowledge of its public servants, the efficiency of their decision-making processes and ability to perform effective supervision and oversight, and the quality of the communication between them and nongovernmental civic stakeholders. Despite the less-than-optimal relationship among its different ministries, which often work more like a federation than like a united body on some issues, Israel has been able to overcome its security, social, and economic challenges thanks to its functioning network of institutions—including its system of government and the professional expertise of its public servants.

Israel's transition to a free market economy, and the subsequent growth of its private sector, has come at the expense of weakening the public sector, with better skilled and more talented people preferring to work in the private sector. This has led to rising tensions between elected and professional officials, and competition for personnel and prestige between the public and private sectors. The coronavirus pandemic exposed structural and professional failures in the government's ability to deal with a civil emergency—it experienced difficulties in designing a strategic policy to plan and analyze data, translating its analysis into a work plan, and executing that plan successfully. There are still pockets of strength in Israel's public administration with the ability to plan long term, but in most ministries, long-term planning is poor, despite the establishment of the National Security Council[3] and the National Economic Council. In light of the complexity of the problems facing Israel—including a growing and aging population, rising tribalism and sectarianism, the conflict with the Palestinians, and ecological and climate threats—it is essential that the country maintain a high-quality public service and governmental think tanks with excellent analytical, planning, and governmental communications systems, which work efficiently, cost less, and achieve better results.

## Local authorities

Israel, as a small country, has two levels of government—central and local. There are 201 municipalities (local authorities) and 54 regional councils. Israel's local government has far fewer powers compared to its central administration—a legacy of the British Mandatory period, when power was concentrated in the hands of the High Commissioner. Most powers are held by central government, mainly the Ministries of the Interior, Finance, Education, and Welfare. For Israel's central government, the local authorities are an executive branch of these ministries, a situation that allows it to maintain centralized control over local government. For years, local democracy in Israel's local authorities was weak. While this situation has improved, adjustments in checks and balances between central and local governments are still required.

In 2022, the government was responsible for setting some 94 percent of all property taxes (*arnona*) collected by local authorities (for comparison, the OECD average is just 15 percent). Local government budgets amount to about 6 percent of GDP, compared to 15 percent in the European Union. In the OECD's measure of the financial independence of local authorities, Israel is ranked the most centralized government in the world (in terms of the central government's power to determine local property taxes). Israel ranks 109th out of 182 countries in the World Bank's local authority centralization index for 2019. Israel's government influences local authority budgets by providing a "balancing grant," such that every citizen receives a normative level of services, with the aim of reducing disparities between wealthier and poorer local authorities. Despite this, Israel has the highest levels of disparities between its local authorities of all OECD countries, a gap that grew by about 5 percent per annum in the period from 2004 through 2014.

However, the role of local government in citizens' lives in Israel is much more significant than public discourse and the media might lead one to expect. Local government has an advantage over central government in terms of its knowledge of citizens' everyday concerns, community and neighborhood structures, and the factors that influence the lifestyles and quality of life of local residents. Israel's local authorities have matured over time thanks to good local leadership and are ripe for taking on more powers from central government. During the coronavirus pandemic of 2020–2021, and Operation Guardian of the Walls in May 2021, Israel's local authorities managed matters efficiently, and helped preserve the fabric of everyday life for residents.

Furthermore, the fragmentation of Israel's local authorities hinders infrastructure development, most prominently in terms of public transportation. A new layer of regional government is needed, a super-authority with the power to coordinate resources for clusters of local municipalities. This would help improve local authority functioning and improve socioeconomic outcomes both locally and for the economy as a whole.

## Development and Construction Bodies

Good urban governance is expressed through the physical planning and construction of residential, commercial, and public buildings, infrastructure, the environment, and open spaces. In view of Israel's rising population density, it is essential that private, commercial, and national life is woven into an integrated fabric that can make the most efficient use possible of the country's limited space. Good high-density residential planning should involve construction that creates aesthetic and functional harmony for residents in the present and in the future, and thus have a positive impact on the economy, in particular the real estate market.

Israel's high population density requires meticulous planning, which is far removed from the scattered, poorly thought-out development of the past, which did not take into account the needs of future generations. Israel's growing population and rising population density require large, well-planned metropolitan areas, good residential integration, proper infrastructure, employment, and public services.

Improving Israel's more peripheral regions requires improving and strengthening existing urban centers in these areas, rather than building more new settlements that will overstretch existing social, cultural, and political resources. Good urban planning takes into account market forces, but also considers long-term development, including how to avoid damage that will negatively impact on future generations. It provides residents with commercial and municipal services, public transport, and employment all within a few minutes' walk of their homes. Israel's high population density demands that planners employ smart urbanization, with mixed land use, urban renewal programs, and building high-rise, high density homes. Urban renewal transforms decaying neighborhoods into modern, urban areas, with mixed land use and public spaces. High-rise construction requires integrating existing low-rise buildings into an urban fabric of commerce, culture, education, and sports.

Most of Israel's land is owned by the state and managed by the Israel Land Authority. The issue of whether state-owned land ought to be privatized is raised from time to time and raises a number of practical questions. Is state ownership of the land desirable? How would privatization occur? Selling land on the private market for a high price would result in a small number of wealthy individuals accumulating land—in other words, a return to feudalism. Distributing land to local authorities would harm those that are less affluent and negatively impact the principles of distributive justice. Land privatization has other implications beyond the economic and budgetary, including the question of land purchases by foreigners. There are advantages to state control of land in a small, overcrowded country, especially when it comes to large-scale projects, such as moving IDF bases to the south, evacuating polluting industries from

Haifa Bay, or undertaking big transport infrastructure projects like the Gush Dan metro system. It would be virtually impossible to undertake such large-scale projects, which ultimately benefit the public, if the land was owned by different persons or bodies.

A successful political system requires a democratic government accompanied by a professional civil service, specialized public institutions providing public services to the population, and an engaged local government and civil society. Also needed are strong legislative institutions and a robust legal system ensuring a system of checks and balances in the government. Over the years, Israel has succeeded in creating a good, albeit not perfect, political system that has been instrumental in building a strong economy. Any harm to this system will inevitably cause damage to the economy.

## Notes

1. E.g., see D. Acemoglu & J.A. Robinson, 2012. *Why nations fail: The origins of power, prosperity and poverty*. New York, Crown Publishers. See also work by Douglass C. North, e.g. North, D. C. 1991. Institutions. Journal of Economic Perspectives, 5 (1): 97–112, and by Andrei Shleifer, e.g. Glaeser, E. L, LaPorta, R., López-de-Silanes, F., and Shleifer, A. 2004. Do institutions cause growth? Journal of Economic Growth 9 (3): 271–303.
2. Ultra-Orthodox leaders had ignored safety warnings from local council leaders, the state comptroller, and the police chief, while no government agency took on the task of enforcing safety rules. In the deadly crush, 45 ultra-Orthodox men and boys were killed and another 150 injured in what was one of the deadliest peacetime tragedies in Israel's history. Mount Meron had, in essence, become extraterritorial, outside the governance of the Israeli authorities.
3. The National Security Council (HaMateh LeBitachon Leumi) is Israel's central body for coordinating, integrating, analyzing, and monitoring national security.

# 32

# Education and Higher Education

## Education

It is an accepted truth among economists that government spending on education is a long-term investment. However, from a state budgetary perspective, education expenditures are considered public consumption, not investments—even though education spending has one of the highest returns of all public investments, especially in today's era of globalization. Education spending also has a long-term impact on the economy. While this impact can be measured economically in terms of its contribution to boosting growth or reducing income disparities, it is impossible to place a monetary value on its role in improving social cohesion or building shared liberal-democratic values. Some of its effects are felt only indirectly, such as improvements in the likelihood that citizens will abide by the law, and reductions in crime and violence, while others are connected with the fact that education gives young people the tools to succeed in the labor market. The quality of education a person receives affects the quality of their life and living standards—and thus also influences the economy and society as a whole.

In Israel's first years of statehood, public education was a high priority for the government in terms of allocating resources. Israel's education system operates according to two pieces of legislation—the Compulsory Education Law (1949) and the State Education Law (1953)—which were intended to ensure access to an equal education for every Israeli. In practice, however, over the years, Israel has developed four completely separate education streams: the state, state-religious, Arab, and ultra-Orthodox. Israel's social and ethno-religious heterogeneity, reflected in these different streams, has reinforced and exacerbated disparities between different populations. Each stream differs in terms of curricula and outcomes for graduates, including regarding positions and earning power upon entering the labor market and acceptance of mainstream Israeli values. The state and state-religious education (and to a large extent the Arab) streams teach core curricula subjects that are in keeping with the needs of contemporary society and provide students with market-relevant skills. However, this is not true of the ultra-Orthodox stream, which does not provide students with adequate labor market skills or instill democratic values. As a result, ultra-Orthodox high school graduates struggle to integrate into the labor market and access the same opportunities as their non-ultra-Orthodox peers. The ultra-orthodox population resist studying the core curriculum that would provide them with human capital necessary to successfully integrate into labor market. Meanwhile, the government allocates the Arab stream far fewer budgetary resources compared with the other, Jewish, streams, which limits students' academic opportunities and is a barrier to integration into the economy. Improving the budgets allocated to Arab schools will help this community integrate into the economy and society. That was addressed by decisions 922 and 550 of the government aimed at correcting this under funding, and now the main issue is the implementation of these decisions. This state of affairs is, quite simply, a public education failure. While, ostensibly at least, Israel's segregated education streams may suggest pluralism, in reality, they undermine the socioeconomic cohesion that is essential for success in the globalized economy that Israel seeks to join.

Education is a public good, even if elements of it are provided by private bodies. The quality of a country's education system, from kindergarten through high school is critical for instilling social, cultural, and economic values. Indeed, a country's strength—economic, military, social, and more—is determined by its education system. The various stages of education, from preschool through tertiary education, are like links in a chain—when one is weak, the entire chain is compromised. Consequently, ensuring equal access to comprehensive education of a high quality is important for children aged between one and three years and is a key to reducing social and economic disparities.

The OECD's Survey of Adult Skills (PIAAC) found significant intergenerational gaps in Israel in terms of problem-solving, quantitative, and verbal skills among ultra-Orthodox men and women aged 16–40 compared to non-ultra-Orthodox Israelis. Education is a multifaceted process that shapes students, personalities and gives them social skills and tools for learning and creative thinking. Education imparts knowledge in diverse fields of thought—including the humanistic, scientific, and technological. Together with training, education is essential for social integration, because both help level the playing field for students from disadvantaged backgrounds, allowing them to participate in and influence society and the economy. Access to a broad education lends real substance to the concept of equal opportunities as a prerequisite for reducing socioeconomic disparities. The more a student's economic background disadvantages them in terms of access to education, the greater the need for a comprehensive primary and secondary education system that can help fill in the gaps.

In recent years, Israel's education system has become mediocre. This despite an increase in the number of high school graduates and the rate of students successfully completing their high school matriculation exams, along with a decrease in class sizes and the number of students per teacher. While there are more teacher education graduates, the quality of their training has not improved. According to the OECD's PISA tests, which measure the ability of 15 and 16-year-olds in mathematics, science, and reading, Israeli students' scores were relatively poor compared to other countries. This is a cause for concern, since these three areas reflect how well students will go on to integrate into the modern world. Moreover, Israel scores among the highest in the OECD in terms of the disparities between students from wealthier socioeconomic backgrounds and those from more disadvantaged backgrounds. Although Israel's investment in education is similar to that in most OECD countries, it takes time for education processes to mature. A population that does not receive a first-world education will not be able to maintain a first-world economy. Israel's educational status quo poses a security and economic risk. Education is an engine for economic growth.

Meanwhile, due to parental and their community leadership's choices, fewer and fewer ultra-Orthodox children are studying science, mathematics, and English. In its first years of statehood, Israel was able to maintain high levels of social solidarity by building a public education system that helped instill the fundamental values of the nascent state and provided children with the relevant skills to integrate into the labor market and society. In these early years, the relative weight of ultra-Orthodox and Arab citizens in the general population was low, and they had little influence in the labor market. Their increased weight in the population has intensified disparities and created some of the problems that have arisen in recent years, including the high proportion of high school graduates who have difficulty integrating into the labor market and society.

The OECD has warned that Israel's education system is a significant obstacle to the development of its economy, given that about half of all children in Israel acquire only a low-level of education in language skills, history, math, and science, which is unsuitable for a modern, advanced economy. Israel's education streams, divided as they are along ethnoreligious and sectarian lines, adversely affect equality and undermine the quality of education the country is able to provide.

Indeed, Israel's self-identification as a high-tech nation is simply not compatible with its "average at best" education system.[1] Its successes in high tech and science are largely a reflection of the results of its past educational efforts, its large population of highly qualified immigrants, and the existence of a privileged class that receives a far superior education than the majority of the population due to their socioeconomic status.

In a world that is increasingly driven by technology and innovation, it is clear that creativity, decision-making, critical thinking, teamwork, self-study, and problem-solving are crucial skills that all children must learn. It is imperative that Israel provide children and young people from less advantaged populations the opportunity to acquire these skills if they are to succeed in the labor market. This includes teaching them how to work with people who perhaps think differently from their ethnoreligious group or "tribe." An "average at best" education only leads to "average at best" productivity. Perhaps it is not surprising that Israel has been unable to improve the low labor productivity that is holding it back in terms of economic growth and living standards, and that is exacerbating poverty and inequality.

Looking ahead, there are three main issues that will determine the quality of education in Israeli schools: inequalities in education provision, teacher salaries and training, and class sizes. First, while Israel's total national expenditure—the combination of public and private outlays—on education is close to the OECD average, its expenditure per student is relatively low due to larger family sizes in Israel. The disparity is amplified by relatively higher increases in outlays by wealthier parents for the education of their children than in government expenditures for all students in the country. The pay gap between newly qualified and more experienced teachers reflects the fact that teacher pay in Israel is extremely dependent on seniority. Moreover, the system is plagued by rigid arrangements with the teachers' unions and over-centralization. In the 2000s, the government carried out two major reforms to improve teachers' working conditions—*Oz LeTmura* ("Courage to Change") and *Ofek Chadash* ("New Horizon"), which, however, yielded only partial results and fell short of expectations.

Studies have shown that the single most important factor that determines the quality of education a person receives is the quality of teachers and principals. For this reason, teachers should play a key role in designing changes to the education system. Moreover, the requirements for teacher training should be raised in all stages of education, while higher standards should be required for those seeking to enter the teaching profession.

Small class sizes are especially important in the early years of education. Overcrowded classrooms undermine the quality of teaching and affect the teacher-pupil relationship, preventing teachers from giving enough attention to each student. Different students have different needs. Some may have difficulty in understanding the material being studied, while others excel and need special challenges. Others may be experiencing personal difficulties. Every student requires special attention and personal input from teachers.

The coronavirus pandemic exposed the weaknesses of Israel's education system. School closures and remote learning disproportionately harmed students from lower socioeconomic backgrounds, which widened existing disparities between students from different populations. Remote learning requires special equipment, and teachers have to adapt content to a framework that is very different from face-to-face lessons. In addition, the pandemic threw into sharp relief the issue of class sizes even under normal conditions, as Zoom instruction is especially difficult when there are many pupils in a class. Even with these problems, the crisis did prove that Israel's education system worked well at a local authority level, thanks to those teachers and principals who were able to provide good solutions.

## Higher Education

Some of Israel's higher education institutions are older than the state and have their roots in the Jewish Yishuv—including the Hebrew University of Jerusalem (established 1925), the Technion—Israel Institute of Technology in Haifa (established 1923), and the Weizmann Institute of Science in Rehovot (established 1934). Indeed, these institutions were an integral part of the infrastructure of the pre-state Yishuv. Until the mid-1990s, most of Israel's higher education institutions were research universities that were organized along the same lines as the Hebrew University. Admission was not available to every student with a high school diploma, due to a lack of infrastructure and because higher education is not equally accessible to all groups in society. As a result of unequal access to the university system, Israel has lost the benefit of the full potential of all its high school graduates to develop science, the economy, culture, and society. Until the 1990s, most colleges in Israel were devoted to teacher education, and only a minority, such as the Bezalel Academy of Art and Design and the Jerusalem Academy of Music and Dance, taught specialized subjects. In 1994, as part of an initiative by the then-Education Minister Amnon Rubenstein, Israel made a dramatic decision to create academic colleges. These would be permitted to award first degrees (in fields such as business, law, education, and other social sciences), but would not be universities, which, among other things, engage in research, teach more costly subjects, such as medicine and engineering, and award higher degrees. This was a dramatic step change that revolutionized Israel's higher education system: indeed, it is difficult to overstate the importance of this reform, which opened the doors of higher education to many Israelis who would have been unable to access it in the past. The number of undergraduates more than tripled, although the country's overall population had less than doubled. The creation of academic colleges was especially important for the labor market, improving Israel's human capital, making higher education less elitist, and boosting social leadership. The rise in the number of graduates positively affected labor market participation rates and GDP. The academic colleges have gradually changed the infrastructure of higher education in Israel, and, by the 2010s, boasted higher undergraduate admissions than the universities. In reality, the creation of academic colleges has shattered the glass ceiling between Israel's prosperous central coastal plain and more peripheral and poorer regions, leading to a rise in the number of Israelis with degrees, and boosting social mobility. The second generation of Mizrahi (Sephardic) Jews in Israel, many of whom came from the socioeconomic periphery, went on to exercise effective economic leadership, and the third generation were able to translate their improved economic status into cultural capital.

Israel's higher education system encompasses a wide variety of institutions—elite universities, universities that offer all types of degree, the Open University, academic colleges, and regional academic colleges—that operate in parallel, create competition, strive for excellence, and complement each other. These institutions, of which there were 62 in 2023, are spread throughout the country, and most of them (90%) receive public funding. The emergence of some private institutions among them has introduced elements of the free market to the higher education system. While competition is essential to provide an incentive for Israel's public universities to change and evolve, they find it hard to compete financially with private colleges. There is also tension between universities and academic colleges over the allocation of government resources. Improving accessibility to higher education was an important aim of the academic college reform and was based on the idea that helping more people to acquire a good higher education would improve earning potential.

Some 25 percent of all academic degrees awarded in Israel are in STEM subjects (science, technology, engineering, and mathematics), which are an important basis for the high-tech industry. Israel is an educated country and is above the OECD average in terms of the number of citizens holding academic degrees. Its higher education system is independent and prosperous and operates according to multi-year plans and goals. An example is The Council for Higher Education. Since the establishment of the Council Higher Education subcommittee, and the Planning and Budgeting Committee in 1977, government budgeting for higher education has been based on five-year plans that provide institutions with a degree of financial certainty, in spite of the shocks that have occurred in public funding. The Council for Higher Education, as the regulator, approves the opening of new institutions and departments, and together with the Planning and Budgeting Committee, facilitates the proper functioning of Israel's higher education system. Public spending on higher education in Israel is one of the lowest in the OECD, at just 0.8 percent of GDP in 2020, compared to 1.2 percent in 2000. There has also been a drop from around 140 faculty members to 100 per thousand people in 2000 to about 80 in 2021. The ratio between senior faculty and the number of students, which stood at 1:7 in 2000, rose to almost 1:11 in 2021. Nevertheless, Israel has four universities that have appeared in the top 100 in a number of leading international rankings and compete against the leading universities in the world.

Public investment in compulsory and higher education is an investment with a very high economic and social return, which contributes to culture, the economy, and national security. The vitality of Israel's higher education institutions is essential for the "Start-Up Nation," whose comparative advantage is, after all, its educated workforce. If it is to maintain and increase this advantage, Israel must ensure that it can maintain its high-quality, broad higher education system. This is key to fostering growth in knowledge-intensive industries, providing technological leverage for traditional industries, and investment in basic research and applied development. The reduction in state research budgets, and the brain drain that has occurred both as a side effect of globalization and the erosion of university and research funding, are worrisome developments. Israel is already a large exporter of academic faculty members in relation to the size of its population. If this trend continues, it could undermine the country's knowledge infrastructure, erode its cultural, scientific, and technological foundations, and jeopardize its qualitative edge.

Israel's high-tech successes can be attributed to its institutions of higher education, to business entrepreneurship, and to the graduates of the IDF's technological units. Meanwhile, the Israeli academy is debating whether it should focus specifically on research that could create commercial opportunities, or on more broad research. Should academic study provide students with a basic toolbox or more specialized training for the labor market? The traditional role of the academy is to impart learning and critical thinking skills for all areas of life, an understanding of basic research, and broad knowledge. More recently, there has been a tendency for universities to be more open to student demands around acquiring relevant labor market skills to improve their chances of gaining employment, amid fears that student numbers may fall if this gap in their expectations is not addressed. Furthermore, there is a growing phenomenon of men leaving academic study. Women, among whom there are increasing numbers of applicants, now make up 62 percent of degree recipients in Israel. Among Arab citizens of Israel, this rate is 72 percent, while among ultra-Orthodox Israelis, some 80 percent of graduates are women, as men are expected to learn in yeshivot and therefore do not acquire an academic education. There is a trend towards young people seeking out shorter paths to employment rather than academic studies.

The percentage of Israelis with an academic degree is one of the highest in the world. Since 1970, the number of Israelis with 16 years of education has increased significantly, and in 2021 they made up about 36 percent of the population. Among non-ultra-Orthodox Jews, this rate was 60 percent. The number of Arab citizens of Israel with academic degrees is also on the rise, but there has been very slow progress in encouraging ultra-Orthodox Israelis to progress to higher education. In addition, OECD studies have found that Israel suffers from the phenomenon of overeducation, whereby a person's level of education exceeds that required for their job—for example, degree holders working in lower-level jobs because their degree has not given them sufficient market-relevant skills. To a large extent, overeducation is related to the degree subject a person chose and is more common among graduates in the humanities and social sciences. This suggests that private and public investments in education are not being optimally used in the labor market, which reduces the personal and social return on investment. Higher rates of overeducation are found among immigrants who acquired their education abroad and do not have a good command of Hebrew. In addition, workers who change jobs after age 45 have a high chance of being overeducated due to the obsolescence of their skills due to rapid technological development and age discrimination.

During the period from 2000–2019, about a third of Israel's university graduates had social science degrees, and their relative excess caused their remuneration to be among the lowest among the graduate population. The highest paid graduates were those with mathematics, computer science, and engineering degrees, which reflects demand in the economy. There is a positive relationship between the number of years a person spends in education and the quality of education they receive, and quality of education influences salary. The average salary for Israel's university graduates is higher than for graduates of academic colleges who studied the same subject; however, academic college graduates do earn more than those without any academic degree.Clearly, there have been advances in higher education in Israel. Still, it is vital to improve education across all ages, sectors, and subjects, especially in a country so dependent on its human capital.

## Note

1. Eytan Halon, "Senior OECD official: Israel education system is 'average at best,'" The Jerusalem Post, Feb. 20, 2020.

# 33

# Infrastructure

## Infrastructure Development

Israel's rapid population rise in its first years of statehood occurred amid a severe lack of modern infrastructure. The government had to rapidly invest considerable resources to develop the nascent state's electricity, water, sewage, roads, ports, and communications infrastructures to meet the basic needs of its swelling population. These investments, as high as 5 percent of the fledgling nation's GDP. Israel's first government instead chose to focus on developing the twin components of economic strength—infrastructure and employment.

At the time, Israel's severe foreign currency reserves shortage was a serious obstacle that severely hampered the development of infrastructure—including power plants, communications, water pumping stations, and cargo shipping—all of which relied heavily on imported materials. When the shortage eased, the government was able to pour a significant amount of foreign currency into infrastructure, especially after Israel began receiving reparations payments in Deutsch marks from West Germany after 1954, as most of the goods purchased were from Germany. Even then, Israel prioritized basic infrastructure rather than projects that would have immediately increased living standards. Nonetheless, the public investment in infrastructure developments, such as electricity stations and large pumping stations for the water system, did contribute to citizens' private wellbeing, including by boosting the growth of business outputs and increasing productivity. Thus, over time, they helped improve living standards.

Ben-Gurion and other leaders at the time took the historical view that the current generation had a duty to take care of the next, and that the country should achieve as much as possible today rather than leaving the effort to future generations—who would also face considerable challenges in order to continue building and strengthening

Throughout the 1950s and 1960s, Israel concentrated on building important infrastructure projects, including the national water carrier and major water projects, the seaports of Ashdod and Eilat, major roads (including the road to Eilat), and oil and energy infrastructures. The exhilaration of development, culminating in "ribbon-cutting ceremonies" where new projects were revealed to the public, played a key role in fostering the young country's sense of pride in "doing and building." In just two decades, Israel managed to build sufficient infrastructure to support a population that had quadrupled in size, and to lay solid foundations for future development and growth.

By the early 1970s, Israel had no shortages in its water, electricity, transport, and energy infrastructures. However, from the mid-1970s through the end of the 1980s, investments in infrastructure dropped dramatically, as a result of the hyperinflation crisis and large hikes in defense spending. The stock of infrastructure investments in the late 1980s was low, largely because of the large jump in Israel's population, which adversely affected productivity and growth. The success of the 1985 Economic Stabilization Plan and the government's new order of priorities sparked a renewal of investments in infrastructure, especially roads, sewage, and electricity stations. However, in terms of percentage of GDP, Israel's infrastructure investments would never return to the heights of the 1950s and 1960s. The Soviet Aliyah of the 1990s increased the need for additional investments in infrastructure, above and beyond merely addressing the deficits that had accumulated over previous decades. While there was a spike in infrastructure spending in the 2000s, it was not enough to meet the needs of the economy. As of 2023, Israel still suffered from serious infrastructure deficits in a number of areas, particularly road transport, electricity, and waste disposal.

Of course, a far higher level of investment would be required to properly address Israel's major infrastructure deficits after the "lost decade" of the 1990s, when infrastructure stagnated while the population grew, boosted by a massive wave of immigration from the former Soviet Union. At just over 20 percent of GDP, Israel's overall infrastructure inventory is lower than the OECD average. Israel's core infrastructure is around 50 percent of GDP, compared to the OECD average of about 71 percent. Between 2018–2022, Israel's investment in infrastructure amounted to some 2.7 percent of GDP, which was lower than optimal for the economy. Indeed, over the past 30 years, infrastructure investment has stagnated at about 2 percent of GDP, again less than the OECD average.

In the 1990s, Israel began to realize that it needed to turn to the private sector to finance and make investments in infrastructure in order to address the accumulated gaps. Private companies, including international firms, have shown an interest in investing in Israeli infrastructure because of the high potential yield involved. To facilitate private sector participation in infrastructure tenders, Israel developed a set of regulatory rules, financing arrangements for banks and institutional investors (pension funds), and a legal infrastructure to encourage private infrastructure investment. However, although Israel has opened the doors to domestic and international private sector participation, investments in its infrastructure have remained low.

By investing in Israeli infrastructure projects, the private sector has operated through BOT, PPP (public-private partnerships), and PFI models. However, not every infrastructure project is suitable for private investment. In 2021, Israel's infrastructure deficits pushed the government to raise the investment ceiling for institutional investors, such as pension funds and long-term saving institutions, in infrastructure tenders from 20 to 49 percent of their funds, on the grounds that these entities had the capital for investment opportunities with a guaranteed return for their partners. Foreign entities, especially of the Chinese, have also been deeply involved in Israel's infrastructure projects. Between 2000–2022, the value of Chinese investments in Israeli infrastructure projects rose to around $17 billion. Chinese companies have been involved in building and operating the new HaMifratz Port (known as Bayport) in Haifa, Highway 23 (known as the Carmel Tunnels), and the light railways in Jerusalem and the central Gush Dan area. The Chinese have brought production capacity, equipment, and work methods that were previously unknown in Israel. As a result of their involvement, these projects ultimately have saved the Israeli taxpayer billions of shekels. However, Chinese involvement in these infrastructure projects has had political ramifications and has caused tensions between Israel and the United States, which considers China its main strategic rival in the struggle for global hegemony.

## Infrastructure Challenges

One of the major challenges it faces is finding a way to invest in infrastructure in order to improve living standards and quality of life as the population continues to grow. Addressing this challenge will involve making investments in advanced infrastructure. However, developing infrastructure in a densely populated country like Israel is a complex challenge that requires considerable thought, planning, and investment. To ensure that it can meet sustainable development standards, Israel must pay attention to environmental sustainability and multisystem planning.

Developing Israel's infrastructure will require long-term multidisciplinary thinking, the centralization of powers, and multi-year budgets for project planning and implementation (such as the Metro Law, which allows for the construction of the underground railway network that is part of the Tel Aviv Metropolitan Metro network in the Gush Dan area). Furthermore, in planning infrastructure projects, Israel must bear in mind the requirements of long-term development, including safeguarding the rights of future generations, as today's mistakes could create irreversible barriers to planning for future generations. All new infrastructure must be of a standard suitable for a country that seeks to belong to the club of leading nations, not least because poor-quality or deficient infrastructure could have a negative impact on growth.

According to estimates, over the next 20 years Israel's economy will need to invest some $500 billion—the equivalent of its entire GDP in 2023—in infrastructure if it is to meet its current needs and address areas with serious shortages, including in sewage and water, ports, drainage, and renewable energy. Overall, Israel must invest in developing its infrastructure to meet the demands of a global economy and to maintain a high standard of living for its citizens The $500 billion that Israel needs to invest in its infrastructure will need to be raised from a combination of private sector partnerships, increased taxation, changes in the composition of government expenditures, and a moderate hike in national debt.

As of 2023, Israel's lack of infrastructure, in particular in its public transport networks, was having a negative impact on its quality of life, growth, and productivity. Future generations should not be encumbered with an underdeveloped public transport system. In 2023, Israel's poor transportation infrastructure was a significant bottleneck that was holding back its economic growth. If existing trends continue, this situation will only worsen.

## Land Transportation

***Road transport*** is essential for Israel's economy and has a direct impact on the quality of life and wellbeing of its citizens. While the number of private cars per thousand people in Israel is not high compared to other countries, its road congestion is among the highest in the world, with negative effects on both humans and the environment. In developing its transport infrastructure, Israel needs to make intelligent choices between various types of land transport, and take into account how these integrate with each other and existing transport networks. Choices also need to be made regarding which land to designate for transport infrastructure or alternative uses, which include long-term considerations, including future investments in light railways and roads, urban density and preserving open spaces. To demonstrate the gravity of these tasks, consider that investment in the underground mass transit system in Gush Dan (the Gush Dan metro in the greater Tel Aviv area) is estimated—conservatively—at about $60 billion over 20 years. However, failure to see the project through could cost the economy, again at a modest estimate, upward of $3 billion per year. If Israel is to successfully develop its transport infrastructure, it will need centralized land use planning, improved project management and execution skills, and more professional personnel (Israel has a shortage of engineers) who can design and build sophisticated transport systems.

Despite the large investments in Israel's intercity roads between 2010–2019, road congestion throughout the country has soared. Israel has the highest road density per kilometer of road of all OECD countries, at a whopping 3.5 times the OECD average. Israel has historically preferred private car use over public transportation, but increases in private car use have outpaced road development. Israel's transportation failures are reflected in its congested roads and the resulting losses of tens of billions of shekels in GDP, half of which are attributable to missed work and leisure hours, and half to road traffic accidents and air pollution. With traffic congestion, referring to a road reaching its capacity, now having reached a maximum point in Israel, considerable investment is needed to address this problem, which exacts a heavy human and economic cost. In fact, studies indicate that time wasted in Israel's traffic congestion has translated into losses of about 3–6 percent of GDP.

Israel's road congestion problem has had a differential impact across the country. Residents of Israel's more peripheral (and less developed) regions suffer disproportionately compared with those in the central coastal plain, in particular in terms of labor market access, since most employment centers are located in the central Gush Dan area. Improving road and rail infrastructure in Israel's more peripheral regions will boost living standards, improve access to the labor market, and raise productivity. Developing rail networks will provide an alternative to private car use, and thus ought to help ease road congestion.

The government should focus on developing synchronized and efficient public transport networks that the public will actively choose over private cars. Such networks should offer seamless connections that enable passengers to easily transfer from one form of transport to another, including using apps to help travel directly from door to door. Furthermore, if Israel is to reduce the use of private vehicles, it will have to allow public transport to operate on Shabbat, which is currently prohibited; otherwise, the public will have no choice but to use cars if they wish or need to travel during the weekend. Realistically, solving Israel's transport crisis will require large investments in mass transit systems, alongside congestion charge schemes that will disincentivize private car use by limiting their entry into city centers. Furthermore, private cars occupy a lot of space, with the average car only driven about 5 percent of the time, while taking up a parking space for the rest of the time. The introduction of realistic parking fees will improve the general welfare, since city parking is currently both in short supply and priced too low, which causes excess demand. Appropriate parking charges will reflect the negative externalities of transport consumption beyond the environmental damage it causes in terms of air pollution, road traffic accidents, and loss of time.

The Gush Dan metro is key to driving significant transport change in Israel's central coastal plain. It will increase the density of businesses and workers in the Gush Dan metropolitan area, have a positive effect on productivity and growth, and improve the quality of life of millions of residents. Ensuring its effective operation will require the creation of a single metropolitan transport authority for Gush Dan, and cooperation between the public and private sectors.

## *Sea and Air Transport*

As a result of the political situation with its neighbors, Israel is effectively an "island state," a reality that the peace agreements with Egypt and Jordan have not changed. Israel's connections with the outside world are therefore by air and sea, and its seaports and airports are a lifeline for the economy and foreign trade—and for the population's links with the outside world.

By the 1950s, Israel had already invested considerable resources in the development of its seaports, with the construction of the Ashdod and Eilat Ports (which were additions to the existing Haifa Port). These state-owned ports were controlled—and often paralyzed—by the powerful Port Union, which cost the economy hundreds of millions of shekels in lost revenues. Although the government attempted a number of reforms to limit the Port Committees' power and streamline work in the seaports, most of these reforms failed. As a result, the government decided to privatize existing ports and build new privately owned and operated ports. The small Israel Shipyards Port in Haifa was privatized as early as 1995, and Eilat Port followed suit a decade later in 2005. In 2022, a consortium of India's Adani

Ports and SEZ Ltd, and Israel's Gadot Group won the tender to privatize Haifa Port. Ashdod Port is slated for privatization in 2024. In 2013, the government decided to create two new private ports, one in Haifa (HaMifratz Port, also known as Haifa Bayport), and the second in Ashdod (HaDarom Port Terminal). Israel's Ashtrom Group and Shapir Engineering won the concession to construct Haifa Bayport, while China's state-owned Shanghai International Port Group won the operating tender. China's Pan Mediterranean Engineering Company (PMEC), a unit of China Harbour, won the tender to complete the construction of Hadarom Port Terminal, while Dutch company Terminal Investment Limited won the operating concession. These two new private ports are almost completely automated and are therefore less dependent on employees. They compete with the old ports, forcing them to streamline and improve.

As of 2023, Israel had six seaports—three in Haifa Bay, two in Ashod, and one in Eilat. Of these, five were privately owned—Eilat Port, the privatized Haifa Port, Hadarom Port Terminal in Ashdod, Haifa Bayport, and the Israel Shipyards Port, also in Haifa. As of 2023, demand for seaport services was on the rise, and by 2030, additional investments will be needed to avoid bottlenecks in the ports. The efficient functioning of Israel's seaports requires efficient land connections, including to the rail network. Given its location on the Mediterranean coast, Israel has the potential to be a "land bridge" that bypasses the Suez Canal via a rail connection between the Gulf to Jordan and Israel. Such a development would help transform Israel's status in the Middle East, in particular in terms of its normalization with the Gulf states, which would open the doors for its seaports and railways to be connected to the regional network.

Since the 2000s, Israel has made considerable investments in its aviation infrastructure, including by building a new international terminal (Terminal 3) at Ben Gurion International Airport in 2000 (the terminal was formally opened in 2004) in response to an increase in air traffic. Israel also constructed another international airport—Ramon Airport near Eilat—which was finally opened in 2019. The volume of air passengers requires additional investment in the form of a third international airport in the densely populated center of the country that can take the pressure off Ben Gurion International Airport, in view of the expected increase in international flights and domestic needs. Due to the shortages of available land in the central coastal plain, such an airport would have to be developed in the north or south of the country.

## *Water and Wastewater Infrastructure*

A central tenet of Zionism was "making the desert bloom." With determination and hard work, this principle has turned Israel into a country with efficient and innovative agriculture. Some 60 percent of Israel's territory is desert, with few natural water sources to sustain the expanding population and the economy. Freshwater sources are diminishing. Some of these come from rivers in neighboring countries, including Syria and Lebanon, which diverted water in the 1960s and 1970s so that it would not reach the Sea of Galilee. A combination of population growth and climate change has turned Israel's water crisis into a major challenge with geopolitical ramifications. Already in the 1980s and 1990s, Israel's natural freshwater sources were not able to meet rising demands for potable water, and water for agriculture and industry. In response to the need for finding and optimizing additional freshwater sources, new freshwater has been created through desalination, water reclamation, and floodwater capture. Since 2011, the government has encouraged farmers to stop using freshwater and switch to treated wastewater instead.

From the first days of Israeli statehood, agriculture had been an ideologically favored branch of industry that benefitted from large state subsidies, including preferential water prices. However, the effective use of a product in short supply—in this case, water—necessitates raising prices for private consumers and agriculture alike. After a great deal of political struggle, Israel's current water prices now meet the costs required to finance a high quality and reliable water supply, including the investments needed to develop the water sector.

Israel has invested in the construction of hundreds of reservoirs for treating wastewater, and as a result has become the first country in the world to use approximately 90 percent of its treated wastewater for agricultural purposes. Additional hefty investments were required for infrastructure to transport treated wastewater to the north and south of the country. In light of Israel's growing population, the government will need to invest in additional wastewater treatment facilities. Since the 2000s, Israel has built five desalination plants on its Mediterranean coast, which currently supply around 85 percent of water for domestic consumption. As a result of Israel's efforts to recycle wastewater and invest in desalination, it has managed to avoid water shortages, even during periods of drought. Indeed, no other country has such high levels of desalination and wastewater reclamation as does Israel, which now boasts a unique and durable water system.

Meanwhile, however, due to climate change, the Middle East is experiencing more and more periods of drought, decreased rainfall, and extreme rain events. These events will increasingly damage water systems and agriculture and may also spark large-scale migrations as people move in search of water and food. Such events will pose significant challenges for Israel, increasing the need for more investments in water infrastructure, including in Jordan and areas controlled by the Palestinian Authority.

The combination of high population density and large-scale urban construction have resulted in increased incidents of surface water flooding in recent years, as drainage systems become increasingly overwhelmed. Agricultural and natural areas have been paved over and transformed into suburban neighborhoods, and roads and highways now cut through Israel's open spaces. Natural drainage basins have been disrupted, and the increase in impermeable surfaces as a result of large-scale, sometimes poorly planned, construction has meant water cannot seep into the soil and increased volumes of water are entering existing drainage systems, which often cannot cope. Excess surface water occasionally combines with wastewater from sewer overflows, polluting groundwater and the sea. In view of increased urbanization and population density, and the resultant increased residential, commercial, and industrial areas, local and central government must make additional investments in drainage infrastructure to help mitigate the effects of surface water flooding, in particular that caused by periodic strong rainfall in short periods of time. Climate change has also intensified the need for Israel to be prepared for extreme rainfall events and develop effective drainage systems that can cope with a sudden increase in surface water.

## Communications

In the 1980s, Israel's communications industry was one of the first sectors to be opened to competition. Following a wave of privatizations, investments in Israel's communications industry were made solely by private entities. In the 2010s, Israel underwent cellular telephony reforms that resulted in lower call prices for consumers. However, Israeli cellphone companies failed to invest properly in infrastructure, which delayed the deployment of fiber optical broadband and 5G. By 2020, Israel had fallen below the European Union average in terms of fixed-line infrastructure, with less than 10 percent of Israeli households connected to fiber optic internet. Israel also lagged behind developed countries in the deployment of 5G cellular networks, dropping to 94$^{th}$ place in mobile (cellular) download speed. However, since 2021, there has been an increase in fiber broadband infrastructure installation, and by 2023, around 50 percent of Israeli households have subscribed to fiber broadband services. As of 2023, the aim was for commercial companies to be responsible for connecting some 80 percent of Israeli households to fiber broadband services, with the remaining 20 percent—those in Israel's most peripheral regions, where broadband infrastructure was still less developed—to be connected with financial support from the government.

A 2016 report commissioned by the World Bank concluded that for developed economies, a 10-percentage point increase in fixed broadband penetration would lead to a rise in GDP growth of just over 1 percent. The high-speed connections facilitated by fiber optic technology represent an essential infrastructure for a developed economy. Delays in deploying fiber broadband in Israel, particularly in more peripheral areas to the north and south of the country, have deepened existing disparities between these regions and the more developed central coastal plain. Digital communication is essential to the economy as a whole, and especially for technological ventures.

The importance of a high-speed, reliable communications infrastructure was demonstrated during the coronavirus pandemic, when a great deal of business and social activity shifted online, and fast, reliable broadband was essential for economic and social interactions. Communications infrastructure will continue to be a vital component in Israel's growth and productivity, including by facilitating remote working, cloud computing, access to government services, information security, and the digitization of public services, and by helping residents of more peripheral regions become more connected. All this will require Israel to make ongoing investments in its communications infrastructure, not least because of the speed of technological change. One important infrastructure development is the plan, announced in summer 2023, by Israel's state-owned energy Europe Asia Pipeline Company to build a 254-kilometer fiber optic cable between the Mediterranean and Red Sea to link Europe with countries in Asia, the Gulf, and Europe.

## Electricity

Electricity is a vital infrastructure for economic development and for ensuring quality of life. In the 1950s, Israel began to invest in building power plants and electricity transmission and distribution infrastructure to guarantee a regular supply to all regions of the country, for both household and commercial use.

As an "island nation," Israel maintains an independent national grid that meets all its needs and is not connected to any regional grid. In this, Israel differs from countries that have created "backup" agreements with their neighbors. In its early years, Israel's power plants relied on imported oil and coal—a major drain on the country's precious foreign currency reserves. From the 2000s, after large natural gas reserves were discovered, most power plants were converted to use this newly available fuel, which eased the balance of payments as well as being more environmentally-friendly. However, the government's commitment to exploiting Israel's natural gas reserves has meant that Israel has lagged behind other nations in terms of transitioning to renewable energy sources. In 2020, only around 6 percent of Israel's energy supplies were from renewable sources, although this had risen to 10 percent by 2023. Israel's target of producing 30 percent of its electricity from renewable sources by 2030 is somewhat lower than the global average and the 50% average of developed countries. As of 2023, most of Israel's renewable energy came from solar power. Solar farms need large swathes of land, which, as a small country, Israel has struggled to find. This can be addressed through regional cooperation with Egypt and Jordan, competitive land ownership and prices.

In 1996, the government announced a decision to grant licenses for the construction of private power plants. However, this work began only in 2018, following the approval of an historic reform that included an agreement with the company and its workers (through their powerful union) for the IEC to sell off its large power plants. The intention was that by 2026, the IEC would own just 35 percent of the electricity generation network. By 2021, most of Israel's electricity generation was undertaken by private companies, while IEC has retained its monopoly over the national grid and as a supplier to private households and businesses. As part of the same reforms, a new government company, Noga-The Israel Independent System Operator, was established in 2021 to manage the national grid in place of the IEC. Noga is also responsible for the electricity-generating market (by both the IEC and private generators), and for developing renewable electricity generation and transmission. In addition, it has been tasked with establishing storage facilities for solar energy, without which transition to this form of renewable energy will be limited. These moves are intended to create a competitive, decentralized, and dynamic electricity market, including a reform of peak hour rates.

Demand for electricity in Israel is expected to rise due to population growth, the widespread transition to electric vehicles, increased use of desalinated water, an expected increase in the number of server farms, and climate change. To meet these increased demands on the national grid, large public and private investments in power plants, substations and switching, renewable energy transmission lines, and renewable energy storage systems will be needed. To ensure a reliable supply of power, Israel will have to continue to use natural gas, despite an overall trend toward using renewable energies.

## Natural Gas

For most of its history, Israel was a net importer of fossil fuels in the form of oil and coal, which was a significant drain on the country's often scarce foreign currency reserves. In 1999, Israel made the first commercial discovery of natural gas in its territorial waters of some 32 billion cubic meters (BCM) in the Noa and Mari-B fields off the coast near Ashkelon. This development heralded a new dawn for Israel's energy use and situation. More discoveries were to follow. In 2009, the large Tamar gas field (223 BCM) was found west of Haifa, with production commencing in 2013, followed in 2010 by the discovery of another large field, Leviathan, with production commencing in 2019. The Karish gas field, which is now owned by the Greek energy firm Energean, began production in 2022 after Israel was able to reach an agreement with Lebanon. The nearby Tanin gas field, which is also owned by Energean, is expected to start commercial production in 2030.

The discovery of natural gas has benefitted Israel financially and environmentally. Fossil fuel imports have decreased considerably, and Israel is now a net exporter of natural gas to Jordan and Egypt (to ensure that Israel will not experience shortages by the 2040s, these exports are carefully controlled). The discovery of gas fields has boosted Israel's energy security and revolutionized its energy market. Natural gas is cheaper and cleaner than oil and coal, although drilling and burning also creates pollution and emits greenhouse gases. Connecting factories and power plants to natural gas instead of coal and oil has advantages, including reducing pollutant emissions and energy costs, and enabling the combined production of heat and power (cogeneration), turning small and medium businesses into small-scale electricity producers. A plan was drawn up some time between 2016–2017 to connect 450 factories to a main transmission pipeline created by the state-owned Israel Natural Gas Lines that was intended to save hundreds of millions of dollars. In practice, connection has been slow, and by 2023, less than a quarter of the target had been implemented, largely due to bureaucratic difficulties with local authorities.

During Israel's transition to natural gas in 2011–2015, there was a lively debate among the public and economists, as the government formulated policy regulations for exploiting these resources. In 2010, the government appointed a public commission, headed by economist Prof. Eytan Sheshinsky, to recommend policies for dealing with the macroeconomic aspects of revenues from natural gas. These were approved in early 2011. In 2015, in the wake of the expansion of gas drilling, the government published its "Outline for the increase of natural gas supply from Tamar gas field and fast development of Leviathan, Karish, Tanin and other natural gas reservoirs," which became known simply as the "Gas Outline."[1] Among other things, the Gas Outline set out gas tariffs as well as the rights for the two companies who owned the four gas fields listed above—Noble Energy (now Chevron) and Delek Energy.

The improved outline for competition (2015) between the two large reservoirs of Tamar and Leviathan, along with the entry of Energean which owns the Shark and Tanin fields, lowered gas prices and enabled long-term export contracts with Egypt and Jordan, which have important economic and political ramifications. Further, in 2022, Israel finally established a sovereign wealth fund as a repository for profits and taxes from natural resources, with gas expected to provide the highest revenues. Known as the Israeli Citizens' Fund, it is intended for the intergenerational distribution of gas revenues, providing a security cushion for exceptional macro events, and preventing a small "Dutch disease," whereby a large influx of foreign cash to exploit a newly found natural resource could lead to a spike in the national currency value, a fall in exports, and a loss of jobs.

Natural gas is considered a transitional fuel between coal and oil and renewable energies. As the world moves toward increased use of renewables, demand for natural gas will decrease. In the meantime, one positive outcome from Israel's switch to natural gas has been a reduction in air pollution of about 70 percent. Israel faces a dilemma over whether to maximize natural gas exploration and production before the window of opportunity to do so closes, or leave its natural gas reserves unused due to its commitment to transition to a low carbon economy. Renewable energy will not provide 100 percent of Israel's electricity needs, and its gas reserves will have to be used for many years to come. The government will have to navigate between energy security, environmental considerations, and economic interests.

## Renewable Energy

A growing awareness of the effects of fossil fuels on the environment, in particular their role in climate change, has caused a global shift toward abandoning them in favor of renewable energy sources. Many countries have set quantitative goals and timetables for this process. In 2021, Israel announced its intention to reduce its greenhouse gas emissions by 2050 and pledged to close its coalfired power plants by 2025, in line with the Paris Agreement (2015) and the Glasgow Climate Pact (2021). As of 2023, Israel has not sufficiently developed its renewable energy infrastructure, due to, among other things, the fact that the discoveries of large natural gas reserves created a sense that two problems—how to achieve energy independence and reduce air pollution—had been solved. In reality, however, drilling and burning natural gas produces greenhouse gases and air pollutants, and reliance on this fossil fuel can only be an interim solution until Israel can transition to renewable energy. As a small and densely populated country, Israel must be steadfast in its efforts to combat air pollution. The climate crisis and the 2021 Intergovernmental Panel on Climate Change reinforced the need for Israel to set ambitious goals for transitioning to renewable energies.

The only way for Israel to increase its use of renewable energy is by investing in solar power. The country has no hydroelectric or geothermal sources and limited wind energy, while its pumped storage hydropower projects are very limited. In 2021, some 18 terawatts of electricity were generated globally. In fact, only solar power has the capacity to provide unlimited renewable energy, and all the more so in Israel. Israel's tardiness in switching to solar power is the result of slow construction of solar panel farms due to a shortage of land for them, and a lack of technologies for storing large quantities of solar energy. Israel also needs to expand its existing solar power transmission networks. Meanwhile, there are opportunities to import green electricity from neighboring countries that have plenty of land for large solar farms.[2] Most solar farms are now located in peripheral areas, as there is limited space around the central coastal plain, where demand for electricity is highest. To expand its capacity, Israel plans to construct new solar farms in the south and in Jordan.

Solar power has a fundamental limitation in that it is impossible to generate electricity at night or on cloudy days in winter. Even in Israel, which has many hours of sunshine, cloudy days in winter limit the total solar power supply. Since it is impossible for Israel—or for any country—to use renewable resources to produce all its energy needs, and, realistically, the country will have no choice but to use backup electricity from its natural gas power plants. It is ironic, perhaps, that Israel's natural gas reserves—a fossil fuel—will be key to its efforts to create a stable solar energy market, since using these reserves is the only way for the country to guarantee a stable electricity supply. Even if Israel can succeed in developing a hydrogen economy, i.e., one where hydrogen can be used to de-carbonize industries that are hard to electrify, such as heavy industry (which would still require a fossil fuel industry), fossil fuels will be needed. In any event, Israel's transition to solar energy, including energy storage and the construction of new transmission lines (which will require overcoming serious regulatory issues) will require large investments of around $60 billion over the next 15 or 20 years.

## The Environment and Sustainable Development

The importance of environmental quality public policy have increased since the 1980s. In 1988, Israel established the Ministry of Environmental Quality. In 2021, a United Nations Climate Panel report noted that an increase in climate damage in the last 50 years was caused by accelerated emissions of carbon dioxide and methane. Heatwaves, storms, and floods have become increasingly common, and there have been a rising number of significant climate precedents. Israel is a partner in international efforts to curb greenhouse gas emissions, even though it accounts for just 0.2 percent of global admissions.

The term "ecological footprint" refers to a measurement of the amount of natural resources required to support an activity or a population. The world has used its natural resources faster than the rate at which they are able to regenerate. Industrialization, energy production, and vehicle use have all caused damage to the environment, despite efforts by developed countries to address the problem. Israel's population increased twelvefold between 1948 and 2023, and its per capita growth has seen a tenfold increase. This has put growing pressure on Israel's natural resources, and led to a concurrent increase in air, water, and soil pollution. Meanwhile, Israel's open spaces are shrinking. The rising incidents of wildfires and floods have made the dangers of climate change, overcrowding, and air, water, and soil pollution all too apparent, and have intensified the importance of environmental protection.

Israel has an interest in the Palestinians' relevant institutions or entities in the West Bank and Gaza preserving the quality of the environment because of their proximity to its population centers. Increasing rates of climate change, which have yet to reach their peak,[3] requires a worldwide political solution based on globally agreed-upon policy. Broad action by just one country, while important, is limited. Only the coordinated efforts of all governments will be able to effect the fundamental changes required to address climate change.

Average global temperatures have increased by around 1.1 degrees Celsius since the Industrial Revolution.[4] Some of the damage already caused by the resultant change to the Earth's climate is inevitable and irreversible, such as rising sea levels. Only a 50 percent reduction in global GHG emissions by 2030 will prevent the situation from deteriorating.[5] Among other measures to achieve this, countries that have joined the Glasgow initiative have agreed to the imposition of a carbon tax of some $50 per ton of carbon—an unpopular but essential move that has created a system of international trading in carbon credits.

As of 2023, Israel lagged behind in most areas, such as carbon emissions, compared to measures taken by other developed nations. To catch up, Israel must tighten existing regulations and enforcement, implement fresh policies to safeguard the environment, raise awareness and improve education around environmental protection, and preserve its open spaces. Globalization has allowed Israel, a small country with a high population density, to trade and import what it cannot produce domestically, and to manage a balanced environmental policy of embracing inclusive growth, which takes into account environmental impact. Environmental protection is one area where there is a large gap between the public cost and the individual cost (price)—in other words, this is a market failure. Israel needs to implement a proactive public policy that embeds environmental considerations in all decisions regarding the economy and society, to safeguard against pollution of the environment, including streams, beaches, and natural areas. Reducing carbon emissions requires developing and promoting clean technologies, generating electricity from renewable energies, switching to clean (electric) vehicles, reducing emissions in industry, undertaking more green construction and waste handling, and maintaining open spaces.

Israel is a dry country. Only 3.2 percent of its territory is covered by natural sources such as trees, grass, and wetlands, compared to 51 percent of Europe. However, Israel is the only country in the world to have entered the 21st century with more trees than it had in the 20th century—which can help Israel meet the challenges of sustainability.

Israel must prepare for inevitable climate-related events, such as ongoing droughts, large-scale wildfires, floods, and rising sea levels. Its biggest failures are in transportation and waste treatment. Ahead of the COP26 conference in Glasgow in 2021, Israel agreed a set of 100 measures that it could undertake to address climate change in order to meet global standards. Waste treatment—in particular of hazardous waste—is a high priority. Today, some 80 percent of Israel's total waste is buried in landfills (compared to around 40 percent in other OECD nations), where it produces planet-warming methane gas. Israel needs to accelerate efforts to move to a "circular economy" that includes maximum waste recycling.

The coronavirus pandemic highlighted the importance of preserving green spaces and agriculture to ensure food security in emergency situations, and to provide "green lungs" and open spaces for the public. Preserving nature and environmental values are important national interests that are inherently in conflict with another major challenge for Israel—infrastructure development and construction. Israel needs to find the correct balance between the two and ensure that national planning authorities adhere to it.

## Notes

1. Grossman Gershon, Evron Yigal. Energy Forum 38: Steps for implementation following the approval of the Gas Outline in Israel Haifa Israel: Samuel Neaman Institute, 2016. Available at: https://www.neaman.org.il/EN/EF38-Steps-implementation-following-approval-Gas-Outline.
2. To this end, in 2022 Israel signed a new memorandum of understanding with Jordan and the United Arab Emirates regarding a UAE-brokered deal under which Jordan will provide solar electricity to Israel in exchange for Israel channeling desalinated water to the Hashemite Kingdom.
3. UN report to the 2021 United Nations Climate Change Conference in Glasgow.
4. See World of Change: Global Temperatures (nasa.gov)
5. UN report to the 2021 United Nations Climate Change Conference in Glasgow.

# 34

## Productivity

At the height of Israel's economic crisis in the 1980s, it ranked 23rd in the world in terms of per capita GDP. Some 40 years later in 2022, despite the enormous changes that had transformed its (and the global) economy, Israel remained more or less in the same place. While Israel has progressed economically and its per capita GDP has risen, the same has happened in other countries, causing the gap between them to stay the same. While many explanations have been offered for this phenomenon, they all can be summarized in one answer: Israel has not managed to achieve more than a moderate increase in its productivity over the past four decades.

What is productivity, and why is it so important to the economy? Productivity measures the differential between economic output (goods and services over a particular time period) per unit of input (labor and capital) as yielded by a worker or labor hour. An increase in productivity means that more outputs have been produced with the same inputs, or that the same outputs have been produced with fewer inputs. A country's productivity explains any growth in GDP that cannot be directly attributed to production inputs but which has occurred as a result of human capital, technology, innovation, production methods, management practices, infrastructure quality, and/or public service capabilities. There is a strong correlation between real growth in a country's per capita GDP and growth in its productivity. Countries improve their living standards by increasing their outputs in relation to inputs—in other words, by improving their productivity, which is the elixir of growth. Achieving a consistent increase in productivity is the key to steady growth in outputs and long-term living standards.

Studies have indicated that rises in a country's productivity have a strong positive correlation with the quality of the systems that underpin its economic, social, and political milieux, including governance, institutions, and level of public services. A good socioeconomic and political "ecosystem" is essential for achieving improved productivity and growth. The larger an economy grows, the more complex it becomes, and the greater the degree to which unmeasurable "soft" issues, such as institutional quality or solidarity, have an impact on its productivity. The increases in productivity that Israel achieved during its first years of statehood can be attributed mainly to developments and improvements in the quality of its capital stock and its workforce. During Israel's first years, public trust and identification with the country's leaders were at their zenith. This, coupled with a strong desire among the working public to help the nation-building project succeed, generated high levels of social solidarity that further enthused and galvanized the population, which contributed to a rise in labor productivity. Indeed, the increase in Israel's productivity in the 1950s and 1960s was particularly impressive considering it was a small, underdeveloped economy whose outputs relied on simple technologies and production methods. The rise in productivity can be attributed to two main factors: the introduction of advanced technologies into the capital and production methods, and improvements in the quality of Israel's workforce, which facilitate shifts to more sophisticated sectors. During this period, workers in Israel's manufacturing, agricultural, and construction industries gained more and more on-the-job experience, and were spurred on by their desire to contribute to both their personal well-being (by earning a living wage) and that of the fledgling state (by improving its economic growth and strength).

However, even as early as the British Mandatory period, certain work practices (and the mentality that accompanied them) had taken root in the culture of the pre-state Jewish Yishuv. Variously dubbed the "shortcut method," "corner-cutting," and "*iltur*" ("improvisation" or "making it up as one goes along"), these practices had proved effective in the primitive economic conditions of the day. Unfortunately, these approaches persisted after Israel gained independence. Over time, *iltur* culture, as opposed to adhering to orderly work processes, became embedded in the Israeli mindset, and to a large extent became familiar symbols of the Israeli approach. Indeed, the ability to improvise was considered to be positive, a sign of creativity and "thinking outside the box"—and *iltur* soon became synonymous with effective, short-term thinking. Today, such practices and mindsets are considered superficial and shallow. As Israel's economy grew increasingly complex and global, its culture of *iltur* and corner-cutting became more of a burden than a virtue.

## The slowdown in productivity

In Israel's first decades of statehood, productivity increased annually in real terms by about 4 percent on average—a high rate—and was an expression of the pioneering spirit, enthusiasm, and solidarity of the nascent society, and a triumph of Israel's good qualities. However, in the mid-1970s, Israel's productivity began to slow, a trend that persisted even after its economy recovered in the wake of the 1985 Economic Stabilization Plan. In fact, Israel's productivity rose by about a mere 1.5 percent each year from the 1980s through the coronavirus pandemic of 2020–2021.

It was the 1973 Yom Kippur War of October 1973 that proved to be a watershed moment for Israel in many ways, including for the economy and productivity. The war was shattering for national security, but also socioeconomically and politically. Now, in the aftermath of the war, there was public criticism of the government as well as changes in the way that the economy and the state were run. The economic reforms of the 1990s, which improved competition by privatizing state-run companies and opening Israel's economy to globalization, did manage to spark a slight increase in productivity. It is clear that without these reforms, productivity would have been in a far worse state.

According to a 2022 report by the Bank of Israel, a number of industries—in particular, banking, hospitality, food, security, and retail trading—have succeeded in improving their productivity since 2015. With the advent of digital banking services, including payment apps, Israel's banking and retail industries have been able to take the quantum leap to online and mobile financial services and ecommerce. Many government services have also moved online.

The slowing in Israel's productivity growth between 1985–2015 has been due, among other things, to a shift in the mix of industries in the economy. In particular, traditional manufacturing shrunk, while the service industry grew in terms of its relative weight in the economy. Since 2015, improvements in these areas have led to increased rates of productivity.

While Israel's traditional, commerce, and service industries have low productivity, its high-tech sector enjoys a far higher level of productivity. In terms of Israel's non-exporting industries—in particular trade, catering, hospitality, and construction—productivity is some 30–35 percentage points below the OECD average. In 2019, Israel was ranked 27$^{th}$ in the world in terms of labor productivity, with an output of $39 per hour, about half that of Norway, which ranked first with an output of $75 per hour. According to a Bank of Israel estimate, in 2019, Israel's labor productivity was 24 percentage points lower than the OECD average rate, a situation that has led to comparatively low wages and stagnating living standards. Given the connection between productivity and wages, inflation can result if wages increase more than does productivity. Israel's standard of living is relatively low in comparison to other developed countries because a large part of the economy suffers from low productivity, accompanied by low wages and standard of living. The generation that entered the labor market in the 2000s works on average about 13 percent fewer hours than workers in the mid-1980s. Nonetheless, Israelis also work more hours per year compared to their peer countries, with the average annual working hours in Israel in 2019 standing at 1,900—a significant 25 percent more than in European countries with a similar population size (Austria, Ireland, Belgium, Denmark, The Netherlands, Finland, Sweden, and Switzerland).

Israel's high-tech industry boasts one of the highest levels of productivity in the world. However, although high tech—which now contributes more than ever before to Israel's GDP—has increased overall productivity, it has not had a particularly dramatic impact on the economy-wide average. A country's productivity is a result of the complex interplay between various "soft" components, including creativity, institutional quality, public vs. private management, openness to global competition, some of which are hard to measure, and it is often also difficult to unravel the interrelationships between and among them. However, these factors play a central role in boosting or dampening productivity. The secret of prosperous economies is that they proactively consider the various factors that affect their productivity.

Israel's low productivity is reflective of its poor management practices at a national, regional, firm, organizational, and individual level. Good management practices are reflected in an organization's planning, thinking, creativity, and implementation. Countries that enjoy high productivity place a firm emphasis on education and experience and have adopted a systemic and multidisciplinary approach to the public and private sectors that integrates many different factors. Such countries also demonstrate a sophisticated approach to financial and exogenous economic issues addressing regarding economic factors and a good understanding of externalities.

The fact that Israel has struggled to increase its productivity to levels typical of comparable OECD economies points to issues within its labor culture and national management practices. The question remains—which are the areas that Israel must address in order to improve its productivity? Technology has become an important factor in increasing productivity, not only in high tech but also in traditional industry and the service sector. Optimizing the use of technology in work processes requires time for trial and error. The resulting combination of technology, management, and organizational culture form intangible capital, which each organization acquires in its own way—and which is often therefore a corporate, industry, or even a national secret. The digital age has increased the importance of intangible capital in the form of software, ideas, brands, distribution channels, patents, research and development, and the knowledge and talents of corporate employees. This differentiates between a modernizing economy based on services and innovation (which Israel is rapidly becoming) and an old-style economy based on traditional industries and services, where old-style physical capital was critical to production and thus of great importance. This is the key difference between an economy based on services and innovation (which Israel is becoming) and old-style economic strategy.

Surveys carried out by the OECD have shown that working-age Israelis lag behind their peer countries in terms of digital skills that affect economic performance and productivity. This finding would seem to contradict Israel's "Startup Nation" reputation. The reality is that Israel's high-tech sector is based on a relatively small, highly skilled, subset of the workforce. Indeed, Israel's "Startup Nation" image should not blind us to wider truths about its economy. In 2021, about 11 percent of the Israeli workforce were employed in high-tech (a high rate in international comparison). Other sectors of Israel's economy that are not considered high-tech are lagging behind. The productivity of an average Israeli worker is about 60 percent that of their average American counterpart—a situation that has persisted since the 1980s, with Israel unable to close the gap. Apart from high-tech, the rest of the Israeli economy is mediocre compared to other countries in terms of productivity and competitiveness.

Israel's status as an isolated "island nation" creates barriers to competition and excellence. The labor productivity of less advantaged groups in the workforce, in particular Israel's ultra-Orthodox and Arab citizens, is below average because they lack the requisite labor market skills. This is largely because both groups do not receive an adequate education. According to OECD reports, Israel's ultra-Orthodox community make the choice not to be taught the core curriculum subjects required for successful labor market participation, while Arab citizens receive a poor-quality education overall, which, among other things, affects their ability to communicate fluently in Hebrew.

In 2019, about 41 percent of the Israeli workforce was employed in the wider public sector, compared to the OECD average of less than 35 percent. This sector includes non-business services—security, healthcare, education, welfare, and administrative services—which are less exposed to global competition and have no incentive to improve productivity. Low productivity in Israel's traditional industries and services is largely the result of a lack of professional personnel and poor professional training provision by both the government and private sectors

Many Israelis who have joined the workforce in recent years do not have appropriate training or labor market skills, and, as a result, have been shunted into occupations in low productivity industries and corresponding meager wages. Since the 2000s, Israel has developed a dual economy, with two separate economic sectors existing side by side. The first is based on high productivity, usually high tech, exporting industries with a relatively small "elite" of specialist, highly skilled workers who are paid internationally competitive wages, while the second is based on non-exporting industries with low levels of competition, labor productivity, and remuneration. To create a more skilled workforce and help it adapt to the changing needs of its economy, Israel must proactively invest in professional continuing education and training schemes. However, as of 2023, such government schemes were severely underfunded, while private sector investment in professional training was also scarce. Israel needs a proactive labor policy that matches its spending on professional training and achievements in boosting labor productivity to meet the level of European countries.

Israel's levels of per capita public capital and private capital per worker have not risen significantly since the 1980s and remain low in comparison to peer countries. Israel's underdeveloped public infrastructure, in particular its land transport, also has negative impacts on productivity. The severe road congestion that is a direct result of Israel's underinvestment in its land transport networks makes commute times unnecessarily long and causes fatigue that affects labor productivity. Meanwhile, investments in business capital per worker are low—only about half those in the United States and just two-thirds of the OECD average. Levels of capital stock in Israel's business sector (including equipment and machinery, vehicles, and buildings) are considerably lower than the OECD average. These factors also influence Israel's labor productivity, which is low compared to the OECD average.

## Innovation

Innovation is also a way to create and dominate markets. There is an argument for extending the Israeli concept of innovation to areas other than the high-tech industry or production. Innovation is the introduction of changes and the adoption of methods that increase productivity across all areas of business. It is not possible to change the face of traditional industry and services without introducing innovation in production, organization, marketing, or management. Innovation is also necessary in public policy to create new tools and methods to significantly improve the efficiency and efficacy of public administration for the good of society and the economy According to the OECD's Digital Government Index for 2019, Israel still ranks low in terms of its interface with citizens.

In Israel, construction is an example of an industry that has been almost left untouched by the technological revolution. A conservative sector, it is lagging behind, largely because of its low levels of innovation and technology adoption, factors that go some way to explaining the high cost of construction projects in Israel. Planning by the central government and local authorities as well as construction also require innovation, not least since Israel's high population density creates considerable complexities for residential, commercial, and employment infrastructure development. A great deal of careful thought around land allocation is needed for effective, long-term planning and long-term to ensure that this precious resource is properly designated for various uses, including when planning cross-city transport services such as metro or light rail lines.

In surveys by the Israeli Central Bureau of Statistics, more than 50 percent of managers in the country's trade, hotel, and business sectors cited employee quality as the most influential factor on output per labor hour in their organizations (mainly small and medium-sized businesses of up to 100 employees). In transportation services, including shipping and storage, and mail and courier services, around 40 percent of Israeli managers indicated that management quality was the main factor affecting labor output, while 38 percent pointed to equipment and technology as being the most influential factor. Meanwhile, in financial services, around 70 percent of managers said that regulatory barriers had the most impact on productivity per labor hour.

Regulatory barriers in trade in services in Israel are among the highest in the OECD report. Overregulation has negatively affected the viability of investments, discouraged new investors from entering the Israeli market, and made it harder for the economy to maximize the growth potential of investment in this industry sector.

Statistics show that, in 2019, around 80 percent of the combined workforce across the OECD was employed in the services sector, with about 75 percent of GDP coming from this sector and 65 percent of foreign investments going into it. In Israel, most of the services sector is characterized by low productivity.

Governance and institutions are a reflection of the ability of elected officials to work with public officials to maintain good and effective government. Elected officials do not have the right skills to allow them to contend singlehandedly with complex and professional issues, and a professional echelon is required as an integral part of good governance. Everything affects productivity—just as the taxation system affects whether citizens are incentivized to work, thus supporting the goal of a fair and progressive income tax, and same principle applies to other incentives, regulation, and bureaucratic processes.

Paradoxically, during the coronavirus pandemic of 2020–2021, Israel's productivity increased. Hundreds of thousands of Israelis were made redundant or laid off, mainly from low productivity industries including hospitality, culture, and commerce. Even industries with high productivity learned to manage with fewer staff, and the high-tech sector flourished. Some employers learned to manage with fewer workers, and there is a chance that this positive trend in Israel's productivity will continue in the future. This would be a good opportunity to eliminate hidden unemployment, which refers to workers with low productivity. Following the pandemic, some of Israel's industries did not maintain their staff cuts and the increased productivity they had managed to achieve was short-lived. If Israel is able to sustain the increase in productivity it achieved over the pandemic, it could lead to improved wages for employees and increased profitability for employers.

# 35

# Security and Peace

## Changes to Israel's political and security reality

Throughout its existence, Israel has been in continuous conflict with its neighbors and the wider region. The many security incidents that Israel has undergone—full-scale wars, military operations, Palestinian intifadas, terror attacks, and the daily reality constant security tensions—are reflected in its unusually high defense budget compared with other developed countries.

Israel is located in a region in constant geopolitical flux and uncertainty. This has often meant unpredictable and rapid escalations from relative calm to states of emergency and full-scale war. The War of Independence (the 1948 Arab-Israeli War) was a comprehensive conflict that severely affected Israel's fledgling economy. The Yom Kippur War (the 1973 Arab-Israeli War) was a significant security event that, owing to economic mismanagement by Israel's leaders, led to a serious economic crisis. Later, the Second Intifada, which dragged on from 2000 through 2005, severely damaged the economy and blighted the lives of the residents of Israel's cities and towns. The Gaza War (2023-2024) continues to be a long and costly war. Both between and following these major conflicts, Israel has experienced scores of security incidents that have affected its economy in the short and longer term.

Since the 1990s, there has been no distinction between the military and the home fronts. This new reality has prompted a dramatic shift in Israelis' sense of security, and poses a considerable challenge for the security services, military, and government. In the past, wars and security incidents had largely occurred on Israel's borders or inside enemy lines. In January 1991, the First Gulf War marked a watershed in this regard when the Iraqi army fired 42 Scud missiles at Israeli civilian targets. Since then, terrorism and two Palestinian Intifadas have damaged Israeli city centers and harmed growth in retail and tourism. In light of Israel's unique security situation, its economic achievements are impressive: despite its complex and fragile reality, it has built a functioning, growing, and advanced economy that belongs in the top ranks of the developed countries However, these achievements should not be taken to mean that Israel's economy and society have not paid a hefty price for the country's long, drawn-out conflicts with its neighbors and the Palestinians.

Israel's signing of a peace treaty with Egypt—a major Arab power—following the Camp David Accords in 1979 and with Jordan some 15 years later in 1994, did trigger important changes in its geopolitical reality. The signing of peace treaties with two of its closest neighbors made a significant contribution to Israel's strategic situation and marked the first steps toward deeper political agreements with these states. The treaties significantly reduced security threats to Israel, and thus had positive economic repercussions by allowing cuts in defense spending, which eased the burden on the Israeli taxpayer. However, the treaties have had almost no effect on bilateral trade or commerce. In effect, the peace agreements ushered in a "cold economic peace" with almost no investment or trade component. The professional and business classes in Jordan and Egypt continue to be antagonistic and boycott Israel, and consider the peace treaties as between governments only, not the people.

Meanwhile, the Oslo Accords, a pair of agreements signed in 1993 and 1995 between Israel and the Palestine Liberation Organization (PLO), have had opposite outcomes to those with Egypt and Jordan. While the Oslo Accords did not end the conflict between Israel and the Palestinians, and Israel continued to have security expenses, they did provide certain economic benefits. Among these were the development of relations and diplomatic ties with many countries that had previously boycotted Israel, the scrapping of the Arab boycott by companies that had previously avoided doing business with Israel, and the expansion of international trade. The international attitude toward Israel improved considerably, with many countries entering into or restoring diplomatic relations with Israel, and businesses that once feared the Arab boycott now began trading trade with Israel. These developments were beneficial for Israel's economy in the 1990s, providing it with greater access to international capital markets and globalization processes. Improvements in the domestic economy helped Israel raise its standard of living as well as absorb immigrants from the former Soviet Union. This is being threatened now, after the 2023-2024 Gaza war.

During the 1990s, initial steps were taken to integrate Israel into the wider region, amid lofty expectations that the peace treaties with the Palestinians and Jordan would herald a "new Middle East." These expectations were eventually realized—albeit informally and through secret, unofficial backchannels—at least with respect to the Gulf states of the United Arab Emirates, Oman, Qatar, and Bahrain.[1] In September 2020, under American mediation, Israel signed bilateral agreements on normalization with Bahrain and the United Arab Emirates. Known as the Abraham Accords,[2] these agreements saw Israel and the two Gulf nations establish full diplomatic relations. In December 2020, Israel signed a further bilateral agreement with Morocco. Israel's ties with the Gulf states are based on economics, trade, and investments, and have begun a new era for Israel in the Middle East. Like Israel, the Gulf states are wealthy, and there is a real capacity for the Israelis to create economic and business ties with them on an equal basis and exploit each other's relative advantages in a reciprocal way. This is in sharp contrast to the situation with Egypt and Jordan, both of which are classified by the World Bank as lower-middle-income countries that are wary of Israel's economic strength. However, normalization with Bahrain, the United Arab Emirates, and Morocco has had no effect on Israel's defense spending since Israel does not share a border and has never been at war with these states. In short, Israel signed peace treaties with Egypt and Jordan to achieve protection and security, while the Abraham Accords (and, as of 2023, the potential normalization with Saudi Arabia) are intended for business cooperation, political advantages, and further integration into the region.

The recent Gaza War, which opened on October 7, 2023 with a surprise murderous attack by Hamas in Israel's communities bordering the Gaza Strip, demonstrated the untenable and complex reality Israel faces. In order to survive securely in the region, Israel must maintain a robust security system, even with its attendant high economic costs.

## The Delicate Balance

Although its economy is at the heart of the globalized world, Israel remains mired in the local problems of the Middle East and in ongoing hostilities with some of the region's countries and non-state terrorist entities, such as Hamas and Hezbollah. Even after normalization with the United Arab Emirates, Bahrain, and Morocco in 2020, Israel has remained isolated in the Middle East. A long and slow process, Israel's integration into the region has occurred against a background of decades of hostilities and anti-Israel sentiment that has been internalized by generations of young people in the Arab and wider Muslim world. The 2023 Gaza War painfully illustrated this reality.

The economic benefits of Israel's peace treaties with Egypt and Jordan were limited to the reduction in defense expenditures that the removal of the conventional threat from these nations allowed. As such, these benefits were exhausted in the 1980s and 1990s.

The direct threat posed by the Bashar al-Assad regime in Syria decreased following the outbreak of the Syrian civil war in 2011, when Damascus focused its resources and energy on attempting to suppress the mass uprisings. Meanwhile, the same period saw the development of two non-conventional threats in the form of terrorism from Gaza and the Hezbollah in Lebanon. Israel also faces an ongoing existential threat from Iran as it pursues its nuclear program and through its proxies in the Middle East. Consequently, since the 2000s, Israel's defense spending has been affected by threats from Iranian-backed groups and regimes, most significantly Hamas in Gaza, the Lebanese Shia Islamist militant group and political party Hezbollah, and the Assad regime in Syria.

In the 2000s, security costs related to Israel's conflict with the Palestinians began to rise as a result of the Second Intifada, its disengagement from Gaza in 2005, and Hamas' rise to power in Gaza in 2007, which resulted in a series of military operations and the October 2023 Gaza War.

Israel's relatively high defense expenditure compared with peer countries is set to continue for years to come. So, too, is the internal debate over what the correct proportion of defense expenditure as a percentage of Israel's GDP should be, and what weight security spending should be given within the country's national priorities. In 2004, Ariel Sharon's government appointed the Committee on the Formulation of the National Security Doctrine (also known as the Meridor Committee)[3], which, among other things, was tasked to address these tensions. The Committee's recommendations, published in 2006, noted that Israel's defense expenditure should increase over the next decade through 2016, when it should stabilize at a rate of 5 percent of GDP. The Brodet Committee,[4] which was established to examine Israel's defense budget in the aftermath of the Second Lebanon War, set out a long-term outline for a moderate increase in Israel's defense budget, improved efficiency, and called for defense expenditure to be stabilized at 5 percent of GDP. In 2018–2022, Israel maintained its defense expenditure at around 5 percent of GDP—in line with the recommendations of the Brodet Committee—which was still far lower than in it had been in the 1970s and 1980s.

In view of the security challenges it faces, the downward trend in Israel's defense expenditure as a proportion of GDP has slowed somewhat to 6% in 2023 before the outbreak of the Gaza War. This situation poses an ongoing challenge for Israel's national order of priorities and for the need to ensure that its defense spending is actually effective. For some years now, Israel's open and global society has not been satisfied with the relatively low levels of public services it receives. This public resentment helped fuel the widespread social justice protests of 2011.

Rapid economic growth will be necessary if Israeli is to reduce its defense spending without harming its basic security needs and ensure that its defense budget can be adequately funded over time.

Israeli and international experience has shown that, above and beyond military and defense spending, small countries must rely on internal resilience and their international status, as was demonstrated again with the Gaza War in 2023. Internal resilience is rooted in an enlightened and progressive society that is culturally and socially cohesive with low internal tensions and socioeconomic disparities and solidarity. A country's military capability, economic power, and social resilience are all irrevocably intertwined. Part of the reason why Israel has been able to sustain its high defense spending throughout its history is thanks to the generous package of military aid from the United States since the 1980s, which has helped it sustain strong security and a healthy economy.

In the final analysis, despite its military, technological, economic, and scientific strength, Israel remains a country under siege that is waging a "defensive war" for its very existence. The pressing issues of defense and security are paramount for Israel's national agenda including in terms of resource and budget allocation. This situation, in which Israel bears exceptionally high security costs, sets Israel apart from other developed nations with which it competes, in international markets, and with which seeks equality in terms of its GDP and living standards. Israel's leaders constantly struggle to find the correct balance of military might and political management that can reduce threats and prolong the periods of calm between the inevitable rounds of violence. Meanwhile, Israel's army, the IDF, has to contend with public criticism that its economic conduct has not improved and that its budgetary and financial conduct is poor.[5]

## The "People's Army" and Mandatory Conscription

Israel's "people's army" model—mandatory conscription for all able-bodied Israeli Jewish men and women, and Druze and Circassian men, upon reaching the age of 18 for 24–32 months—is unique. The concept of the "people's army," as envisioned by Israel's first premier, David Ben-Gurion, was originally intended to allow the IDF to obtain the best personnel for its combat and technology units, and to bring together Israelis from all backgrounds in the name of nation-building. The health of this model, then, continues to have important security, social, and economic implications for the whole of Israeli society.

Over the years, Israel's system of mandatory conscription has drifted away from the "people's "army" model, which was intended to spread the burden of military service equally across all Israeli society. As the ethnoreligious makeup of Israel's population has changed over time, with high birth rates among two populations—ultra-Orthodox and Arab citizens—who are largely exempt from mandatory service, conscription rates have plummeted, with only about 50 percent of able-bodied Israelis joining the IDF each year. This trend poses a challenge to the "people's army." The drop in conscription is mostly because Israel's Arab and ultra-Orthodox communities, who have historically not served in the IDF (albeit for very different reasons) are growing rapidly. The increasing proportion of these communities in the overall population has brought down overall conscription rates. However, even among secular Jewish Israelis, there has been a decline in conscription rates, with many young people preferring to begin building their careers to army service. Israeli sociologist Yigal Levy has argued that the IDF has shifted from being the "people's army" to an "army of the peripheries,"[6] where conscripts from Israel's more peripheral areas are shunted to the IDF's regular ground forces, while those from the wealthier central coastal plain with higher socioeconomic profiles are more likely to be assigned to "prestigious" roles in the Israel Air Force or in IDF intelligence and cyber units, which will later help them integrate into the more lucrative high-tech sector.

There has been a great deal of reflection and debate in the Israeli media, Knesset, and other public forums regarding the concept of the "people's army" and whether it has a future. In the Israeli reality, one must fight for the principles of equality, to ensure that all citizens make a contribution to society, albeit in contexts that are appropriate to their religious and social beliefs.

Service in the IDF is often a consideration in employment screening and selection processes after the army (especially in high tech and communications). In addition, those who serve are granted incentives and rights not available to others. Improper handling of the exemption for ultra-Orthodox men will damage the motivation of other Israelis to serve and also negatively impact the legitimacy of service—a situation that could harm the "people's army" model'. The cost of mandatory conscription in 2023 was directly estimated at about 2 percent of Israel's GDP.

In 2017, the government doubled subsistence allowances paid to conscripted soldiers to incentivize people to serve in the IDF. A hybrid system has begun to emerge, with the old-style "people's army" coexisting alongside a semi-professional military based on those who remain in the army after their mandatory service is completed. In such a system, financial reward could result in selective recruitment, which would determine the scope of the human resources available to the IDF. In light of the security threats it faces, especially after Gaza war (2023-2024), Israel cannot afford to abolish mandatory conscription. The unique challenges faced by the IDF require it to have access to high-quality personnel for its technological and combat roles, and to allow for the professionalization of personnel.

The IDF must find a way of balancing periods of training with time in service for recruits to its technological and combat units. This need is leading to an increase in *keva* officers (conscripts who agree to sign up for longer than the mandatory service period) in these types of specialist units. Under this system, such units receive increasing numbers of experienced soldiers and officers who are not then replaced shortly after their training period ends. Meanwhile, many frontline soldiers serve for a short time, and the state benefits from their going on to study and work after they are discharged. This sort of hybrid model may help Israel preserve its "people's army."

## Threats

Israel's strategic situation is characterized by a severe imbalance between its defense, economic, and technological might, and the gravity of the political and security challenges it faces. Among the most significant of these threats is Iran, which as of 2023 was continuing to pursue its nuclear program while working to intensify the threat to Israel from several arenas. *By Proxies.*

The Palestinian conflict also poses several risks, including the specter of the potential disintegration and weakness of the Palestinian Authority and the lack of governance in their territories along with their battles in the international political and legal arenas. This was reflected in the murderous attack by Hamas in October 2023 and in Hezbollah's actions on the Lebanese border. Long-term, there is also the risk that Israel will slip into a one-state solution—a single binational state for Palestinians and Jews in which Jews would lose their majority status according to democratic processes, thus ending the state's Jewish identity.

The Middle East is an unstable, violent, and badly functioning region, and some of its states continue to pose threats to Israel. Numerous factors demonstrate the extent of systemic instability in the region and its implications for Israel's national security. These include the struggle between Israel and Iran, the entrenchment of Iran, Russia, and Hezbollah in Syria, the volatility of the Palestinian arena, Hezbollah's accumulation of firepower including more accurate missiles, regional competition over energy resources, the deep sociopolitical crisis in Lebanon, and the threat of renewed global jihad.

The Tehran-led axis of resistance against Israel continues to invest in accumulating military power and developing advanced capabilities, including nuclear technology (in the case of Iran), more precise missiles, drones, and cyber-attack abilities. This complex, continually shifting situation illustrates the influence of regional dynamics, the limits of deterrence, and the region's relentless, systemic volatility, all of which demand that Israel formulate a military-defense strategy that can respond not only to emerging threats, but also to opportunities. Israel's goal is to hamper Iran's efforts to become a hegemonic and nuclear power, underscoring that Iranian nuclear ambitions can pose an existential threat to Israel. As long as the Iranian regime is guided by its hardline Shia Islamist ideology and strives to achieve regional hegemony in the Middle East, it will continue to pose a significant threat to Israel. As such, Israel must give its citizens confidence that it has the power to counter Iran through a reliable and persistent strategic deterrence, including the capability to strike Iranian targets.

This is an ongoing situation with occasional outbreaks of violence that have, so far at least, remained below the threshold of war until the recent Gaza War, with Hamas acting as an agent of Iran. Even if the main players (Israel and Iran) are not interested in fighting a lengthy kinetic war, there is always the danger of an error in judgment that could lead to escalation. Iran's nuclear program, coupled with its ongoing ambitions for dominance in the Middle East through its proxies, Hamas, Palestinian Islamic Jihad, Hezbollah, and the Assad regime in Syria—require Israel to continuously spend money and resources to maintain its defense and allow the option of attack. Israel will continue to act according to "theory of rounds," according to which it must proactively develop its national, technological, and social strength between periodic outbreaks of violence and maintain its deterrence between major conflicts. At the same time, Israel must maintain its strong strategic relationship with the United States and develop relations with moderate Arab states to counter Iran and its allies. Reducing the levels of hostility and distrust between Israel and its regional neighbors, with the goal of cooperating with them in the face of shared threats, is a first-order pillar of defense. Political arrangements are part of the fabric of national security and an integral component of moderating the intensity and frequency of severe outbreaks of violence.

The sub-conventional threat posed by Hezbollah, Hamas, and other militant groups, which (in particular Hezbollah) have focused on acquiring long-range weapons caches, and bunkers, has grown considerably over past decades. This threat endangers Israel's rear no less than its front, and as such, civic consciousness has become central to considerations around war and peace, as seen in the confrontation with Hamas in the Gaza War in 2023. The ability for enemy actors from near and far to strike Israel's civilian home front, in particular with precision surface-to-surface missiles that could shift the balance of power between Israel and Hezbollah and/or Iran, has become a serious threat. With it come significant economic ramifications, including the cost of reinforcing and protecting residential buildings, especially in view of the short warning times involved in missile attacks. As of 2023, more than 60 percent of Israeli homes did not have a reinforced security room[7] where residents can shelter during a missile attack, while according to the Israeli Home Front Command, a quarter of Israelis do not have access to a standard air raid shelter. Israel's public air raid shelters can accommodate only about 6 percent of the population, with communal shelters in the basements of residential buildings having room for around 30 percent.

Over the past decade, the emerging threat of cyberattacks has become a huge security and economic risk. Israel's enemies have developed strategic cyber capabilities that could paralyze the country's central infrastructure systems including its electricity, energy, and military capabilities. A cyberattack could be the deciding factor in a war.

In addition to these military and security threats, Israel's relationship with China has become a strategic national security issue, in particular in view of Chinese investment and involvement in key Israeli infrastructure projects. Israel has had to navigate between maintaining strategic ties with its most important ally, the United States, and developing its relations with China, which have economic potential. Since continued support from Washington is critical to Israel's security, Israel must be aware of American public opinion and avoid creating a situation where its relationship with the United States becomes a polarizing political issue.

Israel needs to maintain its military power, its special relationship with the United States, its technological advantages, and its economic power. At the same time, it must preserve its internal solidarity by working to gain public recognition and trust in the righteousness of its actions.

## *The Palestinians*

Israel's occupation and control of millions of Palestinians also comes at a terrible cost to Israeli society. There is a risk of developments that will result in a one-state solution, i.e., a binational state for both Jews and Palestinians. Israel's occupation of the West Bank and its conflict with the Palestinians is a political, governmental, and religious issue and the subject of debate that also has important socioeconomic ramifications. Israel's failure to make decisions on the Palestinian issue will inevitably lead, though inertia, to a one-state solution that would change Israel's character as a Jewish and democratic state.

Israel's lack of a comprehensive strategy toward the Palestinians harms its national resilience, while its existing policy of "managing the conflict" through tactical military and economic tools prevents it from shaping a reality that corresponds with its national security interests. The ongoing occupation of, and conflict with, the Palestinians is a core national security problem that cannot be suppressed or managed through a strategy of "firefighting." Instead, Israel needs to proactively formulate a comprehensive strategy, via a poignant public and political debate, to enable it to make the necessary historical decisions. The lack of such a strategy harms Israel's national resilience.

The Palestinian population, which in 2023 amounted to some 5 million people in the West Bank and Gaza, will threaten Israel's character as a Jewish and democratic state if the situation slides into a one-state solution with Palestinians as residents and citizens of a single, binational state. Any move by Israel to partially or fully annex the West Bank, even if it subsequently granted Palestinians a form of residency status (not citizenship) that would grant them considerable benefits, including social security allowances and government services in health, welfare, and education, but without the right to vote (as it has done with Palestinian residents of East Jerusalem) will come at a heavy economic price.

A one-state solution would not mean that the Palestinian national identity would disappear, and neither would it guarantee peace in the region. The situation could deteriorate into a fully-fledged civil war, due to the Palestinians' desire to establish an identity between a homeland and a state. According to data in 2023, a one-state solution would mean the addition of the 2.7 million Palestinian residents of the West Bank, whose per capita GDP is about $5,000 compared to Israel's $50,000. Economic and civil union between Israel and the West Bank would lower Israel's average per capita GDP to around $32,000 and the Palestinian population would increase to around 40 percent. Economic disparities would be enormous in terms of unemployment rates, wages, and consumption and it is likely that the Palestinians would be in the lower deciles. Economically, Israel would fall to the bottom of the OECD in light of the considerable resources it would have to devote to public services for the residents of a single state (including national insurance, compulsory education, healthcare, and other public services to which residents are entitled). These costs could only be funded by pushing up taxes and slashing services for the "original" residents of the country. In such a scenario, Israel's less advantaged populations would suffer disproportionately.

Israel's ongoing conflict in the Middle East, which mainly revolves around the conflict with the Palestinians, exacts a heavy economic toll on Israel. This plays out in the military arena in wars and security incidents, in the political and diplomatic arena, in the sphere of public opinion, and in the media. Israel also faces pressure from the Boycott, Divestment, Sanctions (BDS) movement, which seeks to undermine the legitimacy of its academic, cultural, and economic ties with the rest of the world. There is a war on public opinion on campuses and social networks with anti-Israeli, anti-Zionist, and antisemitic discourse, and which demands a serious and continuous confrontation. It is difficult to estimate the undeclared damage to Israel's reputation, business, and diplomatic support.

## Notes

1. Although Saudi Arabia were not formally signatories to the Accords, they were deeply involved in the process.
2. Officially, the Abraham Accords Peace Agreement: Treaty of Peace, Diplomatic Relations and Full Normalization Between the United Arab Emirates and the State of Israel. For the full text of the Accords, see: https://edition.cnn.com/2020 Although Saudi Arabia was not formally signatories to the Accords, they were deeply involved in the /09/15/politics/israel-uae-abraham-accords-documents/index.html.
3. I was a member of the Meridor Committee. The report was published in April 2006.
4. Report of the Security Budget Review Committee (Brodet Committee), May 2007.
5. According to a special survey focused on public perceptions of the IDF conducted by the Israel Democracy.
6. See: Yagil Levy (2007) From the "People's Army" to the "Army of the Peripheries," Jerusalem: Carmel Publishing House (in Hebrew), and Yagil

Levy (2022) Shooting and Not Crying: The New Militarization of Israel in the 2000s. Ra'anana: Lamda Open University (Hebrew).

7. A reinforced security room, or merkhav mugan, is required in all new Israeli buildings by law. Most older buildings, however, do not have such a room.

# PART SEVEN

# THE CORONAVIRUS PANDEMIC, WAR AND FUTURE CHALLENGES

## 36

## The Coronavirus Pandemic

### The Nature of the Crisis

The coronavirus pandemic, "the corona crisis", was one of the most intense civil emergencies and public health catastrophes on a global scale. Unlike in previous economic crises, during the pandemic Israel did not have any shortage of foreign currency reserves. Rather, the effects of the pandemic were more akin to those of a multidimensional war, including its devastating impact on public health, with some 12,500 people dying of the coronavirus in the country.

Experience in Israel and throughout the world has shown that large and costly wars often trigger changes to the economic order. The pandemic disrupted global economic functioning to an extent not seen since the Wall Street Crash of 1929. The global public health crisis triggered a worldwide economic, social, and mental health emergency that affected different demographics in different ways. In Israel, as in other nations, the pandemic disproportionally increased morbidity and mortality among older people, who were more susceptible to severe illness. Younger adults faced disproportionate economic harm and suffered more unemployment. Mass school closures severely harmed the education of Israel's children, especially those from socially and economically disadvantaged backgrounds, who emerged from the pandemic with deep scars that will have far-reaching, as yet unknown, consequences. The pandemic also caused considerable economic uncertainty. Israel's most reliable economic metric was the unemployment rate, which peaked at 27 percent—even higher than in previous economic crises. Israel also experienced an acute shock to supply (the result of forced closures of its production facilities), coupled with a similar shock to demand (a consequence of plummeting revenues from employment and economic activity). The damage to supply was a combined result of mandatory shutdowns and restrictions on flights, tourism, and the leisure industry, partial closures of trade and businesses, and disruptions to supply chains, which caused severe delays in shipping and ensuing large backlogs at ports.

To prevent the collapse of (healthy) businesses, including small enterprises, and to avoid inflicting unnecessary harm to physical capital, critical workforce members, corporate knowledge, relations with suppliers and customers, and managerial, technological, and marketing experience, Israel provided a package of government aid to companies, which was intended to bridge the gap caused by the sudden drop in revenue streams and the need to meet ongoing costs, including financial assistance to employees furloughed without pay.

The sudden drop in income for self-employed and salaried workers hit private consumption and short-term investments. However, the slowdown in global trade barely affected Israeli exports, since many of these were high-tech services that remained, or even increased, in demand. Israel's budgetary policy was flexible and permissive, and allowed for an increase in the budget deficit and government debt-to-GDP ratio in order to prevent a continuous slowdown. Israel's fiscal policy played a decisive role in helping to flatten the recession curve, reducing the damage to supply and demand, and supporting economic recovery.

Clearly, the pandemic was a disruptive factor. The economic crisis that the pandemic triggered in Israel created a series of shocks that could be mobilized to drive economic progress, as weaker economic players failed to survive and left the competition in favor of new contenders that could develop, grow, and take the lead. The pandemic had the power to generate positive "creative destruction." Failing to take advantage of this would prove a missed opportunity for significant economic reform. By demolishing old paradigms and socioeconomic arrangements, and building new, long-term capabilities, creative destruction can drive innovation. Indeed, Israel's "change government,"[1] formed in June 2021, introduced a number of structural reforms in its 2022 budget. Even though most of the reforms had little or nothing to do with the pandemic response, the crisis had created the fertile ground for change.

In the spring of 2021, Israel's public health emergency had largely abated following a mass vaccination program. For the time being, the socioeconomic effects of the pandemic had left a temporary mark in the form of increased public and private debt. However, the pandemic had also provided opportunities for entrepreneurship, including for the small businesses that sought and found new revenue streams. Globally, the pandemic demonstrated humanity's incredible ability to mobilize its collective scientific and medical knowledge for the rapid development of vaccines and drugs that accelerated the global scientific-technological revolution of the past decades.

During the pandemic, three lockdowns were imposed, and, as noted, about 12,500 Israelis died from the virus. Considering the country's population size and older age distribution, Israel's death rate was around average in international comparison. The government allocated around NIS 220 billion to its pandemic response efforts, including state-backed loans of around NIS 36 billion. In practice, Israel spent about 180 billion NIS (some 11 percent of its GDP) on its pandemic response in 2020–2022, which included employment benefits for those now furloughed or unemployed, aid to the self-employed, readiness funding for the Ministry of Health, and grants to citizens. Not all of the decisions about aid packages were evaluated professionally before being granted, while decisions on lockdowns were taken with little regard for the economic consequences. Some of the aid packages were not given any in-depth consideration

Despite all these problems, Israel's economy bounced back from the pandemic relatively quickly, amid accelerating digital trends and leaps in cyber and artificial intelligence. The pandemic intensified the importance of the information held by commercial and non-commercial organizations, and there has been a recognition that information is, in fact, the most important asset of any organization. As a result, cyber protection has increased, including technological components, in particular the Internet of Things (IOT), 5G, servers, and migration to the cloud.

## Macroeconomics

Two macroeconomic trends emerged during the pandemic—the strengthening of the powerful (which fueled capitalism) and deep government intervention to save businesses and individuals (a socialist approach). This sort of "combinatorial" thinking, which allows for improvising solutions along non-dogmatic lines, and is long ingrained in the Israeli national psyche, has enabled the country's economy to contend with setbacks and crises throughout its history. At the same time, however, this national characteristic, which often discourages "playing by the rules," is what prevented effective enforcement of government guidelines designed to minimize the spread of the virus in ultra-Orthodox and Arab communities, which resulted in higher rates of morbidity and deaths among these populations.

Israel entered the pandemic with considerable economic strength and benefitted from a variety of resilience factors that helped cushion its economy during the crisis. Among these were a strong high-tech sector, high levels of household savings, a functioning central bank and stable banking system, a surplus in the balance of payments, domestic sources of natural gas, and high foreign exchange reserves. Israel's economic parameters were also favorable: its debt-to-GDP ratio was about 60 percent, its credit-to-GDP ratio about 120 percent, and its private debt-to-GDP ratio was around 43 percent. Israel also boasted a surplus of assets over foreign liabilities amounting to $200 billon, and a low unemployment rate of about 4 percent, while the government's structural deficit stood at about 4 percent. All this was the cumulative result of sound economic policies over 30 years, which had drawn on lessons learned during the hyperinflation crisis of the 1980s.

In 2020, Israel's GDP fell by about 2.2 percent. This was a relatively low drop in comparison to other countries around the world, mainly thanks to Israel's high-tech exports, in particular of communications and computing technology. These benefitted from soaring demand as the world shifted to increased digitalization and remote working and learning. Since tourism constitutes only 2 percent of Israel's GDP, compared to an average of 10 percent in European countries with strong tourism sectors, there was relatively little damage to the economy from the slowdown in this sector, and while Israel's hospitality, catering, and cultural sectors were hit hard, wages in these sectors are typically low. Most of Israel's industrial sector was able to maintain its capabilities, while the commercial sector survived in part thanks to government aid packages. The overall unemployment rate (taking into account workers furloughed without pay) in 2020 was 15.9 percent, while the state budget deficit rose to 11.5 percent of GDP, and the debt-to-GDP ratio soared to 72 percent. Per capita growth fell by about 4 percent, and private consumption per capita dropped by some 11 percent.

Israel was able to maintain a high surplus in its balance of payments of around 5 percent of GDP, thanks to high-tech exports alongside high levels of foreign investments that influenced the appreciation of the shekel. Meanwhile, foreign exchange balances rose from $124 billion at the start of 2020 to $171 billion by the end of the same year. Israel's economic recovery in 2021 was swift. GDP rose by some 8 percent, while the budget deficit fell to around 4.5 percent, and the debt-to-GDP ratio to 68 percent. Overall, the unemployment rate stood at about 10 percent. The surplus in the balance of payments remained high, at around 5.5 percent of GDP, with foreign exchange balances at the Bank of Israel rising to $213 billion at the end of 2021. Inflation rose to about 2.8 percent during the first year of the pandemic. Matters improved in 2022, Israel's economy grew by 6.4 percent, unemployment fell to 4.3 percent, the budget surplus dropped to around 0.4 percent, the debt-to-GDP ratio fell to 61 percent, and inflation rose again to 5 percent. In 2023 the growth of GDP was 2% and the deficit in the budget was 4%.

The pandemic, which appeared unexpectedly and suddenly, forced Israel to speedily find solutions, such as its furlough scheme. However, the fact that the crisis turned out to be relatively short-lived, coupled with Israel's speedy recovery, served to obscure the urgent need to solve these fundamental problems. Furthermore, although Israel's post-pandemic economic recovery has been one of the fastest in the world, it has been accompanied by a rise in inflation—a problem that has been experienced globally, the consequence of supply chain disruptions and the escalation of the Russia-Ukraine War following Moscow's full-scale invasion of Ukraine in February 2022.

## Government policy

The 2008 global financial crisis crystalized a flexible paradigm for managing monetary and fiscal policy. The pandemic reinforced this trend. For Israel, the pandemic was a national "market failure," creating increased risks for households and businesses that required government intervention. This came in the form of safety nets for affected industries and moves to preserve the state's strategic assets, aimed at ensuring that the country could continue to function for the duration of the crisis. The government helped reduce uncertainty by creating future prospects and stability notwithstanding the complexities of formulating long-term policy amid ongoing uncertainty.

During 2019–2022, Israel held five general elections. The lack of an approved budget for 2020 and 2021 severely hampered government functioning and created more insecurity for businesses and households. Decisions on imposing lockdowns were made partly out of political considerations, including as part of a populist move to achieve short-term electoral successes. In the absence of an approved budget, the government operated according to ad hoc budgetary packages reflecting short-term fiscal considerations.

Israel finances its government debt mainly by raising local debt in shekels and external debt in foreign currency at low interest rates. On the eve of the pandemic, Israel's government debt-to-GDP ratio stood at around 60 percent, given that interest rates hovered around 0–1 percent, Israel was able to raise loans and increase its government debt without harming public services. By the end of 2021, the ratio of government debt-to-GDP had crept up to around 68 percent. By reducing government debt to 61 percent in 2022, Israel was able to create a cushion for the next crisis.

Unlike the 2008 global financial crisis, the pandemic was less a monetary crisis than it was a fiscal and real one.[2] The Bank of Israel, supported the real economy in order to prevent a recession, purchasing 85 billion NIS of government bonds in the secondary market and helping the government raise capital at favorable prices. Moreover, the Bank of Israel provided a 10 billion NIS line of credit at a negative interest rate of 0.1 percent and lowered capital requirements from the banks.

## *Expanding monetary policy*

The severity of the pandemic overwhelmed Israel's social security capabilities. The government was concerned about the sudden jump in unemployment and its impact on rising social disparities. Overnight, a large proportion of Israel's young, independent, middle classes realized just how fragile the social and economic safety net was and expressed growing dissent over the results of the government's pandemic policies. In OECD countries, average pre-pandemic spending on welfare had stood at around 20 percent of GDP, compared to just 16 percent in Israel. The pandemic exacerbated Israel's existing social sensitivities, particularly in light of the fact that layoffs and redundancies among those in lower income brackets were far higher than among those with higher incomes—in particular those in the high tech, finance, and public service sectors whose jobs were barely affected. In 2020, Israel hiked welfare spending by about 6 percentage points to help prevent families falling below the breadline. Earlier, in 2018–2019, the government had helped lift some 39 percent of families and 26 percent of individuals out of poverty. In contrast, in 2020 these figures jumped to around 50 percent of families and 41 percent of individuals.

In the short term, the pandemic resulted in the return of "big government" and a decline in free market thinking. Just as during the global financial crisis of 2008, the pandemic also gave rise to a set of illusions, among them that there is such a thing as free credit, that government spending can be financed with zero-interest rates, and that governments can print as much money as they wish without causing inflation. These were dangerous illusions.

## The labor market

Israel's furlough scheme (known as *Halat* in Hebrew) was in effect for a year and a quarter and proved to be a critical tool in the country's pandemic response. The scheme provided the government with the breathing room it needed to manage the crisis. Within days, over a million jobs had disappeared due to lockdowns and other restrictions. In particular, it averted the public unrest that would inevitably have occurred as the result of mass layoffs, a development that would surely have undermined the stability of the government.

By the end of Israel's first lockdown, unemployment hit a peak of some 27 percent (the overall unemployment rate for 2020 was 15.9 percent). Among the hardest hit were young people and workers in lower income brackets. Most of those who found themselves suddenly unemployed or furloughed were under the age of 35. Around half of all Israel's students were also laid off from their jobs. While in 2019, state unemployment benefits had helped lift 2.2 percent of Israel's population out of poverty, in 2020 state benefits paid out under the *Halat* scheme rescued a staggering 23.6 percent of Israelis from falling below the breadline. Thanks to Israel's mass vaccination program in the spring of 2021, unemployment fell to about 6 percent by the end of that year, and in 2022 it finally stabilized at about 4 percent. By 2022, many of the Israelis who remained without employment were from disadvantaged or minority groups—in particular ultra-Orthodox and Arab citizens, young people, and women without adequate labor market skills. As a result of the pandemic, Israel's young people lost at least a year of job experience and opportunities, and when they were finally able to start working, they found themselves earning lower incomes than would have been the case had the pandemic not occurred. Some older adults who were furloughed found it hard to return to the labor market, and their pensions were affected. Women were particularly hard hit and were the first to be furloughed or laid off. Single mothers, who depend on their children being in school in order for them to be able to go out to work, and women over the age of 55 suffered an especially severe blow.

Israel's *Halat* scheme was different from the German-European model, which had been developed during the 2008 global financial crisis to help curb the sudden rise in unemployment, prevent bankruptcies, and maintain workers' skills. The Israeli model was rigid and binary—either a person was employed, or they remained at home and received unemployment benefits. In contrast, under the German *Kurzarbeit* (short-time work benefit)[3] model, which was adopted by most EU states, governments provided subsidies to employers to help them retain their employees. This way, employers retained responsibility for their employees, and were able to maintain an essential workforce on the basis of trust and cooperation between themselves and their employees. This system created a sense of stability and helped keep unemployment rates low.

The scheme ran into difficulties because the country had no organized database for managing the distribution of payments, and because there was no link between income tax and social security data, in particular for the self-employed. This was not merely a technology or computerization issue. It was also a matter of how the relationship between the state, employers, and employees was perceived. The *Halat* scheme was justified by the need to allow the market to adapt to the structural changes set in motion by the pandemic, to prevent wasting public money on propping up unviable businesses, and to reduce state involvement in the labor market. Within the tensions that exist between Israel's model of "letting the labor market adjust" and Europe's approach of "preventing unemployment through comprehensive subsidies," on the one hand, and the need to preserve and maintain consumption and safeguard businesses, on the other, immediate arrangements can be made. These include paying partial unemployment benefits for part-time jobs and preserving employer-employee relationships.

This was a missed opportunity to retrain people who had been laid off, at the cost of paying them unemployment benefits, as an effective way to provide them with new job prospects. Had Israel made better use of job training, the pandemic could have provided an opportunity for Israel to transition a portion of its workforce out of low-productivity and into high-productivity industries.

## Tensions

For Israel, the pandemic was an unusual challenge. Although not a security crisis, it still demanded considerable social resilience, and resulted in a drop in public trust in the government and the civil service. There were expressions of dissent and a sense that social solidarity had been weakened amid tensions between various communities, ethnic groups, and demographics, in particular Arab and ultra-Orthodox citizens and young people, who sometimes expressed different interests and perceptions. During the pandemic, and peaking in 2021, young, self-employed people protested as they had in 2011, against the socioeconomic processes of the preceding decades – but this time, the protests also expressed intercommunity and sectarian divisions and the sense of discrimination that people felt had eroded the bonds of social solidarity. Israel's intercommunity and inter-ethnic tensions were largely rooted in the perceptions of some within these communities around compliance with government guidelines and rules and public discipline. Israel's non-ultra-Orthodox Jewish middle classes struggled to "shoulder the burden" of the pandemic, as they saw it, in light of their perceptions that the country's ultra-Orthodox and Arab citizens were acting as autonomous units and not following government guidance There were high rates of morbidity among ultra-Orthodox and Arab citizens and discrepancies in compliance with, and enforcement of, government guidance and rules, which affected the country's sense of solidarity and equality during the pandemic. Some ultra-Orthodox citizens refused to comply with government guidance and rules to an extent that undermined the country's overall sense of public responsibility and of being "all in it together" as a national partnership. Within the ultra-Orthodox community itself, there was a crisis of trust in the authority of the state as opposed to that of the ultra-Orthodox religious leadership.

In terms of the economy, tensions arose between workers in sectors least hit by the pandemic (mainly public service, high tech, the financial sector, and industry), and those that were disproportionately affected (in particular aviation, tourism, restaurants, culture, and small businesses). The pandemic also exacerbated intergenerational tensions between young people and older adults, as the disproportionate economic burden on young people exceeded the social contract of cross-generational social solidarity. Consumption of healthcare services by older adults was much greater than in pre-pandemic times, while younger people, who were less at risk of severe disease, paid far more in cost-benefit terms than during routine periods, and certainly more than had been envisioned in the National Health Insurance Law (1994). At the same time, the lockdowns had a severe impact on the ability of young people to participate in the labor market and on children's education.

## Implications for the future

Facing the pandemic, Israel had an advantage over many developed countries in the form of its robust healthcare system which managed to cope well both in terms of community medicine (through its system of Health Management Organizations) and inpatient care, creating effective and real-time solutions in the face of a rapidly shifting situation. However, for the first time, Israel's healthcare system faced an emergency where it had the very real risk of being overwhelmed. The pandemic posed challenges around managing public health risk, amid an acute shift in the state of public health that impacted on healthcare costs, drug and equipment stocks, and the availability of hospital beds. The pandemic dramatically accelerated and improved the healthcare system's long-standing processes of digitalization.

In contrast, Israel's education system struggled to contend with the challenges of the pandemic, in particular when it came to managing the sudden shift to distance learning. Compared to other countries in the world, Israel had one of the lowest numbers of fully open school days during the pandemic. The education system discovered that distance learning presents not only a technological issue, but also requires adapting teaching content and delivering it in a different way than previously. The already urgent need to reduce classroom sizes and expand the powers of local authorities and school principals grew more acute. In contrast, Israel's higher education system found it easier to quickly adapt to distance learning, and so was able to minimize the damage caused by college and university closures.

In terms of welfare and work, Israel needs to create temporary programs to help its "new poor"—chiefly, middle-class Israelis who have been pushed toward the breadline thanks to job losses and lockdowns, young people who have not been able to find work, and low-wage workers. One bright spot was the efficient functioning of local government, which demonstrated a good level of professionalism compared to central government. This is proof of the validity of the calls for changes in the balance of power between Israel's central and local government. In Israel's business community, managers invested in organizational changes, digitization, and automation, and benefitted from new technologies and workers who were forced to work from home. There is a chance that Israel's stagnating productivity will rise as a result of companies reducing their workforces and relying more on technology. Companies and businesses that had available technological tools easily shifted to remote working, as did many others over the course of the pandemic.

The pandemic also highlighted issues around inequality and deglobalization, and in response many countries, including Israel, adopted a combination of soft capitalism and government intervention. The Israeli public demanded that the government step in to ensure the provision of a number of public services, which posed a challenge to the political system. The pandemic affected globalizing trends, including global supply chains. Dependence on overseas imports and other factors have strengthened calls to maintain local production, in particular in areas connected with security, health, and food. These developments have helped slow, and in some cases even roll back, the processes of globalization. Meanwhile, Russia's intensification of its years-long war with Ukraine in the form of a full-scale military invasion in February 2022 triggered a global rise in the prices of energy and goods

At the same time, the pandemic increased the need to diversify sources of supply and reduce reliance on imports in several areas. It has arguably also accelerated the "green revolution," as many scientists and environmental scientists associated the virus with humans' excessive intervention in nature. The importance of clean energy and addressing climate change as a threat to humanity, and expediting projects that support a sustainable economy. There is an increased urgency towards shifting to renewable energy, planting trees to create shade for pedestrians and cyclists, and upgrading buildings to meet contemporary green environmental standards.

Although the pandemic receded in 2023, so did the many insights gained from the crisis. Public memory was short indeed.

## Notes

1. In June 2021, Israel installed a new coalition government that both changed the long-standing leadership of Benjamin Netanyahu and his Likud party, but that also promised a change in governance and polices. This new coalition remained in power until Dec. 2022 when Netanyahu returned to power.
2. The term real economy refers to the overall production, purchase, and flow of goods and services in an economy.
3. For more detail, see: International Monetary Fund (2020), Kurzarbeit: Germany's Short-Time Work Benefit. June 15, IMF website. https://www.imf.org/en/News/Articles/2020/06/11/na061120-kurzarbeit-germanys-short-time-work-benefit.

# 37

# Charting a New Course, Including After the War

## Israel's dual economy

The dynamism that has always been an integral part of Israeli culture is one of its positive qualities. Indeed, the ability of Israelis to change and adapt is a key virtue, both for their country's economy and for their embracing their role in a globalized world. However, it is important that changes occur across all of Israel's different ethnoreligious communities and areas of life. In reality, the changes that have occurred within Israel's economy have affected its diverse communities in different ways, spawning tensions that have undermined the processes of change. This discordant reality has adversely affected Israel's economic and social systems. It is reflected in chronic low productivity and deepening socioeconomic disparities, among other things. Furthermore, the economic and social changes that Israel has undergone have not been mutually congruent and have sparked a succession of contradictions and tensions within its economy and society, including the gradual transition from socialism to capitalism and the rapid development of the high-tech sector. These changes, unfolding against the backdrop of increasing globalization and the high-tech revolution, provided the conditions for the emergence of a dual economy and a polarized society.

From a country initially built on a secular Zionist ethos, which glorified hard work and self-restraint, Israel now boasts a market economy by soaring private consumption and even hedonism. The old Zionist ideology of "negating the Diaspora" and creating the "new Jew" has given way to an emphasis on religious issues and the growth of national-religious and ultra-Orthodox populations. The closed economy of Israel's first decades has vanished, and the country now has an open market that is integrated into the global economy. The service industry has replaced Israel's initial reliance on manual agricultural, industrial, and construction labor. Meanwhile, the original Zionist vision of Israel as a "model nation" with high levels of socioeconomic equality has evaporated, and Israel has become a nation plagued by rising inequality and pockets of poverty.

Once a sparsely populated country, Israel now has a soaring population density that is threatening the environment. The youthful demographic of Israel's early years has been replaced by an aging population, its original collectivist character now having metamorphosed into individualism, albeit with an active civil society. Israel's original public economy, which had almost no private capitalists, has been replaced by one with a vibrant private commercial sector and a growing number of wealthy private owners. Originally a nation led by majority consensus, Israel has become a socially divided society, with each community viewing itself as a minority. The early state with its ideology of "ingathering the Exiles"[1] and desire to be a melting pot for global Jewry has become a fractured society riddled with identity politics. Indeed, Israel's increasingly isolated social and ethnic communities fail to identify with each other to the extent that there is a very real fear of a loss of national solidarity. Israel's macroeconomic situation is excellent, but there is a danger that growing tribalism will damage both intercommunity relations and public trust in state institutions.

The changes in Israel's socioeconomic regime have been set in motion by global developments. The technological revolution helped spark the growth of Israel's high-tech industry, which is fueled by knowledge, entrepreneurship, and creativity and rather than by manual labor and physical skills. Globalization has opened the doors to Israel's integration into the international economy. However, the combination of these two revolutions—the technological and the globalizing—has also spawned Israel's dual economy, with its two very different societies in economic terms. Since the 2000s, Israel's economic growth has been distinguished by the high rates of expansion and productivity of its burgeoning high-tech sector. This productivity boom, which is fueled by a relatively small number of highly skilled employees, stands in stark contrast to Israel's traditional economy, which is mired in low productivity and poor growth despite employing most of the country's labor force. Israel's challenge now lies in finding ways to bridge the divide of its dual economy by maintaining the momentum of high-tech growth and exports while improving the growth and productivity of traditional industries and services. Israel's dual economy has produced a dual society with severe income disparities that overlap with patterns of employment, geography, and tribal politics based on religious, social, and ethnic divisions.

Even in the face of continuing social disparities, in the 2000s, Israel began to adopt neoliberal policies that included cuts to welfare budgets, influenced by libertarian ideas from abroad advocating reducing social welfare institutions and social safety nets. Although the Israeli public mainly vote for parties that have advanced neoliberal policies, in-depth surveys show that most also want the trappings of a welfare state, including access to the wide-ranging public services more typical of a Western European social democracy. In this contradictory context, it is important to note that changes in the economy and technological developments have also prompted shifts in economic theory.

Nonetheless, it has become clear that free market economics do not offer an absolute solution to economic and social problems. Rather, countries need to somehow find a balance between a healthy economy, a just society, and government intervention. As the late economist Rudi Dornbusch quipped, "In economics, things take longer to happen than you think they will, and then they happen faster than you thought they could." Israel has experienced this phenomenon many times.

The pandemic and the Gaza War of 2023 have forced the Israeli public to confront and scrutinize the very essence of their government's social contract with its citizens, in particular how risks are shared between citizens, employers, and the state during civil, economic, and security crises. Israel's welfare policies must find a balance in the distribution of these risks between individuals and the state. Over the last decades, Israel has transferred part of the social risk to citizens, including by weakening trade unions and reducing employment protections. The pandemic demonstrated that the government still has an important role to play in protecting the public during major public health emergencies, which cause severe suffering and shock. The latest Gaza war provided further evidence of the government's vital role in defending citizens against security and economic shocks. The success of any welfare state lies in its ability both to be flexible vis-à-vis the economy and to intervene in the event of a major emergency. Finding this balance is a key part of the struggle of post-capitalism.

Israel's less socially and economically privileged populations, in particular its ultra-Orthodox and Arab citizens, are growing rapidly but lagging behind the secular public. There are fundamental tensions: between globalization and local economic activity, and between the growing populations of the conservative ultra-Orthodox and Bedouin communities and modernization and openness.

Although Israel is seen as an innovator and a magnet for leading international and multinational corporations, its scientific, technological, financial, and intellectual wealth coexists alongside deepening pockets of poverty. This socioeconomic polarization, which frequently occurs along ethnoreligious lines, has a strong impact on the broad issues that preoccupy Israeli society, including the country's rising population density and overcrowding, its ethnoreligious makeup, aging population, environmental threats, deglobalization, and the Israeli-Palestinian conflict. These are highly complex, multilayered problems. To tackle them, Israel needs a professional administration with the requisite knowledge and skills to develop effective policy.

The economic system that developed in the wake of Israel's 1985 Economic Stabilization Plan attempted to strike a balance between various conflicting extremes, including economic growth and equitable income distribution, a free-market economy and a welfare state with government involvement. Israel's increasingly neoliberal and capitalist economic regime is facing a population that desperately needs a social safety net. Israel's less socially and economically privileged populations—chiefly, its ultra-Orthodox and Arab citizens and those living in more peripheral and less developed areas outside the wealthy central coastal plain—demand a broad range of public services, the provision of which requires high public spending, which in turn relies on higher taxes. Meanwhile, Israel's secular Jewish, relatively wealthy, and liberal populations, most of whom are integrated into globalization and enjoy higher wages, prefer to keep tax rates low and are more prepared to rely on the private sector for the provision of public services. The socioeconomic tensions and conflicts that have arisen as a result of Israel's increasingly polarized dual economy and society demand urgent answers. If Israel fails to find solutions, it will face serious social and economic crises.

## Tackling Israel's Dual Economy

Generally, over time, there is no stable equilibrium point. Finding an effective balance is often elusive and difficult. Nonetheless, countries must strive to achieve it at all times.

There is no inherent disadvantage to Israel in remaining a small economy—doing so would not prevent it from reaping the benefits of the global marketplace. It is simply not realistic or possible to sustain an economy that has just one strong sector—in Israel's case, high tech. Rather, Israel must find ways to inject and infuse innovation into all economic sectors, including its traditional industries, if it is to maintain a modern, high-quality economy. Technology is versatile and can be implemented and incorporated into traditional industries just as it is in the high-tech sector.

Israel must also exploit the qualities that have been crucial to its past economic development—in particular entrepreneurship, resourcefulness, skill, technological knowledge, and a firm grounding in science. Here, Israel can also learn from the experience of other small, prosperous countries that a long-term strategy of enhancing excellence can be a recipe for success.

Even after 75 years of independence, Israel is still in the nation-building stage and contending with a set of worrying deep-rooted problems relating to the relationship between religion and state, governance, and the rule of law. These issues reverberated throughout the whole of society and economy. Addressing them will require the government to develop and implement wide-ranging and long-term policies that will help to build a functioning economy and society. The attempts in 2023 by the Netanyahu government to make drastic changes to Israel's judiciary, mentioned in Chapters 17 and 24, demonstrated this. Israel cannot allow mediocrity to taint its economy or approach to science and technology, governance, and security. Nor can it continue to permit social divisions to destroy it from within.

In the past, Israel has had stable governments with strong leaders who were able to set and direct priorities that helped the country achieve impressive social and economic milestones. Political crises, such as Israel's five national election campaigns over the four years between 2019–2022 and increasing political nominations that weakened the public service sector, harm both the economy and society. Today, the Israeli economy is attempting to chart a new course, seeking an equilibrium where various, sometimes conflicting, elements can be balanced. These include economic growth based on the evolving demands of the global markets, and the need to address vexing social questions; the desire to maintain a normal economic life amid a complex geographical reality; the need to address long-term economic and social challenges and short-term pressures; the desire to develop the local economy while continuing to integrate into an increasingly global marketplace; and the need to balance between necessary regulation while avoiding populism. Added to all these is the need to allow positive, constructive criticism of government policy while avoiding descent into defiant, humiliating, and paralyzing rants.

Israel's healthy macroeconomic situation, reflected in its low unemployment rate, steady growth, and encouraging debt-to-GDP ratio, makes it harder to impart a sense of urgency around addressing the country's fundamental problems of chronic low productivity, social disparities, high living costs, housing shortages, severe road traffic congestion, and low-skilled human capital. International comparisons consistently point to Israel's strength in innovation but weak public infrastructure, and its overall market efficiency in contrast to its deteriorating economic, social, and political institutions. A sound economy places people and their well-being at the front and center, taking them into consideration when distributing the fruits of various government policies among different communities. Bolstering social solidarity is mandatory for a country that is embroiled in ongoing regional security conflicts.

In Israel, inequality of opportunity is determined by the community or neighborhood in which an individual is born and raised. This is a challenge that reduces the country's potential for economic growth and prevents it from fully enjoying the talents of all citizens to contribute as much as they can to growth, while limiting the personal career opportunities of entire communities. Meanwhile, the digital revolution and the advent of artificial intelligence have exacerbated, and will continue to exacerbate economic inequalities—not just between individuals, but also between small and medium enterprises and more productive large corporations. To help bridge this gap, and boost productivity more widely and equally cross its economy, Israel must encourage and empower its small and medium enterprises to adopt and integrate new technologies and provide them and their employees with professional job training.

Some of Israel's socioeconomic disparities stem from the wealth gap between the baby boomer generation (born between approximately 1946 and 1964) and millennials (born between approximately 1981 and 1996) due to increases in the value of real estate and the expansion of cities. Baby boomers have benefitted from rises in real estate and land prices. The majority of Israel's employment centers—and thus also the greatest demand for housing—are in the more established towns and cities of the central Mediterranean coastal plain. While market forces have driven the growth in prosperity in Israel's central coastal plain, the government does have the ability to shape these market forces through the public services under its control, including public buildings, law courts, and government offices. Further, creating good quality employment opportunities in Israel's more peripheral and less developed regions in the south and north of the country will be key to addressing some of the problems caused by the skyrocketing population density and house prices in the central coastal plain. Improving the availability of suitable jobs in these currently underdeveloped regions and improving infrastructure and services in the periphery would provide an incentive for more people and businesses to relocate to these areas from the center.

The combined effects of the free market, globalization, and privatization have helped create and deepen the disparities between Israel's public and private commercial sectors. These disparities are particularly evident in terms of labor relations. The civil service and government-owned companies often have rigid labor relations and remain centers of power for large and powerful workers' committees, while the private sector has far more flexible labor relations. The pandemic has deepened disparities between the public sector and the non-high-tech private sector. During the pandemic, public sector jobs were barely affected, while in the private sector, hundreds of thousands of workers were furloughed or even fired.

Israel's main issues—how to integrate Arab and ultra-Orthodox citizens into the labor market and to increase productivity, how to address its underdeveloped public infrastructure, what to do about the aging population, and how to fix the country's housing shortages—cannot be solved by the "wisdom of the crowds" either through the market or social media. Instead, what is needed is a coherent, brave, clear, decisive, and non-populist government policy to chart a new route for Israel economically, politically, socially, and culturally. Only this can help Israel lead its economy out of its problematic status quo. Israel is affected by the global agenda. Trends involving globalization and deglobalization, Russia's war on Ukraine, climate change, and now the Gaza War, all have an impact on Israel's economy. The world is on the brink of establishing a new world order in terms of the power balance between the United States and China and the rollback of globalization, and Israel will have no choice but to adapt to this new reality.

## The Main Challenges

The challenges facing the Israeli economy and society are numerous and highly complex politically, economically, socially, and in terms of policy. Failing to respond to these challenges could divert Israel from the course it has been charting for over a century, since before its independence in 1948 through today, and lead it ever closer to an existential crisis. Economists like to focus on the long term. The following are the five major economic challenges facing Israel:

**The education system:** The main way to restructure Israel's dual economy will be by making drastic changes to its education system. Specifically, Israel needs to establish a core national curriculum of general studies that is taught across all its various education streams. This national curriculum must be mandatory for all children, and schools that refuse to comply with it should have their government funding removed. Such a move would be a major step toward helping Israel's ultra-Orthodox population integrate into the labor market, by giving them the right skills and mindset through the study of core, secular curriculum subjects (including English, science, and mathematics). There must be no compromise: there must be drastic reform of Israel's ultra-Orthodox education system to prepare its ultra-Orthodox high school graduates for the labor market. This is an existential strategic move for Israel's economy.

There also need to be changes in how the Ministry of Education operates vis-à-vis local authorities, and in how it confers authority and autonomy on individual school principals. The current low status of teachers in Israel also needs to be improved. The OECD has noted that Israel has one of the most centralized education systems of all the organization's member states.

**The labor market.** The ultra-Orthodox population, with its low rates of employment, is expected to expand considerably. This community's low rates of labor market participation coupled with the rising cost of the numerous special benefits packages it receives, will force Israel into a dangerous period of "treading economic water," with low growth that prevents the economy from improving the standard of living in relation to other countries and its own past.

At the same time, Israel is predicted to have a shortage of productive labor. On top of this, as of 2023 around half of all jobs in Israel were under threat due to predicted changes in the labor market as a result of increased automation, robotics, and artificial intelligence. These and other factors pose a serious risk of causing existing inequalities to soar. The key to upgrading employees' skills, beyond providing them with basic education, is professional job training and continuous learning. Israel should adopt a "flexicurity" model, which provides flexibility to employers in hiring and firing workers, while also providing protection to workers through offering them job training throughout their employment and when they are laid off. Professional and vocational training are critical for upgrading workers' skills and knowledge to allow them to better adapt to changing situations. This is particularly important for Israel's Arab and ultra-Orthodox citizens.

**Public infrastructure:** Israel needs to significantly increase investment in its underdeveloped public infrastructure in order to maintain a high level of per capita GDP and to incentivize people to move away from the overcrowded, expensive central coastal plain. The investment required to improve Israel's public infrastructure is estimated at about $500 billion in public and private financing over the next twenty years. Israel's underdeveloped, public transport, is the Achilles heel of its economy. A large injection of funding is required to develop and improve mass transit systems in the Gush Dan region. Home to about 45 percent of Israelis—the lifeblood of the country's commercial sector—this region stretches from the city of Netanya in the north to the port town of Ashdod in the south, and some 60 kilometers east to the growing new city of Modi'in. Large-scale investment in public transport is needed to facilitate accessibility and mobility in this key region, and should be based on a modern metro, light rail, and bus routes. As of 2023, rates of public transport use in Israel were very low—only about 10–15 percent of the population compared with about 40 percent in similarly-sized metropolitan areas in other OECD countries. Israel's reliance on private vehicles has caused extensive road congestion, traffic jams and gridlocks, road traffic accidents, air pollution, and a considerable loss of productive time. Israel's investment in public transport lags considerably behind the rest of the developed world, which helps explain why its productivity is so low compared to other OECD countries.

**Productivity**: The chronic low productivity of Israel's non-high-tech industries has harmed overall growth and living standards. It has also played a role in exacerbating inequalities between the country's various populations, in particular between residents of the prosperous central Mediterranean coastal plain and those in more peripheral regions. Improving productivity will be critical to ensuring the stability of Israel's economy and its wider society. Doing so is contingent on taking steps in the areas mentioned above.

**The environment and climate change:** The 2021 report of the United Nations Intergovernmental Panel on Climate Change (IPCC) stated unequivocally that global warming is a result of human greenhouse gas emissions. Efforts to mitigate climate change require global cooperation, and Israel must be a partner to these efforts. To reduce its own greenhouse gas emissions, Israel needs to move away from reliance on fossil fuels by switching to renewable energy sources. In 2020, the International Energy Agency named solar as the cheapest and cleanest renewable source in history.[2] Israel, as a country with favorable solar conditions, may benefit from technological developments associated with this lost-cost energy source, including the development of solar energy storage batteries. Israel should cooperate with its neighbors Jordan and Egypt regarding installing solar panels in desert areas in those countries, from which it can import green electricity. Global responsibility requires the imposition of a carbon tax and methane emission reductions, which will increase the prices of carbon-intensive inputs and products.

Israel must also take action to reduce pollution in its streams, beaches, and natural areas, preserve its open spaces, and treat waste, in particular hazardous waste, most of which is currently buried in landfill and produces greenhouse gases.

## The events of 2023–2024

Israel's achievements in the 75 years since its independence have made it an extraordinary success story, even in the face of its complex security situation and the challenges inherent in building a new state and society. Israel has become a flourishing democracy whose accomplishments are the fruit of its entrepreneurial, free, and open society, a progressive and educated country, and a "start-up nation" boasting an impressive array of economic, social, scientific, cultural, and academic achievements.

Nevertheless, 2023 was a watershed for Israel. Two major events exposed it to significant risks – and significant opportunities. As 2023 opened, Israel found itself facing a serious political, social, and economic crisis. By the end of the year, it was fighting a war.

At the start of the year, in a move that has been dubbed the "regime coup" , the sixth Netanyahu government proposed a series of draft laws intended to make changes in Israel's judicial system. By strengthening the power of the executive branch at the expense of the judicial branch this legislation threatened to disrupt the existing balance of power between the branches, thus ultimately undermining Israel's democracy. If adopted, these laws would have inflicted serious damage to the country's liberal-democratic regime by upsetting the balance of the separation of powers and harming Israel's independent judiciary. The impressive growth and development of Israel's economy are rooted, among other things, in the country's robust state institutions and independent, professional, and organized legislature and judiciary. The proposed legislation sparked concerns that the rules of the economic game would be weakened and damaged. Opponents claimed that corruption would soar and foreign investors would fear for the future of their assets, in particular in Israel's high-tech industry. To protest these moves, huge numbers of people poured into the streets, most of them advocates of liberalism, democracy, and minority rights. The mass demonstrations and protests deepened the rift that has emerged over the past few years between Israel's liberal and conservative, religious, and authoritarian "tribes."

The impression that Israel had become weakened by internal divisions likely had an influence on the timing of the heinous and murderous attack perpetrated by Hamas on October 7, 2023 – a plan that the Palestinian militant group had been developing for years. Caught by surprise, Israel incurred heavy losses – some 800 civilians and 340 soldiers were killed in one day, and about 251 more civilians were taken hostage to Gaza. The attack was a severe blow and humiliation for Israel, which responded with extreme force by unleashing a large-scale war on Gaza. The war continued into 2024, with soaring civilian and military costs of some $70 billion. The conflict also spread to other parts of the region, with involvement by Iran's proxies Hezbollah in Lebanon and the Houthis in Yemen. Tensions with Iran have skyrocketed. The war has seriously undermined Israel's international political status and image, which could potentially harm foreign investment as well as international business, scientific, and academic collaborations, so essential for economic progress. The end of the war will see defense spending hikes, even as early as 2025, reflecting the new challenges Israel faces in the region. As of June 2024, it remains to be seen exactly how much Israel's defense budget will rise. But there will certainly be an impact on growth and living standards.

The war in Gaza and the "regime coup" have both served to focus public attention on another controversy – the unequal burden of military service caused by ongoing draft exemptions for Israel's ultra-Orthodox population. This comes amid increasing ultra-Orthodox autonomy in directing resources toward that community's education institutions and yeshivas, reflecting its growing demographic and political strength. Meanwhile, increasing polarization between Israel's liberal and conservative publics has created a deepening rift in Israeli society, in spite of the broad mobilization of the population to provide financial and voluntary aid as part of a collective war effort. Israel's religious-messianic factions have also raised their heads, reflected in the expansion of West Bank settlements and violent confrontations with Palestinians there. Against this background, Israel's Arab population has refrained from engaging in any violence and has proven that they are law-abiding citizens.

The Israeli economy was in sound shape at the start of the war. If the right policies are adopted, it ought to be able to recover quickly, despite the high cost – a staggering $70 billion – of the war. Israeli society has demonstrated high levels of solidarity during the war and in the face of security threats. This has been reflected in its unprecedented levels of volunteerism and financial assistance to groups in need. Israel has one of the most vibrant, robust, and creative civil societies in the world. These qualities have always been an important component of its national security. Furthermore, Israeli entrepreneurship is rooted in a culture of resilience, and the economy has the know-how to continue to function even in the most difficult and complicated times.

The war in Gaza during 2023–2024 has harmed growth and investments and has adversely affected the public debt. As a result, Israel's credit rating has been further downgraded since having been downgraded during the "regime coup" protests. In 2023, Israel's GDP rose by 2 percent, while private per capita consumption fell by around 3 percent. Israel's budget deficit amounted to around 4 percent and public debt reached some 63 percent of GDP. At the close of 2023, foreign exchange reserves stood at $205 billion or about 41 percent of GDP. Estimates for 2024 suggest that GDP will rise by about 1–2 percent, while the budget deficit will soar to 7 percent. Public debt is also estimated to rise, to around 70 percent of GDP. During this difficult period, Israel's business sector has demonstrated, as it has in the past, an impressive flexibility and ability to recover. Israeli businesses have continued to function even during the war, and the country has continued to export despite a severe shortage of human resources, with some 300,000 Israelis having had to leave their businesses and workplaces to serve in the military reserves. Israeli high-tech in particular has demonstrated an astonishing degree of resilience.

The war has made it all the more pressing to find solutions to issues that have been neglected for years. This requires the development of a new sociopolitical system. The failure of Israel's intelligence and security echelons to prevent Hamas' deadly October 7 attack that sparked the outbreak of the war, the management of the war, and its prolongation, have all engendered broad opposition to the government. The political crises and the war may yet produce new rules of the game in terms of the separation of powers and an independent judiciary and professional governance. They may perhaps also prompt a shift in the regional geopolitical situation. In the absence of a far-reaching political solution to the conflict, including Palestinian recognition of Israel's right to exist as a Jewish state, Israel will have no choice but to continue as a mobilized society, with a return to high rates of defense spending not seen in other Western developed countries.

## Notes

1. The concept of "Kibbutz Galuyot" or the "ingathering of the Exiles/Israel" is the Biblical promise made by Moses to the Israelites prior to their entry into the Land of Israel (Deuteronomy 30:1–5). The concept is a key part of Zionism and the establishment of the State of Israel.
2. Carbon Brief. (2020). Solar is now 'cheapest electricity in history', confirms IEA. Available at: https://www.carbonbrief.org/solar-is-now-cheapest-electricity-in-history-confirms-iea/.

# Biblography


Acemoglu, Daron, and James A. Robinson. *Why Nations Fail.* Crown Business, 2012.

*Agreement Between the State of Israel and the Federal Republic of Germany.* United Nations Treaty Series, 10 Sept 1952.

Ahad Ha'Am (Asher Ginzberg). "Truth from the Land of Israel." *Hamelitz.* Multiple: 19-30 Jun 1891 (in Hebrew).

"Austerity Imposed on Israel in Plan to Curb Inflation." *The New York Times*, Jul 2 1985.

Bachar, Joseph et al. *Report of the Inter-Ministerial Team on Capital Market Reform*, Sept 2004 (in Hebrew).

*Annual Reports of the Bank of Israel. Multiple: 1970–2021 (in Hebrew).*

Beilinson, Moshe. "The Point of the Campaign." *Davar*, June 14, 1936 (in Hebrew).

———, "Until When?" *Davar*, Jun 1936 (in Hebrew).

Ben-Bassat, Avi. (ed.). *The Israeli Economy, 1985–1998: From Government Intervention to Market Economics.* MIT Press, 2002.

Berman, Eli. "Subsidized Sacrifice: State Support of Religion in Israel." *Contemporary Jewry* 20, 1999, pp. 167–200.

——————, "Sect, Subsidy, and Sacrifice: An Economist's View of Ultra-Orthodox Jews." *The Quarterly Journal of Economics* 115 (3), Aug 2000, pp. 905–953.

Brodet, David. "Trends in the Israeli Workforce." *Economic Quarterly*, 106, Oct 1980 (in Hebrew).

———, "Research and Development in Industrial Strategy." *Economic Quarterly*, 119, Jan 1984 (in Hebrew).

———, "Balance of Payments Policy." *Industrial-Technological Policy in Israel*, edited by David Brodet et al., Jerusalem Institute, 1990 (in Hebrew).

———, et al. *Report of the Brodet Committee to Examine the Implementation and Consequences of Introducing a System for the Mass Distribution of Government-Held Shares to the Public (the Options Plan).* Feb 1995 (in Hebrew).

———, et al. *Report of the Committee to Examine Aspects of Bank Holdings in Non-Financial Corporations.* Dec 1995 (in Hebrew).

———, et al. *Report of the Committee to Examine Changes in the Capital Market.* Sept. 1996 (in Hebrew).

———, et al. *Report of the Committee to Examine the Defense Budget.* May 2007 (in Hebrew).

Bruno, Michael. "*A Crushing and Quick Blow.*" *Migun*, Feb 1981 (in Hebrew).

Cohen, Avraham. *The Economy of the West Bank and Gaza, 1922–1930. Givat Haviva, 1986* (in Hebrew).

Cohen, Hillel. *1929: Year Zero of the Jewish-Arab Conflict.* Keter Books, 2013 (in Hebrew).

Dahan, Momi. "Income Inequality in Israel: Development and Recommendations." *Lights and Shadows in the Market Economy: The Israeli Market 1995–2017*, edited by Avi Ben-Bassat et al., Am Oved/Falk Institute, 2021, pp. 472–525 (in Hebrew).

Dinstein, Gili. *The Clerk.* Kinneret Zmora-Bitan Dvir, 2020 (in Hebrew).

Eckstein, Zvi et al. *Report of the Committee for Regulating Supervision and Enforcement in the Employment of Palestinian Workers in Israel*, May 2011.

Eckstein, Zvi, et al. "The Labor Market in Israel, 1995–2015." *Lights and Shadows in the Market Economy: The Israeli Market 1995–2017*, edited by Avi Ben-Bassat et al., Jerusalem: Am Oved/Falk Institute, 2021, pp. ADD (in Hebrew).

Elkins, Caroline. *Legacy of Violence: A History of the British Empire.* Bodley Head, 2022.

Freilich, Charles D. "Israel's Classic Defense Doctrine." *Israeli National Security: A New Strategy for an Era of Change*, online ed., Oxford Academic, 22 Mar 2018

Friedman, Isaiah. *British Pan-Arab Policy: 1915–1922: A Critical Appraisal.* Magnes Press, 2012 (in Hebrew).

Galnoor, Itzhak et al. (editors). *Privatization Policy in Israel: State Responsibility and the Boundaries Between the Public and the Private.* Van Leer Institute, 2015 (in Hebrew).

*Gaza-Jericho Agreement: Annex IV—Protocol on Economic Relations between the Government of the State of Israel and the P.L.O, Representing the Palestinian People.*

*United Nations Conference on Trade and Development, 29 Apr 1994.*

Gross, Nachum T. *Not By Spirit Alone: Studies in the Economic History of Modern Palestine and Israel.* Magnes Press, The Hebrew University, 1999 (in Hebrew).

Halevi, Nadav et al. (editors). *Banker to an Emerging Nation: The History of Bank Leumi Leisrael.* Shikmona Publishing Co., 1981 (in Hebrew).

Herzl, Theodor. *The Jewish State*, Wildside Press, 2008.

———-, *Altneuland: The Old-New-Land.* WLC, 2009.

Horowitz, Eli and David Brodet. *Israel 2028: Vision and Socioeconomic Strategy in a Global World.* Samuel Neaman Institute, Mar 2008. (in Hebrew).

*Israel: A divided society. Results of a review of labor-market and social policy.* OECD, 2010. Available at:

Israel Central Bureau of Statistics, Statistical Reports. *Multiple: 1960–2021.*

Jabotinsky, Ze'ev. "On the Iron Wall." *Rassvet*, Berlin, Nov 1923 (in Russian).

Katz, Yisrael et al. *Report of the Prime Minister's Committee for Children and Youth in Need*, 1973, n.p. (in Hebrew).

Kilav, Smadar. *"The Credit Suisse Research Institute's 2021 Global Wealth Report puts Israel among the top six gainers worldwide." Globes*, 20 Sept 2022.
Kimmerling, Baruch. *The End of Ashkenazi Hegemony.* Keter Books, 2001 (in Hebrew).
Levy, Baruch and Amos Zehavi. *"Privatization of Social Services and Government Infrastructure: Public Opinion in Israel." Social Security 114, Sept 2021* (in Hebrew).
Levy, Yagil. *From the "People's Army" to the "Army of the Peripheries," Jerusalem:* Carmel Publishing House, 2007 (in Hebrew).
———, *Shooting and Not Crying: The New Militarization of Israel in the 2000s. Ra'anana: Lamda Open University Press, 2022* (in Hebrew).
Liphschitz, Nili, and Biger, Gideon. *Green Dress for a Country: Afforestation in Eretz Israel, The First Hundred Years, 1850–1950.* Ariel Publishing House, 2004.
Manna, Adel. *Nakba and Survival: The Story of Palestinians Who Remained in Haifa and Galilee, 1948-1956. Van Leer Institute / HaKibbutz HaMeuchad, 2017* (in Hebrew).
Metzer, Jacob. *A National Fund for a National Home. Yad Ben Tzvi, 1979* (in Hebrew).
———, *The Divided Economy of Mandatory Palestine.* Cambridge University Press,
Patinkin, Don. *The Israeli Economy in the First Decade. Falk Center for Economic Research, Mar 1965* (in Hebrew).
Peel, William et al. *Report of the Palestine Royal Commission.* UNISPAL, 1937.
Porath, Yehoshua. *Growth of the Palestinian National Movement, 1918-1929. Am Oved, 1976* (in Hebrew).
*Report of the Committee for Increasing Market Competitiveness* (Chaim Shany, Centralization Committee), Mar 2012 (in Hebrew).
Schwartz, Hans-Peter. *Konrad Adenauer: A German Politician and Statesman in a Period of War, Revolution and Reconstruction: From the German Empire to the Federal Republic, 1876–1952 (Vol. 1).* Berghahn Books, 1995.
Senor, Dan and Saul Singer. *Start-Up Nation: The Story of Israel's Economic Miracle. Twelve, 2009.*
Sheshinsky, Eitan et al. *Report of the Committee to Examine Fiscal Policy Regarding Oil and Gas Resources*, Jan 2011 (in Hebrew).
Smith, Terence. *"Israel Sets Investment Projects."* New York Times, Jun 21 1973.
Strum, Dror et al. *Report of the Committee for Increasing Competition in Israeli Banking and Financial Services* Sept 2016.
Swirski, Shlomo. *The Price of Arrogance, the Price of Occupation: The Price Israel Pays 1967–2005. Mapa, 2005* (in Hebrew).
*The Yearbook of Ultra-Orthodox Society in Israel. Israel Democracy Institute. Multiple: 2016–2021.*
*Twenty Years of Israel's Economy.* Israel Economic Planning Authority, 1968.
Yacobi, Haim and Tovi Fenster. *An Israeli City or a City in Israel?* Hakibbutz Hameuchad—Sifriat Poalim, 2006 (in Hebrew).

Yakhin, Yossi and Inon Gamrasni. *Analysis of the Housing Market in Israel: Long-term Relationships and Short-term Dynamics*. Bank of Israel Research Division, Jun 2021 (in Hebrew).

Yegar, Moshe. *History of the Political Department of the Jewish Agency*. Bialik Institute, 2011 (in Hebrew).

# Index

*Note:* References to notes are indicated by 'n' after the page number (8n3).

www.ingramcontent.com/pod-product-compliance
Ingram Content Group UK Ltd.
Pitfield, Milton Keynes, MK11 3LW, UK
UKHW011808190625
459830UK00011B/2

9 781803 71080